Henry Darrow

Lightning in the Bottle

Published in the USA by:
BearManor Media
PO Box 1129
Duncan, Oklahoma 73534-1129
www.bearmanormedia.com

ISBN 978-1-59393-688-4

Printed in the United States of America.
Book design by Brian Pearce | Red Jacket Press.

Henry Darrow

Lightning in the Bottle

THE TRAILBLAZING LATINO ACTOR'S FIRST
SEVENTY-FIVE YEARS OF LIFE, STAGE AND SCREEN
BY **Jan Pippins** AND **Henry Darrow**

WITH AN INTRODUCTION BY LUIS REYES, CO-AUTHOR OF
HISPANICS IN HOLLYWOOD

Table of Contents

Dedicated to the fans of Henry Darrow — past, present and future.

Acknowledgements

My heartfelt appreciation goes to Henry Darrow for sharing his remarkable life and career with me and for helping me share it with others; this marvelously patient man was part of the process from start to finish. Henry's wife, Lauren Levian, is invaluable to anything in which she takes part and we were fortunate to have her along for this ride. She deserves a big round of applause for donating her considerable insight, humor, time and editing assistance throughout.

The following friends and family of Henry Darrow (listed alphabetically) generously shared their recollections, photos and special perspectives: Raymond Austin, Al Bernstein, Ruth Buzzi, Harry Cason, Frank Catalano, Linda Cristal, Don Collier, Dennis Delgado, Marie Gomez, John G. Herzler, Richard Leder, Denis Lehane, Lee Lowrimore, A Martinez, Patrice Martinez, Catrine McGregor, Francisco Menendez, Denny Miller, Dan Morris, Eric Paisley, Rick Najera, Rudy Ramos, Dorothy Rankin, Duncan Regehr, Luis Reyes, Miluka Rivera, Sally Struthers, Pat Tanno, Michael Tylo, Frank Vallejo, James Victor and Morgan Woodward.

The people who provided their personal stories plus additional assistance merit our special appreciation. Henry's cousin, Solange Rivera Delgado, supplied the genealogy and history of the Delgado family. Kent and Susan McCray answered questions about the entertainment industry and especially, *The High Chaparral*. Penny McQueen lent emotional support, passed along archival material and assembled the manuscript. Luis Reyes contributed his extensive knowledge of Hollywood, memorabilia, editing expertise and the introduction to this book. Michael Druxman pointed us to his publisher, Ben Ohmart of BearManor Media.

Ben Ohmart gets a million thanks for taking a chance on an unproven author, as does Sandy Grabman of BearManor for her assistance. Hopefully, this book will be at least as much pleasure to read as BearManor is to work with.

Although many fans of *The High Chaparral* and *Zorro* provided perspective and encouragement, several need individual recognition. Tina Sweet shared photographs, Tanja Konstantaki translated German articles into English, Daryl McCullough answered *Zorro* questions and nearly a decade ago, Kate Pitts spurred me to keep writing.

Finally, three very significant people deserve a standing ovation. My husband and great love of my life, Mike Pippins, contributed his unyielding support, unbending love, tireless proofreading and an endless supply of take-out sushi. My parents, Lowell and Dorothy Heinmiller, never discouraged me from doing anything, which resulted in a few skinned knees and broken bones, but also in many challenging projects and friendships with fascinating people.

Jan Pippins
Denham Springs, Louisiana
August 24, 2011

Notes to Readers

This book combines recent interviews with archival information. To make this distinct, present tense ("he says") is used when material was provided to Jan Pippins from the individual quoted and past tense ("he said") is used when a quotation is from archived material.

This is a real-life story with a cast of real people. It is told as truthfully as possible. However, readers should bear in mind that much of it is based upon the personal memories and opinions of the individual speaking. Supporting material from books, newspaper and magazine articles and personal files and correspondence is used and cited when available and pertinent. In a few instances, when identities are disguised, that is noted in place.

As of 2011, *The High Chaparral* is available on DVD from Kinowelt GmbH through *www.amazon.de*. The language options include the voices of the original actors in English. These Region 2 [PAL] DVDs do not play on standard North American players; they require "region free" DVD players, which are available in the U.S. and Canada. New World Television's *Zorro* is available on DVD through *www.amazon.com*.

Introduction

I first met Henry Darrow in 1978 on the set of Universal Pictures' *Walk Proud*. He portrayed a youth-gang counselor and I was one of many young Latinos playing Mexican-American gang-members. All of us were excited about working with the actor we knew as "Manolito Montoya" from the NBC series *The High Chaparral*. As Manolito, the scion of an aristocratic Mexican ranch family on the classic TV western, Henry Darrow was one of the few fully dimensional regular Latino characters on television. We and our families had once sat glued to our television sets watching a blazing western drama in which heroic Latinos took part in taming the frontier. For us, Darrow had stature as an actor equivalent to John Wayne.

In person, he turned out to be as down-to-earth and engaging as Manolito, but very serious about his work in *Walk Proud*. He was the professional we all aspired to be. Life imitated art, because while playing the role of a counselor, he counseled us by example to become better performers. Because of this movie, treasured childhood memories of a TV show and its star and our common New York Puerto Rican background, this gifted actor and I became lifelong friends.

After *Walk Proud*, we found ourselves on the Texas plains on the very sets John Wayne used for *The Alamo* (1960) to film *Seguin* (PBS, 1982), a Mexican-American retelling of the story of the Alamo in which Darrow starred as Don Erasmo Seguin, the Alcalde of San Antonio. Always interested in others, Hank frequently asked about my wife, son and daughter. He often spoke about his own son Tom, who was stricken with multiple sclerosis. Hank's painful, private struggle with his son's illness was a matter of fact, not of self-pity.

Before he went to Hawaii to guest-star on the hit TV series *Magnum P.I.* opposite Tom Selleck, I gave him a book about the Hawaiian cowboys known as paniolos. The paniolo tradition began with Mexican vaqueros who went to the islands to teach the natives ranching. Hank used the book as background for his portrayal of an old Hawaiian cowhand dealing with modern times.

When I later wrote and directed the pilot for a Latino family TV series (*Los Alvarez*), Hank agreed to star as the family patriarch. Again he set the professional standards for everyone involved in the production.

Years went by and I was shocked to learn he had suffered a heart attack. We worked together soon after that when he guest-starred along with a fellow Puerto Rican, Oscar, Emmy and Tony-winning actress Rita Moreno, on the series *Resurrection Blvd.* (2001). Hank played a man dying of cancer. He understood the bravery and vulnerability of the character and delivered a superb portrayal. When he and his beloved wife Lauren moved from Hollywood to North Carolina, he left a void in the Hollywood acting community. Hank and I stay in contact by telephone as I love to hear his voice and his infectious enthusiasm for his craft.

His biography provides special insight into a man of humble origins who achieved stardom in a very tough business through hard work, talent, luck and perseverance. Whether playing a good guy or a bad guy, he infuses his characters with dignity, presence and humanity. There is a great creativity and artistry in his body of work on stage, screen and television. Breaking free of prejudice and stereotypes, he paved the way for the Latino stars of today in Hollywood. Trailblazers such as Darrow rarely walk an easy path and his trek to stardom led him through tumultuous times in America and in a changing industry.

Hank's story is presented with uncompromising frankness and paints a vivid picture of the actor's professional and personal life set against a time of tremendous social change in America during the last third of the twentieth century. It is also the story of the Puerto Rican migration to New York and the community's history in the U.S. This triumphant and inspiring life story is part of the American experience and more importantly, the American Dream.

Luis Reyes
Writer/director/publicist
Pasadena, California

Prologue

Backstage in the grand old theater, in a quiet corner, the actor sits alone. Script in hand, he repeatedly runs his dialogue. During a life spent on stage and in front of the camera, from bit parts to international stardom, he has been a complete professional. Prepared, ready to work, he has always known his lines. Now at seventy-five, he no longer trusts his memory.

"Lack of confidence is the worst thing for an actor," he says. "I can feel that lack of confidence. If I dare lose concentration, I'm gone. When my memory was sharp, I could rhapsodize or even go blank, then come back and do a fill in, but I wouldn't chance it now."

He rehearsed before rehearsals began, before auditions. He runs lines as he falls asleep at night. Protecting himself, he carefully explains to youngsters in the play that he cannot, will not, socialize backstage. His whole concentration is on the production, his role, his lines.

The play is a local production of *My Fair Lady*, a classic musical teeming with spirited dance sequences and beloved songs. It has been years since the actor sang or danced on stage. He's game, although he relies on braces to steady his painful knees and threw his back out rehearsing fancy footwork for the big production numbers. His wife worries that he'll practice songs too much and lose his voice.

On the mantle of his home office sits a golden Emmy Award, the winged symbol of excellence from the National Academy of Television Arts & Sciences. In 1967, he shot to international stardom as heroic rascal Manolito Montoya on the television western *The High Chaparral*, but he has also played cops, criminals, Indians, ministers, Don Juan in Hell, intergalactic travelers, Spanish author Cervantes, Shakespeare's Iago, magicians, physicians, ghouls, Zorro and Zorro's father. His name is Henry Darrow and for nearly his entire life, he has made his living as a performer. This time, he is not being paid. He is doing *My Fair Lady* because he is an actor and acting is what he does.

Stay. Learn to love me.

MANOLITO MONTOYA[1]

---

1. The High Chaparral *episode "A Joyful Noise"* © 1967

ACT ONE

Cachet

I was watching Mike Douglas or Merv Griffin and Henry was on. He mentioned that he was Puerto Rican and I was just floored. I was so proud that a Puerto Rican was playing a cowboy on a TV show. In the interview, he said his name was Delgado.

WRITER/PUBLICIST LUIS REYES

Puerto Rico's misfortune is being in a strategic military location, first for Spain which built forts but did little to establish an economic base, then for the United States which has provided opportunities for advancement while often treating the island like a combination weapons testing range and pharmaceutical research laboratory. But Puerto Rico is also blessed with profound natural beauty, resilient people and a rich, ethnically mixed culture. The roots of that culture stretch from native Taino Indians to the Iberian Peninsula, Africa, the Middle East, Europe, Britain, the United States and China.

Writer Harry Cason doesn't pretend to be an expert on Puerto Rico, but during a visit he was struck by the pride and diversity of the people. He saw people in every color and hue and traveling through some parts of San Juan, he felt as if he was in Spain. "You see thin, pale, fine featured ladies and very proud men. It's like they have a direct line back to the blue bloods in the Motherland. You'd swear you were in Madrid."

Blue-blooded, but from Barcelona not Madrid, the first of Henry Darrow's ancestors in Puerto Rico was Don Sebastian Delgado de Rivera. A favorite of seventeenth century Spanish governors, he was granted the island's largest *hato* (farm) in the highlands near present-day Caguas. Delgado de Rivera's marriage to equally aristocratic Marla Antonia de Jesús Manso produced six children and family historian Solange Rivera Delgado notes, "They are described as tall, white and *very* good looking."

Over the centuries the Delgado *hato* was dispersed among descendants, donated to the Catholic Church or given to the farm workers. By the twentieth century, it was gone. Instead of landed gentry, the family brimmed with artists, singers, poets, educators, and respected civil servants like Darrow's paternal grandfather, Emilio Delgado Ramos, Chief of Police in Corozal, a man so large and corpulent that his uniforms were special ordered from the US. He and his wife, Dolores Rodríguez Martinez, had six children — Antonia, Fredrico, Juan, Rosario, Emilio and Enrique, Darrow's father.

Darrow's uncle Emilio Delgado proved to be one of the family's more famous —or infamous — members, depending upon one's politics. A poet and journalist, he was a friend of Fredrico Garcia Lorca and Pablo Neruda and belonged to an influential group of radical intellectuals that included Graciany Miranda and Soto Vélez. Living in Spain at the dawn of the Spanish Civil War, Delgado traded militant nationalism for avid Communism. He joined the Spanish Communist Party and became editor of the Party's newspaper, *Mundo Obrero* (Workers' World). His commitment to Communism did not endear him to the ultimately victorious fascist regime of *Generalísimo* Francisco Franco. Captured when Franco's army took Madrid, Delgado was sentenced to death.

As he awaited the firing squad, a cadre of French mercenaries passed. During the excitement and chaos, blond, blue-eyed Emilio slipped easily into the ranks of the French company. While his Spanish captors searched frantically for a stereotypical dark-skinned Puerto Rican, Emilio marched away with the French, saluting *Generalísimo* Franco as he passed.

Thanks to what some call *cojones* and Solange Delgado describes as innate "serenity of character...a *cachet*," Emilio lived. He married a fiery Spanish lady, raised a family and worked as a correspondent for the Soviet news agency TASS in New York City during the Cold War. He was an outspoken proponent of the Cuban Revolution and civil rights, taking issue with those who claimed that Puerto Rico, unlike the United States proper, was without racism.[2]

Today a high school in Corozal, Puerto Rico is named in his honor, but Darrow says of his uncle, "The family didn't deal with the Communist radical part of his life. His daughters kept quiet that he was their father." However, he remembers Emilio as an interesting person and gives him high marks for intellectual honesty.

He also cites his uncle's comparatively egalitarian marriage as progressive for that time. "Women were subjugated here in the United States and that went double in Puerto Rico," he recalls. "In Emilio's case, his wife was his equal in the political arena, so their marriage was more fifty-fifty."

2. *Ayala and Bernabe, p.133*

Darrow's father, Enrique Pio Delgado, didn't share his brother Emilio's politics or iconoclastic view of marriage. But 6'2" Enrique had the Delgado looks, charm and nerve. He was a hearty drinker who smoked unfiltered cigarettes and loved cooking, chess, women and inventing, although he was more fortunate with the first three. His mechanical engineering skills were enviable and he could fix anything from cars to appliances, but his inventions eluded success. His latch for long-necked milk bottles sold well for several months, then milk companies introduced a bottle without a neck that made them obsolete. A cumbersome invention for scoring fencing matches never got past initial prototypes, but several years later a Frenchman present during Enrique's experiments introduced an improved version.

A fierce chess player, Enrique was a Second Level Master who could play forty-five simultaneous games and once pummeled World Champion Alexander Alekhine. His son Henry learned chess at his knee and played his first game at age five. "Little genius," his father said of the boy who later attained the rank of Expert. Like his father, he would grow up to also love women and cooking, but the elder Delgado's mechanical acumen skipped Henry. Instead, he got a double dose of his mother's passion for performing.

> *She was a diva and she raised him to be a star.*
> *The sun rose and set on him. It was always, "You*
> *can do it! You're the best!" He was proud to be*
> *Puerto Rican and he felt like he could do anything.*
> ACTRESS LAUREN LEVIAN

La Reinita

KEEP ON, one way or another;
Have lots of fun;
You're part of me: your Mother!

GLORIA DELGADO[3]

Henry's mother, Gloria Jiménez, was born in Juncos in 1912, the same year that the town's first movie theater opened. She was the third of four daughters in a prosperous family, with a country home nestled among coffee and fruit farms and a city home bordering the central plaza of Juncos. Personal servants attended to each daughter. On the surface it was a pampered life. Gloria was the family comedian who loved to laugh, but she especially loved to dance and dreamed of becoming a "toe dancer," a ballerina.

Hiding under the bed during violent family fights, she also dreamed of the day when her father didn't beat her mother. One day when she was eleven, that dream came true. Her mother got a divorce and with Gloria in tow, fled to New York City.

"At that time, in Puerto Rico, that just didn't happen," Henry Darrow says. But Gloria's father, Papa Abuelo, was a brutal boozer who once killed another man in a jealous rage and regal, high-born Grandmother Tata wasn't a passive lady; she was a professional gambler and business entrepreneur. In New York, she and second husband Charlie designed and manufactured pricey wedding dresses for Macy's and other upscale stores. Tata also ran a poker parlor — and the family. "The men didn't like it, but what could they do?" Darrow smiles.

"Tata made a million, won a million, lost a million and gave a million away. She was very kind," Henry's brother Dennis says with admiration.

When Tata went to New York, she left daughters Carmen, Grace and Saro behind. That made Gloria think she was the favorite, but Darrow explains, "Unfortunately, the reality was that she was the most vulnerable

3. From an unpublished poem

and the most sensitive of the sisters." Unable to take them all, Tata had to choose.

In New York, Gloria attended convent school until she decided to become a nun. Tata vetoed that career plan, pulled her out and put her in public school. Gloria again dreamed of becoming a ballerina, but it was only a dream. She never had dancing lessons and passing a ballet school, she gazed wistfully at photographs of slender girls in gossamer tutus, *en Pointe* in satin slippers.

Fantasies of dancing on stage gave way to visions of love and marriage. Dating was formal in those days, so when Enrique Delgado wooed Gloria Jiménez, he wore his best suit, starched shirt and tie and brought flowers or candy. After courting her for an appropriate amount of time, he decided to propose when he beat her at chess. "Since he was a Master and she wasn't, that took one very short game," says Darrow.

The couple raised two successful sons. The youngest, Dennis, would grow up to be a respected banker. The eldest, Enrique Tomás Delgado, born in the midst of the Great Depression on September 15, 1933, was inescapably an actor. He had good looks, intelligence, talent, a certain *cachet* and a mother who promoted him relentlessly.

Because little Enrique mispronounced "Daddy" as "Tati," Tati was his nickname at home. He remembers, "It was always, 'Tati, sing! Tati, dance!'"

Darrow's wife says of Gloria Delgado, "She was an incredible stage mother before he was even on stage. She was always upbeat, the sort of person who never felt sorry for herself and never gave up, but so melodramatic! They called her *La Reinita*, the little queen. And Henry was raised to be a prince — or a king."

> *A tiny creature, held so dear.*
> *Year by year, how fast you grew;*
> *A surprise, when you were two,*
> *Tap dancing with your little feet!*
>
> GLORIA DELGADO[4]

4. Ibid.

The New Kid

Saturdays we'd go by train
To dancing school, to mix
With other children, shine or rain,
A little marvel when just six.

By 1933, a full third of the U.S. non-farm workforce was unemployed, great cities like Chicago were on the verge of bankruptcy and homeless families sold the tires from their jalopies to buy food. In the Oklahoma Dustbowl, the hollow eyes of farmers' children told of gnawing hunger. Primitive camps overflowing with dispossessed squatters sprouted across the country. From California to the Bronx, pinch-faced mothers holding lethargic infants huddled under makeshift shelters and unemployed, unshaven men hung their heads in shame as they stood in bread lines. For most, it was a time of making do and doing without. Stalked by deprivation, desperation and uncertainty, many people who lived through the Depression spent the rest of their lives letting nothing go to waste and taking nothing for granted.

Enrique Delgado was among the legion of men without steady employment, but because he took odd jobs he always found work. During one period, he rose early in the morning and dressed in a suit worthy of any executive. Picking up an empty suitcase, he headed out the door and went downtown, where he bought whole hams at cut-rate prices. Stuffing the suitcase with hams, he walked through affluent neighborhoods and resold them door to door.

With money tight, Gloria also worked and her sister Saro took Tati to school on the first day of first grade. His dark hair neatly combed and little trousers pressed, he clutched Saro's hand as she led him through a sea of strangers. His heart pounded and his terrified eyes widened. By the time they reached their seats at the very back of the auditorium, he felt like he was drowning. When he started to cry, Saro made a quick

5. Ibid.

exit. The so-called experts claimed that was the best way to help children adjust. But when she departed, she left a small, miserable boy very much alone in the crowded room.

Seventy years later, panic still clutches at his heart when he faces a group of strangers. He avoids crowds when he can, preferring small gatherings or solitude, but most people never sense his anxiety. Writer Harry Cason says, "I've been around show people all my life and some of them are really crazy, but I've never met anyone who's uncomfortable around Henry. He's so warm and welcoming that you really want to engage with him and he's got personal magnetism in spades."

He learned early to win people over. Asked about his childhood, his memories begin with a litany of Manhattan streets: 125th, 161st, 167th, 168th, 170th, 171st, Thayer, 181st, Dyckman. "It was the constant moving that I can recall, one neighborhood to another and changing schools all the time," he says. "It was awful. I was always the new kid coming in. Sometimes you prove yourself and sometimes you don't."

Gloria insisted on moving whenever *they* moved into the neighborhood. *They* were poor, less educated Puerto Ricans moving up from Spanish Harlem. "And *they* was *us!*" recalls Darrow. His father didn't mind — these were countrymen, after all. But his mother's hand wringing histrionics were a family joke. Agitating to pack the minute other Puerto Ricans moved in, she raised her Tati to be proud of his Puerto Rican heritage, to feel more important, not less, because of it. The mixed message caused a little confusion.

When Tati was ten, he got into a fistfight with the building superintendent's son who was around the same age. "I called him a spic."

And he said, "What?" and started to laugh.

Tati repeated, "You're a spic!"

"So are you! You're a spic!" The super's kid shot back, slamming him hard against a wall. Tati squared his shoulders.

"I'm not a spic. I'm *Puerto Rican!*" he answered.

Incredulous, the other boy asked, "What the hell do you think they call Puerto Ricans in New York?"

The Delgados moved further and further uptown through Washington Heights. The neighborhoods were overwhelmingly Irish or German, although there was an Argentinean family and a Columbian lady in one. "They were more educated, so I could associate with their sons or daughters," says Darrow. "But we just kept moving all the time."

Observes director Dorothy Rankin, "When you have that kind of challenge early in life, you either shut down and become your own solace or you become someone like Henry who is incredibly outgoing and really has a genuine feel for people."

Over and over, *Titi* Saro delivered him to classrooms and auditoriums filled with strange faces. "I think that's your group over there," she would say, urging him forward to join them. Every time, he obediently complied and every time, he felt aching despair when he turned around and she was gone.

Being the perpetual New Kid wasn't his only trouble. During the lean Depression years, his young parents scraped by but meals were usually the Caribbean staple, beans and rice. More nutritious than the mayonnaise sandwiches or cornmeal mush which sustained the desperately poor, it still wasn't ideal for a growing child. Before long, Tati's muscles began to cramp, his bones became soft and painful and his spine curved abnormally. He was diagnosed with rickets. Treatment was a diet richer in Vitamin D, ultraviolet light and traction to straighten his spine. Every day after school for years, Gloria Delgado took her son to the Medical Center. Under glowing blue lights, Tati endured inversion, agonizing exercises and table traction where heavy leather straps pulled his feet in one direction and his shoulders in the other. One of his earliest memories is the terror of riding the elevator to the treatment room, going up, up, up. His physical health improved, but he gained a severe fear of heights.

His grades went down, down, down. A bright little boy, he squeaked by with Ds and Cs. Teachers repeatedly told his parents he could do better. His mother tutored him, but bored and constantly changing schools, his academic performance remained dismal. Other performances came easily. He was the family clown and won approval from schoolmates by becoming the clown in every class. His teachers praised his eagerness to recite poems.

Tati saw his first movie when he was six. His mother scratched together enough money to take him to the show and gave him a choice between Shirley Temple and *Frankenstein*. He picked *Frankenstein*. It gave him nightmares until he was a teenager, but larger than life images on the huge screen hooked him on movies.

His first stage experience as the woodcutter in a grammar-school Christmas play hooked him on theater. Even though he really wanted to be Santa Claus instead of a support player, he relished being onstage where he was somebody else, somebody special and where everyone's eyes were on him. He couldn't count on living in the same place next week and was subjected to painful treatments for his twisted spine, but on stage he had control. It was more than a little magical.

By the time he was eight, Tati no longer went to the hospital after school. With family finances improved, his parents enrolled him in tap dance classes. When he was dancing, his body was strong and agile. Through dance, he found the freedom of expression, the joy of movement, the aliveness of the stage. He felt as brilliant and gifted as his mother always said he was. Dance transported him, pushing away thoughts of ever changing schools where he struggled for passing grades, the relentless parade of new neighborhoods and the past bleakness of the hospital.

After only nine months of lessons, his health betrayed him again and he was stricken with nearly fatal pneumonia. In a grainy black and white home movie, he's a thin, pale child in pajamas dancing frenetically for his uncles and step-grandfather Charlie. Dressed in dark suits and white shirts, they're seated in a semi-circle, enjoying the show while his father rolls the film. Tati put everything he had into the performance, trying desperately to prove he was well enough for classes again, not knowing the money had gone to pay medical bills.

As an adult he attended the play *A Chorus Line* and watching a scene where one of the dancers went upstairs to her class, he inexplicably burst into tears. It took him a while to realize he was grieving for his own long-ago dance lessons and the feeling of mastery he lost when they stopped.

But as the Great Depression ended and wallets fattened, there was fun and even real show business razzle-dazzle. His mother took him to movies, live theater and musical performances. Subway rides were five cents apiece and the subway was a rolling magic carpet that took them to the "Cathedral of the Motion Picture," the lavish Roxy Theater on 7th Avenue. Even past her glory days, the Roxy was Hollywood Heaven with major movies and live stage entertainment. Whether variety shows, ballet, opera, do-wop quartets or epic films, the Roxy had it all and the ushers treated patrons like royalty.

While not as swanky, family gatherings held nearly as much dancing, singing and performing as a good week at the Roxy. Vacations in New Jersey meant swimming, boating, hamming it up for the camera and wide smiles all around. Back in New York, two couples were a party and more were a fiesta. Whether swing or the waltz, they danced. They played games, read poetry, sang and did skits. Movie camera in hand, Enrique Delgado filmed his son imitating everyone from mustachioed Adolf Hitler complete with German accent to samba-dancing Carmen Miranda. As the evening grew late and slow, another Carmen, the dark, sultry aunt, turned the lights down, lit a cigarette and crooned languid torch songs.

The other action was at his grandmother Tata's poker parlor where Henry watched bets go down in a haze of cigar and cigarette smoke and listened as winners crowed and losers groaned. He never had the desire to play Tata at her favorite game, but she was up for anything. "I played board games, Parcheesi, with her," he says. "She hated losing to me or my cousin Sonny. She'd say, "Oh, you're *very* lucky."

Sonny was Grace's daredevil child and Henry's pal even though Sonny was older and stronger. "Sonny could climb a tree, no problem. I'd get about halfway and think, uh-oh, time to turn back." But Henry usually got his licks in when the boys fought, to the annoyance of Sonny's stepfather, Tony. "If I hit him, like once when I clobbered him with a toy gun, really creamed him, there was blood everywhere, Tony yelled at Sonny. 'How can you let Tati do that to you? Jeez!'"

Sonny was Tata's favorite and that annoyed Gloria. "How can I be your favorite daughter and my son not be your favorite grandson?" she grumbled.

She also took issue with her sister Grace. Darrow remembers Grace fondly as an outspoken toughie who had him pegged better than his mother. "She called things as they really were and Mom couldn't take that." When Grace told Gloria the boys had been fighting or that Henry filched Sonny's toys, Gloria's response was always, "NO. Not MY son! Don't be silly. Tati would *never* do that!" Tati got away with a lot and Darrow laughs about Grace nailing him for "toys that I *may* have taken."

World War II gave Enrique Delgado a good job in time for the birth of a second son, Dennis, when Henry was nine and a half. Delgado was foreman for the BG Corporation, a major supplier of spark plugs for the U.S. military. Because his work was vital to the war effort, he stayed home while others fought overseas. Finances were improving, but Gloria still needed to work. Fluent in Spanish, French and English, she was employed as a translator and as always, depended upon her younger sister Saro to take Tati to school.

School remained an indistinct stream of new classrooms full of strangers and he talks more easily about the neighborhoods of the early 1940s. In the neighborhoods, all the kids were baseball fans, especially Henry Delgado, but baseball required the right number of boys, along with mitts, bats and balls. The most popular games didn't take special equipment or a certain number to play, like Ringolevio, a rough and tumble version of Cops and Robbers. At Halloween, the kids had fun with a precursor to Paintball involving Mom's stocking and a big wad of tightly packed flour. Why the flour?

"Well, you had to have something to slap people with. You'd tie it off and go to where your friends lived, and knock on the door. It made a lovely mark on anyone with dark clothing. Like, ha ha! You were hit six times!"

You had to be careful who you hit. "Being chased, swinging it around, the older kids would pop us smaller kids. Every now and then, you'd whap an older kid right in the face. Then it got tough! You're two to three years younger, you smack one of those guys and you really had to get out of there, because they're supposed to win everything."

He regularly got down to serious kid business like putting pennies on the tracks for the trolley to smash. "Then somebody would come up with a .22 bullet. We'd put that on the tracks and bam! Stupid things," he says, laughing. "I remember hitching rides on the back of trolleys, paying five cents for a cherry phosphate and one time, getting sick on candy corn." He grimaces. "Man, that was awful."

He and his friends watched action packed *Zorro* matinees on Saturdays and played "Zorro" in the streets of Manhattan, proof that childhood dreams sometimes come true. "Talk about fantasy as a kid!" he exclaims. "All of a sudden, I'm an adult and I'm playing the voice of Zorro for cartoons. Then I *am* Zorro. And then I play the father of Zorro. Wow! I research the role, see clips of Douglas Fairbanks Jr. doing Zorro and I think, my God, I used to watch this!"

When the game was "Cowboys and Indians," Henry always wanted to be an Indian. At ten, full of Wild West enthusiasm, he took his first horseback ride in New York's Central Park. The horse ran away with him, spinning down winding pathways, clattering over bridges and racing through tunnels. Terrified Henry hung on all the way back to the stables. Cured of ever wanting to get on a horse again, he was an unlikely candidate for future worldwide fame as a television cowboy

Although he was much better at winning pals than handling horses, boys in the neighborhood weren't always friendly. At one point, the family lived on a street close to Mother Cabrini School and the George Washington Bridge. There was a park a block or two away, but Henry knew better than to go there. "That's where these other groups of kids hung out. It was *their* park."

Even before gangs toted knives and guns, entering another group's territory was risky. One day Henry wandered too near the park and several boys beat him up. Bruised and bloody, he limped home. His father handed him a baseball bat and he went back to the park. "There were a couple of boys left. They were laughing, but when I came with the bat they scattered," he recalls. "There are people who believe that if someone strikes you on one cheek, you should turn the other, but I have never found that it works."

He never went close to the park again and as World War II wound down, his father decided his young family needed a different life away from the city. With a partner who shouldered a portion of the financial obligation, Enrique Delgado took out a three year lease on the Bedford Inn in Westchester County's picturesque Bedford Village.

The whole motivation for any performer is, "Look at me, Ma!"

COMEDIAN LENNY BRUCE

Martha Stewart Country

I learned to fight before I learned to win.

HENRY DARROW

Only forty-eight miles from New York City, Bedford Village was a world away. Darrow calls it "Martha Stewart country". The town was a bucolic hamlet of charming homes bordered by rolling hills, dairy farms, estates and woods teeming with deer, squirrels and foxes.

Most businesses were clustered inside Bedford Village, but the Bedford Inn was just outside the town. It was a large, two-story George Washington style building on over thirty acres and running it was a family affair. Enrique Delgado was an enthusiastic chef and the inn gained a reputation for fine dining, garlicky chicken and rice prepared in a special clay pot, robust salads and choice beef. He and Tata's second husband, Charlie, tended bar. Gloria waited tables. Henry prepared salads or chopped wood and visiting relatives helped out in their own ways.

Papa Abuelo, Tata's first husband, came to visit just as he had when the family lived in Manhattan. Even his daughter Gloria called him a "man of low character," but they didn't turn him away. He was still Gloria's father and had no place else to go.

Henry didn't like him, but Papa Abuelo was entertaining. When Henry was eleven, Papa Abuelo was the first one to sit him down and describe the most private female anatomy in captivating detail. And as the old man guzzled rum, he'd sing a drunken lullaby to Henry and Dennis. "*La gallina…está muriendo…y los pollitos…están llorando….*" The more rum he drank, the more emotional he grew. Rather than putting the boys to sleep, their increasingly histrionic grandfather's slurred tune about the dying mother hen and crying chickies reduced them to helpless giggles.

Papa Abuelo appointed himself family guardian when Henry's dad went shopping in New York City. Once when Enrique was gone, a mournful man wearing pajamas and a robe walked to the inn and requested a room. While Gloria hurried to set him up, Papa Abuelo grabbed his machete. For a day and a half, their guest stayed in his room while the old man sat in a chair just outside, sharp machete in hand, drinking and muttering threats and epithets. Fortunately, their intimidated lodger didn't leave the room until orderlies from the local mental hospital collected him.

The inn wasn't only popular with locals, visiting family and escaped mental patients. Movie stars like Humphrey Bogart and Tallulah Bankhead stayed there, but Henry rarely glimpsed famous guests. He was busy with adventures outside. He traveled the woods and fields with his first dog and explored country roads on his first bicycle. He had never been on snow skis before, but when he and his dad found a pair while rummaging in the attic, the crisp winter air and snowy hills beckoned. Henry impulsively strapped on the skis and was soon whooshing head long down the biggest slope. Wandering with his BB gun, he shot stationary targets but when he graduated to a short .22 rifle, he set his sights on live prey. Drawing a bead on a squirrel in a tree, he fired. It dropped lifelessly to the ground. Sickened, he never went hunting again.

Henry's distaste for hunting set him apart from local lads at Bedford's rustic, two-room schoolhouse. Further widening the gap, he jumped at the chance to be in plays. His mother was thrilled when he was chosen to be Santa Claus in the Christmas play ("At only twelve!" she exclaimed. "His voice was very strong and clear!"). In case that didn't draw enough ridicule from denim-clad country boys who thought plays were for sissies, Gloria Delgado wanted him dressed for school like a fine young gentleman in pressed slacks and neat button-down shirt. He was a marked kid.

The other boys elbowed each other in the ribs and snickered at skinny Henry Delgado. Next came insults and he wasn't about to let them pass and came out swinging. He got the stuffing knocked out of him. More fights followed with usually the same result. Finally he wised up and realized he didn't stand a chance.

Unlike the guys, the Bedford girls were crazy about the cute new boy in the sharp city threads. For Henry, it was opportunity knocking. Instead of running with the guys, he hung out with the girls. There was no special crush, just casual dates to see movies at the one theater in town, usually with his little brother in tow.

Heckling from the boys hurt his pride and made him mad, but he needed more than a dimpled smile and a ticket to the flicks to make it stop. He needed leverage and he discovered it inside his little brown lunch bag. When the lunch bell rang at school, lunch trading began with an excited rustle of paper sacks crackling through the classroom. Boys with bologna or peanut butter on mushy white bread eyed Henry Delgado's roast beef sandwiches hungrily. Trading got him more than a bad lunch.

Suddenly, he wasn't just the New Kid from the city, he held the lunchtime Holy Grail. Every schoolboy with a stomach was his best pal.

The schoolhouse wasn't far from the inn and before he had a bicycle, he walked. Then people started to recognize him as Delgado's son, the nice young man from the inn and soon he had regular rides to and from school. After he got his bike, Henry peddled to school past a gated mansion. One day, he saw a young fellow about his age getting into a long, black limousine. He waved. The other boy waved back. For the three years the Delgados lived in Bedford Village, this was the routine every school day. Henry never called hello or approached the gate to talk. The other boy never walked to the gate to introduce himself. Waving was the only contact between the lone boy passing by with the wind in his hair and the isolated boy behind the gate at the mansion on the hill. But yearning makes a slight connection memorable. Decades later at a cocktail party, Darrow was talking about the Bedford Inn and another guest said that he had also lived in Bedford Village. As they conversed, they were astounded. The grownup kid on the blue bike was talking with a man who had been the boy in the big, black car.

When not supervising activities at the inn, cooking or tending bar, Henry's dad took the opportunity to invent and market. His salad dressing was so successful that another man offered front money and a fifty-fifty split; if Delgado would make it, he'd supply the bottles. Henry put the labels on. His father also developed a self-service bowling machine that eliminated manual pin setting. A company put him on retainer while he and Henry worked for a year and a half getting the bugs out of the little machine, then the company paid him off and developed an improved version that made his obsolete.

Meanwhile, Enrique's partner in the inn had been embezzling.

Nearly destitute when their three year lease ended, the Delgados left Bedford Village just after Christmas. They drove back to New York City as temperatures plummeted and snow began falling. The bitterly cold Blizzard of 1948 had started. It buried nearby Bedford Hills under a record thirty-two inch snowfall and paralyzed New York City.

The Delgados moved in with Saro and her family in their tiny Washington Heights apartment. It was only temporary, just until Enrique found work. But while he was running the Bedford Inn, the job market changed. The economy was booming, but companies like BG Corporation no longer needed a massive wartime workforce and returning veterans had priority when positions came open. There wasn't anything left for Enrique Delgado except the sound of doors closing.

Fortunately, Puerto Rico was rapidly transitioning from agricultural to manufacturing economy. Realizing his best chance for work was there, Enrique left Gloria and his sons in New York, paid his way to San Juan and began selling shoes at his brother Fredrico's clothing store.

Months passed before he could bring his family down. During the gray New York winter, Gloria and the boys shared a cramped room barely large enough for two single beds, one for her and the other for fifteen year-old Henry and six year-old Dennis. The apartment was ground floor and Henry peered through the narrow, street-level windows at the feet of passersby. It was a long way from the rolling hills and freedom of Bedford Village and further still from the plantations and personal servants of Gloria's childhood. Even so, the bustling Big Apple was home. Henry did not want to go to Puerto Rico. Checking it out in his geography book, he complained to his mother, "But you can't even see Puerto Rico on the map!"

We know what we are, but not what we may be.
WILLIAM SHAKESPEARE

It Was Television
and It Was *Live*

It was act and sing and dance,
You did so well in plays;
A future actor at a glance;
The path to follow, all the way.

GLORIA DELGADO[6]

In Puerto Rico, there was no snow. In Puerto Rico ocean waves danced to the music of *bomba y plena* on white sandy beaches and sea breezes cut riffs on palm fronds like quick fingers across the strings of a guitar. In Puerto Rico, sugar cane and tobacco matured in the tropical sunlight, coffee beans and fruit ripened where the rivers ran. In Puerto Rico, busy manufacturing plants produced fine textiles, leather, rum, pharmaceuticals and machinery. And in Puerto Rico, Henry's father had doggedly worked his way up to a position with a company in Cayey which made expensive leather gloves for export. For two years, he commuted to Cayey while his family stayed behind in a rented apartment in the San Juan suburb of Santurce.

Gloria maintained order between her sons, but emphasized that it wasn't difficult. When Henry went to the movies, which was often, he took Dennis along. If they fought, Gloria pulled them apart and talked to each one alone, telling Henry not to hit Dennis quite so hard and telling Dennis to have more respect for his older brother.

The Delgado apartment was on the second floor above a funeral parlor. From the balcony, they could hear the indistinct hubbub of work at the mortuary. Since they had relatives who owned a funeral parlor, mortuaries meant mourners, men in suits and children all dressed up. To see bodies being embalmed downstairs required leaning far down over the balcony and nobody was that curious.

---

6. Ibid.

One of Henry's jobs was taking the household garbage out at night for collection the next morning. His route to the curb took him down the back stairs and past the mortuary. He didn't think twice about heading downstairs with the garbage, but as he passed the back of the mortuary a dripping sound caught his ear. To his left, the dim yellow glow of a bare bulb cut the darkness. In the ghostly light Henry saw a body on a table, a thin sheet draped across the bulbous stomach and a tube running to a bucket. From the tube came the steady plop of bodily fluids draining in the lonely night. It was just him, the cadaver and shadows. He dumped the garbage fast and ran like hell back upstairs. When he later had to act a scene that called for sudden terror, he recalled that experience, but once was enough. After that, he always took the trash out during the day.

The most haunting sound from the mortuary came not from a cadaver but from the mentally handicapped young man who moved coffins and bodies. He was normally mute until his fellow employees got him drunk. When he was drunk, he cried. "It was this unforgettably eerie, affecting sound, very soulful, high-pitched," says Darrow.

The apartment above the funeral parlor wasn't the best place for parties, so Grace and Tony's bungalow was the gathering spot. Mango and lemon trees surrounded a covered patio, ideal for Tony's barbeques, singing and dancing. The island's rich musical heritage saturated family gatherings.

At Christmas, everyone serenaded their neighbors in the centuries old tradition of *parrandas*. Going from house to house in the warm, tropical night, spontaneous *parranda* groups of family and friends played guitar, cuatro and maracas and sang *aguinaldos* until dawn. *Aguinaldo* means both a type of folk song and "gift". It's a gift from the performers. Says Dennis Delgado, "It doesn't matter how difficult the economy, everybody's happy, they're doing the fiesta."

Maybe, but emotions were strained at Titi Grace's house. "Sonny wound up really caring for his stepfather, but in the beginning, he was not a good influence. He was harsh," says Darrow. And Grace could be punitive. "She used to smack Sonny when he was disrespectful. One time, he just grabbed her hand and said, 'No more.' She was shocked. He let her go and just walked out the door."

On his own at a young age, Sonny joined the Marines. Meanwhile, Cousin Henry had his own battles. School presented insurmountable obstacles. He was Puerto Rican in New York, but in Puerto Rico he was an *Americano*, the outsider who spoke only English with a smattering of "Spanglish": "Hey amigo, what's that on the roof-o?"

At Central Public High School, classes were in Spanish and exams were torture. Henry strained to translate test questions from Spanish to English, then to translate his answers from English back to Spanish. He says, "I never finished a test. Never." Essay exams were excruciating and he failed the first semester. He would repeat the grade, but not at Central Public.

His parents put him in parochial school at the *Academia del Perpetuo Socorro* (Academy of Our Lady of Perpetual Help) in San Juan's historic Miramar section. "In that school were people who would run the future government. They were kids who studied. They came from families where education was very important," he says.

He remained mostly an indifferent student, waiting until the last minute to cram for tests. Still, for him the *Academia del Perpetuo Socorro* was aptly named. Classes were taught in English and it was at the *Academia* that Henry made his first life-long friends and got the encouragement to begin acting in earnest.

The nuns supported his zeal for drama and English, but urged him to do better in algebra and geometry, which he failed and had to repeat in summer session. Other than being a lackadaisical student, he mostly stayed out of trouble, but recalls one incident with a nun dubbed *La Bizca* (The Cross-eyed One).

"Oh, dear! She had the strongest body odor. She sweated a lot and wore glasses with thick lenses. She had some pimples. She was not attractive in the least." But *La Bizca* was deadly with a ruler. When she caught the boys passing notes, she smacked one then took aim at Henry. He grabbed the ruler and broke it. "All of a sudden," he says, "I became a hero."

The hero was quickly shuttled off to the Mother Superior's office. Punishment could have been much worse than skinned knuckles, but pretty Mother John was no *La Bizca*. She thought he was a charming young man and Henry left her office with skin intact and a crush on the Mother Superior.

Like fictional Bill Starbuck in N. Richard Nash's play *The Rainmaker*, Henry found nearly all women attractive, just attractive in different ways. Whether they were high class, low class or no class, he was interested — and so seductive that his friends didn't want him near their sisters. Nice girls were heavily chaperoned, but suave Henry could slip away with one during picnics and parties for *un beso* or more. When a boy named Gabi noticed Henry buzzing around his sister, he invited Henry to meet him and his big knife in the bathroom. Another pal said it was no big deal. "You know Gabi's only like that when he's drunk."

"But he's drunk all the time!" Henry countered. Gabi's sister was suddenly much less interesting. There were plenty of girls with sober — or at least unarmed — brothers.

"He was always a woman's man, very popular with the girls, a Valentino type," says Dennis Delgado, amazed at the numerous thank-you notes his teenaged brother received from his dates. The girls were grateful, even if their male relatives weren't.

When not charming females of all ages and social strata, going to parties or hanging out with friends, Henry spent time on chess. Passionate about the game, he could play up to twenty-five boards simultaneously but although he was very good, he knew he would never be a champion. "My game was a little bit on the passive side, then I would build up, prepare and go on a counterattack. You have to be particularly good to do that successfully and it didn't always work." Luck sometimes bailed him out, but it didn't blind him. "One time, I was in a classroom with about eighteen other kids. There were six boards left and I was going to lose about four games. Then the bell rang."

However, his enthusiasm for acting increasingly rivaled his fascination with chess. Encouraged by his parents and teachers, he thought more and more of being a professional actor. The question was, how? In chess he learned winning tactics by studying books written by Masters of the game. If there was a strategy for becoming a successful actor, he figured a Master would know it. He went for the top and wrote to the great José Ferrer.

Born in Santurce, Puerto Rico in 1912, Ferrer was the son of an attorney and a planter's daughter. After attending private schools in the U.S. and Switzerland, he entered Princeton University to study architecture. He seemed destined for a well-padded life until his last year at Princeton. His Princeton roommate, also studying architecture, was a preppie from Pennsylvania named Jimmy Stewart, and Stewart was a member of the Princeton Triangle Club acting troupe.[7] Ferrer started hanging out with the actors, joined the Triangle Club, and in his fifth year, was in a play. Without that play, he said he never would have considered a theatrical career.[8] But he had tasted "the addictive drug of the theater."[9] Instead of enjoying the life of a well-to-do architect, he "chose the difficult and arduous struggle"[10] of becoming an actor. He went on to act and direct

7. *He later became a film industry legend and highly decorated WWII pilot*

8. *Reyes and Rubie, p. 468*

9. *Miluka Rivera, p. 70, trans: "la adictiva droga del teatro"*

10. Ibid. *"escogio el espinoso y arduo de las lucha"*

on Broadway and to act in numerous films. Then in 1951, he became the first Puerto Rican and first Latino to win an Oscar for Best Actor in a Leading Role for his work in the 1950 movie *Cyrano de Bergerac*.[11]

To Henry Delgado and many other people of Puerto Rican heritage, Ferrer was a hero. In response to seventeen-year-old Delgado's hopeful letter, Ferrer wrote a humble and insightful response.

Dear Henry:

Thank you very much for your extremely nice letter. I wish that I were all that you think me. By that, I mean I wish I were able to give you advice.

Unfortunately, the theatre is the most hazardous and treacherous of careers. I would not advise anyone to ever take it up without a full knowledge of the many pitfalls which will inevitably confront them. I can only say to you that determination, hard work and a refusal to ever lose sight of one's goal are qualities which one must possess. One must arm one's self with every available weapon, and hope that some day the eventual break may come.

There is no formula for success in the theatre. There is no easy way to achieve that which you desire. I cannot honestly give you any recipe that will in any way aid you in your career.

Thank you again for having written me, and may I wish you all the luck and every success.

Sincerely,
José Ferrer

Although there was no recipe for success, the nuns fostered their students' talent and gave Henry and his friend Ivan Rodriguez a weekly show on the school radio station. Henry and Ivan performed musicals, Shakespeare and *Cyrano*, but the thrill of high school radio was surpassed when Ivan provided a first taste of television acting.

Ivan's father was a representative for Keebler Crackers and Keebler sponsored a fifteen minute variety show on television where the boys were paid to do their stuff in front of the camera. They did short skits in English and Spanish, read poems, recited Shakespeare or just improvised. Henry reveled in it. So did Ivan, who planned on a career as a producer.

---

11. *As of 2011, he is still the only Puerto Rican or Latino to win.*

"It was a little nothing program, once a week for three or four months. We didn't have an audience because it was pretty lousy local TV," says Darrow, adding with a twinkle, "but it was television. And it was *live*."

High school had turned from disastrous to delightful. Henry was popular with the other kids at the *Academia* and they chose him as President of the Senior Class. Among the warm farewells in his high school yearbook, classmates predicted, "Henry is going to be an actor."

That didn't take a crystal ball and of course, Henry agreed. Thinking of José Ferrer, he wrote under his graduation picture, "My ambition is to become a good actor and be another son bringing glory to Puerto Rico, this little island which I hold so dear." Later, Ferrer's warnings about the hazards and treachery of a career in the theater came back to him and he reconsidered. "I thought, nah, that's not going to work. I might as well join the Army."

By then, his dad was manager of the Faculty Club at the University of Puerto Rico in Rio Piedras. When a cousin also employed at the University suggested enrolling there instead of enlisting, his mother begged him to take the entrance exam. Not expecting to pass, he took the exam. He squeaked by with a grade barely good enough for admission.

If nothing is happening, you have to make it happen.

ACTOR JOSÉ FERRER

With Skill
and Insolence

*The stance and magnificent integrity that Mr.
Hernandez displays in his carriage, his manner
and expression, will never flinch in his great
self-command.*

THE NEW YORK TIMES[12]

Fascination with politics and human behavior led Henry to major in
political science with a minor in psychology. He planned on a career in
the diplomatic corps, but the dream of becoming an actor grabbed him
and threw him into the drama section of the English Department.

The director of the drama division was stage and screen actor Juano
Hernandez. He became Henry's first drama coach. In his mid-fifties
then, Hernandez had lived a remarkable life. He was born in San Juan
in 1898, was orphaned very young and taken in by an aunt in Rio de
Janiero, Brazil. Poor, black and illiterate, he survived in Rio by singing,
dancing and doing acrobatics with a troupe of other ragtag kids. He later
ran away and joined a circus which traveled the Caribbean and Latin
America, then boxed professionally under the name "Kid Curley". He
taught himself to read and write, became fluent in several languages and
developed perfect diction. "One thing I learned very soon," he said, "was
that if you speak English with any kind of accent people are inclined
to laugh at you."[13] Hernandez had a rich voice which benefitted him as
an actor and by 1927 he was on Broadway performing in *Show Boat*, a
musical about racism and tragic love. He continued performing in major
theater productions and was one of the first black actors in radio.[14] But

12. *Quoted by Bogle, p. 156*

13. *Quoted by Reyes and Rubie, p. 487*

14. *On the soap* We Live and Learn, *http://www.blackpast.org/?q=aah/hernandez-juano-1896-1970*

while white actors at the New York City radio station used the front door, Hernandez was relegated to the service entrance. In those days, decades before the Civil Rights Era, America and its entertainment industry were both highly segregated. Across the nation, there were separate water fountains, entrances, restrooms, hotels, theaters and hospitals for white and "colored". All white "Sundown Towns" dotted the U.S. and Canada, places that had violently purged themselves of African-Americans (and sometimes other racial, ethnic or religious groups). Black laborers allowed in during daylight were warned to leave before sunset, else risk injury or death. A sign at the town limits of Hawthorne, California in the 1930s spelled it out: "Nigger, Don't Let The Sun Set On YOU in Hawthorne".[15]

The entertainment industry had its own version of Sundown Towns. Whether Broadway, Harlem or neighborhood playhouses, theater welcomed African-Americans before movies, but theater was not a perfect bastion of equality. The daughter of progressive dramatist Paul Green recalled that in the 1920s and early 1930s, her father's "Negro plays" were "done by northern white actors in blackface, attempting to mimic the deep North Carolina rural dialect. They did this because the theatre was not then open to black actors…"[16]

Movies created by major Hollywood studios before World War II targeted white audiences and offered little opportunity to African-American actors. But there was an alternative cinema for black performers. Called "race movies," these independently produced pictures were made with all black casts for black audiences. They paid poorly in money but well in dignity. The giant of the industry was pioneer producer, director and novelist Oscar Micheaux. Juano Hernandez began his screen career in race movies, including three of Micheaux's, then at fifty-one, he starred as Lucas Beauchamp, a proud man wrongly accused of murder in M-G-M's *Intruder in the Dust* (1949). Bogle later wrote Hernandez played the part "with skill and insolence" as he "strode through the film with a haughty arrogance…"[17]

Having such a man for a college drama coach was inspiring. "He was nominated for a Golden Globe for his work in *Intruder* and was considered for an Oscar nomination," says Darrow. "Because he was black, he might have to play a slave, but he always portrayed it with an incredible

---

15. Loewen, p. 23

16. Dr. Janet Green, A Daughter's Biography, *lecture to Phi Theta Kappa in Purchase, NY 1981 http://www.ibiblio.org/paulgreen/daughter.html*

17. Bogle, Ibid.

amount of dignity." Hernandez had starred in *Othello* Off-Broadway and
Darrow vividly remembers the exhilaration he felt when he played Iago
opposite Hernandez' powerhouse Othello in a school production.

Juano Hernandez pushed his students to strive. Henry did not need
much encouragement. He had the leads in *Good News* and in *Cyrano de
Bergerac*, his father's favorite play and José Ferrer's defining role. Because
the drama section was small, Hernandez brought in actors from other
companies — in *Mr. Roberts*, Henry worked with actors from the Little
Theatre of Puerto Rico.

Besides augmenting student productions with outside talent, Hernandez urged his young thespians to go for parts outside the university. When
the Metropolitan Opera Company came to Rio Piedras, Henry sang in
the chorus or had small parts that put him onstage with opera luminaries
like baritone Robert McFerrin, Sr. and veteran tenor Jan Peerce.

Darrow sums up his contribution to professional productions with, "I
was the drunk crossing the stage," but even little roles look good on a
résumé and can be important in unexpected ways. Jan Peerce was legally
blind without glasses, so Henry, playing a helpful peasant, held the tenor's
glasses and led him onstage as they talked. It worked until Peerce shook
off his guide and veered headlong into a heavy cross-cord. When Henry
collected the dazed star, he was more agreeable to being steered.

Henry's dad set him up with gigs at the Faculty Club, where he did
impressions of Al Jolson, Rod Steiger and Marlon Brando. When representatives of the top rated television variety series *Arthur Godfrey's Talent
Scouts* were vacationing in Puerto Rico, they caught his act and offered
him a slot on the New York based show. *Arthur Godfrey's Talent Scouts*
launched impressive careers and Juano Hernandez advised Henry to take
their offer. "If you want to expand your horizons," he counseled the young
man, "you have to leave the island and you must go to Hollywood or New
York." Henry wasn't so sure, so Hernandez tried again more emphatically.

"Look, you've got to get out of Puerto Rico. Your Spanish isn't good
enough to work here." That was hard to argue with, but Henry wanted
to consult his family before making a decision.

Tata thought he should stay in school, graduate and get a real job. His
mother and father had confidence in his abilities, but didn't believe he was
ready to leave home. Henry turned down *Arthur Godfrey's Talent Scouts*.

Patience and shuffle the cards.
                              MIGUEL DE CERVANTES SAAVEDRA

A Svengali
on the Platform

¡Cantemos unidos un himno a la Alma Máter;
Cantemos con fuerza el Himno de la Vida
que anuncie Juventud, Amor y Libertad,
dé gloria al luchador, honra de la Universidad!

(We sing together a hymn to the Alma Mater;
We sing with strength the Hymn of Life
Which proclaims Youth, Love and Liberty,
The Glory of the Fighter, honor of the University!)

"HIMNO DE LA VIDA,"
ANTHEM OF THE UNIVERSITY OF PUERTO RICO
BY FRANCISCO ARRIVI AND AUGUSTO RODRIGUEZ (1938)

Happily for Henry Delgado, University faculty included professors whose renown eclipsed that of talent scouts for a television show. Even better, many of these remarkable men were his father's pals who played chess, shot pool or bowled at the Faculty Club. There, Henry sharpened his skill at billiards while rubbing shoulders with eminent scholars. Before long, he was on first-name basis with men like Nobel Laureate Juan Ramón Jiménez.

Jiménez, a native Andalusian celebrated for his erotic poetry, was one of many prominent academicians who joked and talked with young Henry. Sometimes, they put him to work. "I was the guinea pig student. If they wanted to find out if an exam was too hard, they gave it to me first before administering it to their class," he says, adding, "Of course, I found most tests too hard."

Whether they met Henry over a card game, pool table or test, all the professors were extremely cordial and treated him as an equal in spite of differences in age and accomplishments. He spent good times with poet, playwright and literary critic Elder James Olson and says, "He had wonderful stories. He had seen John Barrymore perform in Chicago in a play by John Galsworthy called *Justice*. Barrymore was so drunk he broke the set. The headline was 'Barrymore Breaks Out.'"

Another talented teacher broke Henry Delgado *into* disciplined habits that paid off throughout his life as a performer. A masterful composer and musical arranger, Augusto Rodriguez founded the University's *a cappella* chorus in the 1940s. As conductor and driving force, he was described by one review as "a Svengali on the platform".[18] Rodriguez was also an outspoken anti-government radical who knew Henry's militant uncle Emilio Delgado well. On the hunt for new talent to fill spots in his chorus, he thought Emilio's nephew Henry was a prospect and approached Enrique Delgado about it. Enrique gave it thumbs up and Henry joined.

Darrow, a baritone, says, "I had a loud voice and I wasn't afraid to blast out. Augusto liked that I was into acting and that I was wasn't intimidated. He was fierce performer. When he directed, he had vigorous expressions and dynamic hand movements."

Rodriguez became a matchless friend and inspiration, but not before he whipped Henry Delgado into shape. "He had a wonderful sense of humor, but he was relentless in his battle to get the best out of you, no matter what," says the actor. "And oh, my God! Augusto had a temper!" If rehearsals alone didn't produce excellence, he lambasted the entire chorus. Face beet-red, he became so angry he pulled hair from his head while shouting that the girls weren't good enough to be prostitutes and the guys weren't real men. Then the master manipulator changed tactics. "After he created turmoil, he smoothed it out. He'd come to each of us individually with compliments and make us feel like a million bucks," says Darrow.

The thirty-member chorus sang like two million bucks, performing a mixture of songs including many from Latin America and the Caribbean. At Christmas, Rodriguez added popular religious selections like *Ave Maria* and *Kyrie, Eleison* and the chorus gave holiday concerts all over Puerto Rico and in Cuba. But the plum was a U.S. tour that included Carnegie Hall, the Washington Press Club, Harvard University, New York City's Pan American Union and Trinity Episcopal Church. Touring was fun and everyone wanted to sing at prestigious venues in the U.S. Carnegie Hall couldn't be beat and President Eisenhower would be at Trinity Church. The U.S. tour was potent motivation to be the best, especially after Rodriguez demonstrated what happened when they weren't.

18. The New York Times, *"Students' Chorus Heard in Concert," 3/28/53*

"We had a tenor in the chorus with a legitimate operatic voice," says Darrow. "He was maybe the best in the group, but he wouldn't cut off and he overpowered the other tenors. Augusto showed him a hand gesture and said, 'When I do this, you have to stop.' He told him several times and it didn't work. Finally, Augusto said, 'You're not going to New York.' That was it. He'd made his mind up."

Henry Delgado wanted to go to New York. He wanted to sing at Carnegie Hall. "Perseverance was the name of the game for Augusto. He drilled it into our hearts and souls! He'd do whatever it took, so I had to develop a different approach. When other stuff was difficult I'd just give up, the C or C-minus student. But with the chorus, I went to rehearsals. I practiced." Henry Delgado made the tour.

President Eisenhower never showed at Trinity Episcopal, but reviews from the performance at Carnegie Hall glowed. Some critics compared them to the venerated Moscow *A Cappella* Choir. A *New York Times* review heaped praise on the choir and especially Rodriguez:

> *Last night at Carnegie Hall…Mr. Rodriguez and the current edition of the Puerto Rico Chorus matched their previous fine performances…Like most good chorus conductors, he uses a highly unorthodox beat. The singers, however, appear to understand it and give him what he wants…Attacks and releases are sharp, incisive and clean…complex rhythms…are deftly managed. It is the sort of pliant, supple choral singing that can be obtained only by hard work under a director who knows his business.*[19]

About the performance itself, Darrow remembers that his opening night nerves caused a screw-up. "At times, we all sang solo and there was a solo in one of the songs that night. Augusto turned to me and made a gesture. And I thought, 'Oh my God, he didn't tell me I had a solo!' But I started to sing anyway," he recalls. "Then I felt a hand on my shoulder. The hand started to squeeze very gently. It was the guy behind me who actually had the solo! Because he had such a wonderful, powerful voice, he drowned me out." He laughs. "When I realized it wasn't mine, I just shut up."

Henry wasn't the only one with jitters. The exacting Rodriguez got edgy before big performances, which sometimes made him fumble. "He wanted everyone set to go," says Darrow. "One time, he got confused and turned to a section and made a cue indicating they should come in. Except, it wasn't their turn. Nobody came in! Not one person! He shouted at us, 'Gracias!' He knew he'd goofed."

The group competed against and bested other *a cappella* choirs. They cut and sold a set of records. For Henry Delgado, the discipline and persistence he learned would lead to opportunities he never imagined. Meanwhile, college life outside Augusto Rodríguez' sphere was business as usual.

> *For a man without prospects*
> *there are only three open roads:*
> *the sea, the church or the king's service.*
>   MIGUEL DE CERVANTES SAAVEDRA

Congratulations, Bring Your Own Sheets

Blue Moon, now I'm no longer alone, without a dream in my heart...

RODGERS & HART[20]

Unsure that acting was a viable career, Henry focused on becoming an officer in the US Air Force and eventually joining the diplomatic corps as a translator. He was already active in ROTC (Reserve Officers' Training Corps) and to learn better Spanish, he got a job as an interpreter at the University. His Spanish improved, but disillusionment followed. "I got involved with some lawyers and I didn't have the smarts back then to understand that some of what was going on was not proper," he says. He felt uncomfortable when asked to pose leading questions or put words in someone's mouth. "After a while, I didn't want to do it anymore. It was easier to just back off."

He still considered a future in the military and cut a striking figure in his ROTC uniform. His cousin Solange Rivera Delgado remembers going to El Manolete, a restaurant near the University. She recalls, "They were playing the tango, *El Choclo*. Henry asked me to dance and we gave a pretty good show." They must have. Someone from Solange's hometown saw them and went straight to Solange's mother with the shameful news that her daughter had been dancing with an American soldier. "She never believed me that he was her nephew," she says. Her mother levied a one dollar a week fine on her, no small amount in the early 1950s.

Dancing, even with a cousin, was more enjoyable for Henry than politics once he got an insider view. In his third year at the University, he dated the niece of the Mayoress of San Juan and saw close up the backstabbing and deals that went down behind the scenes when New York congressmen curried votes in Puerto Rico.

---

20. "Blue Moon" © 1934, Richard Rodgers and Lorenz Hart

"The political realm is not unlike an acting career," he says, but as a student acting was fun and it opened doors. Because he read poetry, performed Shakespeare and *Cyrano* he was welcome wherever creative students hung out. He circulated through different political organizations as easily as he circulated through dance halls, chess clubs, bars and coeds.

With coeds, if poetry, Shakespeare and an impish grin didn't melt their hearts, he sang. It was the thing for boys to congregate outside the girls' dormitories and serenade the girls. The serenades were accompanied by guitars and sometimes even a piano hauled in a truck. Henry's favorite song was "Blue Moon," a classic ballad of loneliness, luck and love. Crooned in his mellow baritone, it was a hit with girls and brought him more luck and love than loneliness.

The saying goes, "lucky at cards, unlucky at love," but what went for cards wasn't true for chess. Even lucky in love, he was good enough at chess to beat the Junior Champion of Puerto Rico. He spent hours a day on chess and memorized thousands of openings. He played blindfold chess, a game where the players can't see or touch the pieces. It was once considered a miraculous display of telepathy, but Darrow notes that blindfold chess is within the scope of any skilled player. "If you've played thousands of games and you've played at all levels, it's nothing unusual," he says dismissively.

But being skilled enough to play blindfold chess or to beat the Junior Champion took practice and practice took time. Between chess, acting, parties and girls, he didn't have many hours left for studying. His University counselor thought he needed to make some choices. Sitting him down, she asked, "How good are you at chess?"

He thought about it a moment. His play could be too tentative. In a match with the National Champion, he offered a draw. His father complained, "Why did you do that? You had him!"

The counselor was waiting for an answer. He shrugged. "So-so."

"Well, I've seen your work as an actor. If you could only do one, which would it be?"

"Oh, actor, I guess."

She nodded. "Then you'd better give up chess, because you're making a lot of Ds in your classes."

He gave up chess. "I didn't have the instinct that the best players have, the persistence to stick it out for the chance to get back in the game," he says.

On the other hand, he knew in his bones he had persistence as an actor. All he needed was a chance. Approaching his fourth year at the university, he bumped into Ivan Rodriguez, who asked, "Are you in the scholarship program? Are you competing?"

"I didn't know what he was talking about," says Darrow about the two acting scholarships available through the Little Theatre of Puerto Rico. They would be awarded to male students. "This was 1954. They did not give it to women. The thought was, their boyfriends or families wouldn't let them go or if they went, they'd get married, have children and they'd stop acting. That attitude was very prevalent in Puerto Rico in the 'fifties."

To compete, applicants put together several three minute scenes. Darrow says, "Of course, being twenty, you do Willie Lohman, things way over your head." His dad helped him rehearse.

He won.

He could get a scholarship to New York's Neighborhood Playhouse, Yale School of Drama or the Pasadena Playhouse in California. Discovering the Pasadena Playhouse was about twenty miles from Hollywood made his decision. Hollywood was movie Mecca and Pasadena was closer than New York or New Haven. His mother sewed five hundred hard-earned dollars into the lining of his jacket and he was on a plane to California.

September 27, 1954
Dear Mr. Delgado:

We are happy to advise you that you have been accepted as a student in the fall class, degree group, 1954.

May we congratulate you on winning the scholarship from the Little Theatre of Puerto Rico. Mr. Esteves speaks very highly of you and we are sure you are a very deserving winner.

Enclosed please find our receipt in the amount of $20.00 covering application fee and room deposit.

We ask all students living in the residence halls to furnish their own sheets (twin size), blankets, towels, etc. The address is 139 North El Molino Avenue. It will save you much trouble if you have your luggage sent directly there.

Enclosed is a form letter concerning costume. Again, let us state that we neither expect nor wish you to purchase any of these items. This is merely to be used as a guide.

May we say again congratulations and we shall be looking forward to meeting you when classes begin on October 4th.

Sincerely,
Margaret Bryant
Director of Admissions

The Pasadena Playhouse

Shaping of the actor came at Pasadena,
EXCEPTIONAL;
Ready to win laurels and fame...
And though we're far apart,
there's one thing I can't hide;
You're so engraved in my heart,
I swell with joy and pride.

GLORIA DELGADO[21]

Ask Dennis Delgado if he's envious of his older brother and his response is unequivocal: "No. Acting is Henry's job." Of his one theatrical experience, the retired banker says, "I don't remember how old I was, maybe five or six. I had to be Santa Claus. The mask would go sideways. I was sweating. I ended up crying and just ran off the stage."

But Henry ran to the stage, not away from it.

He had instructions to go to the Playhouse and telephone his roommate, an actor/dancer he knew back in Puerto Rico, who would take him to the dormitory a few blocks away. But he didn't have directions to the Playhouse. Talking with the girl seated next to him on the plane to Los Angeles, he mentioned his destination. When they landed, she told him she lived in Pasadena. He caught a ride with her.

Since he had completed basic coursework for his Bachelor of Arts degree in Puerto Rico, at the Playhouse he concentrated on theater classes. For once in his life, school was easy. Every aspect fascinated him — building sets, stage managing, costumes, acting, choreography, music, makeup, fencing, saber, tap dancing, ballet. It was a well-rounded education, but even though backstage work was engrossing, being on stage was better. "You did scenes continuously," he recalls. "They started with the most

21. Excerpt from unpublished poem, personal papers of Henry Darrow

difficult Greek tragedy or Shakespeare. Not full productions, all scenes. It was scene after scene all year long." Eventually, when scenes were polished enough, the students performed on the main stage, in front of the curtain. "There were great steps leading up to the stage and we acted on those steps. You could use them in a very dramatic way."

Like his father during the Great Depression and legions of aspiring performers, Hank Delgado took odd jobs to make ends meet. He delivered papers. He worked as a deck hand for ten dollars a day and a discount on beer. He performed in children's theater, which sometimes paid a few bucks. He sold Grolier's Encyclopedias for a time and kept bounced checks from the company so when he made it big, he could show people how far he'd come.

His classmates were from varied backgrounds. Pasquale "Pat" Tanno, a short, wiry veteran of the 82nd Airborne, had tuition covered by the G.I. Bill but side jobs like pumping gas paid for everything else. "Hank and I really dipped into poverty during those early years," says Tanno, who like Delgado grew up in a working-class family during the Depression. "You learned how to get by on whatever you had, which was nothing."

On the opposite end of the spectrum were students like Morteza Kazerouni and Stan Lachman. The son of an Iranian textile merchant, Kazerouni tooled around town in a glossy Cadillac, but like Tanno and Delgado, had sights set on a serious acting career. For Lachman, a good-looking boy from a prominent San Francisco family, being at the Playhouse was more of a lark but like Tanno and Kazerouni, he was one of Hank Delgado's pals.

The young women in Hank's class were as diverse as the men. Among them was Ruth Buzzi, the eighteen-year-old daughter of a respected sculptor. "Ruthie was a riot," says Tanno of the versatile actress who later starred in the 1960s megahit variety show *Rowan and Martin's Laugh-In*. "With her, you couldn't tell where the script ended and the adlibs started. She was great. From her to Lucy, that was the gamut of types."

"Lucy" was sophisticated Louise DePuy from a prominent family in Rochester, New York. Lucy's father made millions manufacturing furniture and she and her siblings grew up in the privileged world of private schools and debutante balls. Bright and innately talented, Lucy was in professional productions with stars like Victor Jory and ZaZu Pitts and later graduated *Cum Laude* from the Playhouse. She attracted Stan Lachman and they began dating, but she caught Hank Delgado's eye.

Delgado's Puerto Rican ways flopped with the girls in California. Female classmates admired his talent and onstage electricity. They were charmed by his mischievous sense of humor and courtly manners. But as a date, his in-charge attitude and possessiveness were off-putting even in the 1950s. His first girlfriend was a prostitute and not as finicky. Recovering from culture shock, he made a few adjustments and had a wider selection of girls to have fun with, but ladylike, confident Lucy DePuy had everything he thought he wanted in a wife. Sure that she was The One, he told Tanno, "That's the girl I'm going to marry."

Although Hank and Lucy had been in class together since the beginning, she didn't notice him until they were in the group organizing background music for *A Streetcar Named Desire*. Lucy later said, "Hank took over completely, directing the group project. I didn't mind; he knew just what he was doing, and I admired his ability to take complete charge of everything."[22] She thought he was dynamic, considerate and comfortable to talk with, but he was also a flirtatious ladies' man and reserved Lucy wouldn't have considered him a serious suitor even if she hadn't been dating Stan.

Patient and intensely determined, twenty-one year old Hank Delgado bided his time. When the relationship between Lucy and Lachman wasn't looking too healthy, he wondered if he had a chance and asked Stan, "What's going on with you and Lucy?"

"Well, Hank," his friend replied, "Lucy was a virgin before she met me and she still is."

To Delgado it was a bright green light and he revved up his campaign to win Lucy DePuy. Lucy didn't see him as a potential husband, but mentioned him more in letters to her parents. They imagined her married to a doctor or lawyer and increasingly worried that she was falling for an actor. Lucy maintained they weren't dating, only friends spending time together.

When Lucy returned to Rochester for the summer, Delgado realized he was in love with her. He wrote long letters. She answered. Since he knew her parents objected to him, he was surprised when they let her return to Pasadena. Back at the Playhouse, she knew she cared for Hank Delgado, but resisted falling in love with him. Nonetheless, after about a week of vigorous romancing from him, her resolve dissolved and fall she did. She wrote her parents about "the man I love" and when they learned he was Puerto Rican, her alarmed mother hopped a plane to California.

The only Puerto Ricans the DePuys had ever seen were in *West Side Story*. Even though Henry Delgado wasn't a switchblade-toting gang member, Mrs. DePuy warned Lucy that dating him was a terrible

22. Screen Stories, *10/68*

mistake. He was nice looking, quite charming and seemed to be from a good family, but his "background" was too different. Before boarding her return flight to Rochester, Mrs. DePuy cautioned Lucy not to do anything foolish and proved once again that parental disapproval is a potent aphrodisiac.

Mano, you are shameless!

VICTORIA CANNON[23]

23. The High Chaparral *episode "The Lost Ones," final script draft dated 5/28/69*

One Suit,
Two Weddings

Jaime: *I hope you understand my position.*

Manolito: *More important...I'm beginning to understand my position.*[24]

In Henry Delgado's second year at the Playhouse, his scholarship was cut in half and the dormitory became too expensive. Playhouse founder and head of the school, Gilmor Brown, offered to let him live in the wardrobe room for twenty-five dollars a month. He gratefully snapped it up. More like a miniature house than a room, it was filled with costumes but had a bathroom, tiny refrigerator and space to sleep. His mother sent him a toaster. He put it to good use since, short on funds, he subsisted mostly on lettuce and pepper sandwiches augmented by commissary specials, cheap restaurant eats and meals scrounged from his friends.

"Him and that beagle nose of his!" Pat Tanno laughs. "Anytime I was cooking, I'd get a knock on my apartment door and there'd be Hank. He had a prodigious appetite. One time the two of us ate a whole ham. I always told him he ought to weigh three hundred pounds, but he burned up a lot of energy. He put it into his work."

His prodigious appetite wasn't restricted to food. Since the wardrobe room was too public for romantic interludes with Lucy, Morteza Kazerouni loaned the couple his apartment. Recalls Tanno, "They were in love and they had a good relationship. She was very bright, so intellectually they hit it off. But life is such a crazy, unpredictable thing."

It could get crazy at Nardi's, a neighborhood gin mill with cheap eats near the Playhouse where Hank Delgado and Pat Tanno hung out. They drank and Delgado hustled chess. "Nardi had a little area in the back

24. *The High Chaparral episode "A Piece of Land"*

where I'd set up my board," he recalls. "I'd drink and play anybody who came to take me on. People drove miles to play chess with me and I'd pick up ten or fifteen extra bucks a week beating them. Nobody ever beat me, except Richard Lupino. The dirty rat! He even took pictures."

Once when Delgado and Tanno were at the long, narrow bar, another patron downed too many drinks and got loud. Nardi, a short, rotund Italian told the drunk he'd had enough and ordered him out. The drunk's buddy sitting next to him said, "Oh, relax, Nardi. He just had a couple."

"You with him?" Nardi asked. The drunk's pal nodded. "Okay! You get out, too!" Nardi grabbed a baseball bat he kept for protection. Brandishing the bat and hollering, he worked his way down the bar until he chased most of his customers out.

"We had a lot of fun with Nardi," says Tanno. "For all of us, going to the bar was a way to blow off some steam and Hank loved to kick and relax with a few beers." But Delgado was Good Time Charlie with a chess player's shrewdness. "The guys at the Playhouse who were in the Master's program, they hung out there, too. They were like gods, because they knew things. Hank the diplomat had the ability to get along with just about anybody. It's an extremely important part of his success as an actor. He has the talent, the looks, the voice, the charisma — all those gifts. But he was also very astute. At Nardi's he would get a lot of information from the Master's students about teachers, upcoming shows, how to play a particular character, available agents, where the jobs were."

He learned the unemployment compensation ropes from struggling graduate actors. Unemployment benefits are based on earnings and he recalls, "The actors I admired were the ones making $55.00 a week in unemployment. That was that was the highest you could collect back in the '50s and it meant, hey, man, you've made it!"

Although Delgado was a long way from earning enough to be eligible for maximum unemployment benefits, his enthusiasm and magnetism on stage set him apart from the others in his graduating class. Actress/comedian Ruth Buzzi says, "Hank was a wonderful, wonderful guy, just full of the devil, the most talented man in school when I was there, certainly the most talented in our class." Onstage, he had surreptitious ways of making her laugh. The audience never caught on. "If people just knew how funny he can be! He should have the lead on a comedy series."

Instead, he was the leading man in a real life drama. Young and in love, he and Lucy steamed up the windows in Kazerouni's apartment.

Hank joked about marriage some day. She laughed. Then she became pregnant and someday turned into right now.

Since Hank was eager to go to the bullfights in Tijuana and Tijuana was also a popular spot for quickie marriages, his friend Martin "Smitty" Smith suggested a trip there could do double duty. Hank thought it was a great idea. He, Lucy and Smitty were off to Tijuana.

Hank wore his only suit. Smitty, a Playhouse graduate and former Coast Guard officer, was Best Man. The colorful, alcoholic New Orleans native was a perfect Best Man for a boozy Tijuana ceremony. After becoming husband and wife, Hank and Lucy toasted with tequila, then he took her to see her first bullfight. Unfortunately, a hasty South of the Border marriage to a struggling Puerto Rican actor was hardly the lovely ceremony the DePuys envisioned for their daughter. They were furious.

To appease them, the couple agreed to another wedding at an Episcopal church in Rochester. Off they went across country, stopping to visit friends from school on the way. Lucy drove. Hank ate everything in sight and his weight ballooned to well over two hundred pounds by the time they arrived in Rochester. They got there two weeks before the wedding so the DePuys could get to know Henry Delgado better and see what a swell guy he was. It didn't work. They still thought he was a no-good bum. Her father made him sign a prenuptial agreement relinquishing any claims to Lucy's money.

"The DePuys were blue bloods, stringent about everything, very straight laced. Uppity," recalls Pat Tanno. "Hank's family wasn't like that. His mother was just a bundle of joy."

Enrique and Gloria Delgado might have preferred their son marry a nice Puerto Rican girl, but they were happy and supportive. Smiling warmly and dressed to the elegant nines, they arrived in Rochester where Lucy's parents gave them a polite but chilly welcome. Tata got off to a bad start with Lucy's father when she insisted on playing cards with the men. Hank became good friends with Lucy's artist brother Charles, but the only others who hit it off were Tata and Lucy's poker-playing aunt.

While the newlyweds were in Rochester, their pal Smitty was supposed to find an apartment for them in Los Angeles. Since looking for an apartment would have interfered with his drinking, Smitty didn't follow through. But just down from Smitty's house on Las Palmas, Hank spied a place for rent. It was a tiny, dilapidated efficiency with a Murphy bed in the living room. At only sixty-five bucks a month, it was cheap, convenient and better than the wardrobe room at the Pasadena Playhouse. Hank thought it was great and signed the lease. When his new bride saw it for the first time, she eyed the garish paper flowers on bamboo poles in the little apartment's sad little flower garden and broke down sobbing.

> *Invent me a means by which I can have love,*
> *beauty romance, emotion,*
> *passion without their wretched penalties, their*
> *expenses, their worries,*
> *their trials, their illnesses and agonies...*
>
> DON JUAN[25]

25. *George Bernard Shaw,* Don Juan in Hell, *http://www.gutenberg.org/catalog/world/ readfile?fk_files=1451939&pageno=108*

A Spanish Barrymore

Actors are strange people sometimes.

DIRECTOR WILLIAM WITNEY[26]

Henry Delgado graduated from the Pasadena Playhouse in 1956. He wasn't *cum Laude* like Lucy, but he had talent and stage presence. People noticed. When the wardrobe master explained the hard facts about acting to the twenty-plus students in Delgado's class, he said, "Almost all of you will fail to make a living as actors. I only see two of you who *might* make it: Ruth Buzzi and Hank Delgado."[27]

"Ruthie was wonderful. I was pretty good," says Darrow, who thought the wardrobe master had a fine eye for talent. "I thought, hey, man! I'm ready! Back then, you got your degree in movie and television acting, got married and went to live in the Hollywood Hills." Armed with a diploma, an attractive wife, skills honed at the Playhouse plus a can do attitude, his future looked golden.

But television and film casting directors weren't as impressed with Henry Delgado's B.A. degree as he imagined they would be. "There I was in Hollywood and I couldn't get a job. It was like they'd circle my name in red. 'Oh no, stage actor!' They thought of stage actors solely as over-actors." Of course, going overboard was his trademark. "At the Playhouse, they used to joke, 'Get the hook for Hank', because I would upstage everyone. They didn't want to give me a pipe or a wig or anything I could use to draw attention to myself," he admits. "But the truth is there's more discipline if you've done stage. You take direction better and you have background. While I was in school, I did thirty, forty different plays. In class you did scenes all the bloody time."

None of that meant spit to Hollywood and since one or two lines on a television show wasn't paying the bills, Delgado joined theater troupes

26. In a Door, Into a Fight, Out a Door, Into a Chase , *p.139*

27. Buzzi's impressive comedy career has spanned movies, television, nightclubs and the stage. She received a Golden Globe award from the Hollywood Foreign Press Association for Rowan and Martin's Laugh-In *in 1973 and was later inducted into the Radio and Television Hall of Fame* and did six to ten plays a year in productions with only a few weeks' rehearsal time. The good ones could run for a month. The turkeys opened and closed within three or four days. Most were turkeys. Eventually, theater contacts brought film and television roles, but that was iffy work, too. "People say, 'Oh Henry did over seventy-five TV shows.' That sounds good. But we're talking two or three lines in maybe seven shows a year and that ain't gonna make it. You've got three appointments this month, four the next, one the next and nothing the next. When the pilot season came around in February or March, you'd do more stuff. But you'd go to one audition and get a little part, then there would be a conflict because you'd get a real job that paid as a day player," Darrow says. "There were many skinny years and many times, I was ready to quit. But once a commitment is made, at what point do you say 'that's it for me?' To wipe out all those years and start over, how could I really do that?" Never a complainer, when discouraged he retreated silently into chess, playing against himself in replicated championship matches from the old Masters.

When he screen-tested at Paramount, they wanted Lucy. "She was a good actress, but she wasn't interested," he says. "She had photos taken, but she didn't build a résumé and she never went on interviews." Instead, she settled into being a housewife, always encouraging him to keep at it. She later admitted that after initial optimism and romanticism gave way to hard reality she wondered how they would survive. Her parents continued to criticize Hank and she cried often during the first six years. "I was pretty easily influenced by my family. If they had lived here, I'm sure the marriage would have been swamped pretty quickly," she reflected in a 1968 interview, adding, "If Hank hadn't been so understanding, I don't know what would have happened."[28]

"Well, you go with the program," he says. He maintained a friendly façade with his in-laws, but knew he would never have their respect or his own until he could support his family. As time passed, responsibilities grew and his income didn't. Respect seemed as elusive as stardom.

"He was an outcast with Lucy's family and that's difficult to digest," says Pat Tanno. "They thought he was just drifting through the Hollywood scene. He has the tendency to be sold a little short. It's a big mistake coming to that conclusion, because Hank is always ahead of just about everybody. He'll come out on top."

28. *"Special: The Wives Talk! At Home with the Henry Darrows," undated magazine clipping, files of Henry Darrow.*

The top seemed far away when Hank and Lucy's first child Denise (Deedee) was born in February of 1957, but at least Hank was working. He was onstage playing the Knight Templar in *Nathan the Wise* when Deedee drew her first breath. In a bit of media misinformation the papers reported he had named her 'Templar' for his role in the play, but the error didn't dim Hank's excitement. When his baby daughter came home from the hospital, he was so happy and grateful he cried. Eleven years later, he still chose her birth as the biggest thrill in his life.[29] Deedee was a welcome addition to the family for everyone, especially grandparents on both sides. Although her bedroom was a closet with just enough space for a crib, the cramped apartment on Las Palmas quickly filled with furniture and toys, gifts from the DePuys.

Hank and Lucy's purse strings stretched to the breaking point, but they got by. Once or twice a week, they ate with Kazerouni and his American wife Sandy at their place. "He'd get $1200 a month from his family in Iran, she'd cook. We'd freeload off them," says Darrow, who rode the bus to auditions until Lucy's father sold them a used Chevy for a dollar. To save money, Lucy cut her husband's hair. Her contribution to the annual household income was around three thousand dollars interest from a trust her father set up for her. Hank's income in 1957 was a lean $680 from acting and odd jobs.

He did carpentry work and moved furniture for a company that employed hungry young actors. He delivered papers part time, riding along with Rita Hayworth's brother Eduardo Cansino in Cansino's blue Buick convertible at 4:30 in the morning, tossing the *Hollywood Citizen News* onto steps along Hollywood Boulevard.

He flopped as a printing salesman, but had better luck working at the Lyceum of Dramatic Arts, an acting school founded by his college mentor Juano Hernandez. During Hernandez' solid career in movies and television, he acted with big name stars who offered to help out if he ever came to Hollywood. When he did, he started The Lyceum and discovered those previous offers of help were just empty talk.

The Lyceum was on Hollywood Boulevard, in a building dubbed "the White Elephant". Every other business there died and Hernandez' school lasted only three years, but for the first year he paid Hank Delgado to teach Spanish accents and pronunciation. "I was there to do scenes with people during auditions. I didn't have the proper education to be a teacher, but I took two years of phonetics at the Playhouse and I could do phonetics."

Hernandez wasn't the only connection to Puerto Rico that came through. The Puerto Rican Film Commission had an office in Beverly

29. 16 Magazine, *"Henry Darrow Answers 20 Snoopy ?'s,"* 12/68

Hills and gave parties to market Puerto Rico to Hollywood. Bacardi Rum supplied the alcohol. Henry Delgado bartended for free and made contacts. "I met producers. I met Joe Ferrer and other Puerto Rican actors. I always thought if nothing happened in my acting, I'd go back to Puerto Rico and work in the film commission department there."

Beginning when he was a student at the Playhouse, his mother wrote encouraging letters to him every week ("Dear Tat, Acting is a part of you. You love it more than anything and you will make it big."). After graduation, Enrique wrote also ("Remember the case of Clark Gable. It took him a long time, too."). When Enrique told Augusto Rodriguez that Henry needed support, Augusto wrote letters urging him to be persistent, to do whatever it took to succeed. Letters from home bolstered him when, as he says, "things got a little thick." He gave himself five years to make it. The first five stretched to ten, then beyond.

In 1958, he had a collection of bounced checks from derelict theater companies and an income of $800 from acting and odd jobs. On the bright side, his unemployment benefits were $28 a week, enough over the minimum that he figured, "Hey, I'm finally making it!"

He joined Projects '58, a professional actor's workshop formed by mostly New York stage actors: Warren Oates, Rupert Cross, Michael Parks, Susan Oliver. "It was a powerful group. These were people I saw regularly on television," he says. "I just got lucky. I was invited to join after someone saw me in a play."

"Basically it was an actors' studio. You got up before the group and set up the premise of what you wanted to attain in a scene, an accent or a dialect. If you wanted to do a Shakespeare monologue, you'd introduce it by saying you wanted it to be in iambic pentameter and also easily understood by the audience." The other members critiqued or applauded.

At one point, Projects '58 had temporary accommodations in the basement of a senior citizens' home. The rules of the place prohibited applause after nine o'clock in the evening, so to show approval the group snapped their fingers. Reflects Darrow, "When you hear thirty or forty people snapping their fingers, it's rather bizarre. I used it later in roles and people would ask, 'What is he doing *now?*'"

Sometimes directors said, whatever you're doing, stop it. "I had a lot of moxie and I just went out and acted over the top. Lots of times I cut my own throat, but I always felt, go out there and give it everything you have, because you may only have that one chance." He also didn't take direction especially well. It wasn't a profitable combination.

William Witney had been a director nearly as long as Henry Delgado had been alive. The respected Witney started with popular, low-budget serials in the 1930s and transitioned to television. In 1958 he was working on Walt Disney's *Zorro* adventure series starring Guy Williams. A director who didn't leave casting to the casting office, Witney was screen-testing actors for a continuing villain role. One of the young hopefuls was Henry Delgado. Witney told him to stop moving his head so much. Says Darrow, "He kept telling me, 'This is a close-up. Don't wave your gun because if you do any movement, you'll be in and out of the shot.' And I thought, he doesn't know what he's talking about." Arm around an actress and prop gun in his hand, he ignored Witney and played it his way. He was pleased when he heard Witney mutter, "Well, it looks like we have a Spanish Barrymore on our hands."

"I went home that evening and wrote my mother. 'He said I was a Spanish Barrymore.' She wrote back, 'Sweetheart, John Barrymore was known for being a hambone, an over actor. They may not have liked your work,'" he says with a laugh.

"Sure enough, another guy got the part, Carlos Romero. He eventually became a friend of mine and guest starred on *High Chaparral*. He was very underplayed, very smooth, but I could hardly hear him! And of course, I was acting all over the place and bombed like a turkey. But rejection when you're younger, at least for me, was hey, you guys made a mistake!"

Eventually, he learned. "At auditions if they said, bring it down a little, there was interest. If they just said 'thank you', you'd gone over the top and that was the end."

On television's small screen, he learned that less is more. "If you do too much, you'll stand out," says Darrow. "If you're one of the stars, then that's proper. But if you're a support player, they'll say, 'That's okay, Mr. Delgado, just dance and turn. Don't get on your knees and shout hallelujah. We're focusing on Mr. Rock Hudson here.'"

> *Without an enlarged ego an actor wouldn't be a performer in the first place. His face and body are as much a part of his working equipment as a carpenter's plane, a painter's brush, an attorney's library; indeed, a reporter's typewriter.*
> UPI HOLLYWOOD REPORTER VERNON SCOTT[30]

30. *The Bucks County (PA) Courier Times, "Every Actor Must Have Enlarged Ego,"* 1/25/69

Too Latin but Not Latin Enough

Andy: *Hey, how you doing? Uh, listen, they like you at Warner Bros. But they think you're not ethnic enough. They wanted you to be more ethnic.*

Rick: *Would a burro and a bandanna have helped? She said I was lucky to have such an interesting background.*

Andy: *That's what she says to you. To me, she said, "They wanted you to be more ethnic."*

Rick: *What about CBS?*

Andy: *They love you, but you're a little too ethnic for them. But they still loved you.*

WRITER/COMEDIAN RICK NAJERA[31]

Henry Delgado was trying to establish himself as an actor, not just a Hispanic actor. Initially he wasn't aware of the endemic discrimination his surname bought. His agents were. One after another, they suggested he change his last name. He persistently refused, although he became more alert to stereotyping's impact on his career.

He was seldom interviewed for non-Latin parts, but Latin roles didn't come easily either. Most Hispanic actors had stereotypical bit parts as servants, border guards, gigolos or other riff-raff, but at least those parts paid. As ex-*Tarzan* Denny Miller observes, "People who are typecast seem to work more than the others, at least in film." Unfortunately for Delgado, typecasting wasn't an option. A tall, fair-skinned New Yorker with brown

---

31. From A Quiet Love (play)

hair and hazel eyes, he didn't fit the popular stereotype. He was "too white," and "not ethnic enough." He was accused of being Jewish and trying to pass himself off as Puerto Rican. One casting director refused to give him a part as a Latin because his English was too good.

Writer/publicist Luis Reyes says, "There were a lot of stereotypes. We were always suffering gang members or their mothers or *bandidos* or *caballeros*. A lot of Hispanic actors like Martin Sheen had to change their names or hide their identities to pursue better roles. Sheen's real name is Ramón Estevez. He'd walk into an interview and they'd be expecting some stereotypical, short Hispanic like Pepino on *The Real McCoys* and this nice looking young man would walk in. They'd get thrown off."

Like Sheen, Henry Delgado defied pigeonholing when he appeared for auditions. Unfortunately, most casting agents sought actors who could be neatly categorized and shuffled into clichéd roles. "Since I didn't fit the criteria," he recalls, "it took quite a bit of time before I started doing my two lines, three lines."

He went through a series of agents including Wallace Middleton (who represented *Superman* George Reeves) and Harold Swoverland, a tough old bird with a seedy office on Santa Monica Boulevard. Swoverland, who specialized in actors for ethnic roles, said Delgado's surname wasn't a problem but suggested he change his first name to Frank. Incredulous, he declined.

His first top agent was Wynn Rocomorra, a cultivated man with elegant white hair who favored cufflinks and sharp blue suits and whose clientele included established actors. Rocomorra had gone to see another actor in a play when he spotted relatively unknown Henry Delgado. Delgado had electric onstage charisma and Rocomorra signed him. "He thought I had something to offer. He sent me all over the place to meet casting directors," says Darrow. But his offstage persona left them cold. "I just didn't have a facility at that time to present myself well in auditions. I talked about theater in Puerto Rico as if it were Broadway or Off-Broadway."

Rocomorra told him that if he had seen Delgado in an interview, he would have never taken him as a client. "You've got nothing going on," he told the actor.

Since competition for roles was fierce, Delgado's inability to wow casting directors left him scrambling for voice-overs, children's theater productions and innumerable other low-paying performances. Not all were legal.

At night in small sound studios on Santa Monica Boulevard, after regular unionized audio work was done, a hidden industry came alive. Through the doors of the little studios crept actors like Henry Delgado to do non-Union work. They were there to dub English language movies into Spanish, English commercials into Spanish or to provide background noises for film or television—laughing, chewing food or muted talking. They weren't paid anything close to Union scale, but they were paid and nobody told them they didn't look Latin enough.

But neither Delgado's marginal employment nor his minimal income dimmed Hollywood's glamour and when one of the first twenty-four hour markets opened blocks from the Las Palmas apartment, the star-struck young actor discovered it was a prime location to see some of the biggest names in the business. Even movie stars need groceries, so Hughes Market was filled with stellar shoppers headed home after Dodgers games. Delgado, a Dodgers fan since they were in Brooklyn, sat in the cramped apartment listening to baseball on the radio. When the game ended, he waited about forty-five minutes, then walked to Hughes Market. He'd buy a quart of cheap beer and stand around hoping to catch a glimpse of Donald Sutherland, Marlon Brando or Marty Feldman. He'd look at what they bought and listen as they talked baseball. After seeing him a few times over the season, sometimes they'd glance his way and say hi.

For low-budget eats in the neighborhood, Delgado visited The Clock or Miceli's Pizzeria ("Hollywood's Oldest Italian Restaurant Since 1949") for a medium cheese pizza. It was the only thing on the menu he could afford. He shared with other struggling actors.

Across the alley from Miceli's, around the corner from the flop-houses, strip clubs and grand old theaters on Hollywood Boulevard was Las Palmas Theatre. Hank Delgado cut his teeth at Las Palmas in productions like *The Tormented*, a stinker about Communists in Hollywood. Veteran character actor John Milford had the lead and Delgado had a supporting role. There were about thirty people in the cast. One night, the 600-seat theater had about fourteen people in the audience. The curtain rose anyway. In Act II, when Delgado went on the audience started walking out. He was trying to perform in the aisle and kept bumping into them, but continued performing. *The Hollywood Reporter* panned the play under the caption "*The Tormented* Torments Reviewer."

I don't want to ruin anyone's dream, so I tell them at least grow some sort of defense mechanism to help you deal with rejection, because you're going to get it.

ACTOR DENNY MILLER

King of the Border Guards

*I did it because I needed the money for basics —
like food, rent and analysis.*

ACTRESS RITA MORENO
ON ACCEPTING LOUSY PARTS[32]

By 1959 Hank Delgado's income from acting jumped to a whopping $1,100 from roles like "bus driver" in *Holiday for Lovers* and a nameless hotel clerk in the *noir* film *The 3rd Voice*. He also had his first starring role in a movie that year. That's the good news. Unfortunately, the movie was *Revenge of the Virgins,* a topless western written by schlockmeister Edward Wood under the pseudonym Pete LaRoche. Wood (*Plan 9 from Outer Space*, 1959) posthumously won a Golden Turkey Award for being the worst director ever. After his death in 1978, his films attracted an enthusiastic following of bad cinema connoisseurs, leading to a well-received biopic directed by Tim Burton and starring Johnny Depp. But back in 1959, Wood was just a box office disaster.

Directed by Peter Perry Jr. (who gave the world 1961's *Honeymoon of Terror* and 1978's *Cycle Vixens*), *Revenge of the Virgins* seemed like a typical low-budget western to the actors during filming. Delgado transcended lousy writing, directing, photography, somnambulant co-stars and rubber rattlesnakes to give a credible performance as double-crossing Wade. Because a good performance in a bad movie trumps no performance in no movie, it would have been résumé worthy. Then Hank Delgado learned footage of explicitly topless "Indian" maidens had been spliced into the film post production. This little trick drew audiences in the days when low-budget films weren't censored and it made his first starring movie role one he couldn't crow about — or even

---

32. Reyes and Rubie, p. 520

mention. Hoping to get parts he could actually list on his résumé, he went shopping for a new agent and landed in the right place at the right time.

The hard L.A. pavement led him to Carlos Alvarado's office on Sunset Boulevard. Alvarado was the only Latino agent in Hollywood and he represented solely Hispanic supporting and character actors. Former casting director Susan McCray describes him as classy, debonair and highly dependable. "He was very kind and the type of man you would trust to bring you the best talent he had to offer," she says.

Heading upstairs to Alvarado's office, Delgado met a tall, dark, mustachioed young man coming down. He asked if Delgado needed an agent. Delgado said yes. "Talk to my uncle, Carlos Alvarado," said the other man. "He might be looking for an actor because I'm leaving to join the Army." Val de Vargas left for his date with Uncle Sam. Henry Delgado signed with the Carlos Alvarado Agency.

Since Alvarado received only scripts with Hispanic parts, Henry's Spanish accent was a problem. He spoke Spanish with a heavy English accent and wasn't convincing in Latino roles. "In the beginning, I tried phonetic substitutions," he says. "But when you're surrounded by legit Mexicans, that's not the thing to do. They're for real and my pretending an accent just didn't make it."

Alvarado had the solution. "He told me to pronounce Spanish words and names properly and they'd think my accent was fine," says Darrow. "Basically, that was the truth. It worked out very well most of the time."

Alvarado got him work and kept him working, but vying for TV and movie roles, Delgado experienced firsthand how completely Hispanic actors were pigeonholed. Theater casting by then mostly hinged on skill instead of ethnicity, but film and television judged differently. "I played Martinez, Lopez, José, Pepé and Carlos for a number of years," he says. A gifted baritone of Russian descent played Daniel Boone's Indian sidekick Mingo, but "Delgado would not be up for the part of Corporal Leutz from Germany."

His first onscreen kiss and first death scene came in a Latin role in Universal's *Curse of the Undead* (1959). It was the same scene. He played the ill-fated Roberto, brother of bloodsucking gunslinger Drago Robles, in one of the few western vampire movies ever made. Unfortunately, the *vaqueros* and vampires genre never caught on. He obviously needed to cultivate wider appeal.

He became "Henry Delgado from New York" instead of "Henry Delgado from Puerto Rico," but to little avail. "It was 'Oh…Delgado…good actor, but we don't have any Latins in this script, Carlos. We can't use him'." Shut out from the get-go, he couldn't make connections through the usual means. He became Alvarado's chauffeur and his natural affability paid off. Driving his agent to the studios, he met casting office personnel and eventually was on first name basis with them. They began throwing him uncredited roles with, if he was lucky, a line or two of dialogue. But Hollywood has been called a meat market and day players with a line or two are cheap ground chuck. He almost lost an eye while in San Diego filming *Manhunt*, a half hour series starring Victor Jory and featuring screen veteran Paul Dubov.

During a dramatic scene, a nervous young actor was pointing a gun at Delgado's head. He says, "He was supposed to shoot at least a foot off the side, but he moved his hand back. I moved my face, because I knew something was going to happen." The fired blank luckily held only a quarter load. It caught Delgado on the left side of his face, just missing his eye. The impact point swelled immediately. Dubov called for a nurse to clean him up and wash his eye out, but the director ordered, "No, just turn the kid around."

"So I turned my face to the other side and we kept going." By the time the nurse saw his wound, it was infected.

Calling Dubov a wonderful actor, he says, "You always met those established character actors that you could follow. You could see them prepare and copy them. I wasn't going to be like a lot of other young actors. Their attitude was, 'Hey man, I'm here doing two lines for two days, one inside the house and one on the porch. I got a two day job!' They'd say their lines and vanish." He knew opportunity when it knocked and hung around the set, watching and learning.

From parts with one or two lines, he moved upward and captured a few plum guest spots on television shows scheduled for cancellation. "Actors who have name value didn't do shows that were going off the air, so that was an opportunity for somebody like me to step in and get a secondary or tertiary guest role. I might only have three scenes, but they would be good ones," he says.

In a film adaptation of Tennessee Williams' *Summer and Smoke* (1961), he played his most frequent role, Uncredited. Rita Moreno was one of the stars of the movie.

Moreno had not yet won her Oscar for *West Side Story*[33] when she made *Summer and Smoke*, but she was getting noticed, mostly as a screen sexpot. A talented actress, singer, dancer and comedienne, she was

---

33. *She was the first Latina to win for Best Supporting Actress and the only one until Penélope Cruz in 2008. As of 2010, she is still the only Puerto Rican Best Supporting Actress. She is among the few performers to win an Oscar, Emmy, Grammy and Tony.*

discovered on Broadway by Hollywood talent scouts who convinced her she could make it big in the movies. First at M-G-M then at Twentieth Century-Fox, Moreno found work mainly in B-movies and television as the stereotypical Latin spitfire, Native American or other "exotic" women. She played these parts the same way, "Barefoot with my nostrils flaring."[34] She needed the money and said in a later interview, "It is important that people understand that there are many indignities that I went through simply because I'm Latina."[35]

Summer and Smoke was average Neurotics Under The Magnolias fare and Moreno's sultry Rosa Zacharias was no real departure from other sexy spitfire parts. But even in a role she disliked, dynamic Moreno enchanted Henry Delgado. During a dance sequence, director Peter Glenville called out, "I need somebody to dance with Miss Moreno!" Awestruck Delgado hesitated for about five seconds, then jumped from his chair. He was too late. Someone else was already swirling her across the floor.

He hesitated to take Rita Moreno in his arms, but grabbed any available acting job, like the gig at the Saturday Children's Theatre which would have paid $19.00 if their check had been any good. It wasn't, but his luck was changing. In 1960, he was Second Mexican Policeman in *Cage of Evil* (the tagline screamed, "Blonde Bait…in a Murder Trap!"). In 1961, movie goers caught a glimpse of him as Pvt. Tonto in the Korean War drama *Sniper's Ridge*. In September of that year, he was at the Music Box Theater playing John Wilkes Booth in *Stovepipe Hat*, the only musical ever written about the assassination of Abraham Lincoln. Lucy was pregnant with their second child.

On September 20, Lucy was supposed to be seated in the first row. Henry looked for her, but she wasn't there. Then his friend Smitty, who was working backstage, brought word that she was in delivery.

In the play, Lincoln never appears, but there's a recitation of the Gettysburg Address with a crowd onstage. History says the Gettysburg audience couldn't hear Lincoln well and responded with just a polite smattering of applause. "And that's how it had been done," says Darrow. "Then at the point where Lincoln gets his little round of applause, the backstage door opened and Smitty came and whispered to me, 'It's a boy!' I went to the curtain and told somebody 'it's a boy, my wife had a boy'. The word spread around in a matter of seconds and at the drum roll where

34. Reyes and Rubie, p. 520

35. http://www.hollywoodchicago.com/news/11671/interview-oscar-winner-rita-moreno-on-her-life-in-america

Lincoln finishes his address, everyone applauded." Thomas Delgado's birth gave Lincoln his biggest hand ever.

As for little Tom's dad, playing John Wilkes Booth and a host of other non-Latino characters onstage didn't open opportunities in film and television. There, he was largely relegated to playing uncredited Latino faces in the crowd or nameless Mexican bus drivers and policemen.

"I was King of Border Guards," he says, but after *Stovepipe Hat* came a discouraging dry spell when he couldn't even find border patrol parts. That dry spell came shortly after Lucy's parents helped them make a down payment on a $16,000 tract house in a Sun Valley suburb.

The house had three bedrooms, two bathrooms, modern no wax vinyl floors and a modest monthly note of $159. It was the kind of home post war, middle class Americans flocked to, nestled on a *Leave It To Beaver* street lined with white picket fences, palm trees and nearly identical houses. The homogeneity of such places inspired the 1962 Malvina Reynolds musical critique "Little Boxes," but conformity wasn't the only story. Crime was low, schools were good, neighbors looked after one another and people in the suburbs, like people everywhere, had their own unique lives, dreams and hopes.

With a house note and two kids, Henry Delgado hoped he could find a job.

For months, he couldn't even get an interview. Income from Lucy's stocks plummeted, expenses siphoned their savings and just when it seemed things couldn't get worse, Henry's unemployment benefits were denied. The disqualifying letter dated May 25, 1962 reads:

> *You restrict acceptable employment to the theatrical field. Your earnings have been low for the past two years and you have not worked since October 1961. Your restrictions eliminate the major portion of jobs available. Your earnings show there is little labor market for you in acting.*

It was a devastating draw to a losing hand and he almost folded. Acting was all he knew how to do. Then the economic development organization of Puerto Rico stepped in, ready to hire him for $6,000 per year plus expenses to encourage industries to locate in Puerto Rico. As soon as he said yes, he got a small television role, then a play. Yes became no and soon he was climbing the Hollywood ladder again.

In a 1963 episode of the Jack Lord vehicle *Stoney Burke*, he's credited as Henry Delgado in the role of "Mexican Border Policeman". In his only significant scene, he greeted Stoney (Lord) and his sidekick Ves Painter (Warren Oates) when they pulled up to the border. Painter was driving and in the first take, Stoney addressed the border guard, "Excuse me, *señor*, how do you get to…."

Painter interrupted. "Stoney, here, let me take care of it. I speak Spanish." In halting, badly accented Spanish, he turned to the guard. "*Señor… por favor…a donde es…*a Buena Vista?"

Delgado's few lines were supposed to be in heavily accented English. Instead, he replied in perfect New Yorkese, "Sure, just take sixteen down to the cross, go about eight miles, hang a right on Cliff and you're there." Lord, not famous for his sense of humor, cracked up but that version was cut. In the final take, Delgado greets the two men with "Welcome to México, *señores*" and continues in lightning fast *Español* while Stoney and Ves stare helplessly.

Others who worked with meticulous Lord found him difficult, but says Darrow, "He always treated me well. He always remembered me and he always remembered me as Delgado."

> *Jack was a very particular person, very picky and always got upset about certain things, but when it came to Henry Darrow, he looked at me and said, "Now there's an actor!"*
>
> CASTING DIRECTOR SUSAN McCRAY

You'll Never Experience Anything Worse

Henry always went in thinking,
"They're going to love me!"
You need that strength to make it in our business.

ACTRESS LAUREN LEVIAN

Slowly, Henry Delgado racked up an impressive list of theater performances and solid reviews, including *Family Portrait* ("Henry Delgado as Judas is striking"), *Blood Wedding, Yerma, Arms and the Man* ("Henry T. Delgado's opportunistic Nicola [was] striking"), *Moon in Capricorn, The Emperor* ("Henry Delgado, on briefly as the Apostle Paul, provides one of the play's better moments") as well as a few television roles in shows like *The Outer Limits* and *Voyage to the Bottom of the Sea.* Then he was offered a continuing part as a shady lawyer on the daytime drama *General Hospital.*

Daytime dramas were bread and butter for a television actor. They could make an entire lucrative career or be a springboard to bigger and better. They were coveted and more than paid the bills. It was the kind of steady work Delgado had longed for. Most young actors would not have walked away from *General Hospital* to take a low paying, temporary stage role, but Henry Delgado wasn't most young actors.

The Theatre by the Sea's production of *Othello* had commanding William Marshall in the lead, but nobody cast as Iago. Joseph Cotton wanted to do it. So did José Ferrer who had played Iago on Broadway with Paul Robeson in the lead. But the production had only seven days left for rehearsals and Cotton and Ferrer needed several weeks more to rehearse. Not Henry Delgado. He said no to *General Hospital* and rushed in. "It's one of the greatest roles in theater," he says. "What else could I do?"

Rehearsals were hectic and emotions between cast members ran a little high. Conflicts resulted and chaos ensued. When the director intervened in a fist fight, he was thrown into the concrete seats, breaking a leg. A new director with two good legs stepped in at the last minute.

With no time to memorize lines, Delgado had a script in hand during rehearsals, using it as a prop. Its Renaissance cover matched the period and he planned on using it during the play. "I established it in the beginning by not reading from it, but perusing it. So when I really needed it, I had it." But the night before opening night, he was given a new script. "It was one of the little paperbacks! The printing was different, the shape was different, the pages weren't turned like mine!"

There was no run-through of the play before the opening, so opening night would be the first complete performance. Mere hours before the curtain would rise, the actress playing Desdemona stormed off. She was replaced by an actress who had recently played Desdemona in another production at another theater.

By the time the curtain went up forty minutes late, the audience was restless. So tense he almost vibrated, Delgado had a death grip on his unfamiliar script, holding it open to mark Iago's sections. As he waited to make his entrance with Bill Marshall, the 6'5" Marshall leaned close and in his deep voice muttered, "I'm going to get your Puerto Rican white ass."

Delgado started laughing, forgetting the book for a moment. It closed in his hand. "Luckily, all the scenes with him I had memorized."

Unluckily, the lovely outdoor location was in a flyway for the Santa Monica airport and planes roared overhead throughout the play. They completely drowned out Desdemona's speech. When Othello spoke, Marshall's robust voice was big enough to hear over the aircraft engines, but his thunderous oration blew out a microphone. "It started an echo," says Darrow. "Then the fog rolled in. And then Rodrigo put his sword in the scabbard, but the fitting broke and the whole thing went flying across the stage." Not to mention the fire on the Pacific Coast Highway and the screaming sirens of passing emergency vehicles.

In another scene with Othello, Marshall forgot Delgado's book was more than a prop and slammed it shut during a heated exchange. Even the end wasn't merciful. The curtain was automatic and took an excruciating twenty-five seconds to close.

The result was what *The Long Beach Press-Telegram* generously called a "rocky" production.[36] Recalls Darrow, "People said I would never experience anything worse. And I never did."

Yet out of the most disaster filled performance of his life, he harvested good reviews.

36. *Long Beach (CA)* Press Telegram, *8/19/64*

"Henry Delgado…makes Iago almost the star of the show with an off-hand kind of villainy that made his evil charming. Even in his areas of reading from the book, Delgado performed with ease and perception, the book hardly perceptible in the performance." (Dale, *Variety*)

"Henry Delgado, a late replacement as Iago, was very promising," (James Powers, *The Hollywood Reporter*)

"Mr. Delgado…played the villain in a casual, off-hand manner that made his poisoning of Othello's mind more convincing and frightening than if he had underscored the evil." (Charles Faber, *Hollywood Citizen News*).

But when the play ended, the great role was done and he was out of a job. He was quickly disabused of the notion that people in television were impressed or even familiar with Shakespeare. When one casting director asked if he had ever played villains, he answered yes, he recently played Iago. Brow furrowed, the casting director stunned him by saying, "I missed that show. Is it going to be rerun?"

Lord, what fools these mortals be!
WILLIAM SHAKESPEARE

The Wonderful Ice Cream Suit

*Hard work pays off. If you want to be good, you
have to practice, practice, practice.
If you don't love something, don't do it.*

RAY BRADBURY[37]

Henry Delgado kept working, mostly at low paying or non-paying jobs in the theater. Rehearsals and performances could run late into the evening. If his in-laws called during the day and he was sleeping, they made snide remarks. To them, he was still a no-talent bum. They would invite Lucy and the children to family events in Rochester, as an after-thought adding, "If Hank wants to come along, tell him he's welcome." He got even by not going.

"That was my claim to fame in a negative way," he says. "It was like oh, yeah, this year I made $1300." He had confidence in his talent as an actor, but his inability to be the breadwinner badly dented his pride. That Lucy and his own parents believed in him didn't negate the fact that he had passed his thirtieth birthday and Lucy still kept the family afloat finan-cially. "I don't think any guy likes the idea of his wife supporting him, but that was the situation." He adds softly, "I was so ashamed."

Acting, the company of actors and actresses and nightlife were a refuge. Along with Janice Rule, Robert Blake, Dennis Hopper, Carroll O'Connor and a number of established actors, he became part of an informal Shake-spearean troupe with hard-partying members. It met at Ben Gazarra's home and didn't pay a dime, but he made connections that paid off later and everyone there knew who Iago was.

"There was a little bar nearby where Blake and I would go with some of the girls." He often didn't get home until early morning, just in time to catch a few hours of sleep before leaving again for rehearsals or auditions.

---

37. *Gene Beley,* Ray Bradbury: the Uncensored Biography *(2006), p.284*

It was an awfully bleak time for normally upbeat Darrow. His career wasn't proving his in-laws wrong, confirming his or his parents' confidence or soothing his wounded pride. Then popular science-fiction writer Ray Bradbury entered the picture with a play about six downtrodden Chicanos who pool their money to buy a magical white suit.

Of producing his own plays, Ray Bradbury wrote, "I talked it over with my wife, told her I thought the plays were more than good, that all the producers were wrong, as well as the bankers, and that I had to try, just once, to see whether or not I was the grandest fool of all."[38]

After saving money for a year the Bradburys rented the Coronet Theater in Los Angeles and successfully staged a production called *The World of Ray Bradbury* followed by a stage adaptation of a Bradbury short story, *The Wonderful Ice Cream Suit*. It premiered March 2, 1965 and ran for six gratifying months.

Although *Suit's* main characters are Mexican-American, in the original production only lovelorn José Martinez was played by a Latino — Henry T. Delgado.[39] But it was skillfully written, heartfelt piece with fine direction and acting. And it was a hit that spotlighted everyone including and perhaps especially, Delgado.

> *The cast of twenty players who flood the stage are uniformly excellent. The six buyers of the suit — Joby Baker, Len Lesser, Henry Delgado, Frederic Villani, Arnold Lessing and Gene Otis Shane — play wonderfully in concert, yet each struts in individual style in his solo moment.* (Cecil Smith, *The Los Angeles Times*)

> *...Each is superbly cast and each makes the others (and himself) shine...* (John Houser, *The Los Angeles Examiner*)

> *The play in its final hour seemed even better than in its premier performance six months ago with some truly remarkable performances by Joby Baker, Henry Delgado, Len Lesser, Fredric Villani and others.* (Cecil Smith, *The Los Angeles Times*)

---

38. *The Pandemonium Theater Company Presents The Wonderful Ice Cream Suit And Other Plays For Today, Tomorrow and Beyond Tomorrow, 1972, p. vii*

39. *Villanezul was played by Len Lesser, Vamenos by Joby Baker, Gomez by Frederic Villani, Manolo by Arnold Lessing and Dominguez by Gene Otis Shane.*

The Wonderful Ice Cream Suit" is a gem of fanciful thinking…the six principals individually catch the mood intended, outstanding, perhaps… (Whit, *Variety*)

These were "money reviews". They boosted Delgado's stock in the theater community, but more than that, Hollywood luminaries flocked to see the play and caught his sterling performance. He met Paul Newman and Ross Martin. James Garner bought him a drink. But he didn't know the man who would be most influential in his career was even in the audience.

David Dortort, creator and executive producer of the hit series *Bonanza*, had gone to see *The Wonderful Ice Cream Suit* because of the Latin characters. He habitually went to the theater to find new talent and needed actors for a new, gritty western with prominent Mexican roles. He was committed to using Latin actors in those parts, which included the starring role of Manolito, thirty-year-old son of the powerful Montoya family. He described Manolito Montoya, as "…The black sheep of the great Montoya family. A fighting man who has no fear and a horseman who looks like he was born in the saddle…and even dissipated, drunk, [and] wild, maintains his dignity of person that is his breeding. He was bred from a long line of noble families and shows it. He is 5 feet 10 inches slender with bright, vivid eyes and dark hair."[40]

Former casting director and Dortort family friend Susan McCray says, "I remember David saying he took one look at Hank and said, 'That's Manolito.'" But Dortort didn't meet Henry Delgado at the theater and when Dortort's people searched for that perfect actor to play Manolito Montoya, Henry Delgado had vanished.

> *That sonofagun got plumb away.*
>
> RENO[41]

---

40. *David Dortort quoted in* Riding the Video Range, *page 342*

41. The High Chaparral *episode "For What We Are About to Receive," script revision 5/1/68*

The Name Game

Starbuck: *What's wrong with my name?*

Lizzie: *It sounds fake. It sounds like you made it up!*

Starbuck: *You're darn right! I did make it up!...The name you choose for yourself is more your own than the name you were born with!* [42]

After finishing *The Wonderful Ice Cream Suit*, Delgado was again on the hunt for an agent. Carlos Alvarado's nephew Val de Vargas had come home from the Army. De Vargas and Delgado were similar in looks and type and Alvarado could use only one of them, so he let Delgado go. Delgado knew it was coming and he and Alvarado parted amicably, but he still needed a new agent.

He could not find one willing to represent him. He wasn't tall enough. He wasn't handsome enough. He wasn't Tony Curtis. In desperation he phoned an old friend, former Playhouse classmate Lester Miller.

Miller had been a professional fire eater until his beard ignited during a performance. He quit fire eating after that, became a hypnotist, then tried acting. His bulbous blue eyes and ragged beard gave him an unforgettably troll-like presence, but he was a lousy actor. He decided to be an agent instead.

When Delgado first met him at the Playhouse, Miller invited him to his apartment in Pasadena. "I said, what do you mean you're a fire eater?" Unconcerned with the apartment's low ceiling, Miller suddenly launched a demo. "And whoosh! He blows the stuff up and the frigging ceiling catches on fire! Oh, God!"

Incendiary tendencies and all, Delgado was fascinated with unconventional Miller. "He was a very smart man and I don't believe anyone in Hollywood had as extensive a collection of Chinese opera records," he

42. The Rainmaker, *p. 76*

says with a laugh. Miller was also a gourmet cook and oenophile who taught him about fine wines. "Les would give me some good wine and he'd say, 'I'm not going to give you any more after you've had a couple. I'll give you a glass of the good wine at the beginning, but after that, you just swallow it. You have to taste it, Henry. You have to swizzle it through your mouth'."

As an agent, he describes Miller as a "tough nut" and after Delgado was turned down for two parts in one day solely based on his surname, the tough nut decided his client needed an image overhaul, starting with his last name. This time, Delgado agreed. Other than Wade in *Revenge of the Virgins* and one guy named Blackie, his film and television parts had been Latino. "Besides, I was tired of competing with Alejandro Rey for roles," he quips.

They thumbed through an old phone book and saw there weren't many Darrows in Los Angeles. With that name, Henry hoped someone might think he was related to the famous attorney Clarence Darrow. When the question arose later, he said no, he was from the Darrows of Puerto Rico. "I must have said it to the wrong people, because they didn't find it amusing at all."

After the name came the image. When Henry Delgado went to interviews, he wore glasses, a suit and had his short hair parted on the side. It was a buttoned down 'fifties look in a mid-sixties world. *My Fair Lady* won the Best Picture Oscar in 1965, but a hurricane of change was blowing through America. Civil rights demonstrators marched in the South. Protests against the Vietnam War escalated. Shaggy haired rock groups like The Beatles and The Rolling Stones were taking the global music industry by storm. Nice boy Pat Boone was out, bad boy Mick Jagger was in. With longer hair, no glasses and a more casual wardrobe, Henry Darrow looked less like the kind of guy a girl brings home to meet Mother and more like the type other men keep away from their sisters.

"We got some new pictures of him showing that rugged twinkle, that spark that he does have," said Miller, "and I did a little double talking and all of a sudden, even some of the same people who'd turned down Henry Delgado were anxious to meet the very exciting and talented Hank Darrow."[43]

Ricardo Montalbán later noted "Enrique Delgado was a highly competent New York actor, a Puerto Rican without an accent...He was

43. TV/Radio Mirror *vol. 68, No 7 June 1968*

encouraged to try his luck in Hollywood. He couldn't get inside the studio door. He changed his name to Henry Darrow and started getting roles…"[44]

The first day after changing his name, Henry Darrow was up for the part of a German. The casting director didn't recognize him, although as Delgado, he had worked with the man before. "At one point, he said, 'you know there's a part here for a Spanish officer. Have you ever done a Latin accent?'" Darrow said no. He didn't get either part, but just being interviewed for a non-Latin role was encouraging.

As columnist Fernando I. Dominguez wrote, whether Latinos in show business use real names or assumed ones is oftentimes a matter of survival itself.[45] Henry Darrow was one who "realized the cold facts soon enough,"[46] but he nevertheless caught flak from Latinos who claimed he sold out. "Latino friends and fans," wrote Dominguez, "people who once had supported and encouraged him, took offense at his new image. They turned their backs and snubbed him, but Darrow never compromised or regretted his actions."[47]

Actor Hector Elizondo agreed that Darrow did what was necessary and said, "The people who criticize actors for changing their names are sort of holier than thou. They're not living in the real world."[48]

"You've got to work," says Darrow, but although it wasn't a rejection of his parentage or heritage, at the time he wondered how his father would react. Enrique Delgado was equally pragmatic. "When I told Dad, he asked why it took me so long."

I've always said an actor by any other name would still smell the same, just like a rose.

ACTOR DENNY MILLER

44. Reflections: My Life in Two Worlds, *p. 52*

45. *Los Angeles* Daily News, *4/5/82*

46. Ibid.

47. Ibid.

48. L.A. Life, Daily News *12/24/84*

You Can't Take Your Eyes Off Him

In this business, a lot has to do with timing and frankly, a lot has to do with luck. That sounds like sour grapes but it's reality.

WRITER HARRY CASON

In 1965, the Pasadena Playhouse was forming its first resident repertory company. It was supposed to consist of twelve paid actors, but Claude Woolman, assistant to director C. Lowell Lees, knew Darrow from the Playhouse and had seen his stunning performance in *The Wonderful Ice Cream Suit*. Henry Darrow became the thirteenth member in the company. The season of repertory paid $6,000. While not a fortune, it was solid income for a small family with a modest lifestyle and marked the first year Darrow made enough money to support his family.

Rehearsals began on August 23 for the premier performance, a double bill of *The Firebugs* and *The Shoemaker's Prodigious Wife*. The Pasadena Star-News called the plays "entertaining though not 'truly great'," but notes in *Firebugs* "Henry Darrow as the leader of the chorus brought back to memory some of the choral effects of Brecht's *Three Penny Opera*."[49]

The Shoemaker's Prodigious Wife featured Darrow as flirtatious Don Blackbird, one of three characters pursuing the young wife of the title. "I cawed and did all sorts of bird-like movements. That was the first time I did bird walking as a comedy routine," says the actor, adding, "There's so much junk you pick up from other folks, things you see. I'd do anything."

The troupe's schedule was tight and turnaround time was rapid. While performing one play they concurrently rehearsed the next. *Firebugs* and *Prodigious Wife* closed on October 16, 1965 and Ibsen's *Peer Gynt* premiered only five days later on October 21.

49. 9/24/65

Peer Gynt featured Monte Markham in the lead and Henry Darrow in a supporting role as Dr. Begriffenfeldt, the director of the madhouse in Cairo. Darrow had recently seen *Doctor Strangelove*, a black comedy filled with madmen, notably the title character played by Peter Sellers. Strangelove's arm often flies into an incontrollable Nazi salute and Darrow thought something like that would work for "the wonderful lunatic" Begriffenfeldt. "I would jerk my arm up and whack the back my neck." Demonstrating, he jumps from his chair, yells maniacally and slaps himself. "At the top of some stairs, I whap myself on the head and go rolling down the steps. Just in the middle of the speech — yaaahaagghh!"

Perky blonde actress Sally Struthers was then a quiet second year student at the Playhouse who had admired Darrow from the audience during rehearsals. She doesn't remember the whack or roll down the stairs, but she vividly recalls being his dresser for that play. "He didn't have any quick changes that I had to yank anything off of him or throw anything on him, but I did have to bring his costume to the dressing room every night and I had to make sure it was cleaned and pressed and that he had all the pieces. And I just remember being thrilled to walk into his dressing room!"

Audiences were thrilled to walk into the theater. *Peer Gynt* was the first sold out production at the Playhouse in several years. Its run ended on November 13 and on November 18, the reparatory company opened George Bernard Shaw's American comedy *The Devil's Disciple*.

The Pasadena Independent called *The Devil's Disciple* a "bright artistic success" with "sparkling and solid staging."[50] The *Long Beach Independent-Press-Telegram* said the play was "performed with near greatness by the highly skilled Claude Woolman, and the much improved and disciplined Henry Darrow as the minister Anthony Anderson".[51] The *Los Angeles Free Press* mentioned that Darrow came to life in Act II when "the script called for a very animated sequence. This scene and his last made the show for him. Up until that time, he was noticeable, but so were the chairs."[52]

The animated sequence that set Darrow apart from the furniture came when he abruptly vaulted over the banister. *The Independent Star-News* stated that as the "preacher who gleefully turns rebel under stress," he did "his difficult change of character with complete conviction. It is foreshadowed by a sudden unexpected leap over a stair railing which was so deftly timed and executed that it surprised the audience into a burst of

50. 11/20/65

51. 11/21/65

52. 11/25/65

applause. It is in touches like that the new company shows its character. It has been a long time since a single movement or gesture has triggered applause in a Playhouse audience."[53]

In reality, that touch showed Henry Darrow's character and ability to generate applause. "No, it wasn't in the script," he says, gleefully. "It was a surprise and a half to everyone!" But then he had to do it every performance and that was a problem. "It was so spontaneous, but then I had to repeat it, to practice it, rehearse it. I became a little fearful and started thinking oh, my foot's going to get caught and I'm going to land on my face. I lost the sparkle." But *The Devil's Disciple* didn't lose its shimmer. It played to full houses every weekend.

While performing *The Devil's Disciple*, the company rehearsed William Congreve's *Love for Love*. The sexually explicit seventeenth century comedy of manners didn't win accolades, although *The Hollywood Reporter* and *Variety* gave high marks to the cast, including Darrow in the lead as duplicitous suitor Valentine. Cecil Smith in *The Los Angeles Times* provided this rather back handed compliment: "Henry Darrow is virulent and handsome as Valentine, but a misplaced cog in the society he keeps which Congreve never intended. His fuzzy wigged madness is fun, but he is much too solid a character to be the frittering, foppish Valentine."

After the unloved *Love for Love* closed on January 15, the Shakespearian tragedy *Richard III* opened on January 20 to good reviews. Claude Woolman was Richard and Darrow played his villainous sidekick Buckingham in what the *Independent Star-News* called "strong interpretations."[54] *The Hollywood Reporter* called Darrow, along with others including Markham and the formidably talented Woolman, outstanding.[55] Darrow welcomed the good reviews and sent copies to his parents, but his shining moment came in the season finale.

The last play of the season was Richardson and Berney's drama *Dark of the Moon*, an Appalachian retelling of Romeo and Juliet infused with the supernatural. It opened the day after *Richard III* closed. Darrow had the lead as John, the witch boy in love with doomed mortal Barbara Allen and the director was Charles Rome Smith. Smith directed Darrow in *The Wonderful Ice Cream Suit* and knew how to keep his star's sometimes overwhelming energy from interfering with his otherwise dazzling performance. In one scene, Witch Boy transformed into an eagle and Darrow

53. 11/27/65

54. 1/23/66

55. 1/22/66

thought of the eerie wail made by the retarded man at the mortuary in Santurce. Unearthly, plaintive — it was a perfect eagle's cry and he copied it exactly. Smith let it go for a couple of rehearsals, then told him to pick another sound. "You stop the play," he said. "It's just too affecting."

To eighteen-year-old Sally Struthers, Darrow more than affecting. He was brilliant. "My jaw just hung there. They usually use this to describe a girl, but he was *touching*." She was transfixed. In her sixties, the energetic actress still bubbles with enthusiasm. "I drooled over this man. His face, the way his cranium is made, his eyes — you couldn't take your eyes off him."

He was just as arresting to most reviewers. *The Hollywood Reporter* said he performed "with the angular grace and freedom of the eagle, whose cousin he is"[56] and a *Hollywood Citizen-News* review glowed: "Henry Darrow as the 'witch-boy' is outstanding: confident, snarling, serpentine as a witch; suspicious, put upon, tender as a human. His is a complex role and he excels in all facets."[57] The *Los Angeles Herald-Examiner* termed his performance "intense" and "persuasive",[58] while the *Alhambra Free Press* trumpeted the role as a "personal triumph," going on to say "Darrow has appeared to be building all season for this particular crowning performance."[59]

The play's run was extended until March 12 and Darrow counted on star billing in the repertory company's new season. He waited eagerly for a letter from the president of the Playhouse Board of Directors, Dr. C. Lowell Lees, inviting him back. When the letter came, it did not say what he had hoped.

Beginning with, "Regarding our plans for next season, I regret to inform you..." the letter said all the star roles had been filled, then threw Darrow a bone. Richard Lupino, of the famous acting family, would be the star of the resident company and had personally requested that Darrow be his understudy. Of course, since Lupino's agent had insisted that Lupino receive a substantially higher salary and Darrow would only be an understudy, his pay would be cut to under $125.00 per week.

To Darrow, it was a stinging slap to the face. He was furious and not about to bow his head and be an understudy. He would also not waste time sulking. It was spring, when pilot episodes for television shows are

56. 2/21/66

57. 2/19/66

58. 2/13/66

59. 3/2/66

filmed and new seasons are shot. It was the best time to find work. He hit the bricks. First he got a part in a movie, a government project for the State of California about non-Union Latin workers, shot in three days. Then Pasadena Playhouse alumnus Robert Totten asked him to guest star in the western television series, *Iron Horse*. Totten respected Darrow and felt he brought strength, dignity and honesty to the role of the villainous, mysterious Apache "Cougar Man". Executive Producer Charles Marquis Warren thanked Darrow for "a truly fine performance" and *Variety's* Daku wrote, "Henry Darrow contributes realistically as the heavy." Television critic Cleveland Amory was not as complimentary. The legend of Cougar Man was that "to see him is to grow ill. To touch him is to wither. To fight him is to die." Amory likened the odd lilt in Cougar Man's voice to an "Irish coyote" and added, "To hear him is no picnic either." But Darrow loved the part. With some of his earnings, he bought a new rug for the Sun Valley house and at thirty-two, fulfilled his childhood dream of playing an Indian. He also came closer to the adult goal of having a viable acting career because Cougar Man was a prominent part. People in the biz liked what they saw and hired Darrow to guest star on *T.H.E. Cat* and *Gunsmoke*.

Meanwhile, David Dortort, creator and executive producer of *Bonanza*, still couldn't locate Henry Delgado to play Manolito Montoya in his new venture, *The High Chaparral*. The network people pressured Dortort to hire an established actor like John Barrymore Jr. or Tony Franciosa. Dortort stalled. He saw Manolito as a risqué, daring version of Ice *Cream Suit's* fun loving Martinez and held out for Delgado.

It might seem finding him would have been easy since he was onstage in Pasadena, not rafting the Amazon. But to locate a screen actor, one queried the Screen Actors' Guild (SAG). Henry Darrow was exclusively doing theater and not listed with SAG. Henry Delgado was listed, but with Carlos Alvarado as his agent. "He no longer represented me," says the actor. "When I was gone, I was gone." Fortunately, Darrow's post-repertory television and film work required SAG membership and permission. At last, Delgado and Darrow were together in one listing and Dortort's casting people called Les Miller about a role for his client in *The High Chaparral*.

Miller asked Darrow what he thought about doing a series.

"Think about it? Are you kidding? I think about it all the time!"

Thou hast seen nothing yet.
MIGUEL DE CERVANTES SAAVEDRA

Gloria and Enrique Delgado, Henry Darrow's parents.

Barefoot in Athens at the
Pasadena Playhouse.

With Pat Tanno. COURTESY OF PAT TANNO

Ready for Hollywood.

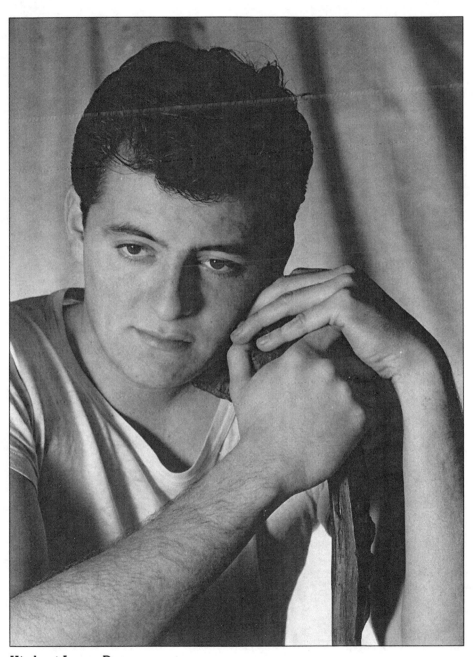

His best James Dean.

A Montgomery Clift moment.

Hank "Brando" Delgado, the kind you don't take home to Mama.

Mr. Wholesome.

In the lead in *Love for Love* (pictured with Gillian Tomlin), Pasadena
Playhouse Repertory Company, 1965

Star turn as John the Witch Boy in *Dark of the Moon,* Pasadena Playhouse
Repertory Company, 1966

The stars of *The High Chaparral,* (front) Linda Cristal and Cameron Mitchell, (back, left to right) Leif Erickson, Mark Slade and Henry Darrow.

A photo op for Mark Slade, Henry Darrow, Frank Silvera, Linda Cristal and Leif Erickson during a party at Linda Cristal's.

Henry Darrow as Manolito.

Practice saves skin when you're swinging bullwhips.

Manolito!

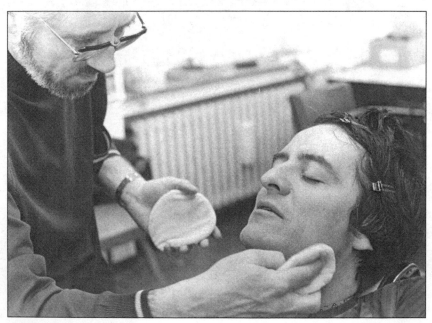

Applying the Manolito makeup.

He got all the girls, like Lenore Stevens in "The Glory Soldiers."

Romancing Patricia Berry in "The Widow from Red Rock."

The High Chaparral's main men (left to right) Mark Slade, Cameron Mitchell, Henry Darrow and Leif Erickson.

With Rudy Acosta (left) and Roberto Contreras (center).

With Cameron Mitchell.

Perlita (Marie Gomez) gives Manolito what-for. COURTESY OF CHRIS CASEY

The Apache camp was busier than it seemed on TV. In this set photo from "Ride the Savage Land," Henry Darrow is on the ground while stuntman Jerry Wills hangs around. Darrow's regular double, Carl Pitti, played four consecutive whip-cracking Apaches in the sequence. (Cameron Mitchell is in the back on the left).

Birthday party on the set for stuntman/actor Jaye Durkus. That's Jaye's father Andy Durkus, Paramount production manager, on the left.

With first wife Lucy, daughter Deedee and son Tom on the set of *The High Chaparral*

That famous squint.

She's alive! Julio Medina, Henry Darrow and Donna Baccala pause for jokes while filming Baccala's dramatic death-scene in "A Time to Laugh, A Time to Cry."

Backstage photo op with Linda Cristal. COURTESY OF TINA SWEET

In Germany for the Bambi Awards. Lee Majors and Farrah Fawcett are on the right.

Belting out the hits at the Bambi Awards.

Playing chess against World Grand Champion Boris Spassky.

Linda Cristal, Leif Erickson, Gilbert Roland and Henry Darrow in "The New Lion of Sonora."

Manolito!

ACT TWO

A Cultural Galaxy Far, Far Away

*This is disgusting! Marlon Brando playing
Emiliano Zapata! How would you like it if I played
Abraham Lincoln?*

ACTOR ROBERTO CONTRERAS

According to historian Allen Matusow, 1960s America "was more divided than at any time since 1861, just before the Civil War."[60] By 1966, depending on which side of the line you stood, the U.S. was either ushering in an era of liberty and equality or going straight to long-haired pinko Communist hell.

President Lyndon Johnson had significantly boosted troops in Southeast Asia and anti-war protests erupted across the nation with the increasingly radical Students for a Democratic Society (SDS) in the vanguard. The Rolling Stones made their first American tour, John Lennon declared the Beatles more popular than Jesus and the LSD counterculture gained momentum as writer Ken Kesey hosted psychedelic parties along the California coast. The Civil Rights Movement was championed by non-violent Rev. Martin Luther King Jr. but also radical followers of black separatist Malcolm X and the Black Panther Party, both of which believed in utilizing "any means possible" to defeat white racism. Race riots exploded in Florida, New York, New Jersey and Washington DC. Nationwide, Black Power gathered steam and so did the Women's Liberation Movement.

Women's Liberation challenged traditional gender roles as women fought for equality and control over their own bodies. A cornerstone work of the feminist movement, *The Feminine Mystique* by Betty Friedan, was published in 1964, but it was not until 1966 that Friedan, Rev. Pauli Murray (the first black female Episcopal priest) and Shirley Chisolm

---

60. *Quoted in Robert J. Samuelson,* The Advocate *(Baton Rouge, LA), 1/17/11*

(later the first black woman elected to Congress and to run for the U.S. Presidency) banded together to form the National Organization for Women (NOW). NOW members demanded legal parity between women and men. They and other Women's Liberationists generally relied on fiery rhetoric and peaceful demonstrations rather than violence.

Another significant group using non-violent protest was the United Farm Workers (UFW), led by Arizona-born César Chávez and California native Dolores Huerta. Captained by vegan, pacifist Chávez and dynamic Huerta, the UFW fought for the rights of migrant farm laborers utilizing peaceful methods espoused by Mohandas Gandhi and Martin Luther King. Marches, strikes and boycotts proved potent bargaining chips and drew national attention to the disenfranchised, mainly Hispanic migrant population, eventually resulting in higher wages and an improved standard of living.

However, on the silver screens of local Bijous and Roxys, Hispanic issues and Hispanic actors were largely absent. Richard Brooks' gritty western *The Professionals* (starring Burt Lancaster, Lee Marvin and Italian actress Claudia Cardinale) introduced Mexican/French Golden Globe nominee Marie Gomez in the breakout role of Chiquita and included other Latinos in smaller roles, but Cardinale played Maria, the Mexican wife of a wealthy Anglo rancher and Jack Palance portrayed fictional Mexican revolutionary Jesús Raza. Shot in Sonora, Mexico, *The Appaloosa* was another western without Latin talent in leading Hispanic roles. Marlon Brando had played a Mexican revolutionary in 1952's *Viva Zapata!* and in *The Appaloosa*, played a Mexican-American buffalo hunter. John Saxon filled the role of bandido Chuy Medina. Emilio Fernández, Alex Montoya, Miriam Colón and Rafael Campos had supporting parts.

Even the Cisco Kid and Pancho had ridden off the celluloid range. It was as if the studios decided hyperactive cartoon rodent Speedy Gonzales provided sufficient Hispanic flavor for nearly all of filmdom. American network television offered witches, cowboys, genies, castaways, spies, country bumpkins, soldiers, bears, dogs, space aliens and super-heroes. But you couldn't see many people who weren't white Anglo-Saxons, although a small, growing number of prominent black and Asian roles hailed burgeoning minority group recognition. However, Latinos were "simply not part of television's new ethnic 'relevance'". [61] In truth, animals were better represented than humans of Hispanic ancestry. Lassie and Flipper had their own shows, but Latino parts had not appreciably improved in the

61. *Lichter and Amundson in* Latin Looks, *p. 60*

years since Ricky loved Lucy and Pepino worked for the McCoys. Latinos mostly appeared as corrupt dictators or sadistic revolutionaries, opponents for heroic spies from north of the border on shows like *Mission: Impossible.*[62]

Charles Ramírez Berg spoke for many Hispanics when he wrote, "Like everybody else, I suppose, who grows up on the nation's fringes, I knew that I was in the United States but felt (and was made to feel) out of it. For one thing, you never saw yourself in the mass media. The homogenized, middle-class, *Leave It to Beaver/Father Knows Best* world depicted in television programs, magazines, and movies belonged to a cultural galaxy far, far away…"[63]

"Most people, most Anglos, don't realize that anytime a Latino was on, it was a big deal. When you turned on the TV, you were going to see Anglos because the people in Hollywood were Anglo and they were telling only certain stories," says writer/comedian Rick Najera.

Then a man named David Dortort got sick.

> *Too often the Mexican in a western is presented as a sullen character useful as background color, or as a foil to manufacture some questionable humor. What about his emotions, his commitment to the land, his dreams?*
>
> DAVID DORTORT, CREATOR/EXECUTIVE PRODUCER
> OF *THE HIGH CHAPARRAL*[64]

62. Ibid.

63. Latin Looks, *p. 191*

64. Arizona Highways, *September 1967*

Changing the Tradition

Nobody told me what to do!

DAVID DORTORT

As a child in Brooklyn, Dortort loved history and later majored in it when he attended at City College of New York (CCNY), where he met his future wife, Rose. He decided to write historical texts for a living and to prepare, took a writing course where he discovered a flair for writing fiction.

During World War II, Dortort headed Special Services at the Army Hospital in Torrance, California. The hospital's proximity to Hollywood insured a steady stream of performers to entertain the patients. This gave Dortort his first taste of show business and provided contacts in the entertainment industry.

Back in New York City after the war, Dortort published his first novel, "Burial of the Fruit" (1947), about the vicious crime syndicate Murder Inc. The book's movie rights were optioned by an independent film company formed by Burt Lancaster and Harold Hecht. Because many sophisticated film artists fled Nazi Germany for Hollywood, some in show business felt movies had become "too European". To rectify this, Lancaster and Hecht planned to do features with particularly American context. Along with Dortort's book, they optioned Norman Mailer's "The Naked and the Dead". Lancaster and Hecht hired Mailer and Dortort to write screenplays of their books, but according to David Dortort, neither he nor Mailer knew beans about screenwriting. They soon learned it required different skills than writing novels. When the studio declared theirs possibly the worst screenplays ever, Mailer hung it up and returned to New York. Dortort stayed and became the first president of the Television Writer's Association and the first writer to become a TV series producer with *The Restless Gun* (1957-1959).

A traditional western about a drifter who solves problems with hot lead, *The Restless Gun* was produced by and starred former Twentieth Century-Fox crooner John Payne. The show rose to number two in Nielsen ratings, but Dortort disliked its typical depiction of the west. Of the real west, he said, "The gunfighter was a tiny part. It was the story of men and women and children, of families, this mass migration to settle the west, their triumphs and hardships, the pioneer spirit. The *family* was the most important thing." He became a man on a mission: to change the tradition of the Hollywood western.

He did it with *Bonanza*, a character-driven western which revolved around wise rancher Ben Cartwright and his three sons — intellectual Adam, kind-hearted Hoss and tempestuous Little Joe. The wealthy Cartwrights lived on the sprawling Ponderosa ranch near beautiful Lake Tahoe, Nevada circa 1860. There were fistfights and gunplay aplenty, but *Bonanza* was unique in its emphasis of family and moral lessons. The series would become a hit, but David Dortort had to negotiate with NBC and RCA before he got the go-ahead to produce it.

RCA, the parent company of NBC, was by 1959 the only manufacturer of color television sets. Color technology was in its infancy and likely to stay there. Filming in color cost approximately 25% more than filming in black and white. Since nearly all shows were in black and white, most consumers saw no reason to spend half the price of a new car on a color TV. Enter David Dortort, who wanted his newfangled western in color. He felt the stunning Lake Tahoe locations would sell color sets and advertising. Projections aside, it was a gamble. The network finally agreed on the strength of the show's concept and Dortort's pitch, which included the promise to kick his own money into the kitty.

Dortort had already chosen his stars — Lorne Greene, Pernell Roberts, Dan Blocker and Michael Landon — which resulted in another round of bargaining. They were unknowns and NBC did not want unknowns. Dortort held firm. "Nobody told *me* what to do!" he said afterward. "If I wanted somebody, I got them. I told the network, 'Television will make its own stars.'"[65]

Bonanza had poor first season ratings, but by the second season audiences warmed to it and clever marketing paid off. Broadcast early on Saturday nights, shoppers could see the show in "RCA Color" on sets in appliance store windows. Color TV sales rocketed and *Bonanza* became the best loved show in America, so NBC urged David Dortort to create another winner for them. Dortort wanted to oblige with a western distinct from *Bonanza*. "In *Bonanza*, we had the ideal family, but in real life sometimes it does not go that way," he said. "Fathers and sons don't always

65. *Retrieved on YouTube, July 2010*

get along." The only thing preventing him from creating a more realistic storyline was time, but when a minor problem put him in the hospital, he finally had the chance to put his thoughts on paper.

Those thoughts focused on the real story of the Southwest and its influential Latino heritage. Dortort would not portray Hispanic men as merely buffoons, Latin Lovers and bandidos. Latinas would not be stereotypical spitfires and prostitutes in flyblown cantinas. "I wanted to go against the grain and show how two families on opposite sides of the border can live together," he said. "My responsibility if I have access…is to educate as well as entertain."

He imagined the saga of two families, the American Cannons and the Mexican Montoyas. His friend Denne Bart Petticlerc, writer and story consultant for nearly forty episodes of *Bonanza*, penned the pilot. Kent McCray, production manager and production supervisor on *Bonanza*, says *The High Chaparral* script, which "had heart, action and depicted the Southwest in its true nature," was Petticlerc's finest. The pilot would be filmed as a stand-alone movie. When completed, Dortort — no slave to modesty — called it the best pilot ever made.

> *Your Pa's different than us, Blue — he's got a dream.*
>
> BUCK CANNON[66]

---

66. *Part 2 of pilot episode of* The High Chaparral, *"The Arrangement"*

Tougher Attitude

Fools don't live very long. And there's one prime rule in this country — survive, keep on living, no matter what.

The High Chaparral bore Dortort's stamp in that it was a period western with a central strong patriarch, emphasis on family relationships and moral lessons. But unlike *Bonanza, Chaparral* featured Mexicans prominently and presented sweaty, grimy Anglos who *looked* like cowhands. Writer/comedian Rick Najera points out, "*Bonanza* was a pretty western. The big house at Tahoe, the Chinese cook, it was like wow! It was nice living in cowboy days! But in *The High Chaparral,* it was a tougher attitude." That tougher attitude meant relationships, although central to *Chaparral's* storyline, were backlit by unforgiving desert and hard-charging adventure.

The story began with the Cannon family's arrival in 1870s Arizona where steely Big John Cannon plans to build a cattle empire. With John are his younger brother Buck ("...hard voiced, big fisted, strongly built man who has led himself a roaring life and loves it..."[68]), genteel wife Annalee and son Billy Blue ("...twenty years old...a curious blend of sensitivity and ruggedness..."). In the first few scenes, Apaches kill the neighboring Ward family and torch their ranch. The Cannons bury the Wards then ride to their own place. It's been ransacked by Apaches, who are retaliating against whites for the Army's killing of Chief Mangas Coloradas. An army detachment welcomes the Cannons to their new home by telling them to get out.

Instead, Buck and Blue go to Tucson to hire ranch hands. While there, Buck pays a saloon girl to perk Blue up with private entertainment. Blue declines her offer of a back room, but it's difficult to imagine that sequence with the Cartwrights. Ditto the next, where Buck hires a pack of drunk,

67. Part 1 of pilot episode of The High Chaparral, *"Destination Tucson"*

68. All character descriptions in quotes are excerpted from the pilot script.

hard fisted cowhands who just tried to kill Blue. The new men — brothers Sam and Joe Butler, Pedro Carr, Ira Bean and Reno — are "a wilted group of ruffians." John shapes them up, but his adversaries are less tractable.

His cattle are stolen by *vaqueros* working for the formidable Mexican *hacendado* Don Sebastian Montoya, who has laid claim to Cannon's land and herds. Meanwhile, Apaches kill Annalee and have the same plan for everyone else. When John rides out alone after a stranded steer, a warrior waiting in ambush takes aim at him. Before the Indian can squeeze off a round, he's killed by a shot from the brush. Cannon's savior steps into view holding a rifle. He appears to be a congenial Mexican peasant, but unbeknownst to Big John, he is Manolito, Don Sebastian Montoya's scoundrel son. After a few pleasantries, Manolito turns deadly serious, orders Cannon to raise his hands and steals his horse.

John Cannon realizes he cannot fight the Apaches and Montoya. Hoping to unite with Don Sebastian against the Indians, he and Buck ride into Mexico to meet the *hacendado*. At a Nogales cantina, they run into Manolito. He happily joins them for drinks. When he learns they're looking for Don Sebastian, he offers to take them to him without revealing his relationship to Montoya.

Attended by a flotilla of servants and surrounded by luxury in the "grand Spanish tradition," Don Sebastian is obviously a man of wealth and class superior to the Cannons. John and Buck are surprised to learn Manolito is his son. They are also charmed by Don Sebastian's lovely daughter, Victoria ("…a beautiful woman in her late twenties, with long dark hair and great dark eyes").

The next morning, Don Sebastian agrees to an alliance only if John marries Victoria to seal the pact. Still grieving John reluctantly consents. When John, Buck, Victoria and Manolito return to the Cannon ranch, Blue is enraged over his father's marriage. After a scathing confrontation between father and son comes a two-fisted battle pitting the ranch against warring Apaches.

Besides action sequences, the script was seasoned with lessons about reconciliation, tolerance and respecting honorable foes. The first people to read it thought it was a darned good story, too.

David Dortort put together something more interesting than Bonanza, *with the harsh environment of the desert and all those people trying to survive.*

WRITER/PUBLICIST LUIS REYES

This Wonderful Script

We're trying to make restitution to what I feel are damaged reputations. High Chaparral *is based on the truth.*

DAVID DORTORT[69]

Dortort was exploring the feasibility of a three-part *Bonanza* shot at historic Parker Ranch in Hawaii. Planning entailed a scouting trip to Oahu by *Bonanza* heavyweights: director William Claxton, cinematographer Haskell "Buzzy" Boggs, production manager Kent McCray and Fenton Coe from NBC. Denne Bart Petticlerc put the screenplay for *The High Chaparral* in Kent McCray's hands at midnight the night before the plane left. Once in the air, McCray began reading. The more he read, the more excited he became. "As I finished a few pages I would pass it over to Bill Claxton. He would read it and pass it on to Buzzy. Buzzy in turn would pass it on to Fenton Coe," he recalled in an interview. "By the time we arrived in Hawaii, we all said, 'What are we doing here? We should be preparing this wonderful script of *The High Chaparral*.'"[70]

Sending the Cartwrights to Hawaii proved too expensive, so the men tackled the new pilot. The polished script needed very few changes, but securing the right Arizona shooting location was key. Dortort liked the "big sky country"[71] around Tucson, so McCray flew out to nail down a deal.

Tucson was unique as a filming location in that Old Tucson Studios was nearby. Built during 1939-1940 for the Columbia Pictures movie *Arizona* (1940), it was a replica of 1860s Tucson and "the first 'big' outdoor western epic location."[72] Instead of movie façades, buildings were real adobe and wood built mostly by local members of the Tohono O'odham

69. TV Guide, *2/20-2/26, 1968*

70. The High Chaparral Newsletter, *"Kent McCray, Destination Tucson" by Penny McQueen, 4/7/07*

71. *From* The High Chaparral *website, http://www.thehighchaparral.com/trivia.htm*

72. *From* The Old Tucson Guidebook, *Terrell Publishing © Pelley Studios Phoenix AZ*

Nation. Once known as Papago, a name given them by the *conquistadores*, their ancestors were the artisans and craftsmen who helped construct Mission San Xavier del Bac. Although a far cry from San Xavier's Moorish-Spanish grandeur, Old Tucson was still an accomplishment. Over fifty structures were built in forty days and the authentic adobe buildings required over 350,000 bricks, which were fashioned from available desert dirt and water hauled by the bucket.[73]

When *Arizona* wrapped, Columbia Pictures donated the set to Pima County. It sat idle for several years, was used briefly for *The Bells of St. Mary's* (1945), then became "Hollywood in the Desert," with the upsurge in westerns. *Winchester 73* (1950), *Gunfight at the O.K. Corral* (1957), *Rio Bravo* (1959) and *Cimarron* (1960) were shot there, but when entrepreneur Robert Shelton saw Old Tucson in 1959, he thought it was underutilized and saw possibilities. He expanded it into a fully functioning movie studio and tourist attraction.

By 1966, Old Tucson had hosted numerous movie and television productions and seemed ideal for *The High Chaparral*. A derelict structure built for a forgotten film could be renovated to serve as the Cannon ranch house and the studio was close to mountains, low desert, old forts and San Xavier del Bac. San Xavier, an imposing eighteenth century mission sometimes called the "Sistine Chapel of the New World," was perfect for Casa Montoya's exterior.

Old Tucson was too good to pass up. Deal struck, Robert Shelton said, "*The High Chaparral* is actually the beginning of a new era of film possibilities for the Tucson area. Its effect on tourism, publicity and economy is bound to be historic."[74]

Location was in the bag, but everything else needed finalizing and hiring the right actors topped the punch-list. Leif Erickson, a strapping screen veteran who had played God on an episode of *Bonanza* was the hands-down choice for Big John Cannon. Erickson began show business as a singer and trumpet player, then switched to acting. Handsome as a Norse deity, his extensive film career mainly consisted of supporting roles because he looked too perfect to be real. After seeing him in the film *The Big Broadcast of 1936*, his son Bill remarked "It's too much. Dad's prettier than Dorothy Lamour."[75] But thirty years had passed since then. At

73. *http://web.archive.org/web/20070424095052/http://www.oldtucson.com/film_office/movie_history/movie_history.htm*

74. Arizona Highways, *Sept. 1967*

75. TV Guide, *"The Dusty Trail to the High Chaparral" by Dwight Whitney, 8/23–8/29, 1969*

fifty-five, Erickson's looks had a rugged patina, ideal for playing a man out to tame the west.

Casting for Buck Cannon hit the wall until Dortort and Claxton got on a plane to Tucson and Cameron Mitchell was a few rows ahead of them. Mitchell, the son of a Mennonite minister, was in high school when a teacher loaned him money to study drama in New York City. When he got to New York, he had never ridden in an elevator or used a telephone, but brazenly wrote the revered Alfred Lunt and criticized his performance in the film *The Guardsman* (1931). Lunt gave Mitchell an audition and was impressed. He and his wife Lynn Fontanne, the premier acting couple in America, became Mitchell's mentors. Mitchell worked on Broadway, in film and on television and immersed himself in his characters so well that his own parents didn't recognize him as an Indian in *Pony Soldier* (1952). When Dortort saw him on the plane, Mitchell was flying to Madrid to do a movie. After reading the script for *The High Chaparral*, he nixed the film to portray Buck Cannon. Dortort believed television made its own stars, but journalist Penny McQueen notes, "Hiring an actor of Cameron's stature gave legitimacy to *Chaparral*."

Hundreds of young actors auditioned to play Billy Blue Cannon. Dortort almost settled on one, but interviewed Mark Slade and changed his mind. A twenty-seven-year-old Massachusetts native, Slade planned on becoming a cartoonist before acting drew him in. After some lean times, he landed a starring role as Hollis the seasick radioman in the TV series *The Wackiest Ship in the Army*. Slade didn't see himself as "the Western type" and was lukewarm about interviewing for *Chaparral*. Since he didn't want to waste the whole day, he loaded fishing gear into his car before driving to the interview. After an emotionally riveting audition during which Slade grabbed David Dortort and hoisted him from his chair, the young actor went fishing. He caught a nice stringer of fish — and the part of Billy Blue Cannon.

"We did have a hard time finding our girl," William Claxton said. None of the actresses who auditioned for Victoria Montoya Cannon had the right combination of class, grit and beauty. Dortort and Claxton focused on Buenos Aires-born Linda Cristal who had made a name for herself in movies and television prior to retiring to raise a family.

Cristal grew up in aching poverty and was thirteen when her journalist parents were killed in an automobile accident. She went to live in France with her older brother Miguel, an artist. She had only a third grade education, but an iron will and studied constantly, becoming fluent in four languages. "In a nutshell, when there is no space behind you to fall back, you have to walk forward," she later observed. When Miguel sent her on a sixteenth birthday trip to Mexico, a film producer offered her a part in a movie. She described it as her first improvisation: "I decided to roll my eyes one way to show grief, the other to show ecstasy." [76] It must have worked. Cristal stayed in Mexico and made twelve films before coming to Hollywood where she acted in movies and television. Then she married businessman Yale Wexler and retired to raise their sons. "I decided to have a marriage and children and give it all I had," she says. "I really don't believe you can do both. You get influenced by so many things when you are in the film business." By the time *Chaparral* was being cast, Cristal and Wexler were divorcing. Cristal needed work, but her agent opposed sending her to interview for *Chaparral*.

Dortort and Claxton were frustrated, but at least they knew where to find Cristal. After his impressive performance in *The Wonderful Ice Cream Suit*, Henry Delgado, the perfect actor to portray Manolito Montoya, was missing in action.

> *Mano's gone! He just went riding off...and he ain't come back.*
>
> BUCK CANNON[77]

76. TV Guide, *"She Doesn't Need a Script" by Terry Galanoy, 6/15–6/21, 1968*
77. The High Chaparral, *"Apache Trust" 4-16-69*

Mr. D in Pleasant Valley

The local rock group down the street
Is trying hard to learn their song
Serenade the weekend squire
who just came out to mow his lawn
Another Pleasant Valley Sunday
Charcoal burning everywhere

GERRY GOFFIN AND CAROLE KING[78]

From the outside, acting seems like a glamorous profession. Mesmerized by sparkling designer gowns, big budget movies and red carpeted Oscar nights, we imagine actors and actresses owning marble floored mansions in exotic locations — Beverly Hills, Boulder or Saint-Tropez. But most actors aren't billionaire megastars. Like many people, if they're comfortably middle class they count themselves successful. Living in Sun Valley and working steadily, Henry Darrow was finally feeling successful.

Sun Valley was only a few miles from Hollywood glitz, but seemed like hundreds. Darrow was the only actor on Remick Avenue, but the weekday routine wasn't so different from their neighbors or people in millions of similar suburban neighborhoods. Hank went to work to earn a living while Lucy kept house and took care of the children. The turbulent sixties were something on television. On the streets of Sun Valley there were Girl Scouts selling cookies instead of rioters throwing bricks. Life was peaceful and safe, but safe and peaceful had an oppressive side. "Everybody played their roles," says Darrow. "I look back on it and it was unfair. Now there are women in positions of real power, but at that time it was, 'Wife, go prepare my home!' and I was part of that."

He was also part of the neighborhood. The teenage boys called him "Mr. D." because "Delgado" was a mouthful for most of them. Summer evenings and weekends, they asked Mr. D to come out and play softball

78. "Pleasant Valley Sunday," © Screen Gems-EMI Music, Inc.

with them. They got a kick out of beating him and that gave him a laugh. "It wasn't hard to do because I wasn't that good," he says. "But because I was the grown up, it was a big deal to them."

His own kids had years to go before their teens. Deedee was nine years old and Tom was four. Hank and Lucy taught them to be respectful but encouraged talent and intellectual curiosity. Deedee was crazy about horses and lobbying for riding lessons. Tom was too little for the neighborhood ball games, but Hank was prepping him. That was going better than teaching karate to Deedee. A petite girl, she gave Hank a kick to the kidneys which put him on the floor. That ended the lessons, but he said, "Lu and the kids and I, we have a lot of fun. There is a lot of teasing — but not in the cruel sense. We enjoy each other. We can talk to each other."[79] When the kids squabbled, Hank was the arbitrator, Lucy was the disciplinarian. Home and kids were primarily her responsibility. On Sundays, she and the children wentto Episcopal services while Hank stayed home studying scripts, reading the newspaper or playing chess.

To his mother's dismay, Hank was no longer a practicing Catholic. To his in-laws' annoyance, he was not interested in becoming a practicing Episcopalian. He made his living pretending to be different people. Attending church was just more pretense, but he went on special days if it was for the family.

He gave Lucy high marks for running their home smoothly. Their marriage was more companionable than passionate after ten years and two kids, but he told a reporter, "Lu and I have adapted very well to each other. I'm not making her suit me; it's working both ways."

"We're both strong willed people," he told another interviewer. But in 1966 it was a man's world. Hank called the shots. "It was a long time before I would allow Lucy to go out to movies and cafés alone," he reported. "But I don't like her to take classes at night or visit friends at night — period. It has nothing to do with Latin attitudes, it's just the times we live in. I don't like the idea of her being in the car alone."[80]

Lucy obliged. "The Latin man is so traditionally the one and only head of the household," she explained. "There's so much pride involved. Hank doesn't go overboard with Latin attitudes, but they are there. I guess they're kind of inbred."[81]

79. TV/Radio Mirror, *Western Edition*, *"How His In-Laws Tried to Stop His Wedding"* by Leslie Steele, June 1968

80. Ibid.

81. Screen Stories Special: *"The Wives Talk"*

Being cagey with a dollar was very nearly inbred. Paychecks were steady, but frugality still ruled. Lucy cut his hair and they were saving for the children's college funds. In the garage were two aged cars, a '55 Chevy and a '61 Pontiac compact. The one television in the house was a basic black and white set. Instead of spendy purebred pets, two mutts, a cat and Deedee's hamster rounded out the household. Hank owned only one suit, the same one he wore to his Rochester wedding nearly ten years earlier. Who needed suits? At work, he wore costumes. At home he was happy in Levi's and t-shirts.

He and Lucy had never been to a Hollywood premier. Instead of black-tie *soirees*, they got together with family and friends for cards, board games, potluck dinners and backyard cook-outs. All in all, Henry Darrow and his family had a comfortable, ordinary life. Then his agent called and asked, "What do you think about doing a series?"

I thought, oh, that's a snap! But it didn't turn out to be that way.

HENRY DARROW

Just Do What You Do

Henry isn't a "Method Actor". But he does have a method.

ACTOR RUDY RAMOS

In those days, if an actor was up for an important part, the script was hand delivered to his agent. The pilot script for *The High Chaparral* was hand-carried to Les Miller's office. Henry Darrow had a meeting at David Dortort's office the next day.

Tired from the day's work but excited about playing Manolito Montoya, he read the script until three in the morning. Manolito had to be credible as a friendly peon, deadly bandido, joking reprobate, teasing (and somewhat contrite) son, Sonoran blue blood, protective brother and fearless Indian fighter. Darrow knew he had the dexterity for the role. He just had to keep David Dortort convinced.

Script filling his head, he arrived at Dortort's office and in the anteroom, met Linda Cristal for the first time. She recalls it was friendship at first sight. "Henry was all smiles, as always." They fell into easy conversation, then Cristal went in for her interview. She read the script to herself, then with typical candor said, "I'm sorry. These lines aren't me, but the part is. I'll prove it." She launched into what *TV Guide* called "a one girl show" consisting of an extemporaneous emotional buffet — Horror, Love, Madness, Sincerity, Happiness and Anger. It ran contrary to conventional wisdom, but won her the part of Victoria Montoya Cannon.[82]

The only major role left was Manolito. When Henry Darrow walked into David Dortort's office, he knew it was not a routine audition. Scrutinizing him was a room full of men who made — or broke — careers: Dortort, Producer/Director William F. "Bill" Claxton, the head of casting at Paramount and several NBC executives. Some actors would have been sweating buckshot. Not Darrow. Outwardly respectful, he was thinking, "I'm going to bust their chops."

---

82. *"She Doesn't Need a Script" by Terry Galanoy ,6/15-6/21, 1968*

David Dortort later told *TV Guide*, "As soon as he finally showed up, I said to myself, 'Boy, is he ever right for Manolito.'"[83] But turning to Darrow, he said, "You know, we've been looking for you for the better part of six months" then started discussing available Hispanic roles with the other executives. Finally, they asked Darrow what he thought.

"I couldn't wait to talk about Manolito!" he recalls. The professorial looking young man flung himself into one hell of a pitch, animatedly doing scenes and talking about how Manolito should come across. He improvised in Spanish and suggested more Spanish to enhance authenticity. While Bill Claxton watched him intently, Darrow acted out the sequence where Manolito appears on the balcony of the cantina. "Claxton was looking at me through the eyes of a director and through the eye of a camera. At one point, I said I wasn't sure, I didn't know how they wanted it played and Claxton said, 'Just do what you do'."

After fifteen minutes, Darrow slowed down and offered to read for the part of Manolito.

"You've done it," said Dortort. "You just did it. You've got the part."

He has a way of bringing life to everything he
does, yet what he does is hard to define.

WILLIAM CLAXTON
DESCRIBING HENRY DARROW[84]

---

83. *2/20–2/26, 1968*

84. The Courier-Times, *12/27/67*

This is the Guy!

I have always had a weakness for style over practicality.

MANOLITO MONTOYA[85]

Grinning broadly, Henry Darrow says, "Man, it was beautiful! It was like I had a license to steal. I was on camera and I was wearing a really great outfit."

The cast selected their own wardrobes. With utmost attention to detail, he created a rakish, bastardized *Californio* look for Manolito. It included a revolver with ivory grip, wide brimmed black hat with silver conchos on the band, short boots and dark purple leather bolero jacket with tooled lapels. Manolito's gun belt was designed by Darrow, inspired by one in an old movie. It had a pivoting, brass-throated holster and unique leather buckle emblazoned with a large "M" pierced by an arrow. Completing the ensemble were very snug wool pants with leather trim to show his physique.

Clothing selections were permanent, a cost cutting measure so master-shots and stock footage (like someone riding through the gate) could be re-used. There was only one problem. All the exterior scenes were filmed on location in the searing Arizona desert. Henry Darrow looked *muy guapo* in the air conditioning at Western Wardrobe but hadn't considered how his sharp threads would feel in Arizona in June. He wasn't the only one. Says Don Collier (*Chaparral's* foreman Sam Butler) who chose a buckskin shirt and chaps, "I thought I looked like a million dollars 'til I got down into this Arizona heat and I felt like two cents."

Darrow was offered standard cowboy boots, but opted for *vaquero* style ankle boots with rubber soles. "That was so I could run in them, but I mainly wanted to look sleek." He laughs. On location his feet swelled from walking on hot sand and rocks. "Wool pants, rubber, leather. Oh my God! What was I thinking?" He later discovered one reason why cowboy boots are a good idea: they stay on. That's a plus around livestock.

85. The High Chaparral episode "A Joyful Noise"

During the ninth episode of the season, "Mark of the Turtle" (guest starring Tony Caruso), Darrow was running when a boot slipped off and his foot landed in a pile of horse manure. "It was so hot, 120 degrees in the canyon and no breeze. Touch a rock and you scald yourself. I got a kick out of working with Tony, but in that kind of heat, you don't want multiple takes." He grimaces. "When I stepped into the horse dung, it was 'Oh, man! Cut!' and yet another take." Swathed in heavy clothes and laden with dark makeup to disguise his pale skin, Darrow dripped real sweat. Melting makeup glued his hair into clumps and he was drained from the heat, much like his first day on the set.

That first day, he had barely introduced himself to Leif Erickson, Cameron Mitchell and Mark Slade when everyone raced to defend against an Apache onslaught. The payoff sequence was a well-choreographed melee of swirling dust, zinging arrows, cracking gunfire, galloping horses and heart pounding stunts. One stunt rider specialized in flipping backward off a running horse. Dressed as an Apache, he galloped into the scene. A rifle boomed and he hurtled backward off the charging horse, slamming hard into the dirt. It was especially spectacular and remarkably a wrap in just one take according to actor/stuntman Bob Hoy (ranch hand "Joe Butler"). After the director yelled "Cut!" the dead Indians could join the living and Hoy helped the fallen rider up. "I always liked to check the boys over after a good fall, but he was fine, dusting himself off and talking," said Hoy. "Except as we lit our cigarettes, a line of blood ran from underneath the black costume wig, across his nose, and down one cheek. No one, not even him, noticed his horse kicked him in the head."[86]

In a sequence so thrilling that a kick in the head went unnoticed, Henry Darrow's performance was mostly forgettable. Looking at the dailies, network big wigs, producers and casting people questioned Dortort's judgment, asking dubiously, "So is this the guy? This is the one you say is going to be Manolito?"

The next day's shoot covered the sequence where Mano saves Big John Cannon's life then steals his horse. Says Darrow proudly, "That had everything in it, the humor of the character and the serious, threatening demeanor." Manolito's rifle was a trapdoor model and Darrow told special effects man Lee Vasqué that he wanted a puff of smoke to come from the breech after he shot. Vasqué told him how to do it and Darrow followed his instructions to the letter. When Manolito opened the trapdoor to extract the spent cartridge, escaping gunsmoke wafted across his

86. Notes from an interview with Penny McQueen

face. It was dramatic foreshadowing in an otherwise disarming entrance. Manolito smoothly reloads while speaking cordially to Cannon, then flashes pure menace when he orders Cannon to put his hands up high. The scene made believers of the producers and casting office. "They were like, oh, yeah! This is the guy! *This* is the one we talked about!"

Production manager Kent McCray remembers best the interior sequence where John and Buck Cannon meet up with Manolito in the Mexican cantina. "Henry came out on the balcony with one of the greatest laughs I've ever heard." It was a joyful, manic laugh and to McCray, set the tone for the free spirited side of Manolito. But audiences would not see free-spirited Manolito or anyone else unless NBC secured the advertising dollars to air the show.

Dortort's production company, Xanadu, was in partnership with NBC, which had financed *Chaparral's* pilot. But that was no guarantee the pilot would lead to a series. After NBC approved the pilot's final cut, the network still had to find sponsors before filming episodes for the 1967-68 season. While rounding up advertisers, NBC tried to keep *Chaparral's* cast working as guest stars in other NBC shows.

"When I'm a guest, I'm wired," Henry Darrow says. "I challenge the regulars and bring them alive. That's another wonderful part of acting." As he waited to hear if *The High Chaparral* was a go, he guest starred on *Daniel Boone, T.H.E. Cat, Gunsmoke, The Wild, Wild West* and most significantly, *Bonanza*.

Bonanza showcased him in a part originally written for Sammy Davis, Jr. The initial script, titled "Cotton," had Davis playing a slave owned by Capt. John Fenner (Gregory Walcott), an ex-Cavalry officer turned comanchero. A good man in the grasp of a bad one, "Cotton" is captured after a bank robbery and held prisoner at the Ponderosa while awaiting trial and certain hanging. But contemporary riots in Detroit prompted revisions in the potentially racially-charged script and "Cotton" became "Amigo," a brow-beaten Mexican peon. Amigo is whipsawed between loyalty to Fenner, love for his wife (Anna Navarro) and unborn child, hatred for Little Joe (Michael Landon) and respect for Ben Cartwright (Lorne Greene). Ultimately, Amigo dies while double crossing Fenner to save his wife and the Cartwrights. Darrow's vivid performance was so absorbing that years later when Lauren Levian watched a rerun with Darrow beside her, she forgot she was watching him. "It's hard when you're with someone not to say, 'Oh, there Henry is on TV!' But I didn't. The role just sucked me in."

Darrow best remembers the "marvelous competition" between himself and Landon. "I did the acting. Michael responded to my acting," he says, explaining, "When you're a regular in a series, you don't always have the goody goody scenes. The guest star gets the goodies and the regular is there to interact with the guest star. I had the dynamite stuff in 'Amigo' and I had a ball because I really zeroed in on the part." It even paid enough that he and Lucy had the house repainted.

I thought, jeez, Landon's been on for eight years!
Maybe Chaparral *will go on forever just like*
Bonanza *and I'll be making fifteen grand a week.*
HENRY DARROW

Christening

Throw him in the watering trough.

BIG JOHN CANNON[87]

The High Chaparral had to be filmed before it could be the gravy train of Darrow's dreams. With advertisers on board, the cast and crew headed back to Paramount's soundstages and Arizona locations to make episodes for the 1967-68 television season.

"Those were incredibly good times," says Darrow. "It was my christening. It was a christening that lasted for four years, in particular the first year. Everything was so wonderfully new and fresh."

He wanted to try everything and to learn everything. Manolito was fluent in the Apache language? No problem! Darrow would teach himself Apache. He planned on buying a textbook before Gil Escandon, an Apache cultural advisor, saved him the trouble. There were no textbooks, said Escandon. Apache was not a written language and seldom used. His people spoke a mix of English and Spanish with only a dab of Apache. As Darrow told the German teen magazine BRAVO, ". . .the few Indians who still speak bits and pieces of Apache — like my friend Gil (his Indian name is Great Servant) — also speak more with their hands than with their mouths."

Escandon became the actor's Apache language and culture guide. An exhaustive researcher, Darrow devoured facts about clothing, customs and folklore. In the margins of his scripts, he scribbled phonetic spellings of Apache words and English meanings and practiced to get it right.

He could not have been more zealous. Whenever anyone said they didn't think their character should say a certain line, he'd ask to take it. "After a while, the producer got tired of me and said, 'Hank, just shut up and do your own dialogue. It's somebody else's turn.'" Come to find out, being in every sequence had a downside. "If I was in the master shot, I'd have to hang around for the rest of the day. Maybe I'd only have one

---

87. The High Chaparral *episode "Destination Tucson"*

line, but I might still be there at two in the morning because I was in the master."

He watched and listened carefully, picking up tips from the cast and crew. He learned from guest stars — character actors, leading ladies and men, future headliners, faded icons and everyone in between.

First year guest stars included Pasadena Playhouse alum Anthony Caruso; physician turned actor Joaquín Martínez; character actors Harry Dean Stanton, Paul Fix and Pat Hingle; screen and stage veteran BarBara Luna; Tony-nominated Fernando Lamas; *Stoney Burke* (and later, *Hawaii Five-O*) leading man Jack Lord; Western Heritage award winner Barbara Hershey; elegant Ricardo Montalbán; and Ramón Novarro, a former silver screen phenomenon.

"Novarro was one of the first real superstars and he was the first Latino superstar," Darrow notes. Handsome Mexican born Novarro was only 5'6," but in his twenties he was a giant of early cinema as Rupert in *The Prisoner of Zenda* (1922) and in *Scaramouche* (1923). When he starred in 1925's *Ben-Hur*, Novarro — hailed as "the new Valentino" — reached fame's highest peak. His biographer Andrés Soares later wrote, "...no other Latin American performer — from Gilbert Roland and Dolores del Rio to Ricardo Montalbán and Anthony Quinn. . ." ever achieved Novarro's acclaim.[88] Unlike many silent film stars, he had a good voice and seamlessly transitioned to talkies, making enormously popular films into the 1930s. Critics adored him. The public adored him. He was exotic, yet not frighteningly foreign — a nice young man devoted to his family and the Catholic Church and as an actor, a consummate professional.

According to his biography, Novarro was genuinely all those things. But he was also a closeted gay man tortured by guilt and self-loathing. In those days, homosexuality was Hollywood's dirty little secret. Even rumors killed careers and the studios hid stars' homosexuality from a disapproving public through any means, including arranged marriages. Novarro refused the pretense of marriage, saying an artist could not serve two masters ("An actor has no *right* to marry...He is public property"[89]). Instead, he hid his sexuality and drank heavily. "We are an illusion," he once observed. "The audience does not look at us as real. We are just an image on a giant screen that can never live up to their expectations as a person."[90]

88. Beyond Paradise, *p. xiv*

89. Ibid. *p. 175*

90. Ibid. *p. 98*

After M-G-M miscast him repeatedly in dreadful movies, audiences cooled considerably.[91] By the mid-1930s, alcoholism ravaged his boyish face. Unable to find steady work, he was a "Hollywood has-been" at only thirty-six.[92] His career revived somewhat in the 1950s, but by the 1960s, he was plagued by poor health and money troubles and mostly forgotten except for publicized drunk driving arrests. His career consisted of occasional movie cameos and sporadic television roles. In 1967, he guest starred on *The Wild, Wild West*. It was a miserable experience. He was given the script a day before filming and had trouble remembering his lines. Painfully nervous while shooting, when filming wrapped Novarro went on a drinking spree.[93]

His next role was on *The High Chaparral* as benevolent Padre Guillermo in "A Joyful Noise". "He was so nervous, always forgetting his dialogue and sweating profusely," recalls Darrow. "He hid Kleenex in his sleeves. He used it to dab the shine from the sweat off his face, just dabbing constantly."

At one point, he extracted a tissue and told Darrow, "This is the most important thing an actor can have!"

Director Richard Benedict realized the best way to avoid rattling Novarro was to pretend they weren't filming. "If we said, 'Action!', if Novarro thought the cameras were rolling, he'd mess up," says Darrow. "So instead, Benedict told him that it was the dress rehearsal, then he shot all those final rehearsals. Novarro did just fine. Most of the footage we used was from the so-called rehearsals. He was good there."

To Henry Darrow, he was an immortal from Hollywood's golden days. "He was very elegant in his white scarf and jacket. He had that old Hollywood glamour, like Gilbert Roland." Ramón Novarro's endearing performance as Padre Guillermo was his last. Several months after *Chaparral*, the frail, sixty-nine-year-old former megastar was brutally beaten to death by two young hustlers.

Decades later, Rick Najera says Henry Darrow taught him to put Hollywood in perspective. "He understood that it's a balancing act. Don't take it seriously, don't buy your own hype, don't make it a measure of you as a man, because it will stop. Enjoy the successes, but know they will stop and take it in stride." But in 1967, Darrow grabbed all the enjoyment he could in front of the camera, mixing with fans or hanging out with cast

91. Ibid. *p. xiv*

92. Ibid. *pp. 206, 207*

93. Ibid. *p. 268*

and crew. Ebullient in spite of blazing temperatures, his enthusiasm was infectious. Says Linda Cristal, "When Henry Darrow came onto the set, it was like the sun came up! That is exactly the truth. The sun came up and was nice and shiny and it warmed you up and that is Henry."

"They told us not to bother the main stars," says Frank Catalano, a first-year extra. "But Hank Darrow would spend time with the extras and bit players."

When ten-year-old extra Frank Vallejo grew bored standing around between takes, Darrow played imaginary baseball games with him. "He'd pretend to pitch," says Vallejo. "And I'd pretend to hit and he'd call it. Oh, too high! Too low! Wow, home run!" He adds, "If you were down, he always knew how to cheer you up."

Leif Erickson warned Darrow to be more leisurely and sit in the shade. "You're always up and about, walking, standing," Erickson said. "It's better if you sit instead of standing. It's even better to lie down instead of sitting."

Constantly on the move, Darrow didn't listen. Did a fan in the crowd work at an orphanage? Okay, he'd go there later and say hi to the kids. "Yesterday I couldn't have given away my autograph with a ten dollar bill," he told an interviewer. "Today I have writers' cramp." And he could thank Manolito Montoya.

Says journalist Penny J. McQueen, "*High Chaparral* characters stayed with fans over the years because they seem so real. That reality is rooted in their very basic, human flaws and Manolito's are such devilish fun. He's lazy, chases women, runs from responsibility, drinks, lies, cheats at cards, steals horses and laughs at his own jokes. But he's so darling that everyone loves him in spite of it."

Kent McCray adds, "Henry's character lent itself to being very flamboyant. And you really saw his character develop and Henry did all that. It was in the script, but he really took the words and made them come alive."

Ask Darrow how he shaped Manolito, he crows, "I stole from everybody!" In the movie theaters of his youth, he cheered as Cesar Romero, Duncan Renaldo and Gilbert Roland successively swashbuckled their way through the *Cisco Kid* movies. Tall, dashing Romero was the first Hispanic to play Cisco and did so with roguish charm. Renaldo played him more as a clean-cut Don Quixote than Don Juan, whereas stylish Roland gave Cisco more flair with the señoritas. Roland's films carried taglines like "HE'S TALL, DARK AND DANGEROUS! A two gun Galahad leaving a trail of Kissing Women and Cussing Men!" Fearless, lawless and elegant, Roland's Cisco donated panache and a bullfighter's stance to Manolito Montoya. But Darrow didn't stop there. From Shakespeare, he borrowed

Mercutio's wit and a taste of Iago's menace. From his own family came a tune about a mother hen and chicks that Manolito often sang, hummed or muttered. It was the drunken lullaby that Henry's grandfather, Papa Abuelo, sang to Henry and his brother Dennis when they were kids. "*La gallina está muriendo y los pollitos están llorando*" ("The mother hen, she is dying and the chickies, they are crying").

Regardless what Darrow says, his brother Dennis maintains the person Manolito most resembled was Henry Darrow. "When I see him in the role of Manolito and the later Cervantes role, he really puts everything into it. It's like watching all the big name stars. But with Manolito, I always kidded him, 'You're not acting, you're just playing yourself.'"

Being himself sometimes earned Darrow bewildering praise. He was congratulated on Manolito's sexy, one eyed squint. "That wasn't inspired acting," he says. "My left eye is weak and the sunlight hurt, so I squinted to protect it." His hairstyle was an attention getter, but like his squint it wasn't a clever affectation. He didn't want to spend the bucks for a barber and that was how Lucy cut it.

As filming progressed, he enhanced Mano Montoya with expressions, gestures and other touches. He listened carefully to comments from the cast and crew and scribbled notes on his scripts. "Someone might say, 'Oh, you looked really sinister.' Since my character had a sinister side, I'd remember that look so I could use it again," he says. "I'd start adding things to my repertoire from the bullshit I wrote down."

It was a winning repertoire. Susan Sukman McCray recalls her first day at work as assistant casting secretary for Xanadu Productions. Her father, award-winning composer Harry Sukman, was hired to write most of *Chaparral's* music and Susan had watched an advance showing of the pilot. Seeing Darrow as Manolito, the young woman was smitten. "I thought, boy is he cute! Is he adorable! Look at those dimples!" He was the star she most wanted to meet, but when she did, he wasn't what she expected. "He was charming, but quiet. He wasn't that flamboyant personality I imagined from watching him as Manolito."

Susan's father was thrilled when Darrow stopped by the scoring stage to hear the uplifting "Manolito's theme" or the regal "Montoya." At parties, Darrow sometimes sang along as Sukman tickled the ivories. "Of course my father beamed!" says Susan McCray. "It was a great combination, the music and the performance."

Sukman's music complimented performances as well as spectacular Arizona locations. The vast desert, high mountains, rustic Old Tucson, grand Mission San Xavier del Bac and other venues set *The High Chaparral* apart from other TV westerns filmed in studio back lots or L.A.'s handy Griffith Park. But location shooting made *Chaparral* more expensive and harder on the cast and crew than other westerns. The whole company was on location for up to six weeks. Fourteen hour workdays weren't unusual and temperatures could soar to 120 degrees, hotter if there was a night time campfire scene. Night scenes were shot in daylight. Darkness was simulated by putting a special filter on the camera lens. Large metal reflectors illuminated faces and raised the ambient temperature while actors swathed in heavy blankets sat on hot sand and rocks around a real fire underneath the broiling sun.

At Paramount Studios, challenges were different than filming on location, but as with location shooting, neither scenes nor episodes were filmed in sequence. If several episodes contained interiors at Casa Montoya, scenes for those episodes were shot together on the Casa Montoya sound stage. Those scenes had to match not only bracketing interior scenes but exterior scenes shot on location days or weeks earlier. Says Darrow, "You have a scene outside the house in Arizona, then days later you're at Paramount doing the rest of that scene in the house. You had to sustain a certain intensity to pick up where you left off. That can be hard."

The script supervisor's job is managing continuity, telling an actor how angry he was in the previous segment, if his jacket was buttoned or if he was scratching his ear. To assist the script supervisor, Darrow took notes. "That way, when they see my sleeves rolled up and ask if I had them that way in the preceding scene, I can check my notes and tell them. It's helpful and it tells them I know what I'm doing."

Darrow definitely knew what he was doing when it came to stealing scenes, but he was a piker next to Cameron Mitchell. "Early on, Mark Slade and I talked about how great it was to be working with Cam Mitchell. Wow!" says Darrow with a laugh. "Then we looked at the dailies. Anytime you'd see our faces, Cam would hug us and turn us around so our backs were to the camera."

Mitchell knew all the tricks and as rowdy Buck Cannon, he got away with them. When he discovered director Bill Witney liked horses, he plied his horse with sugar cubes and carrots. The camera lingered on the nuzzling animal and affectionate man, exactly as planned. Darrow was more comfortable with cats and dogs than horses and says, "Darn! I just couldn't do that! So I'm standing there with egg on my face." Then he snickers. Once — only once — he bested Mitchell. It was in a close-up with Buck and Manolito on horseback.

"When Cam didn't know his lines, he'd tape them to whatever he could find. For one scene, he wanted to tape them on me. I said no, so he taped his dialogue to his saddle." Darrow waited until the camera was shooting over his shoulder straight at Mitchell, who was looking down at his saddle and mumbling his lines. Then Darrow clucked to Mitchell's horse. The horse sidestepped and Mitchell lost his place. They got back into position. Mitchell started to say his lines when Darrow clucked to the horse again. Again, the animal stepped sideways. Again, Mitchell lost his lines and mumbled at his saddle. Knowing he'd been outdone, he flashed Darrow a sourly appreciative look.

"He was a hell of an actor," said another cast member of Mitchell. "He knew how to make you look at him in a scene and that's something you can't teach. Little things, like being the last person out of the room or the last rider out of a shot."[94]

"He would *always* find ways to make sure the camera was on him. It looked like one awful shtick after another. Then you'd see it in the dailies and he was great," says Darrow, then shrugs. He found ways of nicely keeping Mitchell in check. "There were no hard feelings, it was just Cam. You don't fight it. When he grabbed you, you were going to be a prop of some kind, so I'd either fall or let myself slip off camera. They'd yell, 'Cut! Hey Cam, don't hug Henry so tight. He loses his balance.'"

He's very subtle, so it doesn't seem like you're being manipulated.

WRITER HARRY CASON

94. The High Chaparral Newsletter, *"Cameron Mitchell: Ghost of Chaparral,"* by Penny McQueen, 9/24/07

Nuts and Bolts

Pay's real good, real good. Place is lovely to work.
Hours not long, work not hard. Whatcha say?

BUCK CANNON[95]

The nuts and bolts of making *The High Chaparral* were in the hands of many people—producers like William F. Claxton, story consultants Don Balluck and Walter Black, stunt coordinator Henry Wills, numerous directors and production manager Kent McCray. McCray was the ramrod, coordinating everything and everybody from Teamsters' Union drivers to the stars. The cast nicknamed him "Big Daddy" although he was only in his thirties. "A good skipper," one actor called him. "He never was on top of people. Things just ran smoothly."[96]

It took about 300 people to create one episode, typical for a movie but massive for a television show. There were wranglers who only cleaned up cow manure, security guards, a one eyed doctor, makeup artists, lighting technicians, food service workers, stand-ins, stunt doubles and sometimes it seemed half of Tucson worked as extras. Over the run of the series, it took fifty-three screenwriters to put words in everyone's mouths. Cautioning one interviewer against ignoring writers to give all the credit to actors, Henry Darrow said, "Remember, I can't do a thing without the words."[97]

True, but a script is just a piece of paper without actors. *Chaparral* had an abundance, including the eleven regulars. Besides the five stars (Leif Erickson, Cameron Mitchell, Darrow, Linda Cristal and Mark Slade), Don Collier, Roberto Contreras, Bob Hoy, Ted Markland and Jerry Summers played ranch hands and Rudolfo "Rudy" Acosta was a taciturn jack of all trades named Vaquero.

Texas-born Acosta attended UCLA and the Pasadena Playhouse, then received a scholarship to the Palacio de Bellas Artes in Mexico

95. The High Chaparral, *"The Kinsman"*

96. *Robert Hoy in* Trail Dust *magazine, "Three Amigos," quoted on www.thehighchaparral.com*

97. The Tucson Daily Citizen, *11/27/67*

City. Later popular in Mexican and American films, in 1948 he won Mexico's prestigious acting award, the Ariel.[98] Unlike his laconic character, Acosta turned any day into a party and spent weekends bar-hopping in Nogales. One Monday morning, a flotilla of Mexican cabs arrived at the Old Tucson set and disgorged jolly Acosta, drunken mariachi musicians, other assorted revelers and ice chests full of beer. "I knew who was coming back. I told Rudy Acosta to straighten up," reported Roberto Contreras.[99] But it did no good and Acosta was gone after the second season.

From beginning to end, Don Collier played ranch foreman Sam Butler. Collier was a working cowboy at a ranch owned by actor Francis Lederer when Lederer encouraged him to try acting. His riding and brawny good looks made him a natural for westerns and his first part was as an extra in the western movie *Massacre River* (1949). Steady movie and television work followed, including a starring role in the *Outlaws* television series where he met Kent McCray. Collier never brought a mariachi band to the set, but he liked good times and says his favorite drink was "booze". "If I had a dramatic scene coming up, I did not want to be around people," says Henry Darrow. "But if it was a joking kind of scene, I'd hang out beforehand with Don Collier, Bobby Hoy and Bobby Contreras. Wherever they were, that's where the fun was."

Collier has a deep bass chuckle. "Well, we didn't usually have a whole lot of dialogue like Cam or Leif or Hank, so we could relax a little." Once when Darrow collapsed on the set, Collier decided to have some fun. On the daily call sheet, every performer had a number: Leif Erickson was #1, Cameron Mitchell was #2, Linda Cristal was #3, Mark Slade was #4, Darrow was #5 and Collier was #6. As Darrow was being carried out on a stretcher, Collier grinned at Hoy and held up five fingers, then pointed to himself. "Meaning Hank was going to bite the dust and that would move me up a notch." Darrow caught the signal. He wasn't too sick to laugh and he got better fast.

Robert F. Hoy, Collier's running buddy, played Sam Butler's younger brother Joe. Like Collier, he had been a genuine cowboy although he was born in New York City. His father died when Hoy was young and because his mother traveled for work, Hoy attended boarding school upstate. The school was near a dude ranch where Hoy cleaned out stalls, learned to rope and ride and eventually led guests on rides. "I got pretty

98. *Reyes and Rubie, p. 412*

99. Trail Dust *magazine, "Three Amigos," quoted on www.thehighchaparral.com*

good at sizing up a person and which horse was best suited for them," he said.[100] A Marine during WWII, Hoy took up cowboying in Nevada when the war ended. After a year, he gave that up for the movies. His horsemanship got him hired as a stuntman, but his wife Kiva said, "Bobby was one of those rare stuntmen who also became an actor. He was more and more in demand as an actor as his [stunt] career progressed." [101] His first uncredited acting job in *Ambush* (1950) coincided with his first uncredited stunt work in *Devil's Doorway* (1950). By 1961 when he and Jack Williams cofounded the Stuntmen's Association, Hoy had amassed numerous acting and stunt credits.

Jerry Summers was the other stuntman in the bunkhouse. Summers, who played ranch hand "Ira Bean," was a compact man who doubled Sal Mineo and Tony Curtis. He left *Chaparral* after the first season and became one of Hollywood's most famous stuntmen.

Lanky Ted Markland stayed with the show two years. A musician, journeyman actor and standup comic before *The High Chaparral*, his first manager and close friend was legendary comedian Lenny Bruce. Bruce got Markland gigs at big comedy clubs in Los Angeles and New York, but Markland wanted to concentrate on acting and do standup part time. David Dortort saw his comedy routine at the Troubadour Club and created the role of "Reno" for him. When Reno seemed relegated to one line per episode, Markland became restless. "I told David Dortort, give me something to say besides 'Riders coming!' Then Dortort yelled for someone get him more silent actors, because here was another one wanting a bigger part."[102]

Another tall, skinny actor, Roberto "Bobby" Contreras, was on the show all four seasons as ranch hand "Pedro Carr". Contreras, the son of film director Jaime Contreras, was born in Missouri but raised in Mexico City, where he began acting in movies at age eight.[103] By the time he was cast in *Chaparral*, Contreras had been in numerous movies and television shows, including two episodes of *Outlaws* starring Don Collier.[104] During breaks on the *Chaparral* set, Contreras would start a fire in an old oil can and turn up Mexican *musica* on his radio. Then, he'd pull out a little

100. The High Chaparral Newsletter, *5/13/07*

101. The Santa Clarita Valley *(CA)* Signal, *2/8/10*

102. The High Chaparral Newsletter, *"I'm Reno's Dad" by Penny McQueen, 3/24/07*

103. Hispanics in Hollywood, *Reyes and Rubie, p. 444*

104. Ted Markland guest starred in one of them.

skillet and sauté peppers, onions and slivers of meat until he filled the air with the rich aroma of fajitas. "When I wasn't doing anything, I might as well cook," he said.[105]

Contreras was the only chef, but one of several music lovers. Ted Markland would strum guitar and sing. Leif Erickson and Cameron Mitchell, both veteran song and dance men, sometimes broke into favorite songs from the 1930s. They were surprised the first time Henry Darrow chimed in. He wasn't even born until 1933, so how did he know all the words to songs like "Puttin' on the Ritz" and "Lullaby of Broadway"? "My grandmother's adopted daughter had an incredible collection of those songs on LPs," he says. "When I was eleven or twelve, I heard them all the time, but I was as surprised as Leif and Cam when I remembered them!"

Bobby Hoy once called Erickson and Darrow "the backbone of the show"[106] but Darrow demurs. "Leif and Cam, between the two of them, they held that show together." The two men were nearly polar opposites. Erickson was rock steady. "You always knew what you got with Leif," says Darrow. "He was professional, prepared and consistent. He always did his homework. I enjoyed his company when we were together. As a man, he was the most even-tempered person on the show and always helpful."

"Mr. Erickson was incredibly nice," says a New Zealander who visited the set as a child. "I was a shy little nine-year-old boy with a digestive ailment that almost claimed my life earlier that same year. To have Mr. Erickson take the time to come over to us after a hard day's shoot meant the world to me. I think of him often and realize he taught me to always try to treat people the way I'd like to be treated."

Cameron Mitchell had his own devoted fans. "You should see the letters I get," he said. "…I got a forty-seven page letter from a sixty-five-year-old gal in Pittsburg who thinks I'm the greatest thing on her television set."[107] Unlike Erickson, he was intense, outspoken and unpredictable. He changed his hair color on a whim, which played havoc with scene continuity. So did wearing huge, platform "Frankenstein" boots which put him nearly nose to nose with 6'4" Erickson and earned him the nickname "Uncle Boots". Mitchell's shenanigans didn't get him canned

105. Trail Dust *magazine, "Three Amigos" by Bob Anderson, quoted on www.thehighchaparral. com*

106. *Penny McQueen, interview in private papers*

107. *Baltimore, Maryland* The News American/TV Channels, *7/14-7/20, 1968*

because like Don Collier said, "He could act. Nobody could sell a scene like he could." [108]

His sloppiness was as legendary as his talent. "I like to play things for real," Mitchell told one reporter. "As for the dirt, which NBC complained about at first, well, you ride for two hours in that stuff around Tucson and try not to look dirty. I'm that kind of guy anyway. I spill more things in real life than most people." [109]

"At breakfast, you'd lose your taste," says Darrow. "He'd put out his cigarette in the coffee cup. There would be ashes around him! He'd talk with his mouth full. That's why he did those scenes as Buck so beautifully. That was Cam." He adds with admiration in his voice, "But with him, there could also be something intriguing, something interesting, something brilliant because he was really involved in the sequence. He was always challenging but always open and honest."

Mitchell, Darrow, Collier, Hoy and McCray played dominoes, poker or gin during slow times on the set. McCray once played gin on a mule's butt and said they'd do anything to kill time, except play chess with Darrow. Don Collier recalls, "Bobby [Hoy] played him more than I did, but Hank would beat you every time. It wasn't fun."

"Yeah, but I stunk at poker," Darrow says. "My brother Dennis is excellent, but I never had the patience for it and I was sort of chicken and conservative. If I bet, everyone would get out of the pot because they knew I only bet with a good hand."

"Hank never wanted to bet because he didn't want to lose any money," says Collier, laughing. "He's a cheapskate! We'd go out to dinner and he'd scavenge everyone's leftovers, take a big ole bag to his room. He'd collect all the bones and devour them later on. We'd go out to dinner and he wouldn't order anything. He'd snag food off everybody else's plate and say he didn't owe anything because he hadn't ordered. It happened almost every time we got together. One time, me and Bobby went out and Hank didn't go. We had steak and when we got back, Bobby got the idea to stick the bones in Hank's mailbox. The next day, he *thanked* us!"

Nobody called Mitchell a cheapskate, but he was an incessant gambler and lousy at poker. "He'd announce his hand," says Darrow. "He'd say, 'I've got a pair of deuces and I'm going to beat you.' The others believed him and they would raise. Cam would stay and of course, he

108. The High Chaparral Newsletter, *"Cameron Mitchell: Ghost of Chaparral," by Penny McQueen, 9/24/07*

109. *Baltimore, Maryland,* The News American/TV Channels, *7/14-7/20, 1968*

would lose. Everyone knew how he played and anytime there was a game, they couldn't *wait* for him to show up!"

He'd also blow a wad at horse or greyhound races. On a trip to the dog track in Tubac, Darrow and Mitchell brought character actor Albert Salmi along. "Cam bet on the first dog and lost. Albert bet five or ten bucks and his dog won," says Darrow. "Then they bet on the second race and Albert's dog won. Then Albert bet on a long shot in the third race and won again. The guy won the first three races! So Cam asked Albert what dog he was going to bet in the fourth. Albert told him and Cam bet the same dog. Then he asked Albert, 'Why did you bet that dog?' Albert said, 'Well, his name is Levine and my agent is Sam Levine.' So Cam asked why he bet on the third one. 'His name was Doc Gooden and it reminded me of the baseball player.' And so on. Nothing had to do with knowledge of the dogs! And Cam bet the most money on the fourth race thinking that Albert had an in, but he didn't and the dog lost. Oh, it was awful!"

Acting was more of a sure thing for Mitchell, especially partnered with Darrow. Although Mitchell told an interviewer, "Everybody on the show hates me, except David Dortort"[110] he and Darrow had off screen rapport and such onscreen synergy that when paired in "buddy" episodes, they stole the show.

"We had two episodes where Buck and Manolito wound up having their own ranch," says Darrow. "The episodes were so solid, the network people thought they could make us into a spinoff series, but it didn't happen."

Who knows if mercurial Mitchell was eager for a spin off, but he was enthusiastic about *The High Chaparral* and his part in it. "Here in Hollywood, it's another *Bonanza*, but just alone out there in the desert, you have a feeling you're doing something that really happened to somebody 100 years ago," he told *TV Guide*.[111] In another interview, he pointed out additional aspects of the show's and Uncle Buck's appeal.

"Did you know that the English are going for this gray, dirty character who's kind of in between a good guy and a bad guy?" he asked. "Well, they are. And what's more, the Mexicans love the show because Linda Cristal plays Victoria as a regal lady, and a white man, me, is a dirty sloppy kind of bum."[112]

110. Ibid.

111. Ibid.

112. *Baltimore, Maryland,* The News American/TV Channels, *7/14-7/20, 1968*

Cristal and Mitchell had onscreen chemistry but little in common except a predilection for adlibbing (both were frequently told to stick to the script) and rapport with Henry Darrow. "Henry took the best of me and forgot about the worst," Cristal says with a chuckle. "We should do that with all our friends. It's a good philosophy."

Cristal, a self-described loner, was congenial on the set but mostly kept to herself and used free time to study scripts in her room. "But with Henry. I felt comfortable communicating," she says. "When they saw one day that we played so well with each other as Manolito and Victoria, they began to appreciate it. There were many times when a segment would be short and the director would say, 'Could you and Henry adlib something in Spanish? We need about three minutes.' Oh, yes! Of course! We never had trouble with that!" She laughs. It's a hearty, melodious chuckle. "So I came up with something and he picked it up or he came up with something and I picked it up. It was fun! We didn't have to ask, we were just playing and we never knew what the other one was going to do. We each tried to get extreme so the other one would have more fun. It was really great."

"For that you need a degree of trust," says Darrow. "Linda and I trusted each other and the producers and director trusted us to do it right."

But adlibbing in Spanish was tricky. Caught up in the moment, Darrow could let fly with 20th Century Nuyorican slang. "What you'd call Spanglish," he says. "And for those who say Spanish is Spanish, that's not true." He depended on the Mexican actors and Cristal to correct him. "They'd go, 'What? Did he just say something about a subway?' Or I'd use an expression that to me was very mild, maybe something like 'damn' in English and they'd say, 'Oh no, you can't say that! That's a really bad word in Mexico.' It was important to catch stuff like that *before* we taped dialogue."

Highly focused Cristal wasn't above practical jokes. In one scene, she and Darrow were asked to fill a little time. She went inside the ranch house while he stretched out in the hammock on the porch and closed his eyes. When he looked supremely comfortable, she opened the door, stepped across the veranda, picked up one side of the hammock and flipped him in the dirt. "He started laughing that very contagious laugh of his and I adlibbed something like 'Of course you are laughing because you are really crying inside, no?' But I was thinking, "Oh, I *got* you!"

"I particularly liked working with Linda, but it was a wonderful group of people: Cam, Leif, Bobby, Don, Frank Silvera and Kent and Susie McCray," says Darrow. "And Marie Gomez has a great sense of humor and was fun to be around. With her there was never any hanky-panky, just always warm affection."

Gomez, described in a contemporary article as having "a face for *Vogue* and a body for *Playboy*," is a staunch Presbyterian who guest-starred as Manolito's avaricious girlfriend Perlita Flores during the first two seasons. Not the hanky-panky type, she disliked onscreen kisses. Whether she locked lips with Burt Lancaster, Henry Darrow or another handsome heartthrob, she says, "You have lots of people looking at you and the kiss is so professional. Sometimes there is attraction between an actor and an actress, but when I kiss guys in a show, I feel nothing." On the other hand, kisses were stock in trade for Perlita. The site *www.thehighchaparral.com* aptly describes her as "shameless, bold and mercenary, never forgetting to ask Manolito if he has brought her a present before she bestows her favors".[113]

"Marie played such a manipulative character, but she's a real straight shooter," Darrow says. "She's an instinctive actress and a complete professional. She respected me as an actor and we enjoyed each other's company. I think that's the most you can ask for."

"*The Professionals* was serious work, work, work. *The High Chaparral* was fun!" says buoyant Gomez. "Linda Cristal does scenes beautifully, Leif Erickson was always a gentleman, Cameron Mitchell was a pro and Bill Claxton was a great director. Roberto Contreras, we were in *The Professionals* together. What a funny guy he was! But working with Henry Darrow was delightful. I've worked with big stars, bigger than Henry, but as an actor he is in the same category as Burt Lancaster and Lee Marvin except Henry has more joy on the screen than they did," she says. "He is not only a fine actor, he is a man with class and he is very kind. If I was worried and afraid, he would say, 'You can do it, Marie. Any emotion, you can do it!'" A workhorse on the set, Gomez isolated herself to rebuff pushy men and protect her career. Instead of parties or dinners, she studied her script and got a good night's sleep. "When a man, an actor, has been out drinking too much and he looks bad, they say, 'What a good actor! What realism!' When it's a woman, they say, 'What happened to her? She looks terrible!' Women have it tough everywhere."

For other actors, challenges came not from gender but race. Guest-star Frank Silvera played Don Sebastian Montoya so credibly that few people realized he was of Afro-Caribbean heritage. Born in Kingston, Jamaica in 1914, Silvera grew up in Boston and studied law until his stage debut

---

113. *Character description by Lisa McKenzie*

in a Boston production of *Potter's Field* by North Carolina playwright and civil rights advocate Paul Eliot Green. After *Potter's Field*, Silvera abandoned law school and went to New York City where he joined the American Negro Theatre of Harlem and the Actor's Studio. He went on to perform in as well as direct major stage productions.

Although endemic racism limited opportunities for blacks in the entertainment industry,[114] Silvera's light complexion and Iberian surname helped him escape some of the typecasting which hamstrung other African-American performers. He played a variety of ethnicities and races believably and quick thinking never hurt him either. Lecturing at the University of Maryland, he recounted an interview for the role of an African-American elevator operator. The producer rejected him as "not black enough". Silvera left the man's office, then turned and opened the door again. "Am I light enough to play one of the white parts?" he asked. The answer was yes. He got a part.[115]

"Frank was solid, but very unpredictable," say Henry Darrow, who worked with Silvera before *Chaparral* on a series called *The Garlund Touch*. "Sometimes he wanted to rehearse over and over and other times, he wanted to do it right away with no run-through. Either way, he knew *exactly* what he was doing." He summarizes the dynamics between Don Sebastian and Manolito as classically European.[116] Their scenes are rich with dialogue like this from "The Glory Soldiers":

Don Sebastian: *You are a disgrace to the name of Montoya, a disgraceful disgrace. The decent girls of Sonora, at the mention of your name, they are frightened.*

Manolito: *You know, my name was yours before I was born. And by the way, I have heard many stories about you,* Padre Mio.

Don Sebastian: *In my time a man was judged by his virtues. I had the common sense to practice my vices in private.*

---

114. *With sometimes ridiculous results. The 1965 British-made movie* Othello *starred Sir Lawrence Olivier in blackface as the Moor. Columnist Inez Robb ridiculed the performance as "high camp," compared it to Al Jolson and said, "I was certainly in tune with the gentleman sitting next to me who kept asking 'When does he sing 'Mammy?'" (retrieved on www.wikipedia.org, 6/11/10)*

115. *www.wikipedia.org*

116. *University of Western North Carolina, Oral History of Henry Darrow, Part 4*

"Some of the scenes were in the context of comedy and enjoying the tricks and the banter, but then you see anger or a touch of sorrow. It was very Shakespearean and I drew on Shakespeare," Darrow says. "I had many good times with Frank. When he would go 'up', forget his lines, he'd start going, 'Oh ho ho…ah…Manolito…you…oh ho!' Then I'd cover for him. Now that I'm older, I do that when I go up. When I'm onstage and you hear me go, 'Oh…ha ha…ah ah!' I'm telling another actor, 'Say something, kid. Remind me where I am!'" He smiles when he says, "In front of the camera, Frank and Cam Mitchell brought out the best in my character."

The Arizona Territorial agreed, saying, "The scenes between Henry Darrow and Frank Silvera, who portrays the master of the large Montoya spread, are priceless. So much comes through by a shrug of a shoulder, a casual adlib, a fleeting expression of cunning or the betrayal of their particular brand of mutual love and admiration."[117]

Seeing Darrow and Silvera on television confused some fans when they met Darrow's real father. Says Darrow, "One of the times Mom and Pop were visiting, we went on a special tour at Universal Studios. People would recognize me and stop us for photographs. They met Mom and she was already in the habit of saying she was Manolito's mother, so they learned who she was. Then they asked Pop, "And who are you, sir?' He had his little Cesar Romero beard and moustache and he said, 'I'm his father' and they said, 'No, no. You don't look right.' He explained, 'I'm his *real* father, Enrique Delgado.' So then they asked Pop for his autograph and he signed autographs. He and Mom just enjoyed the heck out of it."

> *All those years while he was struggling, we never lost hope that one day he'd make it.*
>
> ENRIQUE DELGADO

---

117. *"Manolito is a Marvelous Rascal, But Henry Darrow was Here First"* by Opal Johnson, 7/10/69

You Always Say Yes, Henry!

If you're casting for the part of a cowboy or a man who rides a horse, all the actors who come in will say, "Yes, I can ride" because they really want the part, bless their hearts.

DIRECTOR RAYMOND AUSTIN

Asked if they could ride, Don Collier and Bobby Hoy told the truth when they answered yes. Not so for Linda Cristal, who told Henry Darrow when they first met at Dortort's office that she had never been on a horse, but "If they ask, I'll say yes of course I ride. You always say yes, Henry!"

"But what do you do when they bring you the horse?" he quizzed.

"I will ride!" answered unflappable Cristal.

Darrow blinked. He had only been in the saddle briefly. When a reporter asked what he knew about horses, he summed up his knowledge with, "I can tell when they don't want me to ride."[118] Handy information, but Manolito Montoya had to look as if he was born in the saddle and Henry Darrow had to make that happen.

The odds were against him. He lacked equestrian skill, had a paralyzing fear of heights and sometimes suffered from immobilizing spinal pain. Still, he was determined to look like a fine young *caballero*.

The "star" horses came from Myers and Wills Stables in California, owned by stuntman Stevie Myers whose father taught Leif Erickson to ride in 1934. Stevie was Darrow's first instructor, but his beginnings as a horseman were as rocky as some of the outdoor locations. One sequence required Manolito to carry his forty pound stock saddle across the corral and put it on his horse. Seventeen takes later, Darrow was whipped and the saddle still hadn't made it correctly on the horse. It finally rested on a rail while the actor exercised his arms and hands.

118. The Modesto (CA) Bee, 5/26/68

But Hank Darrow not only had to carry the saddle, he had to ride like a pro. He needed an onsite teacher and Bobby Hoy turned out to be the best man for the job.

"The film business is all about show; an actor's goods are his looks and voice, just enough to talk his way into everything else," said Hoy. "I've taught more than one good looking actor with plenty of talent but no time in the saddle to ride." The wiry ex-Marine took Henry Darrow behind the barn for horsemanship lessons. "I taught him everything he knows. Not everything *I* know, just everything *he* knows."

"Getting on and off a horse doesn't sound like much," Darrow acknowledged. "But they told me not to hunch over, to pretend I was climbing a ladder and keep my back straight. You make that leg come over the saddle as close as you can. And if there's a blanket or something on the back, you have them take it off. You don't want to put your leg up and bump into the blanket or it's, 'Cut! Next!'"[119] Learning those things gave him more poise, but he was grateful Hoy was nearby.

"When we had a scene with cattle or there was gunfire, that's when stuff happens. You never know what can happen until it does. Bobby protected me," he says, but sometimes Hoy had to rescue him from himself. "One time I thought 'Hey, maybe I can lead this cattle drive.' So I started to move into lead position, then the bad guys showed up shooting and all hell broke loose!"[120] Darrow's horse bolted toward a hill where he ducked under a tree and nearly smacked the actor against a limb. Hoy was in hot pursuit and when Darrow's horse finally stopped, he reined in and asked if Darrow was okay. He was.

"Well, don't do that again because you're going to get in trouble," Hoy advised. "Lay back and follow the rest of us."

Said Darrow, "I just felt so confident whenever he was close."[121] Fortunately he didn't feel confident enough to try leading a cattle drive again.

Instead of risking his neck herding cattle, he augmented Hoy's lessons with rides in the desert during down-time. Frank Catalano, a stranger to horses before working on *Chaparral*, recalls initial rides weren't much fun. "The horn was made out of wood. The horse would stop and I'd hit that horn. Boy, that hurt!" he says with a wince. "I was always afraid the horses would run into cactus, but they're pretty good at avoiding stuff like that."

119. *University of Western North Carolina, Henry Darrow Oral History Part 3*

120. Western Clippings Magazine, *March/April 2010*

121. Ibid.

Darrow's first horse, Diablo, wasn't as good at avoiding Leif Erickson. In the first scene where Darrow did serious riding, he mounted quickly and galloped to the ranch house. "All of a sudden, there was Leif Erickson on foot and I thought, oh my God, I'm going to run over him!" Darrow yanked the reins to turn Diablo, but the animal's hip slammed Erickson into the air. "And that's how I broke Leif's wrist," he says. "Somewhere, there's a picture of him upside down just before he landed." Erickson recovered with no hard feelings, but as long as *Chaparral* aired, whenever anyone was on foot and Darrow rode up, he swears they stepped backward.

In truth, Diablo was too much horse for a novice. Before there were other mishaps, Bobby Hoy provided a mid-season replacement. Because Hoy rode to the rescue if another horse bolted or a wagon team lunged out of control, he needed a fast, reactive horse. Instead, his first mount was a nearly bomb-proof sorrel gelding named Mackadoo. The only thing challenging about Mack was keeping him awake during long scenes, but he was an old trooper who always hit his mark and riding him was comfortable as a rocking chair. He was ideal for Henry Darrow. "Mack knows me and my reactions and I know what he's going to do," he told *Western Horseman* magazine. "In my role as Manolito, I'm supposed to be a horseman and I want to look as well as feel the part."[122]

"It becomes part of your character," he says. "I enjoyed riding in as the sun was going down when maybe only twenty minutes of light was left. When the sun turns from yellow to red, they'd have to put on lights and the entire atmosphere changed. I like working under pressure like that, shooting at the end of a ten or twelve hour day when people are tired. To hit my mark and come through was as satisfying as playing a wonderful emotional scene."

Contrary to macho-man publicity, stars usually don't risk their necks doing serious stunts. They're too valuable, difficult to replace and injury to a star can cause expensive filming delays. If an actor is riding a bucking bronco, it's likely him on a mechanical horse in close-ups and a stunt double on a real horse in long shots.

"Stuntmen are working stiffs who change clothes in the horse trailer, too tough or hard headed to know when they're hurt," said Bob Hoy. Without stuntmen and women, Hollywood would close down. Bruised, battered and bloody, those working stiffs are worth their weight in gold.

Darrow's stunt double was Carl Pitti.[123] When he doubled Darrow on *Chaparral*, Pitti was in his early 50s and shorter than the actor. But

122. *July 1970*

123. *Pitti was later inducted into the Stuntmen's Hall of Fame*

says Darrow, "He would put on the hat and boots and dark makeup and it was no problem. He hunched his shoulders a little bit, so I copied that when I rode. That way, they could use him doing the really good riding up to the last minute."

Besides horsemanship, Manolito's skills included pretty fancy work with a bullwhip and Carl Pitti was an artist with a whip. Susan McCray remembers him as a quiet, almost shy man who grew up working rodeos with his trick-riding father. Says Darrow, "Carl would hold something between his lips and his father would ride by and pop it from his mouth with the whip." Pitti learned to crack the whip with dead accuracy. Darrow couldn't have had a better instructor and Pitti could not have asked for a more obsessive student. Darrow practiced for hours, even using two whips as jump ropes.

"He was like a kid in a candy store, playing with that whip," says actor James Victor, who was in his twenties when he first met Darrow at Paramount. "To me, he was a star already. I'd seen him in *The Wonderful Ice Cream Suit* and I was so proud that a Hispanic actor was finally getting recognition. Then to meet him when I was just getting my feet wet, he was always just a very giving person. That's what I love about him."

The big bullwhip didn't love him quite as much and before long, Henry Darrow sported a bandaged ear. Although proficient enough to cut newspaper into shards, he said, "The going forward part is fine, but I'm having trouble with my ears on the snap back. It looks spectacular but feels terrible."[124]

Good as Pitti was, he couldn't protect Darrow from his dedication to authenticity or his fondness for party tricks. "I tried a few stunts, like going through a table," he says. "It was balsawood and that's soft wood, but I hit it fast and a splinter passed through my skin near my eye. I was hit on the head with a glass that didn't break. The prop glasses were made from sugar, but it hurt and that ended my stunt career."

But he was still the guy who spontaneously leapt over the banister in *The Devil's Disciple*. In an episode called "The Terrorist," one sequence involved Manolito pretending to be drunk so he could outfox a deadly old friend (played by Henry Silva). Darrow recalls, "I told the crew, I'm going to try something, but I can only do it once. I can't repeat it." Two cameras rolled when he jumped on a small table. It was a situation he could control and if he goofed and fell, the fall wouldn't be very far. "They just let me go and I did my phony baloney flamenco on top of the table.

I just did whatever, including almost falling off. When my mother saw it, she said, 'See? I knew you could dance!'"

But it would take more than fancy footwork to change the Anglo-Saxon Protestant face of American television. It would take heroes and a story Hispanics identified with.

> *The High Chaparral was about Arizona and they couldn't help but use Latinos because there were Latinos there. That was a rare exception.*
>
> WRITER/PERFORMER RICK NAJERA

Not Your Typical Bandidos or Peasants

...it certainly is unexpected. I mean — finding such graciousness in this no man's land.

"CAPTAIN THOMAS DABNEY,"
UPON ARRIVING AT THE CANNON RANCH[125]

When it aired on Sunday, September 10, 1967, *The High Chaparral's* pilot preempted *Bonanza*. This positioned *Chaparral* to corral *Bonanza's* enormous audience. The strategy worked. Abundant viewers made the pilot first in the Nielsen ratings that week, but reviews were mixed.

Critics expecting a *Bonanza* clone were disappointed when they didn't get it; others thought *Chaparral* was too much like *Bonanza*. In Los Angeles, William Donnelly of *The Tidings* gave high marks to several actors, drubbed the show's "blood and violence," called the storylines weak and tired, but finished by saying, "For all its faults, however, 'The High Chaparral' may be leading the way towards a new kind of adult entertainment and pointing away from shows that pretend adulthood like 'Mission: Impossible.'" [126] *The Arizona Daily Star* complained, "... its two-hour version was not great television — it was not even good television" and also mentioned the Cannon's "bloody" first days in Arizona.[127] But nobody damned the show's violence as stridently as *Variety*, which called the show as "a lusty, bloody, guts and gore western with an excessive dose of violence" and hammered that opinion home with statements like, "Where *Bonanza* stresses warmth, *Chaparral* has its emphasis on violence."

Meanwhile, at the movies blood was box office bucks. Brutal flicks *Bonnie and Clyde*, *The Dirty Dozen* and *The Born Losers* were among

---

125. The High Chaparral, *"Best Man for the Job"*

126. *William Donnelly, 1/26/1968*

127. TV Highlights, *"Measure of Credibility Big Need of 'Chaparral' " by Tom Riste, 9/12/67*

1967's Top Ten moneymakers. All collected some negative reviews including Oscar-winner *Bonnie and Clyde,* but their success encouraged more graphically violent films. Given the backlash against violence on TV, this would be ironic except that movies differed from television in very important ways. First, television was more personal. To see *Bonnie and Clyde,* people had to go to theaters, but television visited America at home. Second, television was the newest visual medium and some eyed it and its possible impact with suspicion. Parents wondered if the daily bombardment of gunfights, gangsters and Roadrunner's perpetual annihilation of Wile E. Coyote would warp young viewers. Child development experts answered unequivocally "yes," charging that televised violence begat violent children. Although studies have since disputed a link between watching video violence and committing violent acts in the real world, many parents of the 1960's were convinced the experts were right.

In those days before technology gave parents a means to block certain programs or entire channels, the only "parental controls" were early bed times and the word "no." Countless tiny tots who snuck out of bed to watch *The Untouchables, The Twilight Zone, Gunsmoke* or other adult programming proved this wasn't effective. On the other hand, the total elimination of video violence would be effective and was considered in the best interest of the nation's youth and indeed, American society.

Even so, charges of excessive violence weren't necessarily the kiss of death, especially since reviews for *Chaparral* were so contradictory that one wonders if all critics saw the same pilot. Ben Gross deemed the show successfully character driven and not excessively bloody. "What makes this show different from the other Western newcomers is this: It places its stress on characters rather than on mere gunplay and other violent action." He called it "the best of the season" and complimented the "vivid" acting of the principal performers.[128] Likewise, *The Hollywood Citizen-News* called it "a big, brawling Western in which the relationships between the characters are interesting" and noted that although its regular time slot was directly after *Bonanza,* it appeared able to "stand on its own."[129] In America's heartland, the *South Bend Tribune* lauded it as…a solidly professional, rousing and red blooded frontier piece…"[130] Back on the West Coast, Marian Dern praised "high quality production, conception of

128. The Daily News, "What's On?" 9/11/67

129. Allen Rich, 9/12/67

130. 9/11/67

characters, storyline, casting and overall execution," citing David Dortort's involvement as a major reason for excellence.[131]

Whether critics pounded or praised *The High Chaparral*, Dortort's years in Hollywood gave him more faith in viewers than reviewers. "I think audiences generally know and accept something that has a period feeling where violence has to do with the settling of a wild frontier," he said dismissively.[132] Reviewer Bob Foster agreed, noting that shows like the detective series *Mannix* were full of gratuitous bloodshed but violence on *The High Chaparral* signified necessary historical accuracy. It was "the story of one man's fight to establish a ranch in the heart of Apache country and along the Mexican border" and portraying this period of Arizona-Sonora history accurately "without a lot of gun play and violence would be impossible."[133]

Arguments about historical truth aside, Foster stated pragmatically that violence would stay or go depending on the ratings.[134] After starting at #1, *Chaparral* maintained respectable Nielsen ratings, which David Dortort called "excellent, despite the bad hour it's shown".[135] The "bad hour" was 10 p.m. EST on Sundays. The time chafed Dortort because it was later than usual for family-friendly programs and he felt a large potential audience had already been put to bed.

But many youngsters were allowed to stay up past bed-time, because watching *Chaparral* quickly became a special event for families. "When I was a child, watching *The High Chaparral* was something the whole family was looking forward to," said a typical fan. "The rest of the week we would talk about what happened."[136]

It was remarkable that a period western facilitated this rapport during a decade defined by intense intergenerational conflict. By 1967, the rift between the Greatest Generation and their Baby Boomer children was often a deep, angry chasm. Legions of parents struggled to understand sons and daughters with vastly different ambitions than theirs — or with no ambition at all. Many teens and young adults rejected established social values. They rocked the nation with sit-ins and marches — or turned on and dropped out to pursue spiritual enlightenment or sensual gratification.

131. The Hollywood Citizen-News, *"The View From The High Chaparral," 7/13/67*

132. Ibid.

133. The San Mateo *(CA)* Times, *"Screenings," 8/21/68*

134. Ibid.

135. The Tucson Daily Citizen, *11/3/67*

136. "Vlammetje" on Internet Movie Database (IMDB.com) User Reviews

High Chaparral's producers, writers and directors drew insight from contemporary generational battles. In doing so, they left behind the idealized white-bread world of previous family oriented shows like *Father Knows Best, Leave It To Beaver* and *Bonanza.* Instead, they created ethnically diverse, imperfect heroes struggling to survive in a hostile environment. This infused *The High Chaparral* with appealing relevance for families who often felt they, too, were struggling for survival in a hostile land.

Decades later, the TV mega-hit *Lost* proclaimed "All the Best Cowboys Have Daddy Issues."[137] It's an apt description of Manolito and Blue as they struggled to define themselves from their fathers, but *Chaparral* reached beyond daddy issues. Parents identified with Big John's and Don Sebastian's hopes and frustrations. The relationship between stepmother Victoria and stepson Blue resonated with blended families. John's and Victoria's marital ups and downs had relevance for couples. Sibling connections — protective, humorous, contentious — were illustrated by John and Buck and by Manolito and Victoria. The affectionate extended family bond between Blue and Uncle Buck charmed viewers; Buck wasn't always civilized, but he always had his nephew's back. An example of devoted friendship was that of Buck and Manolito, sometimes trading punches and sometimes risking their lives for each other. And everyone worked together — Cannons, Montoyas and bunkhouse boys — although they didn't always see eye to eye or even like each other much, not unlike a modern office except with cattle and drunken brawls.

These essential relationships echoed real-life ties binding viewers to family, spouses, friend, lovers and coworkers. But realistic interpersonal relationships weren't for everyone. One fan remembered Michael Landon berating *The High Chaparral's* emphasis on father-son conflict. "Mr. Landon insisted America didn't want to see this type of realism," she wrote. "He may have been right to a point, but I think it *was* this realism that made the show memorable. All of the main characters were lovable yet they were all far from perfect. Meanwhile, many of the villains had qualities that made the viewer identify with them ...."[138]

Apaches, often vilified in westerns, were presented to show their common human bond with non-Natives. "It was one of the first to show Native Americans in a positive light, that they're just like us," said a Wisconsin fan.[139] As David Dortort noted, the Apache "...could and did fight

137. Lost, Episode 1:11, 2004

138. "Bmeskunas," IMDB.com User Review

139. From The High Chaparral online DVD Petition

like a demon, but he had reason to. He was fighting for *his* homeland. Ruthless, granted. But we mustn't forget his courage and honor, nor the many outrages perpetrated against him...."[140] Indeed, in the pilot John Cannon says the Apache are just like anyone else fighting for their homeland. This didn't inhibit his determination to keep some of their homeland for himself and his family, but he voiced a reality contrary to the white-bias permeating western mythos, western films and TV and American history texts at the time. Apaches responded by choosing Leif Erickson as their guest of honor at the forty-fifth annual White Mountain Apache Tribal Fair.[141] A Navajo man spoke for other Indian fans when he wrote that he was delighted to see Native Americans play Native Americans "as real people, good and bad."[142]

Latinos were also portrayed as "real people, good and bad". Critic Marian Dern noted that *Chaparral* owed some of its unique realism to Mexican characters "pictured as real human beings and not either the comic sombreroed character leaning on a cactus plant or the murderous bandit..." However, most Anglo reviewers — i.e., most reviewers — didn't mention non-stereotypical Latino characters, the number of Latinos hired (a groundbreaking 250 or so over four years) or record number of Hispanic regulars. Anglo reviewers generally missed the significance of these accomplishments because they were not personally affected by them. For many Latinos, the show was profoundly personal.

"There weren't a lot of Latinos on television, so it was a big deal. It was 'Oh, wow! *There goes us!*'" says Rick Najera. "*The High Chaparral* was more than a TV series. We were actually watching our history." It was a proud chapter of history, the grand tradition of vast Mexican and Southwestern *haciendas* personified by the Montoya family. "I always thought the Anglo family was kind of trashy. Those guys looked like they didn't take a bath too often, but that was the history. The Mexican *caballeros* and *vaqueros* taught the Anglos how to be cowboys, but both sides gained from each other and they needed cooperation to survive. On *The High Chaparral* we saw Latinos who were land owners, people in charge. Not your typical bandido-peasants, but people with class and graciousness."

The portrayal generated ethnic pride and self-respect. It influenced the lives and careers of countless young Hispanics, including award winning

140. Arizona Highways, *September 1967*

141. The Tucson Daily Citizen, *8/29/70*

142. From The High Chaparral *DVD Petition, provided by Penny McQueen*

writer/comedian Najera and accomplished actress Patrice Martinez, a graduate of the prestigious Royal Academy of Dramatic Arts.

When Martinez was growing up in Albuquerque, New Mexico, her father urged his children to read or play outside instead of watching television. He made an exception for *The High Chaparral.* "Every week, we would gather around the TV," Martinez says and recalls pretending to be elegant Victoria Cannon when she played dress-up. "I actually wanted to be Victoria when I grew up. Linda Cristal was so beautiful!"

She credits *The High Chaparral* and especially Henry Darrow as Manolito Montoya for prompting her to become an actress. She says, "For a young Latina girl, his character was very inspirational. He projected warmth and humor and he was a special character to children." He was so special that meeting him was a dream of hers. "I had two dreams. One was to visit Spain, because I wanted to be a flamenco dancer. The second was to meet Henry Darrow."

"A lot of Latinos were really proud of Henry. Everyone admired him," says Najera, noting the cultural validity of Darrow's character. "Manolito had that freewheeling sense and the old Spanish grandeur and he really symbolized the *vaqueros*, the whole *vaquero* culture."

> *Isn't it nice to see Mexicans on a show as something other than servants or clowns? The Cannons and the Montoyas are absolutely equal! I am really happy to give Latin-Americans a hero they can identify with.*
>
> HENRY DARROW

A Very Hot Article

...I have the honor to present Manolo Montoya, a man both arrogant and foolish, though some feel he has a certain loveable charm. He is conceited, though not totally without cause. A harsh judge of his fellow man, though not without compassion. A man of some humor. Religious, in his own way...

MANOLITO MONTOYA[143]

"Henry Darrow, as a dashing Mexican scapegrace and Big John's brother-in-law, steals every scene he's in and should be given more to do" (*The New York Times*).[144] "And now in '*The High Chaparral*'...we have a non-hero coming up very fast along the trail. He is Henry Darrow and he's going to be a very hot article in the acting business. In fact, he may be just that right now" (*The San Diego Union*).[145] "...'*The High Chaparral*'... a solidly professional, rousing and red blooded frontier piece...is most notable for unveiling a young actor who, as they say in baseball, has it all; Henry Darrow, handsome, elegant, tough, funny, wholly commanding and magnetic, not to mention his talent" (*The South Bend Tribune*).[146] "Mitchell and Slade are good in their roles, while Henry Darrow offers an excellent, sparkling characterization as the brother of the second wife" (*Variety*). "... perhaps the meatiest role goes to Henry Darrow as Miss Cristal's brother, and as a fascinating rogue he made the very most of it" (*The Hollywood Citizen-News*).[147] "Henry Darrow, as the ne'er do well son of the Mexican land baron, dominated every scene he was in..." (*The Arizona Daily Star*). "Darrow has been compared to a young Gilbert Roland" (*The Pensacola*

---

143. The High Chaparral, *"A Joyful Noise"*

144. 9/11/67

145. 9/26/67

146. 9/11/67

147. 9/12/67

News-Journal).[148] "They are calling him the star of tomorrow, and a young Gilbert Roland…" (*The Modesto* (CA) *Bee*).[149] "…[Darrow] stole most of the thunder… with his lively Latin ways…Manolito should be simpatico with the kids, if they can stay up that late on Sunday nights, and he's obviously going to wow the ladies" (*The Binghamton* (NY) *Press*).[150]

Reviewers who panned the show praised Henry Darrow and those initially unenthusiastic about him warmed up fast. Curmudgeonly *TV Guide* reviewer Cleveland Amory first complained that it seemed Darrow would never stop laughing, then later said he deserved an Emmy. He wasn't nominated, but *Photoplay* magazine selected him as their 1967-1968 "Most Promising New Actor" — quite an honor, especially for the lowest paid of the show's stars.

Besides being low man in wages, Darrow was originally scheduled to appear in only half of the first season episodes, just above the minimum to be a regular. In the end he was in all but one and featured in most. "You see more of a character once that character starts to hit," he says. "It also staves off logistical problems. I was approached fairly quickly about doing other projects and that's a hassle. 'Henry's going to be doing *Gunsmoke* next month, so write him out of that episode', et cetera. It was easier to pay my $950.00 per episode and call it a day, even though I might only be in a few scenes here and there." A portion of his first paycheck purchased a new color television and part of the next paid for new household furniture.

Having steady work and steady pay was good, but fame was wonderful. After fan mail began pouring in, Leif Erickson remarked, "I'm the darling of the grandmother set…the 45-year-old set. The teens go for Henry Darrow." Rather than being jealous, Erickson said at his age he was pleased to get *any* fan mail at all and congratulated the younger star on being "the big smasher of the show".[151] Letters from adoring fans were just one of the bonuses. Darrow had great, free seats at baseball's World Series, football's Super Bowl and other sports events. Service in restaurants improved dramatically. Reporters called to talk with him. "I look forward to interviews and the whole bit," he told *Screen Stories*. "People want to know 'What is a Henry Darrow?' and I think that's groovy."[152]

148. 10/15/67

149. 11/5/67

150. "He'll Win Kids and Wow the Ladies" by Charles Witbeck, Special Press Writer, 9/30/67

151. The Syracuse (NY) Herald-Journal, "Grandmas Like Erickson" by Joan E. Vadenboncoeur, 1/14/68

152. May 1968

As always, he sent articles, reviews, photos, magazine covers and entire magazines to his parents. The Delgado's scrapbook collection, which Gloria proudly maintained, ballooned. So did Darrow's bank account.

His 1967-68 per episode pay was $950.00 and his agent periodically negotiated a $150 per episode bump.[153] Although not generous by Hollywood standards and lagging behind the salaries of the other stars, it amounted to a solid living even in pricey southern California.[154] A solid living while it lasted, that is. Hank Darrow was acutely aware that he could be a "young Gilbert Roland" one day and riding the bus to auditions the next.

"I look back over the years and a lot of memories are burned in the mind. It's easy to forget hard times when things are going well for you, but some things you always remember," he said, cautioning, "You've got to keep your feet on the ground. The whole thing can be zapped out from under you so fast, just as fast as it happened for you, particularly if you get carried away and lose your cool. I don't think that will happen to me."[155]

It sure sounded good.

"Yeah, but I was getting a lot of attention. It was great, but I wasn't used to it," he says. "And I had to learn all aspects of being a public persona."

On location in Arizona, fans stood mere yards from actors filming scenes and Darrow worked the crowd of star struck autograph seekers with amiable dexterity. Nobody would have guessed he battled intense social anxiety. "It's not being in a crowd that I have trouble with. The problem comes in approaching a crowd. Once I'm in, I'm okay. Before that, I see all these people who expect something from me. I don't want to disappoint them and there is a terrible feeling which goes along with that," he says. "And it was much worse then because I didn't have years of going to events."

One of the first places to invite him as a "celebrity guest" was White Front, a chain of Southern California megastores. White Front staged extravaganzas with battling rock bands, full sized circuses, beauty queens, celebrities and hoards of shoppers lured by the razzmatazz. More terrifying than all the classrooms of strangers he'd ever faced, but people wanted to meet him and the money was sweet, between $500 and $700 for about an hour of signing autographs.

---

153. *About $6,000 per episode and a bump of $939 in 2010 dollars*

154. *About $25,000 in 1967 (approximately $155,000 in 2010 dollars)*

155. Screen Stories, Ibid.

"The more you do, you gain a facility in talking to people," says Darrow. "At first, I wore the Manolito costume but not the dark makeup and gloves. People were puzzled, because I didn't look like Manolito. So the next time, I put on the makeup and wore the gloves." Practice decreased his panic about entering crowds and he became known for never passing the chance to appear at grand openings, charity fundraisers, parades or any other event. "I became good at promotional events for businesses and charities. I'd tell a story and it might be the most boring story in the world. But I'm a celebrity and the people at that particular event never heard it, so it's 'Oh, he was so charming! He imitated Leif Erickson and Cameron Mitchell and Frank Silvera and Linda.'"

He would have gladly told stories and turned on the charm to promote his father's restaurant, but TV scheduling quashed those plans. Enrique Delgado was in his late fifties and still managed the Faculty Club at the University of Puerto Rico, but he had lupus and decades of heavy smoking, hard drinking and rich food had given him high blood pressure, heart problems and breathing difficulties. Nonetheless, he had long dreamed of having his own restaurant. He opened El Tauro, figuring that after *The High Chaparral* premiered in September 1967, Henry could make a few appearances and pack in the customers. Unfortunately, *Chaparral* didn't premier in Puerto Rico until 1968.

"The restaurant did so-so," says Darrow. "If the show had started in Puerto Rico when it did here, it would have made a difference for me to go down once a month. But when later *The High Chaparral* was shown there and I would take the kids to visit, Pop didn't use us to promote. He had a picture of me in the restaurant and he and Mom were thrilled, but that was it. After a few years, the place closed." When it did, Enrique Delgado dusted off and went on to the next venture. "Moneywise, he always did better as a manager for other people than working for himself. In his own place, he treated customers as if they were guests and gave them meals and drinks on the house. He enjoyed it, but he lost money."

Gloria Delgado enjoyed having a famous son, but a postal problem rained small drops on her parade after Henry went to Arizona to film the first year's episodes. She sent a letter to the Hilton addressed to "Henry Delgado". Unfortunately, there was nobody registered by that name. When her letter came back marked "Addressee Unknown," the dramatic little woman was beyond flustered. From then on she used "Darrow," unless she was introducing him to someone, that is.

"After *Chaparral* aired in Puerto Rico, she would introduce me as Manolito. It was amazing. She would call people and say, 'This is Gloria

Delgado. I am Manolito's mother.' Even my grandmother Tata introduced me as Manolito. She had *never* been pleased with my choice of career and there she was, calling me Manolito!"

Once *Chaparral* was solid in the ratings, Darrow sold the twelve-year-old Chevrolet to a friend for a buck and bought an economical used AMC Rambler compact for Lucy. A reporter challenged his description of it as "new" and Darrow replied, "I've been so used to riding the bus to work that anything that runs on gas with over two cylinders is 'new' to me."[156]

"If the series is renewed," he said, "I may have my teeth capped."[157] When *The High Chaparral* was renewed, Darrow paid off all his debts, but didn't get his teeth capped. He vaulted from unknown to being "the ultimate Latin heartthrob"[158] with his naturally dazzling, bad-boy smile.

Parents named babies after him. At least one twelve-year-old girl named her first hamster "Manolito". Fan mail gushed in. Casting directors tried to lure him away to other projects — although he didn't have the time, it was gratifying to be asked.

But being the "ultimate Latin heartthrob" didn't mix with suburban life. Before long, comfortable Sun Valley wasn't so comfortable anymore. Formerly friendly neighbors grew aloof. "They sort of backed off. They didn't want it to look like they were sucking up to me," Darrow says.

Lucy and the children avoided the public eye, but with Hank's star ascending, maintaining a normal family life was difficult. They didn't live in a gated community, so fans and paparazzi showed up uninvited, disturbing everyone on their street. Completely protecting the children was impossible, but Darrow controlled information and photos by dispensing selected items to friendly reporters. It seemed to work, then a stalker followed Deedee home from school. "That wasn't right," says Darrow. "It was scary. I wasn't aware of it then, but NBC had a couple of private detectives who could take care of situations like that."

He replaced their backyard fence with a privacy wall, but a neighbor complained and wanted it taken down. Darrow planned to invite the man in for a beer, explain the situation and hope reason prevailed. If not, he would take the wall down for the sake of harmony, meanwhile he and Lucy went house-hunting. "We looked at a more expensive place

156. The Cumberland *(MD)*Times-News, *5/18/68*

157. The Record *(Troy, NY), 3/2/68*

158. From IMDB.com mini-biography

in a lovely area, but I was afraid if *Chaparral* ended, we'd be stuck with something we couldn't afford," he says. They stayed in Sun Valley, but put in a swimming pool and renovated the family room with help from Lucy's youngest brother, Charlie.

Darrow quit attending his children's school events, but not by choice. "Even sitting in the back, I was a distraction for the other kids. They'd see me and turn around, so I had to leave. After a while, I just stopped going." He and Lucy did their best to shield the children from publicity. "We don't want them turning on the charm for the cameras," Hank said in an interview. Deedee threw herself into music and dance. Tom became nearly invisible. "When he started public grade school, he just sort of disappeared. Lucy wanted to send him to a private school and we did that for a while. And for a while, he did better."

"You shouldn't have to sacrifice your private life or your family's privacy, but that's what happens," he says. "It's an unpleasant part of fame. You can't really prepare for it. We were not prepared."

Initially when he was on location in Arizona, Lucy and the kids joined him on weekends or school holidays. The cast bunked at the Hilton Hotel, which had a pool and a little train the kids enjoyed riding. Tom and Don Collier's son Don Jr. played together and got into a little mischief, like filching cigarettes and sneaking off to smoke. Deedee didn't like crowds and preferred reading. As for Lucy, longtime pal Pat Tanno remembers she always seemed bored. Tanno had put acting aside and settled in Tucson to concentrate on the family automotive business. "Tucson was a small town then and there wasn't much she liked to do there," he recalls. "Hank took her out to dinner, but that was about it."

"All the wives and kids could really do was hang out by the pool," says Don Collier. "We weren't available because we were working all the time."

Families, including Hank Darrow's, eventually stayed home.

"On location, we'd do fourteen hour days and that could be awful. You did what you could to make it bearable," he says. "You'd go to bed at three in the morning, get up at six and you were on location at seven and ready to go at eight. Some of the guys could do that and function. I couldn't. When I had a lot to do, dialogue-wise, I left the set, came back to the Hilton, had dinner and went to my room to study lines."

When he didn't have many lines, it was playtime. Says Pat Tanno, "I was never a party boy like Hank. He has the ability to socialize with everyone and he loves to go to a bar, kick back and relax."

It was easy to find a watering hole or a hole-in-one in Tucson. Ever since 1922 when the Tucson Sunshine Climate Club began luring travelers to their city, resorts, guest ranches, galleries, golf courses, restaurants, bars and other attractions proliferated.[159] In spite of these up-town diversions, the area retained an Old West swagger. *Fiesta de los Vaqueros* rodeo and parade flaunted wild and wooly heritage, but bulldogging and busting broncs weren't why Tucson had once been called "a paradise for devils."[160] Booze, drugs, gambling and prostitution came with the package. Depending on the times and legalities, enjoyment of such pastimes might be surreptitious, but the West was always long on independent cusses who figured the law be damned.[161]

In the 1960s, bars and saloons peppered the city and on Speedway, there were nightclubs with dancing. Over on Oracle Road was Gus & Andy's where *Chaparral* extra Frank Catelano played timbales in a band called *Los Caballeros*. "I think Henry liked us because we played salsa and Latin jazz and mambo music from Tito Puente, Puerto Rico music," he says. "For a while, Lynda Carter was our singer. We hired her when she was fifteen and we had to lie about her age when we played Las Vegas. We hired her for her looks. She didn't sing very well. I tried to tell her how to breathe so she wouldn't go flat and she said, 'We're even. I don't know how to sing and you guys don't know how to play.' But we were known to play the best music in Tucson and a lot of famous people went to Gus & Andy's. Actors from *High Chaparral* would show up when they got bored at the Hilton."

Around the Hilton, girls lined up to score with the actors or guys who knew the actors or knew guys who knew guys who did. Actors and others who were single or living like it were neck-deep in willing women. Some of the girls woke up on the wrong side of weird, like the legendary subject of a Don Collier song. Whenever she saw the *Chaparral* actors approach, she ducked around a corner to hide for an ambush. It didn't work. Her huge breasts stuck out past the wall, earning her the nickname "Watermelon Mary." "I think she may have been a local hooker," says Darrow with a laugh.

Away from the hotel, he and his pals found another breed of cat. Jester's Court Restaurant and Lounge on Tanque Verde kept two live black panthers. On E. Broadway, Leopard's Lair ("Tucson's newest intimate

159. Just Memories, this is not a book *by Roy P. Drachman Sr. at www.parentseyes.arizona.edu/drachman/0201.html*

160. Arizona Highways, *September 1967*

161. *After Arizona outlawed prostitution, Tucson mayor Olva C. Parker refused to shut down the rollicking red light district as long as there were more men than women in town. (Eppinga, p. 77)*

restaurant") featured a live leopard, African masks, leopard carpeting and waitresses dressed in safari jackets, miniskirts and pith helmets. The leopard lent a certain fragrance, like a big kitty litter box according to a wag from *The High Chaparral* who dubbed the place "Panther Piss". But the Hemingway Meets Hooters theme targeted a particular clientele and Hollywood types weren't it. The owner of Leopard's Lair made that clear when he said "...we've decided to provide a completely masculine atmosphere for our local men".[162]

Even without sham safari *je ne sait quoi*, enough booze can turn any establishment's "completely masculine atmosphere" aggressive. "I was youngish and I was drinking a lot," says Darrow. "I could start bragging and posing or make a pass at a cowboy's girlfriend and you did *not* want to do that. If I was by myself, the situation could get scary. I'd have to work my way to the bathroom and out the back door."

On location, the actors and stuntmen went out as a unit. "That was your protection, to be in the group. A problem would only go so far. A word or two from one of the stuntmen would do the trick." But if somebody saddled up and threw a punch, the stuntmen were all in. "They'd grab pool cues, you name it. Those guys could fight and it would be over quickly." Like on the set, the stuntmen took the licks, dished them back double and the actors kept all their teeth.

Sometimes, the guys wondered if the group was enough protection. A couple of nightspots allegedly run by crime syndicates attracted a worrisome clientele. "People getting drunk at the bar would be wearing cowboy hats and jeans and then these short-haired guys in jackets would show up. They were FBI and they didn't want to blend in. The idea was to make sure everyone knew they were there. It was like 'Oh, gosh. What are we getting into?'"

If a member of the *Chaparral* group needed to get away from overzealous fans without seeming rude, they had a discrete little distress sign. It was a common gesture, but signaled in context brought buddies to the rescue. It came in handy for everyone, especially Darrow.

"He had a lot of fans and he could have a difficult time with them. The lack of privacy was a pain in the neck," says Don Collier, but helpful friends like Collier and Hoy could give Henry a hard time, too. One evening in the Hilton's lobby, Collier and Hoy watched Darrow preen while a bevy of attractive ladies fawned over him. When he inadvertently made the signal, Hoy and Collier knew he didn't mean it, but rushed to

162. The Tucson Daily Citizen, *10/4/69*

save him anyway. Darrow tried shooing them away. It didn't work. His buddies made excuses to the disappointed women and hauled off the "star of tomorrow" in spite of his struggles and protests of, "Guys, no. Go away. I'm okay. Leave me alone."

Female adulation was one of stardom's perks for Darrow, but he told Donald Freeman of *The San Diego Union*, "Overnight success, right? It's taken me ten years to reach the point where people say, 'Hey, you look familiar…didn't I see you in a *Gunsmoke* two years ago?"[163]

His brand of unpretentious good humor was a hit with women reporters and one gushed, "Handsome he is not, but winsomeness, charm, wit, love for his fellow man, for his craft and tolerance of human frailty are his in great measure. He has great dignity of manner and an 'old world' type of courtly manners. These are coupled with a bubbly and slightly off beat sense of humor add up to a fascinating personality. He is never 'on' — he is simply Henry Darrow." Finally, she vowed she would always treasure "his gentle kiss on the cheek" and softly spoken farewell.[164]

Darrow's ability to charm women — and make grown journalists rhapsodize like schoolgirls — relied greatly on a pervasive, effortless, leonine sensuality. When Mano tells Victoria he knows more about women than she knows about men, nobody doubts he knows more than nearly anyone.

"He got all the girls! Beautiful ladies were always fighting over him," says Luis Reyes. But he and other young men idolized Manolito for other qualities and Reyes points out, "He was fiercely dedicated to family, even though he fought with his father and didn't always agree with his sister." When Victoria is taken hostage, Mano clashes with Big John about how to save her and hisses, "If he hurts her, the first bullet will be for him; the second one for you."[165] Viewers believed the threat and the understated promise in his eyes — here was a hero who would kill for his sister.

Emmy, ALMA and Imagen winner A Martinez (no relation to Patrice) was a teenager just starting to break into acting when *The High Chaparral* aired and Manolito Montoya caught his attention. "He was so suave and good looking and fiery and capable, just the epitome of cool."

163. 9/26/67

164. The Arizona Territorial, *"Manolito is a Marvelous Rascal, But Henry Darrow was Here First," Opal Johnson, 7/10/69*

165. The High Chaparral, *"The Ghost of Chaparral"*

Film director Francisco Menendez recalls, "I was eight years old, growing up in El Salvador and I thought, 'Wow! Here's a Latin character and he's not on a Mexican soap.' He was an incredibly fun character. That's who I wanted to be when I grew up, this crazy guy who got away with a lot! Everything about Manolito was just fabulous."

But his Anglo last name confused some viewers, including Francisco Menendez. "His was the first Latino face I saw in an American TV show. I was in El Salvador, watching Henry dubbed into Spanish and I always wondered why his name was Darrow."

Confusion was one thing, but there were Latinos who criticized David Dortort for casting an Anglo as Manolito or presuming Darrow was Anglo, berated him for playing a Mexican. Upon hearing him speak off screen, some people complained, "You can't be Hispanic. You sound like a Jew from New York City."

"I *am* from New York City!" he would reply and later told one reporter, "It was hard to take sometimes, but I don't look back."[166] There would always be malcontents, including those who felt Puerto Ricans should only play Puerto Ricans, not Mexicans. Darrow laughs. "If I only played Puerto Ricans back then, those *two* roles would not have paid the bills. I liked it when Mexicans would come up to me and say, 'Man, we know you're Puerto Rican, but we like the way you *play* a Mexican.' That happened. It still happens and it makes me feel good as an actor."

It also felt good that once he became a television star, Lucy's family accepted him. The DePuys invited him to all their family events, proudly introducing him to wealthy, powerful relatives and friends. He gleefully participated while they showed him off like a prize pony. "Once I paid my own way, that changed the whole operation. I became part of the family," he says.

"What can I say? Behind every successful actor is a surprised mother-in-law," Lucy's mother quipped to a reporter. For the son-in-law she used to consider a bum, being famous was sweet payback.

"Lucy's father dressed well and he reeked of education and wealth, but he had a very up tempo way. He was fun to be around, whereas his wife would get a few drinks in her and she would turn nasty. One time, she walked home from a party without him and took a shotgun and shot a hole through the front door. She'd complain about our 'little Puerto Rican kids'. When she got loaded, it wasn't good," he says. "So after I became acceptable, for Christmas I gave her a month in rehab. Of course, she was offended." Still, she didn't kick Hank Darrow, television star, out of the house like she probably would have Hank Delgado, marginally employed Puerto Rican actor.

But neither the DePuys nor Darrow knew then how famous he was, how famous he would become or the impact it would have, especially since *Chaparral's* lackluster U.S. ratings didn't shout superstardom.

The High Chaparral's first season spawned merchandise like comic books, lunch boxes, bubble gum cards and paperback books. But unlike *Bonanza*, *Chaparral* wasn't among the year's Top Ten. In spite of a loyal following, it never cracked the top thirty. Hoping for better ratings, David Dortort promised the show's second year would have a "younger approach revolving around such things as a young man finding his way".[167] He also vowed the Arizona Territory would be a kinder, gentler place in keeping with country's anti-violence trajectory.

Public opposition to violence on television soared in 1968 after the assassinations of civil rights leader Martin Luther King, Jr. in April and presidential candidate Robert F. Kennedy in June. In response, President Lyndon B. Johnson, whose escalation of the Vietnam War made him the subject of the anti-war chant, "Hey, hey, LBJ, how many kids did you kill today?" incongruously created the National Commission on the Causes and Prevention of Violence.

In Hollywood, the Screen Writers' Guild responded to anti-violence fervor by passing five resolutions against TV and movie violence. Commenting on this, Bob Foster wrote, "Television will make an honest effort to cut back on violence. The cutback on violence will not be a token…" Foster presumed this would last as long as ratings supported it. He also argued against the notion that bloodshed on TV bred a violent society, stating, "the violence shown on television is a reflection of our time". [168]

Commercial television networks vowed to eliminate gratuitous brutality, especially on shows in child friendly, early time slots. Since *The High Chaparral* had finally moved from late Sunday night to 7:30 on Friday as David Dortort long wanted, it was solidly in the sights of the anti-violence forces. To put everyone at ease, Dortort declared a shift in theme. "The Cannon family will still have to battle the savage wilderness. But they'll also face the more difficult problems of learning to live with each other," he told *The Hollywood Citizen-News*.[169]

167. The Hollywood Citizen-News, *"TV Week", 7/13-7/19, 1968*

168. The San Mateo *(CA)* County Times, TV/Radio World, *"Screenings" 8/21/68*

169. "TV Week" 7/13/68

As it turned out, compliance with the new, ostensibly voluntary no-violence rule didn't help mediocre second year ratings, but it certainly affected realism. "I'll give you one example," Leif Erickson said. "A few weeks ago we were filming an episode and the script called for Manolito to see a man on the roof about to attack us. He raises his rifle, fires, the stunt man reels, clutches his chest and then falls off the roof. Then, as directed, Manolito goes over to the body, examines it and shouts to me, 'He's just wounded, Big John. He'll be all right!' I don't really know what that proves...but we're following the rule to the letter."[170]

Unlike actor James Stacey (*Lancer*) who said, "The whole idea of a Western is violence. Take that away and you haven't got much,"[171] Erickson later became convinced that reduced violence resulted in better shows.

"This edict against violence on television is giving us the best scripts we've ever had," he said. Since writers couldn't use gunfights and fisticuffs for conflict resolution they had to "invent an honest and plausible solution out of characterization and the basic elements of drama." As an actor, he appreciated enhanced character development but wasn't sure how the public would respond.[172]

The public responded as well as they had previously. Ratings were just adequate for keeping *Chaparral* on the air, in spite of well-written, well-acted and often critically acclaimed episodes. One was a source of special pride for Production Manager Kent McCray. Called "The Buffalo Soldiers," it centered on the heroic all-black 10th U.S. Cavalry and was full of rip-snorting equestrian sequences. It won the National Cowboy Museum's Western Heritage Awards 1969 Bronze Wrangler for Fictional Television Drama. Guest stars included a unit of contemporary Buffalo Soldier reinactors from Los Angeles and professional actors Rockne Tarkington (believed to be the first African-American on *The Andy Griffith Show*[173]) and Yaphet Kotto. Kotto said of his "Buffalo Soldiers" character, "I hope Negro kids see the pride and strength in this man — especially since he is in the nineteenth century. It all comes down to the kids." Educators agreed and used this episode to show children how African-Americans helped build the United States.

170. The Arizona Republic, *Television News*, "*Big John with a smile...? It may never happen*" *by Harvey Pack, 10/6/68*

171. The San Mateo *(CA)* County Times, "*Theatre World*" *8/2/68*

172. The Beckley *(WV)* Post-Herald, "*Edict against violence improving TV Scripts*," by Cecil Smith, *6/23/69*

173. *IMDB.com biography*

Unfortunately, when *The High Chaparral* went on filming hiatus this stand-out historical episode inspired Cameron Mitchell to make a movie. It involved Buffalo Soldiers, Henry Darrow, carnivorous wild animals, snowstorms, male accountants in drag, snakes, Jesus Christ and O.J. Simpson.

> *In his "Pensees," Blaise Pascal, the French scientist and religious philosopher, said, "What a chimera then is man! What a novelty! What a monster, what a chaos, what a contradiction, what a prodigy!" Which, in relation to Cameron Mitchell, isn't as far-fetched as you might think.*
>
> JOURNALIST LESLIE RADDITZ[174]

---

174. TV Guide, *"Everybody on the Show Hates Me", 4/27-5/3, 1968*

One of the Other Guys
Pulled the Leopard Off

*I don't know how Cam raised the money. He got
people to loan him horses worth $50,000, but it
was just a mess.*

HENRY DARROW

"The dream of my life — and I believe in God, by the way — is to film
the story of The Man of Love." Cameron Mitchell described with intensity
his desire to someday make a movie about Jesus. "I would love to do it truthfully as it has never been done before, with all the violence of his day…"[175]
After *Chaparral's* second season filming ended, he finally had his chance.

"I've worked *for* enough idiots in my career," he said. "I wanted to be
the idiot myself." He was both director and executive producer but added
that God was his co-producer.[176]

To portray Jesus Christ, Mitchell tapped Henry Darrow. His mother
would have been delighted, but he said no. Mitchell wanted him to wear
a real crown of thorns. "I said, 'You're out of your friggin' head' and he said,
'No, it'll be fine. If there's a problem, we'll have great surgeons standing by.
I just got back from Europe and I had a full body lift, face and everything.
They've got the best doctors in the world. I'll get those guys and they'll
be right there.' I said, 'You really *are* out of your friggin' head. What the
heck are you talking about?'"

Mitchell pulled his hair back and just inside his hairline were scars
from the lift. He said, "Look, I've had the work done and it's great!"
Darrow was unswayed. Instead of playing the Son of God, he portrayed
the dissolute son of a Mexican aristocrat in the film. Called *The Dream
of Hamish Mose*, it was shot in the boondocks of Texas and New Mexico
and it was the kind of dream you have after too much cheap wine.

175. *The Hayward (CA) Daily Review, 9/2/73*

176. *The Tucson Citizen, 6/21/69*

The story involved a group of Buffalo Soldiers (the spirited group of reinactors from the *Chaparral* episode), lost near the Mexican border. When they find Rockne Tarkington hanging from a tree, they cut him down. Even though he can't speak after being hung, Tarkington proposes to lead the soldiers across the River Jordan, or as they call it in Texas, the Rio Grande.

"In the process, they're kidnapped by Indians," recalls Darrow. "We didn't have any Indians in the cast, but that wasn't a problem for Cam. He got burlap bags and made holes for eyes and put them around the soldier's heads. He put them in arm bands, feathers, stuff around the ankles. So, now they're Indians."

They also didn't have any women in the cast. When a sequence called for a woman, innovation ruled. "The only woman was the associate producer, Sharon Gless before her acting career got going," says Darrow. "Maybe Cam thought she was wrong for the part, because he made do with one of the accountants, a very short, blond, effeminate gay guy. They dressed him in drag and sort of fuzzed the lens so you couldn't see him very well."

The Manolito-esque *hombre* played by Darrow meets the soldiers and joins the trek to River Jordan. While he treks, he talks. A lot. Without a script. "Cam would turn the camera on and say, 'Talk about your father, talk about your past, talk about the history of your family' and he'd just leave the camera rolling. That wasn't too bad, but then he wanted me to hold a rattlesnake up to my face and I said, 'No! No poisonous snakes!'"

"What about a bullsnake?" Mitchell wheedled. "They're not poisonous and they look sort of like rattlers."

Grimacing, Darrow answered, "I don't know, Cam. Let me see what you want me to do." Enter a wrangler with a bullsnake. The wrangler held the snake up to his own face. "Pow! It bit him and just hung on to his cheek! I said, 'That's it! Forget it!'"

That might have been a bad omen, but Mitchell wanted more animals in the movie—lions, tigers and bears. He got them when a freak snowstorm stranded Bill Burrad and his wild animal show at the same motel. "If the movie had ever been shown, there were sequences with the wild animals which would've been very exciting to watch, because they were very exciting to film," says Darrow. "Once, Cam had the grizzly bear coming straight toward the camera. Cam was standing by the cameraman, but the bear picked up speed as he came toward them, so Cam started backing away. But he was telling the cameraman, 'Stay there! Keep shooting! This is good footage!' The camera guy said, 'F___ you! I'm outa here!'"

Mitchell had borrowed expensive horses for the film, some worth $50,000. When the bear and big cats arrived on the set, one uneasy horse owner stood by with a 30.30 rifle in case a fake attack turned real. Maybe he sensed the leopard was a Method actor. "One of the soldiers was holding the leopard and they were playing a scene where something dangerous is about to happen," says Darrow. "Lo and behold, it did. All of a sudden, the soldier started yelling, 'Is this…this…what the…oh, shit! His teeth are around my leg! CAM!' One of the other guys pulled the leopard off him."

Sulfur springs bubbled at one location, adding a rotten egg odor to the ambience. Either Cochise or Geronimo had come to the same springs for healing, but there wasn't enough mojo for the movie's maladies. "At the end, it was snowing and we all crossed the River Jordan. There were rows of tall trees and when the snow stopped, the sun came out and the rays shone through the branches," says Darrow. "Then O.J. Simpson[177] appeared in a Civil War uniform, talking and making no sense whatsoever."

The whole project made Darrow's head hurt. He left the location in his Mexican peasant threads and ducked into a saloon for a couple of beers. "About ten minutes passed and the bartender was ignoring me. There were a couple of men at the bar, but nobody came to serve me a drink." He had been with the group in a restaurant when a knot of white locals took exception to the Buffalo Soldiers being there until Mitchell turned it into *High Chaparral* time and suddenly, everything was fine. But this was a different place and Darrow was by himself. There was an undercurrent in the bar, mean as an ax handle. He sat a bit longer. "I said, 'Hey, what's up, guys?' The bartender answered in this very unhelpful tone, 'What can we do for *you*?' So I said I was down there shooting a movie and that changed the whole dynamic. It was *High Chaparral* time again. 'Oh, for God's sake! You're that guy on TV! I didn't recognize you!'"

When filming started for *Chaparral's* third season, Darrow wasn't sure he recognized Manolito either. "Suddenly," said Darrow, "Manolito's friends could not be bandidos and the Cisco Kid elements of his character went in the toilet. The worst thing I could do was get firewood."[178]

The network, or the government really, made us change.

ACTOR/STUNTMAN BOB HOY[179]

---

177. *Football Hall of Fame running back who went into acting. In 1995, he was tried for the murder of his ex-wife and a friend and acquitted. In 2007, he was convicted of armed robbery and kidnapping and sentenced to 33 years in prison.*

178. The Tucson Citizen, *2/11/80*

179. Ibid.

If Anybody's Shot, It's By Accident

Just killing them is not enough. I want to humiliate them!

VILLAIN DISCUSSING MANO AND BUCK[180]

Lyndon Johnson's creation, the National Commission on the Causes and Prevention of Violence, reported decisively, "Violence on television encourages violent forms of behavior, and fosters moral and social values about violence in daily life which are unacceptable in a civilized society".[181] Those findings could be argued *ad infinitum*, since later longitudinal studies said otherwise. However at the time Commission findings were accepted truth and there was a pervasive feeling that the networks had a moral responsibility to decrease televised violence. Of course, nobody wanted to be morally irresponsible. Networks, vying for advertising dollars and viewers, panicked.

The Commission was constitutionally prohibited by free speech guarantees to mandate a reduction in violence, but it recommended that NBC, CBS and ABC *voluntarily* limit TV violence and air "adult" programs with "significant violence content" after 9 p.m. The Commission's secondary agenda was to make recommendations that would increase government funding to the Public Broadcasting Corporation for more children's educational programming.

Chaparral producer/director William Claxton said later, "We weren't a particularly violent show to begin with, but they [the network] wanted to change us into another *Bonanza*."[182]

"If a guy is thrown by a horse, we must show him get up and walk away," said Leif Erickson, who thought the dedication to non-violence

180. The High Chaparral, *"Sanchez" in "Friends And Partners"*

181. Wellsville *(NY)* Daily Reporter, *9/26/69*

182. The Tucson Citizen, *2/11/80*

had turned silly. "When you draw a pistol, you don't point it, you hold it sideways. If anybody's shot, it's by accident."[183]

Nonetheless, NBC continued to pressure Executive Producer David Dortort for less violence. Dortort acquiesced and made more changes. Those resulting changes, said Kent McCray, brought a decline in quality.[184]

First, mounting network emphasis on family-friendliness and budget caused the show's venue to shift from action sequences filmed at expensive but spectacular outdoor locations to interiors where interpersonal dynamics held the floor. Then in April 1969, *Variety* reported that producer William Claxton had left the series and David Dortort was searching for his replacement.[185]

Dortort called Claxton "a wonderful director". Beloved and respected by *Chaparral*'s cast and crew as both a producer and director, Claxton returned to directing *Bonanza*. In his place, Dortort hired thirty-one-year-old James Schmerer, head of Creative Development for Xanadu Productions. Dortort's decision, Kent McCray said, was "a big mistake as far as I was concerned, but that's history."[186] For two years, Claxton had directed "roughly every other *Chaparral* and really was the thought behind the show," said McCray of his friend. A quiet man with a low speaking voice, Claxton had a good sense of humor and many friends in Hollywood. "The stunt people were big fans of Bill's. He really was a great believer in stunts and loved the stunt people. Henry Wills was our stunt coordinator and Bill thought very highly of him and would never do any kind of action stunt without Henry's input."[187]

Schmerer was a relative newcomer, in Hollywood since 1961. When he began producing *Chaparral* he was allegedly the youngest producer in prime time television. But if NBC wanted nonviolence, Schmerer said he was determined to give it to them, even if he didn't like it. "Through the years, I was constantly going up against the networks and the studios when they wanted me to do something I knew wasn't right," he told interviewer Ron Miller.[188]

183. The Beckley *(WV)* Post-Herald, *"Edict against violence improving scripts" by Cecil Smith,* 6/23/69

184. The High Chaparral Newsletter, *7/23/07*

185. 3/2/69

186. The High Chaparral Newsletter, *7/23/07*

187. Ibid.

188. Retrieved from http://www.thecolumnists.com/miller/miller59.html, 11/11/10

It wasn't just violence. When activist Native groups protested the portrayal of Indians on television, NBC issued an edict demanding that no Indians be killed on any of their westerns. According to Schmerer, he complained to NBC that the show took place "in 1880s (*sic*) Arizona and there were hostile Indians out there," but the network wouldn't budge.[189] As a result, said Bob Hoy, if an Apache was shot, he had to get up and scoot away afterwards. The sponsors loved it. They were among the few who did.

Lively dead Indians, changes in established characters and newbie producer Schmerer created tension on the set before NBC turned up the pressure for better ratings. Individual episodes had rated better, but the series itself wasn't in the Top 10 or the Top 20. It pulled only a respectable Top 40 audience share. To make matters worse, as a period western filmed on location, it was expensive to produce. According to Kent McCray average cost per episode for *Chaparral* was $225,000. When NBC executives compared that to around $200,000 for ratings frontrunner *Bonanza*, *Chaparral* looked like a lot of outgo and not much return. The network's purse strings tightened on *The High Chaparral* like a hangman's noose.

Even though *Chaparral* wasn't a ratings barnburner, by 1969 Henry Darrow's star shone across the U.S. Even so, cost cutting and other changes on the series made him wonder when the next paycheck would be the last and how soon he'd be competing against Ricardo Montalbán and Alejandro Rey for guest starring roles.

Happily, while he was acting his brains out on *Chaparral*, opening megastores and riding in parades, in the foreign market Henry Darrow had become a superstar. In some European and Scandinavian countries *Bonanza* held the top spot as it did in the U.S., but with a significant difference — *Chaparral* was giving it a run for its money. Great Britain chose *Chaparral* as 1968's Best Color Series[190] and Darrow squinted seductively from the cover of British teen magazine *Fab 208*.

Many Germans believed *Chaparral* was too "rough" for young children, but the show attracted between 60-75% of that country's TV viewers, about 15 million people who rated it either good or very good. And they couldn't get enough of Manolito, the "dark rascal from Mexico".[191] Readers of the German tabloid BILD, the bestselling newspaper in Europe, devoured news about Henry Darrow. *BRAVO*, a Deutschland combo of

189. Ibid.

190. Hör Zu TV Magazine, *July 1969*

191. Ibid.

Screen Stories and *16*, featured the "smiling *vaquero* with the sad eyes" in articles with full-color close-ups.

In Sweden, *The High Chaparral* was, as they say in radio, number one with a bullet. Manolito was *the* favorite character and Sweden sent more fan mail than any other country. Tabloids with Henry Darrow on the cover sold like cold beer in Tucson and Swedes from six to ninety-six longed to meet him. It was great, except being an overseas sensation didn't put any jingle in his pockets. When NBC sold the show to foreign markets, the stars got nothing—no percentage, no residuals. So when Michael Landon started talking about his recent, lucrative tour of Sweden, Darrow's ears perked.

> ### *Kom snart, Manolito!*
> COVER HEADLINE ON SCANDINAVIAN EDITION
> OF GERMAN TABLOID BILD[192]
> (ENGLISH TRANSLATION "COME SOON, MANOLITO!")

192. 8/28/68

Big in Sweden

Actors like Darrow, with a little something going for them beyond the ordinary, maintain a precarious balance.

WRITER CAROLYN SEE[193]

In Sweden, Michael Landon did his "Little Joe Cartwright" stage show for thousands of adoring fans. The Little Joe Show was about thirty minutes of stunt fights and songs accompanied by a backup guitar. It netted Landon a healthy profit and Darrow and his agent Lester Miller figured they could do even better. After all, Manolito — not Little Joe — was the Swedes' number one cowboy. There was just one problem. Darrow didn't know what the Swedes expected. "…they're very big for the character of Manolito," he said in a *TV Guide* interview. "What would the character of Manolito do for an act? *I* can do all those imitations. But how would *Manolito* do imitations?"[194]

A studio rep suggested he wear Manolito's blue formal outfit "the tight costume, the sharp costume." For the grand finale, the rep continued, Darrow could crack his bullwhip around a pretty girl and reel her in for a kiss. After nearly taking off his own ear with the whip, the actor wasn't so sure. "I'd kill her, probably," he said.[195]

When Darrow's Sweden tour was a go for August 1969, he prepared his act with whip tricks minus the girl, imitations of movie stars and a few tunes. His practice run was on Celebrity Night at the Seven Seas Restaurant on Hollywood Boulevard. Lucy went along, and so did Dixieland jazz musician Matty Matlock and his guitarist son Buddy, Darrow's musical accompanist in Sweden.

"Seven Seas was this cheesy Hawaiian joint we'd go to, but that night I was the guest of honor. I performed for free since they let me have the

193. TV Guide, *"Zap!," 11/2-11/8, 1968*

194. Ibid.

195. Ibid.

stage. I went on after the hula dancers and the ukulele guy," Darrow says. "I wanted to see if my act worked. It was a test to see what I could get away with."

Backed by Buddy Matlock, Darrow sang pop hits ("The Look of Love," "Little Green Apples"), Broadway show stoppers ("Rich Man" from *Fiddler on the Roof*), a drunken version of the Mexican *Ranchera* standard "Cielito Lindo" and a little comedy number called "Rancho Grande" which featured imitations of his *Chaparral* costars including Linda Cristal. Using the microphone as a prop, he added an extra flourish. "I practiced flipping the cord like I'd seen Bobby Darin and Sammy Davis Jr. do," he recalls. It was safer than a bullwhip and the lei-laden audience loved the show. A columnist there with his wife and mother-in-law wrote, "Henry displayed a fine baritone…Even more surprising than his vocal expertise were his impressions. Some of his outstanding voice characterizations included José Ferrer, James Mason, Boris Karloff, Kirk Douglas, Dale Robertson, Rod Steiger, Senator Dirksen, Otto Preminger and Bela Lugosi." Bill Claxton was in the audience and the writer, not knowing Claxton was gone from *Chaparral*, guessed the producer was so impressed that he'd soon look "for ways to redesign Manolito's part in the series."

Sweden greeted "Manolito" with open arms and more. "After we landed, somebody gave me a list of thirty girls who wanted to sleep with me," Darrow recalls. He gave the list to bug-eyed, unprepossessing Les Miller. Darrow chuckles. "He was delighted throughout the whole tour!"

As Darrow's bus rolled from one venue to the next, a long caravan of cars followed. Screaming devotees applauded wildly when he performed. Young women brandished signs declaring their undying love. It was like being a rock superstar. "It was really something! Holy cow! I loved touring and performing all over the world. That was a wonderful experience," says Darrow.

Guitarist Matlock was joined by a group of Swedish musicians who became part of the tour and added full orchestral sound to musical numbers. Then Swedish singer Lill-Babs joined Darrow on stage. She was a bona fide superstar with a long list of hit songs and film credits, but Darrow was even more dazzled by a thirty-two-year-old Russian named Boris Spassky.

The reigning World Chess Champion, Grandmaster Spassky was a marvel in international chess from boyhood on. In a public relations coup, Henry Darrow faced him across the board on a balcony high above a sea of onlookers. For Darrow it was an incredible moment. The Grandmaster was also impressed by his opponent, although not initially for his skill at chess. Before the game started, an attractive girl with flowers in her long hair appeared suddenly. She ran to Darrow, squealed "We love you, Manolito!" and kissed him fully on the mouth.

Spassky looked at the actor in frank admiration and said in his thick Russian accent, "Must be *nice* to be American television star!"

The match was timed for five minutes. Says Darrow, "Finally, Spassky had three and a half minutes on his clock and I had twenty seconds left on mine. He asked if I played professionally. Let's just say he brought the best out. I did hold my own, but I was no professional and I said so. He said, 'You play good enough. I offer you draw.'" Since Enrique and Gloria Delgado didn't raise any stupid sons, he accepted.

At Gröna Lund Amusement Park in Stockholm, a whopping 16,000 fans showed up screaming for "Manolito". It was the second largest crowd ever drawn[196] and considerably larger than Michael Landon's. Newspapers crowed that *The High Chaparral* had its revenge on the Cartwrights. Translated to English, one caption read "Manolito Wipes Out Little Joe".

"They liked the gun, but they *really* liked the whip." Darrow laughs. "Unfortunately, I was cracking two whips on a small stage and yanked a light down on top of me. I just flung the whips backstage and that was the end of those!"

Fans were generally mannerly, but could be frenzied in the overwhelming crowd. "They would try to yank out my hair for souvenirs. All you could see was this mass of arms and hands reaching out and grasping. I wasn't used to anything like that." The memory makes him shiver. "A guy almost punched me through an open window of the bus. He was Spanish and thought his ticket to the show should've been free, but he had to pay and he was upset with me because of it." He didn't focus on unpleasant episodes, not when the tour was a sparkling triumph.

"My greatest memory from there was being on stage at Liseberg, and seeing thousands of people there. It was my only afternoon performance and my one opportunity to actually see the audience. I remember the flowers and the buildings. It had had been raining that afternoon and during the show, the sun came out. The audience was so marvelous that I started crying at the end of the show."

The thunder of applause and adulation shining on the faces of thousands of fans feed an actor's soul. Darrow made more money on the tour than he earned in a year's worth of *High Chaparral* episodes and money puts food on the table and feeds self-worth. But there's a tradeoff.

---

196. *World Heavyweight Boxing Champion Floyd Patterson held the record with 18,000*

"The audience wasn't there to hear me sing or imitate Boris Karloff. They wanted Manolito, not me," he says. "'Rancho Grande' was in keeping with the character of Manolito, so it worked. But people weren't there to see Henry Darrow and I had to remember that or risk disappointing them."

A female journalist traveled with Darrow's group and years later in California, she called him. "Do you remember me?" she asked. He said no and she told him that she had been on the tour.

"Was I nice?" he asked. "Was I a gentleman?"

"Well," she answered, "I remember that you drank a lot."

He's this incredibly high profile, sexy guy and he walks into a restaurant in Hollywood and the place stops dead because oh, my God! He's Henry Darrow! He had ten thousand Swedish girls throwing underwear at him. How could anyone not have their head turned at least a little by that?

WRITER HARRY CASON

You are Manolito!

Blue: *Hey, Sam. Did you see the way that girl looked at Manolito?*

Sam: *Yeah, they all look at him that way.*[197]

After touring Sweden, Henry Darrow was offered $2,500.00 to cut a record of "Little Green Apples" and "El Rancho Grande." Feeling cocky he said, "Nah, it's five thousand or nothing." Les Miller suggested they flip for it and Darrow won. "I did one take on each side and walked away with an extra five grand!"

Darrow's fame also put a little jingle in son Tom's pockets. A little sharpie, he'd tell the other kids that his father was Manolito. When they didn't buy it, Tom told them to put their money where their mouths were. After the bets went down, he wagged the kids home and after Darrow was surrounded by gaping little boys, Tom would say, "See? I told you Manolito was my father. *Now* do I get my quarter?"

Unlike Tom, Deedee didn't see much benefit in having a television star as a father. In her teenaged eyes, he was like any annoying, embarrassing parent. "You could see the typical sullen body language," Darrow recalls. "And that voice. Oh, my! 'Do I *have* to go to the restaurant with *you?*' Or, 'No! Don't drop me at *school!* Drop me off half a block away and I'll walk.'"

Darrow's adolescent fans probably said the same things to their parents, but they sent fan mail to him. His killer smile graced the covers of teen publications like *16* and *Tiger Beat*. Countless young women carefully taped his pictures on their bedroom walls, gazing at Manolito as they drifted off to sleep. It looked like they would be dreaming about — and watching — Mano for a quite a while longer, too.

Despite misgivings, *The High Chaparral's* third year contained some of the most appealing episodes of the series. "A Piece of Land" and "Friends and Partners" spotlighted Henry Darrow and Cameron Mitchell.

197. The High Chaparral episode "The Firing Wall"

There were adroit dramatic episodes ("The Brothers Cannon," "Generation"), nimble comedies ("The Reluctant Deputy," Mi Casa Su Casa") and tender romances (for Manolito in "A Time to Laugh, A Time to Cry" and for Buck in "Lady Fair"). Action sequences were still included, but several episodes conveyed an anti-violence message ("The Time of Your Life," "The Lieutenant" and "The Guns of Johnny Rondo"). Ratings were excellent for *The High Chaparral* although it was pitted against the award-winning spy spoof *Get Smart* (CBS) and family comedy *The Brady Bunch* (ABC). Finally hitting its stride with viewers, *Chaparral* copped critical accolades. Linda Cristal–nominated by the Academy of Television Arts and Sciences for a Supporting Actress Emmy in 1968–won the Hollywood Foreign Press Association's 1970 Golden Globe for "Best TV Actress."

Neither the Emmys nor Golden Globes gave a nod to perennially overlooked Henry Darrow. "It was a waste!" says Cristal. "He is unique, very special. He goes on screen and you are *with* him. It was a waste that the industry didn't see it. I see so many people in the front row who don't deserve to be there. And here is this talented man, Henry, sitting in the back of the theater."

However, Europe put Darrow in the front row, rolled out the red carpet and threw rose petals. In 1970, German multinational multimedia giant Hubert Burda Media honored him with their prestigious Bambi award. The award is named for the title character in the 1923 wildlife novel "Bambi: A Life in the Woods" by Austrian writer Felix Salten. Later turned into a Disney cartoon feature, the original "Bambi" is a serious book, banned in Nazi Germany as an antifascist allegory about the treatment of Jews. Hubert Burda Media chose the heroic fawn as the symbol of media excellence in 1948 and ever since, has awarded Bambis to performers with "vision and creativity who affected and inspired the German public." Winning put Henry Darrow in elite company with previous winners like Gina Lollobrigida, Horst Buchholz, Sophia Loren, Rock Hudson, Maria Schell, Omar Sharif and *Bonanza's* Lorne Greene.

Darrow went to Germany to collect his award. He and agent Les Miller left balmy Los Angeles on a Lufthansa jet and disembarked in the midst of an ice cold German winter. The two men fastened every button on their heavy wool coats. Miller, misery in his bulbous eyes, pulled his collar up, his hat down and shoved icy hands into his pockets. Darrow's wide grin lit up his face as he slung his suit bag over a shoulder and strode across the frigid tarmac. Thousands of screaming fans would converge wherever he went and he would be treated like royalty. After the U.S. awards brush-off, he was ready for rampant adulation.

He was being paid for a short performance at the Bambi ceremony and figured the routine he used in Sweden would have the audience in the palm of his hand. Then he discovered he would be sharing the stage with top performers. Worried, he told the producer he felt bad going on stage in that company. The man replied, "No, no, no. They're here to see Manolito. *You* are Manolito. The others are not. Whatever you do will be fine."

The producer was right. As Darrow walked to the stage and as he performed, worshipful smiles and enthusiastic applause embraced him. He beamed and he put on a show. When he looked at the golden statue of the fawn, it reflected the face of a star.

Back in the United States, a rising number of zealous fans hung around the set in Los Angeles, Old Tucson, the hotel or public appearances. He savored the attention, but not rudeness or having his private life invaded. He learned to walk through crowds with determination. To thwart ambushes, he depended upon "fantastic peripheral vision".[198]

Still, he didn't like dodging kids and usually took special care with them. When a young fan who lived near Old Tucson wanted to meet Henry Darrow, she got on her pony, rode to the set and met her hero. She recalls fondly, "Mr. Darrow was so nice to a little girl with a crush."

Says writer/performer Miluka Rivera, "He knows how to relate to any age, but kids love him. My kids are fans of Henry's since they were very little."

His soft spot for children sometimes got him bushwhacked. Don Collier remembers a family with two mentally handicapped sons who approached Henry in the hotel lobby. "They had made some drawings and he talked to them for a while," says Collier. "They showed up almost everywhere he went while we were in Tucson. Then we went back to Hollywood to shoot and about a week or two later, there was a knock on his front door and it was those people. They followed him out there."

Says Darrow with a shrug, "It's one of those things, 'Yeah, yeah, come see me sometime.' But you don't expect them to do it. Then bam! Their camper was in my driveway. But they were harmless. They were very loyal fans who hung in there with me for years and years. Now they've all died except the mother."

He still sends her a card at Christmas.

198. The Tucson Daily Citizen, *6/21/69*

Makeup artist Beau Wilson told *The Tucson Daily Citizen* about a Puerto Rican lady who waited hours on the Old Tucson set to see Darrow. There were days when as many as forty tourists fainted from the intense summer heat and she was one of them. She was put into the golf cart outfitted as a mini-ambulance and given an ice-pack for her head. "Henry heard what had happened and came over and talked with her," said Wilson. "It was the best treatment possible. She figured fainting was worth it." [199]

Some situations bred humility. After Darrow signed an autograph for a grateful woman, she gushed, "Oh, thank you so much, Mr. Slade!" [200]

He laughed about that, but not about resting in his dressing room between takes when two girls opened the door, shoved a microphone inside and demanded an interview for their high school newspaper. Then there was the time someone opened his dressing room door, saw him lying down, shook his foot and asked if he was sleeping. "It was a nice old lady or probably I would have done my first rude bit," he said. [201]

When he felt ready to snap, he retreated to the solitude of his hotel room. "People see you as a role model and there's a certain responsibility as to how you represent yourself," he says. "There are a number of things that I look back on and think, 'Wow! If that had gotten in the papers it would have reflected badly.' There are those moments when I would have lost my role model quotient."

Those moments mostly involved women, booze or both.

In *TV/Radio Mirror*, the actor said the most important thing to him was being home with his family. "I leave the set, I get in the car...and bam! I'm home with the kids and take out the garbage and what-have-you. I'm back to normal living." Early on, when *16 Magazine* asked what girl in the whole world he'd most like to meet, he answered, "I met her some time ago. She's my wife, Lucy." [202]

But the number of ladies who wanted to meet him had mushroomed. Marie Gomez recalls, "The young girls, the women, would come looking for Henry. 'Where's Henry Darrow? Where's Henry? Manolito! Manolito!'" Darrow had become what *Screenland* called "the suavest, most superior sex symbol of all — the Latin Lover". One of *Chaparral's* producers said, "Henry has done more for our relations with Latin America than the whole state department" and *Screenland* answered, "...girls of

199. 7/24/70

200. The Tucson Daily Citizen, 7/21/69

201. The Tucson Daily Citizen, 6/29/69

202. "Henry Darrow Answers 20 Snoopy ?s," 12/68

all ethnic groups who have been waiting so long for the Latin Lover to bound back into their lives will reply, 'Henry has also done more for romance than the whole town of Hollywood!'"[203]

He was doing more for romance than most people knew. Marriage never meant monogamy to him and now, to find available women he just had to open his twinkling eyes. The restraint of previous decades was floundering and casual sex was losing its stigma. The Pill distanced sex from procreation and "Make love, not war" was a more popular anti-Vietnam War slogan than "Hell no, we won't go." The average guy's chances of getting laid had improved considerably, but for a TV star like Henry Darrow, doors were thrown wide open especially on location in Tucson. It was a different world, full of the front line troops, victims, guerillas, non-coms, lifers and mercenaries of the Sexual Revolution.

The combination of hedonistic times and his own fame got Hank Darrow into more beds than moonlight serenades and dimples ever did. It beat taking out the garbage and he believed Lucy didn't know. Always complimentary to her in the press, he was discrete about liaisons. Occasionally, the tabloids reported gossip or ran photos that upset Lucy, but she put on a game face in public, warmly describing him and their marriage in interviews. Meanwhile, the children heard her crying in private when he wasn't around.

"As a boy, I learned that if the husband took care of the wife and kids, it was acceptable if he also had mistresses or girlfriends," he explains. "That is what I saw. That was the Latin culture I knew. I took care of my family. I came home at night and spent time with them, but I didn't really pay attention to them." He pauses. "While I was with them, I was thinking about getting together with my girlfriend later. I did not take the marriage seriously and I did not truly respect women."

When he and Lucy visited Puerto Rico, the women went to the kitchen while the men talked politics in another room. "It was the 1960s and one time, Lucy brought some of the women into the men's room. The attitude of the men was 'What's this? You can't be here. Go back to the kitchen. Yeah, that's Hank's wife. She's American, she doesn't know any better.' So that was the status of women at that time in the Latin culture." Second-class citizens though women were, wives were jealously protected possessions. He ended a casual friendship with a man who kissed Lucy on the cheek. "I couldn't absorb that. You know how men are — we're dogs, for God's sake!"

---

203. Screenland *High Chaparral Bonus*, "Henry Darrow: Doomed to the Fate of Latin Lovers? Why the Women Chase Him!" *undated clipping from files of Henry Darrow.*

And it's said every dog has his day — or maybe, night. Darrow kept a steady girlfriend or mistress or two, then filled in spare time with one-night stands. He found women at bars, restaurants, parties and clubs. Some waited at the hotel or were brought to his room. They cozied up to him at public appearances. However, there was one group of women he never scored well with. "For some reason, I struck out with nine out of ten of my romantic interests on the show," he says. "We'd be leaving the Paramount lot at the same time at night, walking to our cars together. It's quiet and dark and everything is very nice, then all of a sudden it's, 'Goodnight, Henry. See you tomorrow!' And that's it, pal! I asked one of my leading ladies out to dinner and she answered that she was married. I said, 'So what?' That did not go over well. They just were *not* interested. I never figured it out."

Maybe they didn't like crowds. An admiring male extra on *Chaparral* recalls, "The ladies loved him! It's not Hank's fault they went crazy for him. He was just born that way." But Darrow doesn't excuse himself as easily.

"I've been watching *Mad Men*," he says. "It's a series about advertising guys in the 1960s. The husbands all lie and cheat and try to make out with the secretaries who work at their office. They have wives and steady girlfriends and occasional girlfriends. Unfortunately, I was part of that program. That is what I was like and it's awful. I drank a lot; I've been a shining example in that area. I smoked when I drank, so I smoked a lot. And I never walked away from situations with women."

However, he ran from situations with potentially lethal men. He dropped one woman fast when she informed him that she was only sleeping with him to get back at her policeman husband. "That kind of trouble I did *not* want," he says.

He wished he had walked away from a mother-daughter team before they tried to blackmail him. The daughter wasn't very attractive, but seemed hot to trot. "Of course, I was looking to score," says Darrow. "Then the mom showed up and it got strange really quickly."

The duo insinuated that he had smoked marijuana at a recent party, an allegation that could have jeopardized his career. "Indeed, there had been a party," he admits. "But anybody who knew me knew I *never* smoked marijuana. If they'd said, 'Oh, he got drunk!' That would have been like, 'Yeah, what else is new?' Nobody would have cared. But the other was different and it was a little scary."

"It was just a little hint of blackmail. They hinted that if they had money from me they would keep it quiet," he says. He offered no money and sure enough, a rumor circulated that he'd smoked grass at the party. That's when he called NBC and explained the situation. The network promised to send the ex-FBI agent they employed to resolve problems like his. Meanwhile, Darrow went to the bar at the hotel, where he ran into someone who knew the would-be extortionists. "I played stupid and said, 'Gee, I don't know what's going on. I hope they haven't done anything wrong, but NBC is sending an ex-FBI agent down here to handle it.'" Within twenty-four hours, the rumor was dead and word came back from a mutual acquaintance that the blackmailers had only been joking. But bad experiences didn't put the brakes on his womanizing.

"I thought I was single. I thought I really was Manolito," he recalls, but his conquests were sometimes disappointed by differences between the character and the actor. Some of his liaisons were used to seeing him in costume, including dark make-up. All was going well with one until he undressed. Frowning, she gawked at his naturally pale body, then whined, "I thought you were Latin, but you're so *white!*" Then she turned and left his room, slamming the door behind her.

Working and work's corollaries consumed nearly as much time as women. *Chaparral*, paid public appearances, charity events, favors for friends and promotions for Puerto Rico left little time for a personal life. "I let the acting take over everything that I was about in terms of my family, my kids, my marriage. I just was engulfed in being a glad hand. I made the trips around the country, got to travel around the world because of it, all those are the plusses. Then all of a sudden, I'm shorting the other situation, the real life."

Darrow's absorption with work, frequent absences from home and gusto for other women contributed to simmering resentments. His marriage grew more distant. He remembers Lucy's intensifying coldness and later, her anger. "Once, she came at me with a hammer and broke my class ring. Everything was crumbling."

But his greatest anguish wasn't from conflict with Lucy. While he spent time with children of friends and delighted little fans, he was slowly becoming alienated from his own daughter and son. Realizing how estranged he had grown was like a knife in the heart. "I lost contact with Deedee and Tom. Then later I circled around and came back to deal with them—or tried to. You try to put it together again. You don't know it, but it's too late."

> *He was a slightly soiled character, but you always knew he would do the right thing because his heart was in the right place.*
>
> LUIS REYES DESCRIBING MANOLITO MONTOYA

We of the Spanish-Speaking Origin

*Our goals are simple and our intent is genuine. We
seek only to work within the system, with abilities
we have, to improve the image and ambitions
of those 12 million persons of Spanish-speaking
origin in the United States."*

ACTOR RICARDO MONTALBÁN[204]

One of four children in a prosperous, devoutly Catholic family, Ricardo Montalbán was born in Mexíco City and as a teenager, moved to Los Angeles. He lived with his brother, attended church and concentrated on his studies until the high school drama teacher urged him to take part in student plays. From then on, acting hooked him.

By age nineteen, he was in New York City making three-minute musical movies which played on Soundies jukeboxes. Stage productions followed, then M-G-M planned a film of John Steinbeck's novel *Tortilla Flat* (1942) with a Mexican cast and asked Montalbán to screen-test for the crucial role of Danny. "I made the test with Lina Romay playing the role of Dolores Sweets Ramirez. We were told that the test was very successful," Montalbán wrote in 1980. "But Hollywood being what it was, our roles were cast with John Garfield and Hedy Lamarr. The other Mexicans in *Tortilla Flat* included Spencer Tracy, Ralph Morgan, Akim Tamiroff and Sheldon Leonard."[205] He was offered a small supporting role, but instead returned to Mexico to be with his gravely ill mother. She recovered, but he stayed. He became a star in the booming Mexican film industry before returning to the U.S. to play the hunky matador in M-G-M's 1947 musical *Fiesta*. From *Fiesta* onward, he galvanized a solid reputation in movies, television, theater and radio. In the muscular

---

204. Henry Darrow, personal papers

205. Reflections, *p. 62*

noir classic *Border Incident* (1949), he starred as Mexican G-man Pablo Rodriguez, but by the mid-1960s he had played many ethnicities, notably Japanese, Middle Eastern and Native American.

As one of the few working Hispanic actors in Hollywood, he took some parts he was not especially proud of. He avoided the most demeaning, but was so often cast as the stereotypical Latin lover that Clara E. Rodríguez later dubbed Montalbán and native Argentinean Fernando Lamas "Quintessential Latin Lovers".[206] The often-married Lamas whose exploits tagged him "First of the Red Hot Lamas"[207] railed against being professionally limited by the stereotype but embraced it in his private life, saying "It was a great image to have off the screen, but a pain in the ass in the movies".[208] However, Montalbán's issues went beyond typecasting to pejorative meaning. He wrote, "If being a Latin lover means needing a new conquest every day, preferably two, then I find nothing admirable in such a man. Of course it is easy to be obsessed with the chase and to seek the thrill of change. But that doesn't take much imagination. Dogs do the same thing." Montalbán said his father was the epitome of what a Latin lover *should* be. "For fifty-three years he was always faithful, always respectful of my mother. He enjoyed an active sex life to the end of his days and he was never bored. Imagine the romanticism that it took to keep a love affair going all those years! To my mind, *that* is being a Latin lover."[209]

Montalbán found Hollywood's Hispanic stereotypes — whether Latin lover, bandit, lazy peon, spitfire or other stock cinema characters — damaging. Recounting a conversation where a Mexican-American child's definition of Mexican was the Frito Bandito, the ubiquitous animated mascot for Fritos® Corn Chips, he said, "The boy's only connection with his heritage was a cartoon caricature...in a corn chip commercial. It's tragic. The boy did not realize what his people had achieved."[210]

In movies and on television, positive Latino role models, fictional or real life notables, remained largely absent. Says Luis Reyes, "There were vicious gang members or their suffering mothers or bandidos or caballeros. Movies were told from the point of view of the Anglo teacher who went to help the poor Hispanic family. The Hispanic family wasn't the center of the story." While the story of an "urban missionary" teaching

206. Heroes, Lovers and Others, p. 112

207. IMDB.com biography

208. Heroes, Lovers and Others, p. 114

209. Reflections, p. 22

210. Ibid., p. 150

Hispanic youth to rise above poverty and violence might seem preferable to showing Hispanics as vicious bandidos, it ain't necessarily so.

When "poor Hispanics" served only to illustrate the nobility, heroism or altruism of their White Savior, the message was that inferior Hispanics couldn't help themselves. Gang bangers relied on the noble Anglo teacher just as good Mexicans depended on the heroic gringo cowboy to rescue them from bad Mexicans.[211] Charles Ramirez Berg wrote, "Viewed as a tool of the dominant [Anglo] ideology, the creation and perpetuation of stereotypes in the movies and in the media function to maintain the status quo by representing dominant groups as "naturally" empowered and marginal groups as disenfranchised."[212] The White Savior was the White Man's Burden retold. Once it was neocolonial exploitation disguised as the moral imperative to "improve" so-called inferior people, played out in places like United Fruit Company's Central American and Caribbean banana plantations. In the 1960s it played out more covertly in movies with social issues themes like *Up the Down Staircase* (1967) and *Change of Habit* (1969).

Of course, colonial and neocolonial subjugation has not been limited to Hispanics. And, it can be successfully argued that cinema and television have been boundless repositories of racial, ethnic, regional and sexual stereotypes. However, empirical research strongly supports the conclusion that conspicuous exclusion and pervasive negative representations are historically greater for Hispanics than other groups.[213]

There were exceptions. Charles Ramírez Berg named "Katy Jurado's strong portrayal of the resourceful businesswoman in *High Noon* (1952), Ricardo Montalbán's intrepid Mexican government agent in *Border Incident* (1949), and Anthony Quinn's dignified, defiant vaquero in *The Ox-Bow Incident* (1943)" as "three rare cases where Hispanics are depicted as more than simplified caricatures in U.S. studio films."[214]

In television, one show is routinely singled out. "One of the few exceptions…was the western '*High Chaparral*'," wrote Lichter and Amudson. "To be sure, the series still presented semiliterate Hispanic ranch hands, but these portrayals were overshadowed by the Montoyas."[215]

Ricardo Montalbán guest-starred twice on *Chaparral* and until his first guest appearance, he and Henry Darrow had never met. The two

211. Latin Looks, *p. 76*

212. Ibid., *111*

213. Ibid., *p. 5 and elsewhere*

214. Ibid., *p. 104*

215. Ibid., *p. 60*

men had more in common than may have been immediately obvious in 1968. Two years later, their shared convictions compelled them to become emissaries of social change.

In 1970, Montalbán and several young Mexican-American men met together at a Los Angeles drugstore cafeteria. The younger men — Gilbert Avila, Robert Apodaca, Luis De Cordoba, Val De Vargas and Rodolfo Hoyos — wanted to change Hollywood's ignominious depiction of Hispanics, but felt they had no real entrée to studios and networks. "We need a key to open those doors," Avila told Montalbán. "You could be the key."[216]

Never before an activist, Montalbán considered their proposal. Warned by friends that rocking the boat could harm his career, he decided the risk was worth it. He would do it his own way, by forming an inclusive organization called *Nosotros*. "It means 'we,'" he explained. "Therefore, it signified We of the Spanish-speaking Origin. Not only Mexican, but South American and Spanish, too."[217]

Montalbán spelled out the primary goals of the group. First, to "Improve the image of the person of Spanish-speaking origin as he is portrayed on the screen". Second, to "Seek acting opportunities in the industry in all types of roles that we are capable of performing". Third, to "Train our members to become better actors and actresses in theater workshops and ultimately to seek talent in the barrios in an attempt to train creative youngsters to enter our chosen profession".

The first official meeting of *Nosotros* contained nearly as many stars as the clear night sky at Tehachapi Pass. Desi Arnaz, Anthony Quinn, Carmen Zapata, Anna Navarro, Fernando Lamas, Vikki Carr, Mario Machado, Linda Cristal, Henry Darrow and myriad others came together to extend a helping hand. The initial Executive Board of *Nosotros* consisted of Inez Pedroza (Public Relations Director), Richard Hernandez (Legal Counsel), Valentin De Vargas (Treasurer), Carlos Rivas (third Vice President), Rodolfo Hoyos (second Vice President), Ricardo Montalbán (President) and as first Vice President, the guy Montalbán called "a highly competent New York actor": Henry Darrow.

"It was partly that European tour that did it," he told *The Los Angeles Times* reporter Cecil Smith. "I got back from Europe and I began to think of all the good that happened to Henry Darrow and I decided it was time to think of what good Henry Darrow could make happen to someone else."[218]

216. Reflections, *p. 148*

217. Ibid., *p. 149*

218. "TV Times" *7/26-8/1, 1970*

Recalls actor James Victor, "Henry didn't have to get involved in *Nosotros*. He was already established when *Nosotros* came around. He was doing a series. He was one of the first guys, Hispanics from New York, who were getting opportunities. You could count them on your hands — Perry Lopez, Eugene Iglesias, Rafael Campos, Henry Silva, Henry Darrow. But he was a pioneer and one of those inspirations for any young Latin actor coming to this town."

"When we first started meeting, we met in a borrowed office around Beverly Boulevard and La Cienega," says Darrow. "The people who loaned us the office told us, 'When you fellows use the building, please bring your own toilet paper'."

Free toilet paper would have been hospitable, but it was critical to have phone calls returned. Ricardo Montalbán's lengthy career made him well known and Henry Darrow was easily the most prominent Latino face on television. They had the kind of name recognition that commands attention. Together, they tackled crucial education and outreach. They met with Hollywood executives, gave interviews to the press, spoke with community groups and appeared on television talk-shows.

"Some people felt they should be doing that instead of us, but they didn't have any name value," says Darrow. "So there was a jealousy aspect, but who's going to tune in to see someone whose film career consists of six close ups in one movie? With Ricardo Montalbán, something happened. People tuned in and they listened."

A favorable 1970 news article[219] enumerated *Nosotros'* concerns and goals, and called Darrow "one of the group's best spokesmen...an engaging man, vital, filled with humor..."Then surreptitious prejudice weighed in with this:

"Darrow speaks faultless English."

Nosotros had a boatload of work ahead.

Montalbán was courteous and diplomatic, but also very persistent and focused. As for himself, Darrow says, "I'm very good in situations where I present the package. At the beginning, I can sell it, I can act it, I can raise tens of thousands of dollars." He adds, "Later I lose interest, enthusiasm and drive and I need someone else to organize the details. My mother was like that. Mom was very good at originating things, getting things, then she would lose interest. But in the beginning, it's all great."

---

219. The Beckley *(WV)* Post-Herald and Register, *"Latins Unite To Get Better Shake In Show Business" by Vernon Scott, UPI Correspondent, 7/19/70*

Ricardo Montalbán and Henry Darrow traveled the country making personal appearances. There were dinners at the posh hotels and gatherings in the East L.A. *barrio*, interviews on local and national talk shows. "Rick would do shows like Johnny Carson," says Darrow. "I would do Joey Bishop and Regis Philbin. People would hear us talk and they would learn about the lack of opportunity and the cost of prejudice."

They spoke with Hollywood big shots and conferred with leaders of other community action groups, like radical Black Nationalist Stokely Carmichael. Recalls Darrow, "He said, 'Look, if you want to get it, you gotta throw a brick through the window. Being nice and polite and gentlemanly, it ain't going to happen.' But we were low-key. Ricardo was soft, not harsh. There were a number of radical groups. One called *Justicia* (Justice) would rant and rave and threaten to blow up the studios. We'd wear jackets and ties and we'd go in very politely to see the network people and we'd get stuff like a makeup program or a writers' program. One group played off the other."

"I like to believe that advances were achieved by a combination of their militancy and our own gentle persuasion," Montalbán agreed. "Together we managed to get rid of Frito Bandito."[220]

First appearing in 1967, the Frito Bandito replaced the blond, blue eyed Frito Kid as the "spokestoon" in Fritos® Corn Chips commercials. The Bandito was a "...type familiar to American movie audiences since the days of Pancho Villa..."[221] A chubby character with a thick accent, he sported a gold tooth, handlebar moustache, cheek stubble, huge sombrero, pistol in each hand and bandoliers across his chest. He sang a little song to the tune of "Cielito Lindo" ("Ai-ai-ai-ai, I am the Frito Bandito...") and given the repetitiveness of commercials, was likely the most visible Hispanic character on television. The National Mexican-American Anti-Defamation Committee (NMAADC) and other community action groups condemned him immediately. However, their protests and boycotts failed to move Frito-Lay. The company believed these groups didn't speak for the majority of Mexican-Americans who, according to Frito-Lay, found the character cute and appealing.[222]

"Why didn't you make him the Frito Amigo, giving the chips away, sharing them with everyone because he loves them so?" Montalbán asked the president of Frito-Lay. "No. You made him a bandit, stealing

220. Reflections, *p. 152*

221. *www.toonopedia.com/frito.htm*

222. Ibid.

the chips. Because that's the only way to think of a Mexican — as a bandit."

The executive admitted he'd never thought of it in those terms.[223]

Pressure from activists resulted in a makeover which included removing the pistols, but the Bandito stayed on the air until 1971. It took a lawsuit by the NMAADC and others against Frito-Lay for malicious defamation before Frito Lay laid him to rest.[224] That's four years of effort by several groups to eliminate one offensive cartoon mascot, an illustration of the uphill battle *Nosotros* faced against overt prejudice and unconscious discrimination.

Initially when Montalbán and Darrow met with the networks to talk about hiring more Hispanic actors, Darrow says, "Some of them would point to art directors. For some reason, there were a lot of Hispanic art directors. That was good but not enough. You never saw a Hispanic first or second Vice President of a network, except for one Mexican gentleman who was a Vice President during *Chaparral*. You did not usually see Hispanic actors up for roles that were not Hispanic. If your name was Rodolfo, you played Rodolfo. When Hispanic parts weren't being written, you didn't work."

Unless, like Darrow and myriad others, you Anglicized your name. "I am the first Puerto Rican to appear in a regular series," he told an interviewer. "When I go back…, they call me 'mano. That means 'brother' [from *hermano*]. It is a touching thing to see the pride and affection on their faces. I am one of them. I would like to change my name back again [to Delgado]. But it is too late. Everyone knows me as Darrow now."[225]

Darrow told *The Los Angeles Times*, "In some of our meetings I get zapped about changing my name, but I tell them the reason for *Nosotros* is that this will never be necessary again…"[226]

"We were asking employers not to reject a prospect because of his name," Montalbán wrote. "Give him the dignity of being able to present his talent. Then if you don't think he's suitable, hire someone else. But at least give him a chance."

"The basic problem of course went beyond actors," says Darrow. "A Latino television reporter would be doing a show on immigrants or the

223. Reflections, p. 152

224. www.toonopedia.com/frito.htm

225. The Beckley (WV) Post-Herald and Register, "Latins Unite To Get Better Shake In Show Business," by Vernon Scott, UPI Hollywood Correspondent, 7/19/70

226. TV Times, by Cecil Smith, 7/26-8/1, 1970

Mexican restaurant that just opened. He would not be given the chance to do a front line news story, unless it concerned crime in the *barrio*. Of course, Latino television reporters were rarely seen, like Latino actors. When we asked the networks why they didn't hire Hispanic actors, they would tell us, 'Wait a minute! We've got a 25% Latin hiring,'" says Darrow. "Yeah, almost all of them worked in the commissary or cleaning the sound stages! On one hand, it was work. People had jobs and they were going to get pensions. On the other hand, we wanted people behind the camera but we first wanted them in *front* of the camera. They'd tell us there weren't any qualified Hispanic actors. So, we'd ask, 'What are you going to do to help them qualify?' Of course, they were doing nothing."

Nosotros planned to implement an acting workshop for Latino performers, but didn't have the necessary funding. Antonio De Marco suggested a benefit show at the Hollywood Bowl. "We were staggered by the prospect of filling the place. But Tony convinced us we could do it," said Montalbán, who sent letters to entertainers inviting them to take part. Frank Sinatra said yes, then Dionne Warwick agreed. Other luminaries followed: José Ferrer, Charlton Heston, Jack Webb, Antonio Aguilar, Yvette Mimieux, Tony Martin and Glenn Ford. The musical director was noted Afro-Cuban jazzman Eddie Cano, whose orchestra provided instrumental accompaniment. Looking sleek in Manolito's formal outfit, Henry Darrow introduced the sensational Peruvian soprano Yma Sumac and did duets with her on "La Pampa y La Puma" and "Good Lovin.'" He says, "I did what I always wanted to do with an orchestra, which was to say, 'ONE...MORE...TIME!'"

Variety raved, "'*Nosotros*' Bash a Beaut."[227] In that one star studded night, the organization netted $30,000.[228] The acting workshop became reality, one of many achievements to champion Latino talent. But for Ricardo Montalbán, doors shut. Misquoted and misconstrued, he became known as a trouble-maker. Producers and casting directors offered him a few Mexican parts, but otherwise turned him away. For four years until he became bankable again, theater and voice-overs in Chrysler commercials helped him survive. Montalbán wrote, "I believe *Nosotros* accomplished some good, though not necessarily for Ricardo Montalbán...." Yet, he had no regrets. [229] "You choose a route, you go with it, and you pay the consequences."[230]

227. 8/18/70

228. Daily Variety, *9/1/70*

229. Reflections, *p. 153*

230. Ibid., *p. 154*

"Anyone who puts his life and career on the line is taking a risk, especially in a place like Hollywood," says Luis Reyes. "We didn't have cable then, so we didn't have a lot of options. It was ABC, NBC, CBS or the major movie studios. Some people resented the actors who got together and tried to tell the studios what to do, but it was very important at the time to work for better opportunities."

"It really hurt Ricardo Montalbán more than anyone else," says Miluka Rivera. "He took the chance to organize Latinos and the rumor got around that he was trying to start a Latino union. He was not, but he was blackballed. I respected Ricardo tremendously. I respect Henry Darrow; he was one of the few actors other than Ricardo who was willing to sacrifice his career to help his brothers. When he was at the top of his fame with *High Chaparral*, he was the hottest Latino at the time and he wasn't afraid to lend a hand."

> *Henry survived when a Latino actor couldn't be just good, he had to be beyond great. He had everything it took to be truly a star. Instead, he was a trailblazer for other Latinos. He was opening doors and mentoring people. So that's the kind of tragic part, but I never once found bitterness in Henry.*
>
> WRITER/PERFORMER RICK NAJERA

Business and Programming Judgments

*Those of us here directly connected with the
production of this fine series are equally unhappy
about the decision, but we also realize that it was
made as a business and programming judgment
and not as a reflection upon the series.*

THOMAS SARNOFF,
NBC WEST COAST VICE PRESIDENT[231]

Meanwhile back at the *rancho*, the 1969-1970 season seemed like all aces. *Chaparral* was garnering handsome third year Nielson ratings and was one of two most watched shows worldwide.[232] Undisputed trail boss *Bonanza* aired in an astounding ninety-one foreign countries, but *Chaparral* played in approximately fifty and was #1 in many. When production for the third season wrapped in mid-December 1969, *Chaparral* sat tall in the saddle.

Then early in 1970, *Variety* reported a split between *Chaparral* and Paramount Studios. "After filming almost entirely on location in Tucson, NBC's *High Chaparral* series will shoot at the Warner Bros. studio in May for the 1970-71 season. Long term agreement has been made with David Dortort, exec producer and creator of both *Chaparral* and *Bonanza*. Latter is leaving Paramount after eleven years to lease at WB, as first reported Fri."[233]

Later articles reported that either Warner Bros. lured *Bonanza* and *Chaparral* away from Paramount[234] or that Dortort jumped ship after eleven "great years" because WB's facilities were superior[235]. "We had no

231. *Letter to Henry Darrow dated July 10, 1970 in personal papers of Henry Darrow,*

232. *Advertisement in* Daily Variety *placed by David Dortort*

233. Daily Variety, *"Chaparral To Shoot on Warner Lot Also" 2/2/70*

234. Daily Variety, *3/4/70*

235. Ibid., *"Light and Airy" by Jack Hellman, 5/11/70*

back lot [at Paramount] and it became difficult to turn out nine months
of hour shows," said Dortort, adding that Warner's had "the sharpest
team" and "the best facilities" in Hollywood. But production manager
Kent McCray and others say leaving Paramount wasn't Dortort's idea. It
happened because someone with a vendetta bushwhacked *Chaparral*.[236]

The story is David Dortort had fired an employee of Xanadu Productions. This happened when Xanadu and Paramount Studios were entering
negotiations concerning *Chaparral's* lease-renewal. As bad luck would
have it, Dortort's ex-employee landed a job in Paramount's leasing department and he nursed a very robust grudge. He refused to renew *Chaparral's*
lease, thinking that would kill the show. To put another — hopefully
fatal — bullet in the back, Paramount also refused to sell Xanadu the
sets from *Chaparral's* pilot and previous seasons. Instead, even though
the studio lost money doing it, they struck the sets. With sets destroyed
and without a studio, *Chaparral* was in a nine-line bind.[237]

True, to preserve the show's authentic look, Dortort intended to film
65% in southern Arizona and at Old Tucson Studios, which had duplicate
exterior sets at their new sound stage. But 35% of the show was to film
in California. In only a few months, shooting had to begin for the next
season. It was a rotten time to be homeless.

Dortort and Warner Bros. quickly struck a deal. On February 1, Dortort moved Xanadu ratings leader *Bonanza* along with *Chaparral* to
Warner Bros. A huge boost to Warner's sagging television division, the
maneuver saved *The High Chaparral*.[238] WB sent people to Old Tucson
so the sets they created from scratch would be identical to those Paramount destroyed. Meanwhile, Old Tucson's owner, Bob Shelton, went to
Paramount and bought what was left of the interiors.

The High Chaparral would be ready to shoot season four, but changing
studios under duress ruptured the budget and economic realities super-
seded that authentic, on-location look. When filming began in May, it
was at Warner's.

"*Bonanza* and *The High Chaparral* will have a new look next year," wrote
Variety's Jack Hellman, "It may not be totally visible to the set huggers, but
the production values will be considerably enhanced on the move from
Paramount to Warners studio."[239]

236. *Kent McCray in public forum at The High Chaparral Reunion 2007*

237. Ibid.

238. Daily Variety, *"With Full Crew Aboard Now, WB Sets Its TV Prod'n Sails," 2/11/70*

239. *"Light and Airy," 5/11/70*

The High Chaparral did indeed have a new look. Months before the cameras began rolling at Warner Bros., Mark Slade (Billy Blue Cannon) was off the show. According to contemporary press reports and later recollections, Slade either quit[240] or was fired[241], because he wanted more money or to make a movie[242] or to finish his movie or because he had outgrown the role[243] or because the other cast members had to babysit him[244]. Or, he never left at all; he was still on the payroll and would again be seen when *Chaparral* was picked up for a fifth season. But in any case, the audience wanted "fresh young blood" for "fresh and provocative stories" on the show and Slade wouldn't do for that.[245] Then again, perhaps he would return later as a more mature Blue Boy, since he was a "fine young man, good actor, cooperative and hardworking."[246] That is, unless he was "expendable" and a "detriment" to other members of the cast.[247]

Fortunately for continuity's sake, Slade's character was written out late in the third season in "Generation," "an episode that shows he has a future as an artist, a reason for him leaving the old homestead to seek fame and fortune in the outside world."[248] According to some sources, the write out was both inadvertent and fortuitous since supposedly nobody knew Slade would be absent in the fourth season. It also wasn't a complete write-out, since Blue came home at the end and was still there in "Auld Lang Syne," the episode which aired after "Generation."

Unfortunately for continuity's sake, Blue was never mentioned in the fourth season. Silence plus the episode "The Badge" (written as if Blue and his mother never existed and "probably the most universally panned episode of the entire series"[249]) abruptly erased a beloved character along

240. The San Antonio Express, *"TV/Hollywood Line," by Marilyn Beck, 11/17/70*

241. The Corpus Christi Caller-Times *"Whatever Happened to Baby Chinook?" by Dick Kleiner, 7/ 26/70*

242. The San Antonio Express, *"TV/Hollywood Line" by Marilyn Beck, 11/17/70*

243. Daily Variety, *"Light and Airy," Jack Hellman, 5/11/70;* The Tucson Daily Citizen *6/10/70; and Marilyn Beck, "TV/Hollywood Line,"* San Antonio Express, *8/18/70*

244. The Corpus Christi Caller-Times *"Whatever Happened to Baby Chinook?" by Dick Kleiner, 7/ 26/70*

245. The San Antonio Express, *"TV/Hollywood Line" by Marilyn Beck, 11/17/70*

246. The Tucson Daily Citizen, *6/10/70*

247. The Corpus Christi Caller-Times *"Whatever Happened to Baby Chinook?" by Dick Kleiner, 7/ 26/70*

248. The San Antonio Light, *"Westerns Keep Going," 5/10/70*

249. *www.thehighchaparral.com*

with three years of interpersonal dynamics integral to major plotlines. Yet, according to *The Tucson Daily Citizen*, "Dortort said Slade's character, Blue, would be kept alive 'because of the affection we have for Mark.'"[250]

Although Slade's name would not be listed when the credits rolled on fourth season episodes, there was every reason to believe those credits would continue rolling. *The High Chaparral* finished its third year in the Top 20.[251] Top 20 shows pleased networks, so did being #1 in its time slot, where it clobbered *Get Smart* and *The Brady Bunch*. In April 1970 the expected official word came down; NBC renewed the show for another season of twenty-six episodes "firm" for 1970-71.[252]

David Dortort was initially undecided whether or not to replace Mark Slade.[253] But, he had "stories we couldn't tell because we didn't have young people."[254]

"They missed the boat by not using Henry Darrow to the hilt in episodes," says Linda Cristal. "They should have said, 'Everyone loves Manolito, what else can we do with this character?' If I had been the producer, I would have gone to the bank with Henry. He is a performer! But they had lack of vision. They were married to their ideas and you must never marry your ideas."

The casting call went out for an actor to play "Wind," a teenaged, half-Pawnee drifter. "We're going to try something novel," Dortort said. "Instead of the artificial, stock characters on television, perhaps including some on our own show, we want to go back to the facts of history." He talked about Civil War veterans going west and meeting friendly tribes whose hospitality meant offering a traveler one of their women. Half-Native children like Wind resulted; he would turn out to be Buck Cannon's son.[255]

Two hundred hopefuls vied for the part. Only five were screen tested. The last young man to audition was a nineteen-year-old unknown of Mexican heritage who had only one TV credit on his short résumé. His name was Rudy Ramos and he got the part.

Ramos was from the toughest, poorest side of Lawton, Oklahoma. His was the only Latino family in a neighborhood of blacks, Kiowa and

250. 6/10/70

251. The News *(Van Nuys CA)*, 6/23/70

252. *Letter from David Dortort to Don Durgin, private papers of Henry Darrow*

253. Daily Variety, *"On All Channels," 3/18/70*

254. The Pomona *(CA)* Progress-Bulletin, *7/28/70*

255. The Tucson Daily Citizen, *6/10/70*

poor whites. Rudy's friends were black and Kiowa kids. Of his Kiowa pals, Ramos says, "Some of them are still my friends. I think that is why I have always been embraced by the culture even though I am not a Native. As for Wind, we were and are very much alike. I honestly think that is why Mr. Dortort cast me." In his interview, someone started to put a hand on him when Ramos stepped back and said, "DON'T touch me." It was exactly how Dortort envisioned Wind's reaction.

"He sat me down and asked me how fast I would be ready to go to Tucson," Ramos says. "I replied that pretty much everything I owned was on my back."

Before he stepped on the set, a producer took Ramos aside. "He was concerned about Henry Darrow's reaction to me, that he might be jealous to have a younger Latino man in the cast," he recalls. "That couldn't have been farther from the truth. I can't imagine *anyone* thinking that about Henry." The whole cast welcomed him warmly and Ramos especially loved Cameron Mitchell, who was like a big brother. "But my first day on the set in Tucson, Henry was the first one to come by my dressing room and welcome me. He didn't hang out much, but he was such a gentleman."

The advance publicity on Rudy Ramos wasn't any more accurate than what he'd heard about Henry Darrow. Says Kent McCray, "We were told Rudy could ride a horse, that he was brought up on a ranch. Denny Allen was head wrangler. I said, 'Well? Was he brought up on a ranch?' And Denny Allen said, 'Yeah, a *chicken* ranch.'"

Even though Ramos knew more about plucking pullets than herding heifers, Darrow thought he was a good addition to the show and a positive sign for Latinos. "Tom Sarnoff, who was a Vice-President at NBC, visited the set and told me about Rudy," says Darrow, then first Vice-President of *Nosotros*. "It looked like a strong indication that NBC, which led the networks in creating opportunities for Latinos, would continue to create those opportunities. Tom reminded me to get the word out to *Nosotros* and the Latino community."

It seemed like a sure bet that as long as *The High Chaparral* aired, it would be in the vanguard with worthy roles for Hispanic actors and actresses. All signs pointed to *Chaparral* staying on the schedule. In a phone conversation, producer James Schmerer told Henry Darrow that NBC sent a memo on June 1 trumpeting its great regard for the show.

Then on June 11, another actor was gone, this time due to a tragic accident. Fifty-six-year-old Frank Silvera (Don Sebastian Montoya) decided to repair his kitchen garbage disposal unit. That's usually a mundane task that blows an afternoon. When his son dropped by later, Silvera was dead on the kitchen floor of his Pasadena home. He was being treated for high blood pressure and a heart attack or stroke seemed the likeliest killer. Instead, the coroner found he had been electrocuted by the garbage disposal. "He forgot to pull the plug on the disposal and there was water on the floor," says Darrow. "It was a freak accident, but the coroner said it was just a matter of time before he was going to have a major heart attack."

Frank Silvera's obituary in *Variety* detailed a life full of accomplishments as actor, director, producer and civil rights advocate. On *Chaparral*, he left a legacy of fine performances and also, a big void. But, so did Mark Slade. Since neither Blue Cannon nor his absence were ever mentioned, it was anybody's guess how Don Sebastian Montoya's disappearance would be handled.

Fourth season filming continued and talk was upbeat. Henry Darrow was especially optimistic. As a leader in *Nosotros*, his input was actively encouraged to make Mexican-themed episodes strong and dimensional. "If there were things in a script which the Latino community might find offensive, I suggested changes," said Darrow. "This freedom to exchange ideas showed a willingness in NBC and *Chaparral* to cooperate with *Nosotros* and its goals. What an ideal situation. And I could let the Latino community know that things were happening in a positive way."[256] That was especially important because the U.S. was in a deepening recession. NBC had already experienced staff cutbacks and many actors were out of work.

After Frank Silvera's death, Henry Darrow had lunch with Fenton Coe, a Vice President at NBC. When Coe said Gilbert Roland was hired as a regular, Darrow was thrilled. "He was a hero of mine. I remember seeing him all the time in *The Cisco Kid*. He was a real movie star. I thought, wow! This is going to be big!" There was even more exciting news. With Roland in the cast, more episodes would have Mexican themes and Darrow would be prominently featured.

Then an ominous message from NBC shocked everyone from David Dortort down. Based on "research," the network unilaterally made a "business and programming decision" to cut the number of fourth season episodes from twenty-six to eighteen. NBC planned to pre-empt *Chaparral* midseason for eight straight weeks of specials.

Tense, sometimes rambling telegrams and letters sped between distraught David Dortort and network brass. "We're not arguing about an economic decision the network feels it has to make," wrote Dortort. "We

256. *Henry Darrow's notes, private papers*

understand that things are rough, and that certain belt tightening is necessary. What we don't understand is why THE HIGH CHAPARRAL has been singled out, of all the shows on the schedule, to absorb all the punishment by itself...we have no choice but to do anything in our power to try to persuade you and the network that your action is unfair, discriminatory and ill-advised."[257] Praising his stars and *Chaparral's* value to the Hispanic community, Dortort called the decision a "death blow."[258] Cast and crew agreed that NBC had "given the needle" to its own show. With the future suddenly unsure, production staff and crew began fleeing to more secure employment.

Everyone was upset, but of the show's stars the decision hit Henry Darrow hardest. Leif Erickson and Cameron Mitchell were guaranteed pay for twenty-six episodes regardless of how many were actually shot. Darrow had no such arrangement. If there were only eighteen episodes, he would be paid for only those. It meant making $20,000 less than expected for the year.[259] At $2,500 per episode, his annual salary was finally at a comfortable level, but it still lagged behind other star paychecks on *Chaparral*.

Linda Cristal recalls one day during *Chaparral's* first year when she and Darrow were talking. "I said, 'You know what? I want more money. I'm working very hard, it's very hot here and I want more money.' And Henry said, 'Oh, nonono. I don't think it's a good idea at this point. Wait and see if we're picked up for next year.' And I said, 'No, I want it now while we are working.' Henry would never do that, but you have to do those things! You have to knock on the door and say, 'I'm unhappy about this.'" Three years later, Darrow still preferred being friendly and subtly persuasive but NBC's alarming edict left him angry, worried and not at all interested in being quiet.

He met with David Dortort on July 1 to discuss his concerns. Was this retribution for his activism or was *Chaparral* sacrificed because Anglo researchers and the network were blind to the large number of Latino viewers? Did NBC, the leading network in providing opportunities for Hispanics, not really care about minority hiring?

Dortort thought Darrow's questions were understandable. NBC's decision attacked Darrow's pocketbook and "will result in a drastic cutback of

257. *Letter from Dortort to Don Durgin, President of NBC Television Network, 7/13/70, private papers of Henry Darrow*

258. Ibid.

259. *Equal to $112,597 less in 2010 dollars.*

employment for Spanish-American actors, because more than any other show on the air, THE HIGH CHAPARRAL has been the principal source of employment for them...the only show that has made a point of not treating them solely as bandits, knife wielders and people too lazy to work."[260] As rumors spread in Hollywood and at NBC, more people became embroiled. Letters were more strident. The media quoted Dortort maybe accurately or maybe not, quoted Darrow maybe accurately or maybe not. Maybe the network brass read or heard the interviews. Or perhaps not.

On July 10, NBC's West Coast Executive Vice President Tom Sarnoff wrote, "Dear Henry, I am both hurt and very disappointed by the reports I have received about your recent interview with the press and about the alleged reaction of the *Nosotros* Organization as expressed by David Dortort...To charge that NBC is deliberately discriminating against the Spanish-speaking people by this cut back is totally unfair; and, you, of all people, know this is not so. Surely you cannot have forgotten so soon the reception you and Ricardo Montalbán got in my office and the encouragement we gave you and the *Nosotros* Organization...It is perhaps ironic, but nevertheless true, that our show was chosen for this cut back not because it was considered a weak show, but rather because it is considered by all to be a strong one...it would not suffer from the hiatus...Indeed, had we decided to cancel the show, we would have stopped at the end of thirteen episodes and not scheduled new shows after the hiatus."[261]

Typically mellow Darrow was livid. What he just read could easily be interpreted as "Sit down, shut up, get your people in line or you'll never eat lunch in this town again." If "strength" was the criterion, NBC had stronger shows to pre-empt like *Rowan and Martin's Laugh-In* (#1), *Wonderful World of Color* (#9), *The Bill Cosby Show* (#11) and of course, #3 rated *Bonanza*. Furious, he attempted to frame a constructive response. "This is the reward for a 'strong' show?!!" he scrawled in heavy red ink. Other sentences careened down the page and turned illegible. Later, in neater black ink he wrote, "I am certain that you have thought, does Henry know what he is doing and what possible repercussions can come from it? Of course, Tom; the networks have kept actors cognizant of what happens when you get too outspoken." The recent battle between *The Smothers Brothers Comedy Hour* and CBS was one example. First CBS censored the Smothers' biting anti-war, anti-Oval Office satire to the point of not

260. *Letter from Dortort to Don Durgin, President of NBC Television Network, 6/13/70, private papers of Henry Darrow*

261. *Private papers of Henry Darrow*

allowing one particular episode on the air. Next, the network president suddenly cancelled the highly rated show.

Darrow continued writing, carefully choosing words, then striking them. "My anger, frustration and disappointment over the present situation are not directed in any way to you. How can you condemn me? I've stated repeatedly when interviewed that NBC is the leader in opportunities and recognition for Spanish speaking people...." After sheets scored with heavy pen strokes, words emphatically underlined and sentences finished with exclamation points, he penned a civil, focused reply to Sarnoff. But his indignation hadn't cooled. He was still steaming when Cecil Smith of *The Los Angeles Times* interviewed him.

"They say we are so strong a show on Friday nights that they can afford to take episodes away from us to do specials which they couldn't do with a weaker show," he said. "Suppose we get stronger? Will they take us away altogether?"[262]

Hotly, he continued. "In the Mexican community, *Chaparral* was known as a program that portrayed a Mexican with dignity as a man of substance and worth. In Mano's father's home hangs a Goya! It was also a program that employed many Chicanos. But with the cutback in the number of shows, they will shrug and say: 'It is to be expected; what is good for Chicanos will be destroyed.'" Smith writes that here Darrow paused, "dark eyes troubled" and added, "It's an attitude we can't afford."

NBC would not budge. Beginning with the Orange Bowl on New Year's Day until February 19, the network would replace *Chaparral* with specials about animals and nature, plus the network's yearly circus show.[263]

Variety called the two month interruption of *Chaparral* "unprecedented" and "startling". It charged that NBC President, Dan Durgin, had a "deepening commitment" to specials and was "determined to accommodate the maximum number possible." As to why *The High Chaparral* was sacrificed, *Variety* had answers. The Friday time period was perfect for family-friendly specials, NBC had total control since the show was owned by them, it was an established show better able to withstand the hiatus and as a western, it allegedly drew older viewers that advertisers didn't court. "NBC is, of course, fully aware of the risks. There's a school of thought (at CBS, for instance) that excessive interruption can destroy a series. However, Durgin and other web execs believe the return of *Chaparral*...may have a

262. *TV Times, 6/ 26-8/1, 1970*

263. *Daily Variety, 7/29/70*

certain value, like a second premier...."[264] Right, just in a more swan song way. What *Variety* didn't mention were new Federal Communications Commission (FCC) regulations which made "specials" highly desirable and shows that drew older viewers unappealing.

In 1970 the FCC enacted the Prime Time Access Rule (PTAR). At the time, the networks owned four hours of peak viewing a night. PTAR would change that. It mandated one of those hours be remanded to local stations for local-access programming. When PTAR took effect in September 1971, the networks would have only three hours for their programming, except for shows exempt from PTAR which allowed a network more than its Prime Time allotment. Live sports, some children's programs, news shows and "specials," like the ones which pre-empted *The High Chaparral*, were the exceptions. PTAR made specials *very* special, but it would still take a bite of network programming time. ABC, CBS and NBC started tightening their belts and sharpening axes.

With advertising dollars at even more of a premium, what was good for Madison Avenue was good for the networks. Madison Avenue pandered to the young, urban and trendy — the audience most likely to buy what it was selling — and the networks would, too. ABC, CBS and NBC lost their love for rural sitcoms like *The Beverly Hillbillies* and westerns which attracted an older, un-chic demographic. And westerns were damned by a problem that the Clampetts never faced, no matter how ornery Granny got.

The western genre had nearly been ridden out of town by anti-violence groups. Across the board, the networks had capitulated with less action and more interaction. Vernon Scott, UPI's Hollywood correspondent wrote, "Even such series as *Gunsmoke, Bonanza, The Virginian, Lancer* and *High Chaparral* have come to wrist slapping and dirty looks instead of a left hook to the mandible."[265]

"The networks have panicked and overcompensated," said Robert Herron, President of the 140-member Stuntmen's Association. "They have mistaken action for violence. Where action is called for the television people are cutting it out — leaving gaping holes in their stories."[266] It also left many stuntmen with gaping holes in their pockets due to dwindling TV work and it changed the very nature of westerns.

264. Ibid.

265. The Lowell *(MA)* Sun, *"Entertainment," "TV stuntmen up in arms about ban on violence," 10/31/69*

266. Ibid.

"…with low violence scripts, the [westerns] of yore have turned into period drama," wrote *Variety's* Les Brown. Noting that period dramas weren't popular with the young crowd that Madison Avenue adored, he called westerns a "tough sell". So tough that they really *weren't* making 'em like that anymore.

In spite of Top 10 shows like *Gunsmoke* and *Bonanza*, there wasn't a single new western on the 1970-71 TV schedules of NBC, ABC or CBS. Western movies were still solid box office,[267] but the TV western had taken a bullet. It was more than a flesh wound. Situation comedies, variety shows, detectives and doctors homesteaded nearly all the prime time real estate where westerns once staked their claims. Both CBS's short lived *Lancer* and NBC's long running frontier saga *Daniel Boone* had bitten the dust, leaving only *Gunsmoke, Bonanza, The Men from Shiloh* (formerly *The Virginian*) and *The High Chaparral* to ride the shrinking video range.

"One of television's better weekly series steals through each season relatively unnoticed. It's NBC's *The High Chaparral*, a kind of a *Bonanza* with bravado, a Ponderosa with punch," wrote Ernie Kreiling in Van Nuys' *The News*. Instead of a "relatively sterile morality play with sharply stereotyped characters" like *Bonanza, Chaparral* used "real people". Perhaps they "aren't quite as loveable as those at the Ponderosa, but I find them much easier to respect, as would anyone who prefers people to icons."[268] *The High Chaparral* was soon even less popular than before and that didn't go unnoticed by NBC.

According to *www.thehighchaparral.com*, "Season Four…stirs up more controversy among fans than any other season" and soon as it premiered on September 18, 1970, the fan base started slipping. By October 28, the former Top 20 series was #40 in the ratings. Perhaps a reflection of pervasive anxiety and anger, comedy episodes and family themed shows that were handled so deftly and that viewers loved were largely gone. Although the fourth season included outstanding drama, viewers didn't get the variety they liked. Mark Slade fans, angry that Blue had been completely erased, switched channels.

Wind, the new character well-played by Rudy Ramos, received mixed reviews. A defiant young man seeking his place in the world, he appealed to teens who related to his "otherness" and problems with authority.

267. Little Big Man, The Ballad of Cable Hogue, The Cheyenne Social Club, Chisum, A Man Called Horse, Monte Walsh, Rio Lobo, There Was a Crooked Man, They Call Me Trinity *and* Two Mules for Sister Sarah *were all popular 1970 cinema releases.*

268. *"A closer look at television," 6/23/70*

Unfortunately, he was also "almost a mystic warrior."[269] He was a better marksman than everyone else, a more skilled rider than Joe, nobler than Big John and smarter than Manolito, who had forgotten everything he knew about the Apaches but luckily had Wind around to educate him. Ramos needed time for his character to develop, but with eight episodes cut, emphasis replaced time. It seemed beloved, established characters got the short shift when, to paraphrase Manolito, Wind used up all the good rocks.

Cameron Mitchell, Leif Erickson, Linda Cristal and Henry Darrow all put in stunning performances. Don Collier was back as ranch foreman Sam Butler after a long absence in season three (he had been working in a John Wayne movie). Fans warmed to Wind. Ratings slowly improved.

The tenth episode, "Too Late the Epitaph," aired on Nov. 6, 1970. It was twenty-fourth in the ratings, the best thus far in the season.[270] The lightest episode of the season, it was a solid Manolito vehicle guest-starring Henry Darrow's Pasadena Playhouse classmate Monte Markham. It was filmed after NBC's decision to preempt eight episodes, and Darrow was noticeably careworn.

For Henry Darrow, the brightest light that year was the brightest star. When it was time to film the eighteenth and final episode, Gilbert Roland swept onto the soundstage cloaked in Old Hollywood magic. Born in Juárez, Mexico but raised in Los Angeles, the graceful matador's son was a silver screen legend from toes to the tip of his elegant cane. He had been a leading Latin Lover in silent movies and early talkies until his audacious off-camera womanizing nearly ended his career. "He was blackballed when he was caught messing around with one of the top producer's wives," Darrow says, incredulous. "The big guys in Hollywood all knew each other. They played poker together!"

Rather than becoming an embittered has-been, Roland used those little parts to showcase his considerable talent. Better movie roles, like the popular *Cisco Kid* series, and TV work eventually came his way. On *Chaparral*, he played Don Domingo, Don Sebastian's wastrel brother and the new head of the house of Montoya. The episode introducing Don Domingo was a two-parter encompassing Don Sebastian's death.

Susan Sukman McCray says when Gilbert Roland sauntered into the casting office, "He was the epitome of a star and he was still a charmer. You could not resist that feeling of your heart pounding when you looked at him."

269. www.thehighchaparral.com

270. Daily Variety, 11/11/70

If Henry Darrow's heart pounded when he first saw Roland, it was not entirely due to the older man's glamour. In the Cisco Kid movies, Roland had a particular way of placing his hands on his hips. "Not with the thumbs to the back," says Darrow. "He'd do it like a bullfighter, with his thumbs to the front." Imitation being the sincerest flattery, Darrow copied the pose and was comfortable using it until Gilbert Roland appeared on the set of *The High Chaparral.* "All of a sudden, he was walking toward me. My hand was on my hip and I was thinking, oh, my gosh, this is his bit! That's the man I stole this from! I didn't know where to put my hands at the beginning." Darrow shrugged off his embarrassment. "Then I thought, ah, what the heck! It was a pleasure working with him. He exuded such confidence and style, it was a delight."

Roland traveled with his own wine, a 1966 Pommard, and promised fellow oenophile Darrow a bottle. But at the end of the wrap party, Darrow was without wine. "He shakes my hand, gives me *un abrazo.* I'm saying goodbye, it's been a pleasure and I'm thinking about the wine, that he's not going to come through."

Catching the younger man by surprise, Roland said, "Henry, come with me to my car." Reaching the sleek white Cadillac convertible, Roland opened the trunk and withdrew a bottle of Pommard, declaring, "When Gilbert Roland gives his word, he keeps it."

If only life had more honor and fewer hard knocks.

The Recession of 1969-70 brought higher interest rates and unemployment. At NBC-TV, staff cuts were not news anymore. The network was looking down the barrel of the Prime Time Access Rule as advertising dollars evaporated. NBC had partially put the advertising noose around its own neck when in July 1970, NBC News did an exposé on the misery of migrant workers in Florida citrus groves. The groves were owned by the Coca-Cola Company. In December 1970 Coke's advertising buys on NBC were up for renewal. Coke didn't renew. NBC was still smarting from that in January 1971 when the Public Health Cigarette Smoking Act went into effect banning cigarette advertising on TV and radio. The ban alone lost the National Broadcasting Company about 10% of its advertising revenues.

Darrow followed economic news and knew times were hard, especially for NBC without Coca-Cola's big bucks. But between NBC's assurances that they wouldn't cancel the show and happy talk about season five with Gilbert Roland, he says, "This was the first time I was confident that we would be renewed."

Still, he liked to hedge his bets. When season four filming wrapped, he guest-starred in an episode of the CBS adventure series *Mission: Impossible*.[271] Then both ABC and CBS approached him about doing pilots. It would be additional income even if neither became a series, which was especially attractive after his eight episode pay cut. He went to the NBC brass and asked about the pilots. "I told them how things were," he recalls, "They said no to the pilots because my contract with them was good until April 9."

But when "The New Lion of Sonora" aired after eight weeks of pre-emption, his basic optimism got a boost. Positive reviews pointed to better times ahead. *Variety* said *The High Chaparral* came "storming back with two hours of violent drama. The incentive was two-fold; to strike hard at the rating table while the parent is sorting out the survivors for next season and the assurance of profits in overseas sales. It has a winning look both ways."[272]

A winning look wasn't enough. Previously *Chaparral* was the ratings leader in its time-slot. Half hour sitcoms *Get Smart* (CBS) and *The Brady Bunch* (ABC) had been followed by shows without the horsepower to rustle ratings from *Chaparral*. Then in January 1971, ABC made a scheduling change that buried "New Lion" in the ratings. Says Darrow, "ABC cancelled the poor performer following *The Brady Bunch* and moved *The Partridge Family* in its place. With them back-to-back, it was a delightful family hour. We got wiped out."

On March 3, 1971, the week after "The New Lion of Sonora" aired, *The Tucson Daily Citizen* ran an article with the header "Rumors Say 'High Chaparral' Is Done."[273] David Dortort is described as "shocked by reports from television industry sources" that *Chaparral* would be dropped. "When the series was pre-empted in mid-winter for a series of specials, I was assured by network officials that it was a temporary situation and was promised the show would be renewed. All the actors in the continuing cast were given the same reassurance."

The article then quotes a "network official in New York" who told the reporter "this is the rumor season" and "decisions on next year's shows have not been made yet."

Responded Dortort, "I hope this is not another act of betrayal on the part of some money minded executives in New York City who will not face up to their social responsibilities…"

271. *"Blast," original air date 1/30/71*

272. *Daily Variety, "Telepic Review" by Helm. 2/22/71*

273. *By Micheline Keating, staff writer*

On March 9, NBC-TV issued a press release saying they had cancelled *The High Chaparral*.[274]

"Usually when you get kicked off a show, you get two weeks' notice. 'You're closing, pal!'" says Darrow. "I found out *Chaparral* had been cancelled when I read it in *Variety*. Nobody even called me to say it was over."

Henry taught me to enjoy the red carpet, but realize you might end up vacuuming it.

WRITER/PERFORMER RICK NAJERA

274. *The Tucson Daily Citizen*, 5/5/71

Hosting the Latino TV variety show *Bravo* (1972) in "Manolito's" formal outfit.

As "Alex Montenez" in *The New Dick Van Dyke Show* (1973-74).

Lauren Levian and Henry Darrow, wedding photo.

Henry and Lauren roughing it in Bryce Canyon, Utah.

Lauren and Henry onstage in *The Roar of the Greasepaint, the Smell of the Crowd.*

With a young friend at a March of Dimes fundraiser.

Stars of Seguin (PBS *American Playhouse* TV special). A Martinez
(left rear), Henry Darrow (right rear), Rose Portillo (left front) and Lupe
Ontiveros (right front).

With Will Sampson in the TV series *Born to the Wind* (1982).

Darrow was the first Hispanic to play Zorro in TV's *Zorro and Son* (1983) costarring Paul Regina.

Author/playwright Ray Bradbury *(The Wonderful Ice Cream Suit)* with Zorro (Henry Darrow).

Jumping ahead a few centuries and changing species, Darrow played worm-eating Vulcan Admiral Savar on *Star Trek: The Next Generation* in 1988.

Darrow as Don Diego de la Vega in *Zorro and Son*.

The Champion of the 1989 World Chess Convention
Celebrity Tournament relaxing at home.

Taking aim at another cop role in the feature *The Last of the Finest*
(1990) with guidance from director John Mackenzie.

The stars of New World Television's *Zorro* in 1990. (Left to right) Juan Diego Botto, Toronado the horse, Patrice Martinez, Duncan Regehr, James Victor, Henry Darrow and Michael Tylo

On the set of *Zorro* in 1990 with guest-star Doug McClure and leading man Duncan Regehr.

Don Alejandro (Henry Darrow) and son Don Diego (Duncan Regehr) share a moment.

Don Alejandro uses his powers of persuasion on Sgt. Mendoza (James Victor).

Patrice Martinez, Darrow and guest-star André the Giant on the set of *Zorro*.

With *Zorro* costar Patrice Martinez *(left)* and guest-star Donna Baccala *(right)*.

Midlife Manolito.

Henry's son Tom Delgado with a furry friend.

Henry with Lauren *(left)* and daughter Deedee *(right)*.

The silver fox.

With writer/actor/comic Rick Najera in Najera's autobiographical play
A Quiet Love.

That certain Darrow as *That Certain Cervantes.* COURTESY OF MILUKA RIVERA

The High Chaparral's original three amigos *(left to right):* Bobby Hoy ("Joe Butler"), Henry Darrow ("Manolito Montoya") and Don Collier ("Sam Butler"), pals for over thirty years.

With fellow *Resurrection Blvd.* guest-star Rita Moreno.

The guy!

ACT THREE

This Could Be Held Against You

In Europe an actor is an artist. In Hollywood, if he isn't working, he's a bum.

ACTOR ANTHONY QUINN

First Henry Darrow found out in *Variety* that NBC had cancelled *The High Chaparral*. Then he got a form telegram from the network saying he didn't have a job anymore. "But I didn't feel depressed until they sent a personal letter saying it had been good working with me," he recalls. "I felt like I was right back where I'd been six years earlier." But he wasn't.

Six years before, he was working. So was his life. His future as an actor held promise, his marriage was at least friendly, fame hadn't invaded his peaceful neighborhood and disrupted his family's relatively pleasant life, nobody stalked his children or him and neither of the kids were argumentative teenagers. He had filled his family with pride. He had honored his beloved Puerto Rico and all the people who believed in him. Then stardom crashed the backyard bar-b-que. Like a crazy lover, it gave him unsurpassed approval, undreamed of love and unequaled ecstasy before coldly casting him aside and walking out the door. It took paychecks and perks with it. He was still a hero to his family and to many Latinos, especially Puerto Ricans, but he worried that disappointment would erase their pride in him just as neglect, booze, women and simmering resentments eroded his marriage.

Neither he nor Lucy was willing to give up and file for divorce, but their marriage was frosty. Power struggles between Lucy and teenaged Deedee upped the ante for tension at home. "Lucy and Deedee are very much alike — fragile, but also very stubborn," he says. "Deedee had a wonderful talent for music and she was good at pursuing things but there was an attitude problem. Because we wanted Deedee to study piano, she studied the accordion. When we said, okay, that's fine, she dropped it and took up the flute. She and Lucy really fought hard against each other."

Away from home, there were too many mistresses and girlfriends vying for his attention and one was especially a handful. While shooting the *Chaparral* episode "Only the Bad Come to Sonora" the year before, a drop-dead beautiful brunette showed up on the set. Wherever Darrow went, she went. She was hard to miss and guest star Bruce Dern nudged Darrow saying, "Boy! She's really after you." Dern didn't know it, but heiress Eve Black[275] took "after you" to new heights. When Darrow was onstage in California, she came from her home several states away to see him perform. If he made a promotional appearance, she was there. She dressed to the nines, always packed a pearl-handled pistol and knew how to use it. Stepping from her chauffeur-driven Cadillac limousine, she dripped money and sexual obsession.

"She was very unstable," Darrow says. But except for the crazy stuff — only calling him "Manolito," never "Henry" or "Hank" and stalking him from state to state and event to event — Eve was the stuff of male fantasy.

"Besides, Henry has always had a thing for limousines," says Lauren Levian.

Turn Eve down? You've got to be kidding. She became his mistress.

"I guess she bought me for a while," Darrow says. Another guy on *Chaparral* was the beard. When Eve blew into Los Angeles, she phoned the beard and he passed messages to Darrow. "That's how we'd arrange to meet. She was very determined and it wasn't a happy association. There was always chaos."

Although dalliances were diverting, his professional life took precedence. Looking for work stunk and it was an especially bad time to be unemployed, but he had a family to support.

On the radio, Janis Joplin was singing about being "busted flat in Baton Rouge" with Bobby McGee and feelin' good, but being busted flat in Los Angeles didn't have much in its favor. Hollywood's job market was more depressed than Henry Darrow and a lot of people were singing the blues. Headlines shouted "Hollywood Job Crisis — 50% out of work"[276] and "Much of Hollywood Found in Unemployment Ranks."[277] Unemployed actors weren't news — at any given time, 95% of the Screen Actors' Guild didn't have jobs. But the current crisis affected every trade-union and guild in what *The Los Angeles Times* called "an unprecedented

275. *Not even close to her real name*

276. *The Los Angeles Times, by William Endicott, 6/16/71*

277. *Piqua (OH)* Daily Call, *by Bob Thomas (Associated Press), 4/22/71*

depression."[278] The Screen Extras Guild reported 94% unemployment and 65% of the film editors' union were out of work.[279] Financially strapped television networks produced fewer shows and laid workers off, but the film industry was hit even harder; fat subsidies and cheap labor in foreign countries had lured a majority of U.S. film productions away from domestic soil. Major studios shut local offices and cut production. In desperation, the movie industry petitioned the U.S. government for a 25% tax exemption on gross income from domestic films. It was a little like General Motors asking Ford for help: the U.S. government was the American film industry's biggest competitor. Uncle Sam spent about $500 million annually making training, military and industrial films with cost saving non-Union actors and non-Union labor.[280] No help came from the government.

With Disneyland-sized lines at the unemployment office, Henry Darrow was especially happy when he was chosen as Grand Marshal of the Wilmington, North Carolina Azalea Festival Parade. Lucy usually didn't accompany her husband to events, but she went with him to North Carolina. Arriving at Wilmington International, she wore a weary smile but was chic and pretty in a white Nehru style jacket and short, layered hair. Darrow was so tired and immersed in frenetic festival activities that he hardly knew she was there.

Sporting Manolito's jacket, white shirt and bandanna, his feet barely hit the tarmac before he was whisked off to perform in the evening variety show. He arrived late to a standing room only crowd. Wilmington took "variety" seriously. Besides Darrow, the show featured Maureen Reagan (daughter of then-Governor of California Ronald Reagan), other TV actors, local celebs, beauty queens, a donkey derby and fireworks.[281] Back to back appearances, performances and interviews made Darrow's time in North Carolina a blur, but he recalls lunch and a kitchen tour at a Greek restaurant. "There was a kid in the back and I signed some photos for him," he says. In Wilmington thirty years later, he met the city's new mayor, Bill Saffo. "Saffo said, 'We met before. Do you remember the Greek restaurant? I was the kid in the kitchen.' You meet all these people in life — directors, producers, film students, fans, other actors, all kinds of other people — then years pass and all of a sudden, there they are again. It's amazing."

278. The Los Angeles Times, by William Endicott, 6/16/71

279. Ibid

280. News article in private papers of Henry Darrow

281. The Wilmington (NC) Morning Star, 4/16/71

Wilmington was charming and people were friendly. He hoped he didn't disappoint or offend anyone. "Everyone was just great, but it was intense and I was exhausted. There may have been moments of not being a good role model. 'Yeah, he was just some jerk Hollywood actor.' When I came back, I asked people, 'Did I behave properly?'"

The local paper said yes: "An observer of Mr. Darrow here on his AF [Azalea Festival] visit said of him that, 'he takes time out to say the good words for everybody from on the Cradle Roll to the Golden Age.' Mr. Darrow, obviously and humanly, holds that all of us from toddlers to trotters are an essential part of the scene."[282]

Meanwhile, in California David Dortort ramped up his campaign to convince NBC that *The High Chaparral* was essential to the TV schedule. But the network's attitude toward him had changed since 1965 when *Bonanza* was a ratings bonanza and *TV Guide* described NBC executives eager to please Dortort because "Top 10 shows are the crown jewels of any network, and...*Bonanza* is the gaudiest—and sometimes the only — adornment in the NBC tiara."[283] *Bonanza* was still a ratings winner in 1971, but NBC had brighter baubles. The most lustrous was innovative *Rowan and Martin's Laugh-In*, featuring Ruth Buzzi, Henry Darrow's funny Pasadena Playhouse classmate, as a regular. Filmed inexpensively at NBC's Burbank studios, *Laugh-In's* manic gags and trendy satire appealed to critics, hip viewers and network accountants. It earned numerous awards, was #1 in the Nielsens for three years running and it wasn't David Dortort's baby. The older NBC execs respected his past accomplishments, but Hollywood is a "What have you done for me *today?*" kind of town.

Dortort was furious over losing *Chaparral* when "it never had a chance" and was "getting better all the time."[284] He aimed both barrels at NBC-TV and charged that the network had committed a "breach of faith" by canceling the show.[285] Then he implored the U.S. Congress to investigate how networks determined which shows to cancel, meanwhile lobbying NBC to put *Chaparral* back on the air. Neither Congress nor the network jumped to accommodate him, but when he asked Henry Darrow to fight for *The High Chaparral*, Darrow immediately agreed.

282. Ibid, *Editorial, 4/20/71*

283. *"David Dortort, "The View from the Top," 6/13/65, quoted on www.ponderosascenery. homestead.com*

284. *The Hamilton (OH)* Journal-News, *1/22/74*

285. The Tucson Daily Citizen, *"Pressure Mounts to Save 'Chaparral' " by R. Kent Burton, 4/10/71*

"I had enjoyed this wonderful part in a series because a producer — David Dortort — believed in me. It opened many doors for me and for other Latinos," he says. "And when David asked if I would do TV and newspaper interviews to promote the show being reinstated, of course I said yes." Shortly thereafter, NBC vice president Fenton Coe invited him to lunch. "He said, 'Henry, David Dortort is doing this for his own reasons. If you continue, this could be held against you down the line, so think about it. Think about how far you want to go with this.' He spoke to me as a courtesy. I thought about it and the message was clear." *Keep it up and you'll be lucky to play Border Policeman Number Three.* "So, I backed off."

However, David Dortort wasn't about to back off. He remembered when CBS axed *Gunsmoke* in 1967 and public pressure brought the series back. Figuring the same could happen for his show, he penned impassioned letters to civic leaders and fan clubs. To Ricardo Montalbán, by then Past President of Nosotros, Dortort wrote, "I sincerely ask that you raise your eloquent voice, and obviously the united voices of NOSOTROS as well, in protest against this evil deed. This is tantamount to spitting in the face of every man with Mexican blood in his veins, and I'm certain that no real man will silently accept that kind of treatment."[286] Dortort cc'd the letter to Gilbert Roland and the new president of Nosotros, Robert Apodaca.

Apodaca wrote NBC president Julian Goodman and politely asked him to keep *The High Chaparral* on the air. "The 10 to 12 million persons of Spanish speaking origin in the United States will have no other programming that reflects their lifestyle or historical background. We ask you to take a step forward with us. Cancellation of '*Chaparral*' is a step backward. We feel in years to come, that this giant step will be applauded by millions of persons in the United States. And we, in Nosotros, will join in that applause...."[287]

Civic leaders in Tucson and surrounding Pima County sounded the alarm over lost revenue. People connected with *Chaparral* spent about $75,000 per week in the area — big money for the time. The show also attracted tourists from across the nation and all over the world who contributed to the local economy. The Pima County Board of Supervisors asked NBC-TV to reconsider ending the series.[288] "We just can't let

286. *Letter in private papers of Henry Darrow, dated 3/11/71*

287. *Letter in private papers of Henry Darrow*

288. The Tucson Daily Citizen, 5/5/71

'*Chaparral*' slip away like this," declared a panicked Chamber of Commerce official.[289]

The outcry grew louder. Robert Shelton of Old Tucson Studios told a reporter that several southwestern governors had urged NBC to salvage the show. Fans inundated the network with postcards and letters.[290] "One of my most gratifying experiences," said Leif Erickson, "was seeing all the mail that poured in to protest the closing of the show."[291]

But efforts, though sincere, passionate and gratifying, were failing. *The News* of Van Nuys cautioned, "Talk of the reprise of *The High Chaparral* on NBC next fall seems to be premature."[292] Eventually, even the most stubborn supporter realized it was over.

When *Variety* announced that *The High Chaparral* would be sold into syndication, it didn't mean big money for the cast.[293] Those who had residuals coming, like Henry Darrow, would be paid for only the first ten rerun episodes. After that, they got the same nothing they got from foreign distributors who were by then airing *Chaparral* in fifty-four countries. But, mortgages had to be paid, kids needed braces or college tuitions, ex-wives expected alimony and working actors want to work.

Cameron Mitchell adamantly reminded everyone that he was a 'name' decades before Buck Cannon came along. "I refuse to knock TV because it's been too good to me," he said. "But there are all kinds of people around who do not remember that I was pretty good in the original version of '*Death of a Salesman*' on Broadway. No, I'll take that back — I was damned good."[294] He waved goodbye to Uncle Buck and scored stage, screen and television credits at home and abroad.

Linda Cristal worked in American and Mexican television and movies, but grew increasingly frustrated with the roles offered to her. She retired again and discovered a knack for making profitable investments. "If what they offer you is not what you enjoy doing, pick something else that you enjoy doing!" she says. "I like money, so I create money and that's very exciting!" As for *Chaparral*, "We all have a span of time to be in the light,

289. The Tucson Daily Citizen, *4/10/71*

290. Ibid

291. San Antonio (TX) Light, *"Leif Erickson Still Going Strong" by A. Michael Avalos, 10/31/71*

292. The News *(Van Nuys, CA), column by Ernie Kreiling, 4/1/71*

293. Daily Variety, *3/30/71*

294. Newspaper Enterprise Associates syndicated column, "He Can't Get Off His Chaparral Horse" by Roger Doughty, 2/21-2/ 27, 1971

but everything has an end. We feel embarrassed when it ends, but why feel embarrassed? The train is coming, get off the tracks and do something else!"

Leif Erickson probably felt like he'd been hit by a train when his son Bill died in a tragic automobile accident. When *Chaparral* was cancelled only a few months later, he didn't feel like smiling, shaking hands, riding in parades or looking for work, but soldiered on. He said the cliché about a series killing an actor's career was false; he had never worked more steadily in his life.[295] Besides acting jobs and public appearances, Erickson and his wife Ann barnstormed the country to promote syndicated reruns of *The High Chaparral*. "We're having a heck of a good time," he said. When Ann chided him after one taping for mentioning Linda Cristal but not Henry Darrow, he quipped, "It's a tough business, but Henry's working and Linda isn't. It's every man for himself, but Linda isn't a man, is she?"[296]

No, but Henry Darrow wasn't working very much. Contrary to Erickson's experiences, Darrow says, "Nobody wanted to hire me because I was too associated with Manolito. The irony is that you want to establish yourself. You want to embed your character in the hearts of your audience, but if you succeed it can keep you from getting other jobs."

Veteran director Raymond Austin agrees. "The sponsors of a show are paying the money. Sponsors don't want people watching their show and Henry Darrow comes on and the people watching have completely lost the advertising message because they are remembering *High Chaparral* or they're trying to recall where they've seen Henry before," he says. "Henry can switch himself to any part, but it's getting through the door. With the network people, the casting directors, they're not seeing the transitional character, they're not seeing someone in the makeup. They're thinking of the past."

Minus TV and movie work, Darrow polished his variety act, made paid public appearances and did freebies for charity. He was active in the Screen Actors' Guild, chaired Nosotros' scholarship committee and performed again in Nosotros' Hollywood Bowl Fundraiser. For some time, he had gone into the East Los Angeles *barrio* to talk with school kids about staying off drugs then realized, "I knew nothing about drugs and I thought, why am I doing this? I'm an actor, I know about acting. So then I started doing theater projects, what's called 'expressive theater', with the kids."

295. The Burlington *(NC)* Times-News, *12/31/71*

296. The San Antonio *(TX)* Light, *"Leif Erickson Still Going Strong" by A. Michael Avalos, 10/31/71*

He was also developing his own TV pilot, *Just Ask Mr. Drivas*, about an East L.A. probation officer. A respected cameraman had signed on, a top screenwriter expressed interest and Mr. Drivas would favor a character viewers already loved — Manolito Montoya. "I have to use the salable points I have," Darrow stated, "and the only one that I have is Manolito."[297]

He hoped NBC would make *Drivas* part of *The Bold Ones*, the umbrella title of several dramas in regular rotation. However, *The Bold Ones: The Protectors* already had a black cop, played by Hari Rhodes. "Black cop or Latino cop, back then they only wanted one," says Darrow. "The bottom line was, there were more blacks in the country." NBC passed on *Mr. Drivas*.

Henry Darrow's masterful portrayal of Manolito Montoya on The High Chaparral *is...the one figure that young men of the widely supported Chicano movement can look up to, can identify with, can root and cheer for. Should we not be grateful that we, rather than another network, enjoy the services of so magnificent a young actor as Henry Darrow, who can produce so much esteem, so much good will for us amongst all the vast Spanish-speaking community, though his charm and appeal transcend even that great group.*

DAVID DORTORT[298]

297. The Fayetteville *(NC)* Observer, The TV Observer, *"Name Change Created New Image" by Nancy Cain 5/8-5/15, 1971*

298. *Letter to Don Durgin, NBC-TV President, 7/13/70, private papers of Henry Darrow*

Consummate Professional

Except for the character actors, very few people survive doing a television series.

DIRECTOR RAYMOND AUSTIN

Determined survivor Henry Darrow says, "I've always been more a character actor than leading man or the Latin Lover." True, but his reputation in the industry really saved his bacon.

Former casting director Susan Sukman McCray speaks for many others when she says, "Henry is the consummate actor and professional. I always knew if he was available and I hired him, I would get the best performance of anyone I could ever hire."

Both artist and craftsman, Darrow was the guy who never used a teleprompter or cue cards because he always knew his lines. He was always on time and never a pain in the rear. His characters were spot-on. In short, he delivered. "There's so much crap out there. I just try to do my best. I want to leave a good mark wherever I am," he explains. "If I replace another actor, I try to be better than. Not just as good, but better — and different." People in the industry remembered and after a slow start, his career took off again.

He gave knockout performances in stage productions like *The Tavern*, *Ping-Pong* and *Sunday*. The only play George M. Cohen wrote for himself, *The Tavern* is a manic, melodramatic farce. Darrow played the lead — a "mysterious, whimsical vagabond" — with "great verve, zest and agility" in a strenuously athletic performance which involved "prancing back and forth across the wide stage, leaping up on chairs and tables — even at one point perching himself on the mantle of the fireplace."[299] Rather than imitate Cohen, Darrow lent "a certain effective charm of his own plus a thoroughly professional approach."[300] *Ping-Pong*, a comedy/drama, centers on a bitter married couple, their lovers and their sexually experimental

---

299. Daily Variety, *"Legit Reviews" by* Mish., *7/10/73*

300. Ibid, *"Legit Reviews" by* Mish., *7/10/73*

son, all of whom arrive at the family vacation cabin on Christmas Eve. Darrow played the father and earned *Variety's* kudos for mixing "suave sophistication with strong will and a vulnerability that arises from not being able to give the proper priorities to his responsibilities as father and breadwinner."[301] Critics panned *Sunday*, noting the "good cast was defeated by the material" — except for Darrow, who starred as an aging bullfighter. He alone transcended the material and played his role to the hilt.[302]

His do-my-best attitude was good for his résumé and his bank account. It led to prominent roles in feature films, but television was his bread and butter. In demand as a series guest star, he worked on all three networks during the 1970s. On ABC, he did *The Mod Squad, The FBI, The Man and the City, The Streets of San Francisco, Kung Fu, Baretta, Gemini Man* and *Vega$*. People watching CBS saw him in shows like *Hawaii Five-O, Bearcats!, Kojak, The New Adventures of Wonder Woman, The Waltons* and *Sara*. At NBC, Darrow was featured on *Primus, Rod Serling's Night Gallery, Chase, The Invisible Man, McMillan and Wife, Jigsaw John, Quincy, Kingston: Confidential, Police Woman* and *The Bionic Woman*. He had the lead or co-starred in series pilots and TV movies *Hernandez, Houston P.D., Brock's Last Case, Hitchhike!* and *Aloha Means Goodbye* and had support roles in *Portrait: A Man Whose Name Was John, Night Games* and *Halloween with the New Addams Family*. He was in the cast of megahit miniseries *Centennial*. Although the odds are against anyone starring in more than one series, he costarred in both *The New Dick Van Dyke Show* and *Harry O*. He played an Eastern European, Hawaiians, Native Americans, a Frenchman, Hispanics and Anglos, criminals, lawyers, doctors, cops, aristocrats, a shopkeeper, an ambassador, a villain who uses massage to ingratiate himself with female victims, a sleazy talent agent and a very lifelike dead man. But his first television role after *Chaparral* was as a Mexican adventurer in 1914 Arizona.

Robert Totten, who had directed Darrow in episode of *Iron Horse* in 1966, still preferred hiring fellow Pasadena Playhouse grads in 1971 when he was tapped to direct the new CBS series, *Bearcats!* Half western, half detective series, *Bearcats!* starred Rod Taylor and Dennis Cole as pre-World War I troubleshooters and in the episode, "Ground Loop at

301. Ibid, *"Legit Review" by* Edwa., *3/5/76*

302. Daily Variety, *"Legit Reviews" by* Edwa., *8/7/79*

Spanish Wells,"[303] they meet swashbuckling biplane pilot Raoul Esteban. Totten thought Hank Darrow was perfect for Esteban.

The episode was filmed partially at and around Old Tucson Studios. On June 30, Darrow was on location and *The Tucson Daily Citizen* announced "Manolito Rides Again."[304] In the heavily nostalgic article, Darrow said, "It was almost like coming home after being away a long time. I look around, expecting any minute to see Cam Mitchell or Linda Cristal or Leif Erickson come walking up and then I realize that all that's over, now. It's done, it's history."

Dashing Esteban, "sort of the *Rojo* Baron," had possibilities of becoming a reoccurring character, but Darrow only played him once more.[305] NBC's runaway hit *The Flip Wilson Show* killed *Bearcats!* in the ratings and it was canned after thirteen episodes.

At the other end of TV's success spectrum was Jack Lord's iconic crime drama *Hawaii Five-O*. By its fourth year, *Five-O* was an established winner for CBS and Lord had an iron-clad reputation for perfectionism. Costar Kam Fong, a cop in the Honolulu police department prior to becoming an actor, described Lord as a "real hard taskmaster."[306] When a speeding car peppered one of the bit players with gravel and made him forget his lines, Lord grabbed his shoulder and snapped, "Concentration, that's what it's all about. Concentration!"[307]

The uncompromising Lord decided immediately whether he liked someone or didn't. If he liked you, you were one of the select. Luis Reyes says, "Jack Lord got along with almost nobody." However, Henry Darrow, who got along with almost everyone, thoroughly enjoyed working with him.

They first met when young Henry Delgado played the Mexican border guard with a surprising command of English on Lord's first series, *Stoney Burke*. Too often, series stars were dismissive if not downright rude to guest stars and bit players, but Lord was congenial although exacting. Since Darrow could out perfectionist nearly anyone and had a knack for making Lord laugh, they worked well together. Later, on *The High Chaparral*, Darrow warmly welcomed Lord when he guest starred on the episode "The Kinsman." Lord appreciated Darrow's hospitality

303. *Original air date Sept. 23, 1971*

304. The Tucson Daily Citizen, *by Don Schellie, 6/30/71*

305. Ibid.

306. The Syracuse *(NY)* Herald Journal, *Associated Press, 1/22/98*

307. *Quoted on www.mjq.net/fivo/ retrieved 3/23/11*

and professionalism and called on Darrow to play an ambitious small-time hood in the *Hawaii Five-O* episode "No Bottles...No Cans...No People."

Darrow guest starred on *Hawaii Five-O* twice more, first as a mob snitch in "Loose End Gets Hit" then as a distraught father whose children are kidnapped, in "The Cop on the Cover." Susan McCray was casting the latter and Darrow was the first person who came to mind.[308]

In "The Cop on the Cover," petite British film star Jean Simmons played a reporter. She had rocketed to fame as a teenager in *Great Expectations* (1946), *Black Narcissus* (1947) and *Hamlet* (1948), but after winning a contract dispute against powerful Howard Hughes she was mostly relegated to supporting roles. Movie critic Pauline Kael called her "one of the most quietly commanding actresses Hollywood ever trashed."[309]

By the time Jean Simmons guest starred on *Hawaii Five-O* she was middle-aged, depressed by the lack of good roles and in the midst of a disintegrating marriage to the formidable director Richard Brooks. She was, however, a gifted and well-regarded actress and McCray says, "I knew there would be nothing to worry about if I hired Henry to be in the same episode with her. They had a great rapport and they complimented each other. Both gave great performances."

"Sue McCray really changed casting on *Five-O*," says Darrow. "Instead of just flying the guest star in first class, she'd offer to fly in the husband or wife and the kids first class as well. Because of that extra touch, she was able to bring in the superstars like Jean Simmons. Jack Lord was thrilled to have Jean on his show. She was very elegant and had a delicate approach and set a beautiful tone."

Darrow and Simmons had the same return flight back to Los Angeles and the airline treated them like royalty. The plane was a Boeing 747 with a first class lounge on the upper deck. Simmons and Darrow had the lounge to themselves, complete with a nice dinner for two. It beat riding the bus to auditions, but when they disembarked at LAX, Richard Brooks was waiting for his considerably younger wife. Brooks wasn't noted for a mellow disposition and fixed Darrow with a deadly stare. After a curt introduction, Brooks ushered Simmons away. Darrow, who generally tries not to annoy renowned filmmakers, exhaled with relief.

308. *Then known as Susan Sukman*

309. The New York Times, *"Jean Simmons Dies at 80; Actress Whose Talent Exceeded the Parts She Played" by Aljean Harmetz, 1/23/10*

Unlike his brief meeting with Richard Brooks, working with Jack Lord was always a treat. Whenever he guest starred on *Five-O*, Lord always followed up with gracious handwritten notes.

What a joy to work with you!
You were, as always, brilliant. Come back soon.

Aloha, Mahalo, luv and peace, Brudda
Jack [310]

And:

Dear Henry,
I am aware of how casual some series people are when it comes to recognizing the contributions of their guest stars.

We are not. Your work was exciting and exceptional. It was valued. It was a joy to have you. You are a consummate pro.

Come back soon.
Love, Aloha and Mahalo,
Jack [311]

"Jack was marvelous!" Darrow exclaims. "He could be sort of a tight ass, but I understood that. If you're starring in a series, your energy is up at the beginning of the season. Then it drags on and the days last fourteen, fifteen, sixteen hours. It doesn't matter if you're on location in Hawaii or where the hell you are. If you're a lead actor, by the time you go home and get up at six to be on the set for eight, you don't have time to study your lines in the new script. You're the star and you're not prepared. There's pressure and you're tired. I like to work under the best conditions and the best conditions are if the star needs to rehearse and wants to run dialogue, I'll do that."

With Lord, the dialogue could change because he liked to change scenes. "Maybe we'd start out with me seated at a desk surrounded by five bodyguards, waiting for Jack's entrance, which was going to be rather subdued. Then Jack would walk in and say no, no, no. The final scene

310. *Letter dated 6/13/71 from personal papers of Henry Darrow*
311. *Letter dated 10/28/75, personal papers of Henry Darrow*

would be me at my desk with no bodyguards and Jack storming in and shaking his finger in my face." Athletic Lord had a unique way of prepping himself for angry scenes. "He did pushups at first to pump himself up. Then later he ran around that huge soundstage until he was short of breath. It gave him energy, force and fire. He would have a controlled intensity when he spoke," says Darrow.

In *Hawaii Five-O*, Lord had an unbeatable formula and knew it. "Jack protected Hawaii on the show and made Hawaii look wonderful," Darrow recalls. "The show was a great commercial once a week for twelve years — wow! That's really something." Other actors in positions of power wanted to interject personal politics, but Lord resisted the temptation. Anthony Quinn didn't. "Tony, when he played the mayor on *The Man and the City*, wanted to do things on Vietnam and other issues important to him. But the networks aren't into political stuff on that kind of show. They just want you to go out and do your guy and leave the politics mostly alone. There are other shows that handle politics."

Filmed in and around Albuquerque, New Mexico, ABC's *The Man and the City* starred Anthony Quinn in the groundbreaking role of a Mexican-American mayor. Henry Darrow guest-starred in the episode "The Handwriting on the Door" as a Hispanic policeman accused of using unnecessary force against another Hispanic; Mayor Alcala (Quinn) faced resulting community outrage.[312] Don Page in *TV Times* called Darrow's performance "exceptional" and "TV Scout" reported Quinn "couldn't wait to get to work in the mornings when they were filming tonight's episode…"[313]

Quinn, a bona fide star on stage and in major films like *Lawrence of Arabia* (1962) and *Zorba the Greek* (1964), was taken aback by television. "You have to walk a tightrope," he told Don Page. "You have to please everybody — the network, sponsors, critics, the cook. It's the first time in my life that I'm standing out there naked. On my own. And my amount of freedom is limited!" Quinn did not accept limitations or measure his success by the low ratings *The Man and the City* fetched. "What is success? What is failure? Who is qualified to judge it?" he asked Page rhetorically. "I'll tell you — I'm the judge of my success. I know best. People don't really know what is good. They're terrified of making a decision. You have to tell them."

312. *Aired on 10/27/71*

313. The Lowell *(MA)* Sun, *10/ 27/71*

"Tony was big and boisterous, loud and dynamic, full of energy," says Darrow, who preferred making his own decisions. "He would change scenes like Jack Lord did and he didn't solicit input. My character was a cop and he was calling the other cops 'fuzz', things like that. It wasn't legit and I told Tony, 'My character wouldn't say that.' So Tony yelled out, 'Get the limo for Henry! He's going home!'" He grins. "But when I got there the next day, he had new dialogue for me." Darrow not only got better lines, he was given the white cowboy hat Quinn wore on the show.

The Man and the City lasted only fifteen episodes, but was nominated for an Emmy and won a Directors' Guild of America award. Jay Rodriguez, a Nosotros spokesman, singled out Quinn as an actor of Hispanic background who "has broken the mold and played a variety of roles." He also named *The Man and the City* as one of two dramatic series which elevated the image of Latinos on television — the other was *The High Chaparral*.[314]

You can be destroyed but not defeated.

ACTOR ANTHONY QUINN

314. The Anniston *(AL)* Star, *"AP Hollywood,"* 1/15/73

Sometimes the Magic Works

When an actor comes to me and wants to discuss his character, I say, "It's in the script." If he says, "But what's my motivation?" I say, "Your salary."

DIRECTOR ALFRED HITCHCOCK[315]

Michael Druxman, Darrow's friend and former publicist says, "Henry will do almost anything and that wouldn't work out for a lot of people. But people meet him and they remember him. That's kept him working." Besides providing a paycheck, exposure and contacts which led to more work, seemingly insignificant projects paid off for Darrow and others in unexpected ways.

Insight was a syndicated anthology series produced under the auspices of a Roman Catholic religious society, the Paulist Fathers. It aired across the country in the wee hours of Sunday morning, just before the national anthem and station sign off. A hit with insomniacs, drunks and shift workers, it ran for twenty-three years, featured established stars as well as young actors and won Emmys for outstanding religious programming.

In the episode "Eye of the Camel," Henry Darrow played the father of a twenty-three-year-old actor named A Martinez. For A, working with Darrow was dream come true. "He was my role model and I was a wide eyed kid just thrilled to meet him," says A. "Being in the acting game, you have occasion to meet people you've admired from a distance and sometimes they disappoint you. That's happened a couple of times, but not with Hank. He gave me good advice about dealing with that kind of actor who thinks the way for them to succeed is to see you fail. He was the coolest."

A Martinez was gifted enough and motivated enough to carve out a highly successful career. "He's a fine man and a fine actor," says Darrow, who worked with Martinez repeatedly over the years.

315. Retrieved on www.wikiquote.org 2/17/11

Unlike syndicated religious shows, student plays and unaired pilots which may bear fruit years or even decades later, a feature film always looks like a golden opportunity for right *now*. Appearances can be deceiving, but Henry Darrow was thrilled to have a shot at a part in a movie starring the famous comedian Bob Hope.

The film was *Cancel My Reservation* (1972) and Darrow was up for a support role as an Indian. So what if Hope's last seven movies were flops? He was one of the best known comedians in the world, a folk legend and wealthy super-patriot who hobnobbed with U.S. Presidents. Known for rapid one-liners, it was said Hope would put on a show for a cigar store Indian, just to be performing.[316] That line that could have been used to describe Henry Darrow, who was ecstatic to learn he would meet Hope at his audition.

In fact, the audition was for Hope himself at the comedian's nine-acre Toluca Lake estate. Darrow was ushered through Hope's rambling home, through the award packed trophy room and into the great room where Hope received his visitors. From the picture window, Darrow had an impressive view of the backyard golf course but he was less concerned with being impressed than making a good impression on Hope.

"I wanted him to see I had a sense of humor," he says. When Hope asked him about his career, Darrow considered Chief Dan George, who was already cast in *Cancel My Reservation* and who had guest-starred on *High Chaparral*.[317] The Chief had also starred in the film *Little Big Man* and Darrow described to Hope the scene in that movie where the Chief lies down to die. "He closes his eyes and Dustin Hoffman, who's playing his grandson, is crying. Then it starts to rain and it hits Chief Dan George's eyes and he blinks and opens his eyes. And Hoffman says, 'Grandpa, it didn't work! You're alive!' And the Chief says, 'Well sometimes the magic works and sometimes it does not.' That's my career, Mr. Hope."

Hope said, "Hey, the kid's got a sense of humor." Then he asked, "So, are you an Indian?" Darrow nodded. "What kind of Indian?"

"Borinquen." Darrow answered.

"Borinquen?" Hope's brow furrowed. "Where are you from?"

"New York," Darrow deadpanned.

"New York!? Wait a minute! Are you *Puerto Rican*?"

"Yeah!"

Hope laughed and said, "The kid's in."

316. Arthur Marx, p. 182

317. He played "Chief Morales" in the episode "Apache Trust"

Darrow was delighted, but unfortunately *Cancel My Reservation* would not be a delight to make or for most people, to watch. It all began when Hope's production company bought the rights for a Louis L'Amour novel, *The Broken Gun*, intending to produce it as a serious western starring a dramatic actor. That kind of intention in Hollywood is the road to Hell. *The Broken Gun* involved an 1870s murder mystery and the twentieth century writer who travels to Arizona to solve it. The book's publisher called it a "blistering novel of action"[318] and with twenty-nine murders and vicious killers in two centuries, it was *not* funny. To turn it into a comedy, Hope hired two writers primarily known for that genre, Robert Fisher and Arthur Marx. Marx recalled telling Hope's assistant that there was no way to turn L'Amour's novel into a Hope vehicle. "It wasn't constructed for comedy and just putting funny lines into the mouth of the main character wasn't going to help. You needed a script that led to comedic situations." He suggested they torpedo the script based on *The Broken Gun* and write an original screenplay better suited for Hope.

The assistant responded that Hope wanted to keep the L'Amour book and, "If you want the job, you'll have to make something out of that pile of shit." Then he warned Marx and Fisher that Hope wouldn't pay until he saw a screenplay he liked. On that happy note, the writers began writing.

Hope liked the finished script and hired Paul Bogart to direct. Bogart (later director of the cutting edge hit comedy *All in the Family*) and Hope argued constantly about what was or wasn't funny. When Hope's *coterie* of outside gag writers gave him lines he liked, he added them to the script over Bogart's objections. Tension on the set escalated when Hope's gag writers came up with "funny" subtitle translations of Chief Dan George's lines, Indian jokes in such bad taste the old man almost quit. Bogart, who was Jewish, was offended by anti-Semitic humor from Hope and Forest Tucker, who played a villain. Keenan Wynn, who played the sheriff, just stayed drunk. Then there was the heat. *Cancel My Reservation* was filmed in the Arizona desert in mid-summer. Poorly insulated metal trailers served as dressing rooms and by late morning, they were ovens. Bob Hope's trailer was the only one with air conditioning.

"It was just amazing," says Darrow. "Hope was taxing. He would keep everyone waiting in the heat. Then there was Eva Marie Saint, the marvelous Academy award winning actress, who was also in the movie. And she *hated* being in it! She hated her wardrobe. She hated her make-up. She hated her hair-do. She and Hope didn't even do their offstage

318. Retrieved on www.amazon.com 2/16/11

dialogue — stand-ins did it. One time I was reading a sequence and they just walked off the set because he was going to play golf with the President. I got pissed and told Paul Bogart about it. He said, 'Hank, Hank, you get an extra two weeks because he's not coming back.' So I ended up getting paid for three weeks work when basically I had a week's work. But it didn't make up for that kind of insult."

Cancel My Reservation insulted most viewers with its stale quips, strained hipness and dreary acting. Critic Pauline Kael called it "a new low." *Variety* dunned the "fumbling plot" as "contrived hokum."[319] Most of the principals "phoned in their performances with forced menace and-or chuckles" and it showed.[320] But Henry Darrow, onscreen for a short time as Joe Little Cloud, the uncle of a girl Hope is accused of killing, effectively underplayed a tense, serious character as if *Cancel My Reservation* had merit.

It didn't have much merit. When it premiered at Radio City Music Hall, Paul Bogart said it was the worst work he'd ever been associated with: "I couldn't imagine this turkey playing in that beautiful theater." Bob Hope and his wife attended the premier and it's rumored that Hope decided then never to make another film.[321]

Henry Darrow went on to the next project. A couple years earlier, he had been in Cincinnati, Ohio substituting for the vacationing regular host on *The Paul Dixon Show*, an early morning TV talk show. The audience loved him and it was a nice change from playing Manolito. He interacted with guests, did impressions, a little singing, some dancing. When he returned to L.A., he brought back a tape of himself strutting his stuff on *Paul Dixon*. Time passed and KNBC-TV in Los Angeles needed a host for a Hispanic variety show called *Bravo*. Darrow showed the producers the tape from Cincinnati and they chose him to host *Bravo*.

"It was a local show, but I got to sing and dance and I enjoyed that. And I used my wardrobe from *Chaparral*, the white shirt with the ruffles and the vest," he recalls. "I looked pretty sharp and there were mariachis and everything. It was shot at Paramount and Bob Hope had a very elaborate dressing room at Paramount. They gave me the use of his dressing room during *Bravo*. Hope ran in one day while I was there. He didn't stay long, but he was friendly. He said, 'Here, knock yourself out, kid' and handed me a bottle of champagne."

319. Ibid.

320. Daily Variety, *by* Murf. *9/20/72*

321. "Jake" IMDB.com *user review, posted 8/1/02, retrieved 2/16/11*

Even before the champagne, Bob Hope was not the most difficult person Darrow encountered during his career. Fifty-plus years of prima donnas, incompetents, egomaniacs and jerks couldn't hold a candle to an actor who was simply very, very quiet.

"Richard Widmark was the most difficult person I ever worked with," he says of the star in a TV project called *Brock's Last Case*. "He just wouldn't talk."

> *Henry can tell stories all night, but he doesn't have to dominate the conversation. He's everybody's friend! He's fascinated by people and amazingly well informed, He can talk about so many subjects. And as an actor, he's very inclusive. He's always eager for feedback: "Now tell me, what needs work?"*
>
> DIRECTOR DOROTHY RANKIN

Brock's Last Case

It's good to shut up sometimes.

MIME MARCEL MARCEAU

Movie, stage, radio and television actor Richard Widmark won numerous awards during his lifetime including Career Achievement Awards from both the Los Angeles Film Critics Association and the National Board of Review. Widmark became a *film noir* star playing mostly villains — hard boiled, cold blooded, psychotic or simply shady characters — although he could also play the hero (in the 1950 Elia Kazan thriller *Panic in the Streets*) and even appeared in an episode of TV's classic comedy *I Love Lucy*. When they acted together in the NBC pilot *Brock's Last Case*, the renowned performer nearly drove Henry Darrow crazy.

A mix of comedy and crime/drama, *Brock's Last Case* starred Widmark, Darrow and Beth Brickell. Several years earlier, Widmark starred in the tough cop action drama *Madigan* and NBC hoped to capitalize on that successful film with *Brock's Last Case*, casting Widmark again as a crusty city detective. This time he played Max Brock, who is sick of policing New York City and retires to a ramshackle California citrus farm where he intends to grow oranges and relax. Instead, he's drawn into a murder case. His ranch manager, affable Indian Arthur Goldencorn (Darrow) has been charged with murdering the sheriff.

Scenes between Darrow and Widmark have the natural flow of two excellent actors. Widmark could hold his own against superstars like Gregory Peck, Burt Lancaster and Spencer Tracy. He and Darrow were well matched as opposites. Although their characters grow to appreciate each other, Widmark remains the salty, dyspeptic New York cop and Darrow's mellow character retains his ironic sense of humor.

One might think Richard Widmark and Henry Darrow would have hit it off in real life. Both men were dedicated actors and basically gentle men who enjoyed playing psychotic villains. Both were intelligent and articulate. Darrow was a political and social liberal. So was Widmark.

Widmark had friends who were blacklisted for allegedly being or associating with Communists during Sen. Joseph McCarthy's career-killing Hollywood witch hunts; Darrow had friends who spoke out against McCarthy and his Uncle Emilio Delgado actually *was* a Communist. Widmark's son-in-law was Baseball Hall of Fame pitcher Sandy Koufax; Darrow is a baseball nut. However, outgoing Darrow is a gregarious talker and an interested listener who can keep conversation rolling non-stop for hours. On the other hand, Richard Widmark preferred silence and was effective at shutting conversation down and other people out.

"He was partially deaf in one ear," says Darrow. "If he didn't want to talk and he usually didn't, you could be sitting right next to him and you could say, 'Dick, what do you think about…?' And he'd just go 'Ehhh?' and push his ear at you. Gradually people caught on, leave him alone. It was hard being with him during breaks because he just wouldn't talk! He always had a book and he would take out his book and put his glasses on and that was it!" The most agonizing breaks involved scenes where the two men were in an old jalopy. Setting the scenes up took time. "You set up the camera, you're moving around, the camera starts, you go and you shoot it from one way, then the other way, and it goes on and on." Meanwhile, Darrow sat in excruciating quiet while Widmark read.

One morning, inspiration struck when he was again confronted with Widmark's stony silence. "I looked at him and thought to myself, I wonder if I can do that? So I kept my mouth shut and didn't interrupt him or bother him." Widmark was probably delighted, but how did that turn out for Darrow? "I got a perverse kind of pleasure from it," he says with a triumphant twinkle in his eyes. "After that, I used it in other situations with people when I was tired or my memory was starting to go or it's the end of the day and I'm beat. I sit by myself and open a book or just sort of close my eyes and pretend I'm sleeping. It does keep people away. I'll tell the assistant director, keep an eye out! I'm out here to get some fresh air. I'm not out here to meet people. If I want to do that, I go somewhere and become available. There's so much junk you pick up from other folks. I would write down on little pieces of paper and stick them in my wallet. Then I'd look at them later and wonder, what the heck *is* this? I never knew, but I'd keep writing it down!" He laughs. "But yeah, Dick Widmark was the most difficult person I ever worked with. However, as an actor, he was a total professional. He gave it his best. He was just as focused and intense during my close-ups as he was during his close-ups. When I later did *Magnum, P.I.* with Tom Selleck, Selleck was the same way. Neither Selleck nor Widmark phoned in scenes."

Brock's Last Case became a little like NBC's version of the pieces of paper Darrow stowed in his wallet. Once the pilot was finished, prospects for becoming a series faded and NBC shelved it. Instead, the network developed a *Madigan* TV series for Widmark which lasted only six episodes. Meanwhile over a year went by before *Brock's Last Case* aired on *NBC Monday Night at the Movies*. Reviews glowed. *Variety* said it was a "smart production" with wit, style and crisp editing. The reviewer additionally commended it for ripping action sequences, "rich humor based on local customs, both eastern and western" and "strong windup" and noted "Henry Darrow comes across especially strong as the easygoing Indian."[322] Darrow hoped everyone would respond as warmly to him as the star of a prospective new series called *Hernandez, Houston P.D.*

> *Success in Hollywood isn't about making money.*
> *It's about survival.*
>
> FILM PRODUCER ED FELDMAN

---

322. Daily Variety, *"Television Reviews,"* by Tone. *3/6/73*

That Offbeat Quality

Henry Darrow is likeable, genuine and sensitive as a Mexican-American police detective.

CRITIC ALAN R. HOWARD[323]

After *The Man and the City*, skittish network execs were reluctant to try a second dramatic series with a Latino star but NBC-TV went forward with the pilot for *Hernandez, Houston P.D.* starring Henry Darrow as a Mexican-American police detective in the eponymous title city. Darrow resigned from the SAG Board of Directors[324] to make time for *Hernandez*, noting the show was in keeping with his desire to see "Americans of Latin ancestry more equitably represented in movies and video."[325]

Entertainment reporter Vernon Scott emphasized Darrow's "tremendous warmth and charm" but noted the public "rejected" Anthony Quinn in a Hispanic starring role the previous year and asked, "Will you, the public, go along with a Mexican-American cop in Houston, Tex., as the hero of a television series?"[326] Actor Raymond Burr (*Perry Mason, Ironside*) who worked with Darrow on *Portrait: A Man Whose Name Was John*, owned the rights to *Hernandez* and apparently thought so.

To appeal to Latinos and everyone else, Detective Juan Hernandez of the Houston Police Department would have "a sense of humor and the style of Manolito Montoya." Unlike Manolito, Hernandez had a difficult mother (played by Spanish actress Amapola del Vando), a brother and only one girlfriend.

Created by TV mystery writer Robert Van Scoyk, *Hernandez* was produced by David Levinson and directed by Richard Donner, all well respected Hollywood "names." A trio of veteran character actors — Dana

---

323. The Hollywood Reporter, *"Television Reviews," p. 8 from Henry Darrow's files, exact date unknown*

324. Daily Variety, *2/20/73*

325. The Long Beach *(CA)* Independent, *"Chicano seek TV breakthrough," 2/12/73*

326. Ibid

Elcar, Ronny Cox and G. D. Spradlin — had supporting roles. Nevertheless, NBC wanted to avoid gambling and possibly losing on *Hernandez*.
The network had a string of top rated shows (*Sanford and Son*, *The Flip
Wilson Show*, *Ironside*, *Adam-12*, *The Wonderful World of Disney*) and liked
it that way. Although minority roles, especially for African-Americans,
increased in sitcoms and variety shows, most dramas still had Anglo stars.
Of course, since most dramatic leads were Anglos, the bulk of cancelled
dramas had Anglo leads. Never did network brass worry that a show failed
because an Anglo lead didn't draw enough viewers. However, when *The
Man and the City* failed to pull good numbers, all three networks grew
concerned. Based on a sample of one, they worried that a Hispanic star
couldn't attract viewers to a dramatic series. To protect itself, NBC didn't
schedule *Hernandez* as a weekly series. Instead, the network decided to air
the pilot once as a "Program Development Project" and see what happened.

Initial reviews were optimistic. *Daily Variety* said *Hernandez* looked
good for a series. The plot was fairly routine, but the "Darrow energy"
raised it above humdrum and the concept of "a Chicano cop deep in the
heart of Texas has mucho going for it if the proper vein is tapped." The
same review noted "great potential in Henry Darrow in the title role"
but warned against making Hernandez too amiable: "Darrow can easily
dominate his characterization without playing Mr. Nice ...the overingra-
tiating bit doesn't do anything for the action."[327] However, *The Hollywood
Reporter* called Darrow's portrayal "humorous, resourceful and courageous
without false bravado" with sensitivity which was "neither coy nor senti-
mental" and gave high marks to the show for warm family relationships
with rare ethnic appeal."[328]

A few days later, *Variety* sniped, "Now ethnicity is all the rage, and
the odd part of *Hernandez, Houston P.D.* is not that the titled detective is Spanish-American, but that anyone should choose Houston as a
dramatic locale." After proving some people in L.A. don't get out often
enough, the reviewer turned favorable attention back to the series and
especially to Darrow. "...[D]espite the potboiler pilot...there would seem
to be a nice place for star Henry Darrow in just such a series. Darrow
has that offbeat quality that seems to be scoring well on TV drama cur-
rently, and he did an excellent job in establishing an intriguing central
character despite a flaccid script." Nevertheless, the same reviewer found

327. Daily Variety, *"Telefilm Reviews" by* Tone. *1/17/73*

328. The Hollywood Reporter, *"Television Reviews," p. 8 from Henry Darrow's files, exact
date unknown*

creator/writer Robert Van Scoyk's grasp of police procedural and Hernandez' "Spanishness" lacking[329] and raised concerns about absence of Latino influence behind the cameras. "Although Richard Donner did a firstrate job with the thin teleplay, a good case could be made for finding both a Spanish-American director and writer to deal with the theme."[330] However, *The Hollywood Reporter* praised Van Scoyk for robust character development and color, called Richard Donner's direction "excellent," complimented cinematographer Bill Butler's "resourceful" use of Houston locations, deemed Ronny Cox "properly menacing" as the villain, noted Jess Walton's "deft flair" as Hernandez' girlfriend and called the casting of Dana Elcar and G. D. Spradlin as fellow cops "off beat and intriguing."[331]

In January 1973, buoyant Henry Darrow was busy promoting *Hernandez* in New York City when the Associated Press interviewed him about the future of Latinos in television. "I think we've been fairly successful in a number of areas," he replied. "Not only in front of the camera but in the arts and crafts. The thing I see is the young performers with talent getting breaks earlier than I did. It took me ten years to star in my first show. That has to be an indication of progress. There is an awareness within the industry. It happened with the blacks. They started getting roles, then their own movies. Well, will it happen with Latin actors?" He was optimistic that it would.[332]

Quoted in the same article, Jay Rodriguez, Nosotros spokesman and community relations manager for KNBC-TV in Los Angeles, noted an increase in Latino executives at television networks and local stations. "In television we're making headway, moreso than in the movies," he said. "Television seems to have more social consciousness than the movies. Many [Latino] people are now getting so-called Anglo roles." He emphasized that *Hernandez*, with its Spanish-American star portrayed as "a hero, a take charge guy," was an important sign of progress.

But some things hadn't changed. Says Darrow, "I was in this celebrity softball league and when one guy on our team learned about *Hernandez*, he became irate. He didn't know I was Puerto Rican. He was critical of

---

329. *Six years later, Van Scoyk won the Edgar Allen Poe Award from the Mystery Writers of America*

330. Variety, *"Television Reviews" by* Mor., *1/24/73*

331. *The Hollywood Reporter, "Television Reviews," by Alan Howard, from Henry Darrow's files, exact date unknown*

332. *The Cedar Rapids (IA) Gazette, "Television's 'Hernandez' Is Putting Henry Darrow Back Where He Started" by Jerry Buck, 1/16/73*

my being in the role, because as far as he knew, I wasn't even Hispanic. Neither was he, but his wife was Mexican so when it came to the show, he felt he had a special right to critique it and my fitness to star in it. He married a Mexican, so he knew what Mexicans were about!"

While NBC decided the fate of *Hernandez*, Darrow was in Cincinnati, Ohio again guest hosting *The Paul Dixon Show*. He told the local paper, if the network gave the go ahead to *Hernandez*, he wanted to be out of town to celebrate. "And if I did not make it, I didn't want to be around to have friends feel sorry for me."[333]

Unfortunately, like *The Man and the City*, *Hernandez* had a doomed time slot. It followed *Bonanza* (in its final season death throes) and pre-empted *The Bold Ones: The New Doctors*, also in its last year. Opposing it were #17 rated *ABC Movie of the Week* and #3 *Hawaii Five-O* on CBS, which left few viewers to watch Henry Darrow thwart crime in H-town. With ratings for *Hernandez* predictably low, NBC abandoned it as a potential series. However, the show captured three awards from Nosotros at the organization's annual ceremony.[334] Albert Dorskind of Universal Studios, which produced the pilot, received a Special Award "as the one person who assisted most in enhancing the image of those of Spanish-speaking origin in the entertainment industry." Universal and its Studio Chief, native Texan Sid Sheinberg, garnered an award for making the "television pilot most beneficial to the Latin image." Creator/writer Robert Van Scoyk received the award for the Best Creation of the Latin Image for a TV Pilot; Henry Darrow accepted the award for the absent Van Scoyk.[335]

The Hispanic community wasn't nearly as pleased with Darrow's next feature film, 1973's *Badge 373*. As for reviews, when they glowed, it was mostly with outrage.

Sometimes I give myself over to a part heart and soul. At other times, it's just technique. There's nothing in particular to say about it except it's work. But I love to work!

HENRY DARROW

333. The Cincinnati Enquirer, *"Darrow's Series Miss Brings No Tears" by Steve Hoffman*, 4/11/73

334. Daily Variety, *"Nosotros Honors Dorskind Et Al," 3/5/73*

335. *At the same ceremony, Darrow's former agent Carlos Alvarado was honored as "most loyal artist representative".*

Badge 373

A few scenes exploring Puerto Rican identity are interesting, like those featuring an immigrant crime boss (Henry Darrow)...but the movie gets lost in one trite cop movie trap after another.

WRITER/FILMMAKER PETER HANSON[336]

The police melodrama *Badge 373* seemed to have a lot going for it. A major release from Paramount Pictures, it was inspired by New York City police detective Eddie Egan, who likewise inspired multiple Oscar winner *The French Connection* (1971). Egan had a small part in *Badge 373* and also served as technical advisor.[337] The producer/director on the movie was respected TV and film veteran Howard W. Koch. Among his credits were films *Come Blow Your Horn* (1963) and *The Odd Couple* (1968) and TV's *Maverick* and *The Untouchables*. Syndicated columnist and bestselling author Pete Hamill penned the screenplay; Hamill had ties to the Puerto Rican community and wrote numerous sympathetic articles, so it was reasonable to assume his screenplay would be even-handed.[338]

Eddie Egan's avatar, hardnosed cop Eddie Ryan, was played by Robert Duvall. Duvall first hit the big screen as Boo Radley in the iconic *To Kill a Mockingbird* (1962). More recently, he had portrayed Major Frank Burns in the big screen hit *M.A.S.H.* (1970) and reaped critical kudos as consigliore Tom Hagen in *The Godfather* (1972). Costar Verna Bloom (Ryan's girlfriend Maureen) had noteworthy stage (*Marat/Sade*), television and movie work (1969's *Medium Cool* and 1973's *High Plains Drifter*) to her name.

Ryan's nemesis, Harvard-educated Puerto Rican crime boss "Sweet William" Salazar, was based upon an actual Harvard educated Puerto

336. *http://every70smovie.blogspot.com/2011/01/badge-373-1973.html retrieved 4/24/11*

337. *According to IMDB.com, "373" was Det. Eddie Eagan's badge number*

338. *Pérez, Richie "From Assimilation to Annihilation: Puerto Rican Images in U.S. Films"* in Latin Looks, *p. 156*

Rican gangster who was doing time in prison. Although incarcerated, the real life "Salazar" still controlled or influenced a number of New York City enterprises. He let it be known that he wanted to be played by a Puerto Rican actor. Since he could have used his clout to pull people off the movie, it made sense to oblige.

Henry Darrow won the part of Sweet William and star billing. It was his first time to play a Puerto Rican character. "I had to work on my accent," he says. "After years of playing Mexicans and of being in California where my friends were mostly Mexican, I spoke faster than Puerto Ricans speak and my speech was also more deliberate; Puerto Ricans take more short cuts. When I went back to Puerto Rico, people would say I sounded *muy México*. I did not want Sweet William sounding *muy México*."

He usually does exhaustive research for a role, but didn't meet with Sweet William in Sing Sing Prison. "Sweet William had protection in Sing Sing, because people always want to off someone in prison who's in a power position. That includes actors like me. It's like, 'Hey, why not? I killed three other guys, I might as well do a celebrity.'" When they spoke by phone, Sweet William seemed like a "fairly articulate, intelligent man" and the idiosyncratic gangster definitely inspired a flashy role for Darrow.

However, Darrow almost didn't make it through filming. In his big finale, the severely acrophobic actor was supposed to climb onto a ledge. "I told the director that I had an incredible fear of heights and I'd be on the ledge but I wanted chains attached to my feet and a net and several other things. By the time I finished telling him what I wanted, he said, 'Okay, Henry. We're going to do something else.'" The sequence was rewritten, moving Sweet William from the ledge to a mammoth shipyard crane. With a little movie magic, a thirty foot ladder doubled the 150 foot crane in the film. For Darrow, the thirty foot ladder was about twenty-nine feet too high. From the ground, he mulled the problem of climbing up while holding the machine gun and crushing anxiety gripped him. "I started to think, 'Let's see…I've got my hand here and I'm holding the gun…' and all of a sudden, I weigh 400 pounds and I can't move."

Director Howard Koch decided to get him going with a bribe. Darrow likes to take his wardrobe with him after a production wraps. He wears clothes from old shows everywhere — dinner with friends, public appearances and in new projects. "I'd go to an interview and I'd get a partial check because I'd use my own wardrobe, which was the wardrobe from some other show. I'm a slob and the only nice clothes I had were from some show I did and in *Badge 373*, I wore three great suits," he recalls.

Koch told him every time he went up the ladder, he'd get a suit to take with him when the movie wrapped.

The first time Darrow went up and down the ladder went fine. Then he climbed up again. "Bam! It started to drizzle, then raining harder. Koch yelled, 'Cut!' and everyone was leaving and going inside. I yelled, 'Hey, I need some help to get down!'"

Someone hollered back, "You can't get down?"

"No! I've got this machine gun in my hand. Send somebody up!" Darrow answered, white knuckled and pelted with cold rain.

One of the stuntmen clambered up and said, "Give me your hand."

"If I could reach out my hand, I'd be down already!" Darrow replied. "I need you to take the machine gun away from me, because I'm not letting go." The stuntman eased the machine gun away and finally got him down.

Darrow says, "So that was another suit. Then they shot a close up of me on a ladder that was about ten feet off the ground, but it was made to look like the top of the crane. It was top heavy and in the excitement I was moving around and I almost fell off. Koch wound up giving me the last suit."

Darrow remembers Robert Duvall was dating a Cuban lady at the time and although he wasn't overly chummy, "Bob was an incredibly hard worker and very engaging. I had good scenes with him. Sweet William was the favorite character of the writer, Pete Hamill, and he gave him interesting dialogue, like in the first scene with Duvall: 'Hey, you guys taught me. I took the lessons to heart. Why should the Italians or Blacks take over my Puerto Rican neighborhood and screw my people when I can screw them myself?' And there was a nice scene by a wishing well with Felipe Luciano, the young terrorist."

Real-life Puerto Rican poet/activist Felipe Luciano had his first screen role as *Badge 373*'s intense revolutionary Ruben Garcia. An East Harlem native, Luciano co-founded the Young Lords Organization, a civil rights and community improvement group modeled after the Black Panthers. Luciano was a proponent of the Puerto Rican independence movement, which had been recently approved by the United Nations General Assembly. Puerto Rican independence was also central to the movie's plot and the young activist took part in the movie because he was promised the opportunity to make a speech in support.

However, in movie making, the finished product can surprise and disappoint even those involved. An actor may have only the broadest sense of the plot, characters and set up for his scenes — "The ship left without you and you know you're going to die" — because movies aren't filmed in storyline order. Scenes at the waterfront are shot together, all the interiors at the police station are shot in a group, all the nightclub exteriors are done on Tuesday, nightclub interiors are shot on the soundstage next month in California. A film editor puts it all together pursuant to the wishes of studio heads, directors, producers or powerful stars, sometimes leaving all of a supporting actor's scenes on the cutting room floor. Sequences may be spliced together — from the car chase, cut to leading lady in the garden, back to car chase, back to leading lady crying in the garden. Scenes can be added after the actors have picked up their checks and gone home. Henry Darrow learned that in the 1950s when the innocuous, low-budget western he'd just finished hit the theaters with added scenes of topless women.

Felipe Luciano's pro-independence speech was filmed at a rally in Central Park. The speech was probably passionate and moving, but when *Badge 373* was released, it was interrupted with a chase sequence and most of it was lost.

The finished movie was definitely *not* pro-Puerto Rican. *The New York Times* critic Roger Greenspun wrote, "All the evil is perpetuated by Puerto Ricans, either innocent but violent revolutionaries who run around shouting "Puerto Rico Libre!" or the uninnocent but equally violent nonrevolutionaries who manipulate them."[339] However, when it comes to evil one could argue that brutal cop Eddie Ryan perpetuates his fair share. He's the type of "good guy" who made many viewers root for the "bad guys." On a bloody quest to find his partner's killer, Ryan shoots unarmed men, terrorizes civilians, spouts bigoted epithets that would have made Archie Bunker blush and has a chip on his sociopathic shoulder considerably bigger than his I.Q. The film's tagline, "A gun in his sock, a tire iron in his belt & no badge" describes his ethics pretty well and Greenspun concluded "unless you care to hate Puerto Ricans (or Irish cops) I don't see how the movie can have anything for you." *Variety* panned it as "ploddingly paced…with racist and fascist undertones."[340] *The New York Times* found "absolutely nothing to praise" about *Badge 373*, "from Howard Koch's helpless direction to the dumpy performances by all the cast" but mentioned "Pete Hamill's screenplay has at least the interest of its overblown prose and its curiously devious intentions."[341] Roger Ebert was in the minority when he complimented it as an "intelligent and

339. 7/26/73

340. Daily Variety, *by* Beau. 7/16/73

341. The New York Times, *by Roger Greenspun, 7/26/73*

thoughtful crime movie."[342] Ebert cited Duvall's portrayal as outstanding, but *Variety* charged that he lacked the "warmth and charisma necessary to make the obtuse, bigoted, ruthless antihero palatable" while praising Luciano ("displayed impressive intensity") and Verna Bloom ("does what she can") as Ryan's girlfriend.

As for viewers, some loved it ("simply, the greatest movie ever made"[343]), but most concurred it was a "clichéd glob of trash". One commented that out of the 2,600 films he had seen, *Badge 373* was "the WORST."[344]

Even though the movie mostly flopped with critics and audiences, both categories either agreed Henry Darrow was the best thing in it or excused him since he didn't write the screenplay. *The New York Times* called Sweet William possibly the worst written role in recent movies, but didn't pan Darrow's acting.[345] On the other coast, Richard Cuskelly of The Los Angeles Herald-Examiner wrote, "Henry Darrow has the unenviable task of making believable a Harvard educated Puerto Rican gangster with a 'Little Caesar' complex."[346] Cuskelly didn't say if he thought Darrow succeeded, but another California paper reported he did: "Henry Darrow… is excellent. We believe him, but don't condone him when he tells why a Harvard educated man has become a gangster."[347] *The Los Angeles Times* skewered the film, but noted the "…good acting…especially from…Henry Darrow as a sophisticated, embittered gangster."[348] *The Hollywood Reporter* eloquently called Sweet William a near miss: "Were it not for Hamill's overwriting, Darrow's characterization might have been extraordinary; his whole body seems to sink behind the cool sunglasses and raincoat he sports to hide the ache of corruption." The same reviewer added that the scene between Darrow and Luciano at the wishing well was "almost" truly moving because both actors transcended their dialogue.[349]

Most of that dialogue belonged to Darrow, because as *The New York Times* critic Greenspun observed, "nobody else can manage much more

342. The Chicago Sun-Times, 7/26/73

343. IMDB.com user review by ianlouisiana from the UK, retrieved 2/12/2011

344. IMDB.com user reviews retrieved 2/12/11

345. The New York Times, by Roger Greenspun, 7/26/73

346. Movie Review "Egan Back on Rampage," 8/3/73

347. Paper unknown, clipping in personal files of Henry Darrow, "Badge 373 continues story of Eddie Ryan" by Dale Harvey, 8/10/73.

348. "Eddie Egan Inspires Another Police Film" by Kevin Thomas, 8/2/73

349. "Movie Review" by Alan R. Howard, p. 3, undated clipping from personal files of Henry Darrow

than monosyllables."[350] This was troublesome for Roger Ebert, who complained that the final shoot out was "marred by all the dialog" Darrow had to remember."[351] One cheeky viewer suggested Duvall shot unarmed Darrow just to shut him up, but added that Darrow was effective as the gangster.[352]

Badge 373 opened at New York City theaters and outrage followed. Robert Taylor of the Oakland *Tribune* presumed Howard Koch and Pete Hamill "must have decided that Puerto Ricans don't go to movies and therefore wouldn't get the chance to be offended."[353] But, Puerto Ricans do go to movies and many were incensed.

Like other contemporary movies with tough guy (Anglo) vigilante/protagonists (and most films in general since the 1950s), *Badge 373* presented only Puerto Rican characters who were viewed as social misfits by the majority of both Latino and non-Latino moviegoers: drug dealers, pimps, crooked cops, prostitutes and gangsters.[354] However, to these omnipresent media stereotypes, the movie added "the image of the discontented, misguided and ultimately ineffective 'revolutionary'."[355] According to former Young Lords member Richie Pérez, in so doing the film criminalized the Puerto Rican independence initiative, making it appear that law abiding, rational Puerto Ricans didn't support the movement.[356] Of course, *Badge 373* didn't acknowledge the existence of law abiding, rational Puerto Ricans in the first place. The Puerto Rican Action Coalition cried foul, labeling *Badge 373* racist, insulting and degrading. Marchers picketed Gulf & Western, Paramount Picture's parent company and there was a call to boycott not only *Badge 373*, but all Paramount projects. In a meeting with Paramount Pictures brass, the Coalition demanded a public apology, withdrawal of the movie from all national and international theaters and formation of a committee comprised of Coalition members to review all Paramount scripts involving Puerto Ricans. Paramount rejected their demands.[357]

350. The New York Times, *by Roger Greenspun, 7/26/73*

351. The Chicago Sun-Times, *7/26/73*

352. *IMDB.com user review by sol1218 (Brooklyn, NY), retrieved 2/12/11*

353. The Oakland Tribune, *"Stage and Screen: Tin Star," 7/20/73*

354. Latin Looks, *p. 75*

355. Ibid, *p. 157*

356. Ibid

357. The New York Times, *"Paramount Tells Puerto Ricans It Won't Withdraw 'Badge 373,'" by Sanka Knox, 8/11/73*

Felipe Luciano and Henry Darrow were hammered for being in *Badge 373*. The Puerto Rican community lambasted Luciano for selling out. Role model Darrow caught more flack for playing Sweet William than for any other part in his career. He held his tongue, but when the media in Puerto Rico attacked him, his mother picked up the phone or her pen and gave them what-for.

"How dare you criticize my son for playing the Puerto Rican mobster! He has played Iago! He has played John Wilkes Booth! Should he not also play that character in *Badge 373*?"

"He was the shining Hispanic star," says Luis Reyes. "And it was a difficult time. It was the time of the civil rights movement and for him to play a Puerto Rican villain in a movie like that was disappointing."

Someone will always be disappointed. "I did *Badge 373* because it was a chance to get into a feature film. My part was just a part for an actor who happened to be Latin," says Darrow. "Sweet William sent word that he liked how I played him. He was okay that his character died in the movie. His ticket was, 'But I didn't die. I'm still here running things.' The lottery, the numbers game, prostitution, the unions — he was still controlling all that from Sing-Sing. Then a few years after the movie came out, I was at a gathering and all of a sudden, I felt this heavy hand on my shoulder and a husky gangster voice said, 'You played Sweet William in 1973? We'd like you to sign three color photos for his nephews.'" At least the people who could have killed him were happy.

> Badge 373 *was kind of here nor there, because the Manolito character was so powerful it stayed with you no matter what he did.*
>
> WRITER/PUBLICIST LUIS REYES

The Next One

You can't go around to the theaters handing out cards saying, "It isn't my fault." You go onto the next one.

DIRECTOR PRESTON STURGES

In September 1973, fans wrote entertainment columnist Dick Kleiner wondering where Henry Darrow, "the Mexican with the fantastic dreamy smile on *The High Chaparral* series," had gone. Kleiner answered that he was "coming back to TV" on *The New Dick Van Dyke Show* (CBS) in a continuing role as the Mexican stage manager. "He is bringing his smile with him."[358]

Created by Carl Reiner, *The New Dick Van Dyke Show* starred Van Dyke as an Arizona talk-show host and Hope Lange as his wife. After decent ratings the first year, it was switched to a new time and the ratings plunged. A three-year contract between Van Dyke and CBS saved the show from cancellation and a complete makeover included adding costar Henry Darrow as station manager Alex Montenez. *Variety* said the revamp paid "handsomely" and emphasized Darrow's "highly competent support" in the opener, a "continual round of hilarity."[359] Episodes which highlighted Darrow's flair for funny jumped the show into the "comic stratosphere."[360]

"It was a nice change of pace for me, but it was competitive," he says. "After a dress rehearsal, we were sitting around and people started doing 'humble stories.' Humble stories are where you make fun of yourself. It's the embarrassing stuff you would never, ever tell except now you're successful and you tell them and it's like, 'Wow, that guy, he's really solid.' Dick Van Dyke and Hope Lange and other very funny people were all doing humble stories — and trying to top each other. 'Oh, no no no. I have one better than that!'"

358. The Columbus *(NE)* Telegram, *9/11/73*

359. Daily Variety, *"Telefilm Reviews" by* Daku. *9/12/73*

360. Ibid

One episode focused on competition between station manager Alex Montenez and TV star Van Dyke. In the initial script, Montenez stole equipment from Van Dyke's show for his own. "I was the only Latino character and I told Carl Reiner, 'Carl, no, this is not going to happen. We're not going to have me stealing.' Instead we did a variety number," he recalls. "The competitiveness between Dick's character and mine was shown through song and dance numbers."

Not long into the season, Carl Reiner had a dispute with the network and left the show. Ratings stayed high, but Van Dyke refused to renew for a fourth year without him.

After *The New Dick Van Dyke Show* ended, Henry Darrow guest starred on the Telly Savalas detective series *Kojak* as cat burglar Kevin Le Jeune in the episode "Before the Devil Knows."[361] In the well scripted plot, crafty Le Jeune and his partner (played by Jerry Summers, formerly "Ira Bean" on *Chaparral*) steal from the wrong man. The victim, a mobbed-up embezzler, kills Le Jeune's partner and hires a hitman to off Le Jeune. Kojak convinces Le Jeune to be bait for the killer. "It was a nice script and a good role and I was able to play it low key," says Darrow. "Louise Sorrel was the embezzler's wife. She and I were in league and she was also trying to double cross me. I had a nice little love scene with her."

Reviews cited Darrow's "capable acting support" and ability to brighten up the scenes.[362] The grudging, uneasy alliance between Le Jeune and Kojak played well on the screen and Darrow had the opportunity to turn the role into a continuing part. He passed. The grudging alliance was real; Darrow disliked Telly Savalas too much to work with him again. "Oh, he was full of himself! And he brought girlfriends to his trailer on the set while we were filming and that was a problem," says Darrow.

Stuntman/actor Denis Lehane recalls Savalas spent time in his trailer with women, but says with a chuckle, "Along with fame comes all those *other* things. I never had any problems with Telly, but I never worked with him. I drank with him. He was a pretty arrogant guy and I can see why Hank didn't think much of him."

Darrow felt completely dismissed by Savalas and it didn't go over well. "Telly had a close up in one of our scenes and had written his dialogue on a sticky note. He reached up and slapped it on my shoulder. He didn't ask, he just stuck it on me. I said no, so he stuck it on the wall behind

361. Original air date 2/27/74

362. Uniontown (PA) The Morning Herald-The Evening Standard, "TV Staff Previews," 8/ 28/74

me and read his lines off of it. Then came my close up and he just walked off and went to his trailer with a girl. His stand-in started to read his dialogue and the guy couldn't read worth crap. I was basically talking to the camera with nobody playing off me, so I asked, 'Where's Telly?' It got quiet and I asked, 'Does Telly not do offstage dialogue or what?' By then, the trailer was rocking and jumping, moving back and forth. They hesitated, but they got him out. I did my close up and Savalas raised his hands, clapped three times and left again. The next day we had a sequence in a pool hall with a lot of dialogue interspersed with a lot of action and before we shot it, Savalas had several martinis at lunch. He didn't know he was messing up his lines over and over again. I could have bailed him out, but I thought, 'Oh, screw you!' He knew I intentionally didn't help him and I was okay with that."

"Then the next day, he came up to me and said, 'Hey Hank, I just wanna let you know I'm not gonna be able to do any offstage dialogue for you. I've got an appointment.' And I said, 'No problem, Telly. Thanks for letting me know.' And I meant it. I'd put in as many years as he had and all I wanted was some respect."

Henry Darrow had respect in spades, plus a full measure of hero worship on his next project. The lead in the TV movie *Aloha Means Goodbye* was Sally Struthers, his star-struck dresser when he was with the Pasadena Playhouse repertory company.

Struthers had worked her way from regional theater to dancing on TV variety shows to feature films to becoming an Emmy winning star on Norman Lear's groundbreaking CBS sitcom *All in the Family* (1971-1978). Playing "Gloria Bunker Stivic" on *All in the Family* made Struthers one of the most recognized faces on American TV. She was totally unprepared.

"I was just another actor who was lucky to have a job," she says. "The first director sat us all down and said *All in the Family* is either going to be thrown off the air tonight or it's going to be the biggest hit and none of your lives are going to be the same. And you know, we hadn't considered it." The negative side of celebrity caught Struthers by surprise as it had Henry Darrow. "People like Henry and me, we're just artists. Our aim was not to be famous, it was to act! The fame came with it. People believe if you wanted to be an actor, you wanted to be famous and you *wanted* the loss of privacy. Well, that's just not true! I learned I could not leave my garbage in my hotel room. I have to carry it out of my room and stash it somewhere myself. Otherwise, people sell it." Now it's to collectors on eBay — back then, it was the tabloid press, eager to make much ado and headlines.

When CBS offered Struthers the lead in *Aloha Means Goodbye*, the rest of the the cast was already chosen, including Darrow. "I said, 'Oh my God! I know him from the Pasadena Playhouse!' No matter how old you get, you always remember that first crush you had on somebody in the career you've chosen for yourself," she says. Darrow was her "first idol worship" when she was a shy Pasadena Playhouse student. "And now I'm starring in a movie with him? It was amazing."

Aloha filmed on the gorgeous Hawaiian island of Oahu. Struthers played a vacationing teacher with the same rare blood type as the son of a desperate tycoon. When the son needs a heart transplant, teacher Sally is the unaware prospective donor. Darrow played the Hawaiian doctor who falls in love with her. The only trouble in paradise was when Struthers she sliced her big toe on a piece of coral. After getting three stitches at the Kahuku Medical Center, the script was changed to eliminate scenes where Struthers was supposed to run. The show went on. Energetic, warm hearted Struthers adored working in Hawaii with Henry Darrow.

"Besides being a brilliant actor, Henry is such a good man. That's not always the case and that makes him even more special," she says. Reporters and fans swirled around both of them and she was especially impressed with his graciousness even when tired and needing to decompress. "He spends time signing autographs and visiting with anyone who says, 'Aren't you…? Don't I know you from…?' You're stared at, you're stopped, some days you feel like an animal in the zoo, but gracious people like Henry never let the person approaching them know that's how they feel. It's a gift."

Darrow had a birthday while they were shooting and Struthers took him out to eat. "That was just thrilling for me," she says. "Even though we were in the movie together and I could've felt we were contemporaries, I was still idol worshipping him. He's the professional I'm going to be when I grow up! So to be able to buy him dinner for his birthday was great."

"Sally is so entertaining and so professional," says Darrow. "I liked working with her very much and I thought back to the Playhouse. *All* the guys were hitting on her. She was very young and it upset her terribly and I told her, 'If you can't take it, go home to Oregon and forget being an actor because it only gets worse.' But she hung in there and has had this wonderful career in movies and being a TV star and then she turned to the stage where she's done well. I'm really glad she didn't listen to me!"

Modern Screen magazine later ran set photos from *Aloha* in an article about Sally Struthers' "last fling" before marriage. The largely fabricated piece misidentified Henry as *Aloha Means Goodbye* co-star "John Darrow" and insinuated he was the "fling." Abounding inaccuracies are a clue not to believe everything you read at the beauty salon. But Sally Struthers' name was spelled correctly, the grainy photos are obviously Henry Darrow and they co-starred on *Aloha*. That made it just the kind of article that friends showed to Lucy's mother. Mrs. DePuy flew into a swivet, then phoned Lucy.

> *After seeing all the dailies and knowing how you ride a horse and have a beautiful smile and all those other nice things, I now have to add one more to the long list: on film you are a great lover (your wife will have to answer to the offstage). It's all there, Henry, and I can only say thank you for making my job so easy.*
>
> PRODUCER SAM STRANGIS
> (*ALOHA MEANS GOODBYE*)[363]

363. *Letter dated 6/28/74, from personal papers of Henry Darrow*

Harry O and Manny Q

I am many things, but I am not a "Milt Bosworth".
HENRY DARROW

Spaghetti Western star Clint Eastwood was an even bigger hit as the violently macho antihero in *Dirty Harry* (1971) and following that film's phenomenal box office, Warner Bros. asked writer Howard Rodman to create a *Dirty Harry*-based TV series. Rodman, who designed *The Man and the City* for Anthony Quinn, gave it a shot. He ended up keeping only the name "Harry." *Harry O* featured Harry Orwell, a jaded ex-cop on a disability pension who did his sleuthing unarmed and traveled by bus. The role was created for Telly Savalas, but he became *Kojak* so David Janssen was chosen for the lead.

Janssen was only twenty-five when he was chosen to star in his first series, the CBS drama *Richard Diamond, Private Detective* (1957-1960). From 1963 to 1967 he starred on the Emmy winning dramatic series *The Fugitive* (ABC) as Dr. Richard Kimble, a doctor on the lam after being wrongly convicted of killing his wife. It was his best-known role for which he received several Emmy nominations and won a Golden Globe. But after four seasons, Janssen was too exhausted to continue. *The Fugitive* ended with a finale which gleaned the highest ratings of any episode in all of TV history up to then.[364]

Like Henry Darrow, David Janssen almost never turned down work. "Oh, you know me," he said. "I'll open supermarkets if they ask…I'm from Nebraska and I feel guilty when I'm not working." He starred in numerous B-movies, had supporting roles in major releases, did commercial voice overs and sound recordings, was a fixture in TV Movies of the Week and starred in the short lived Jack Webb produced series *O'Hara, United States Treasury*. Not the classically handsome hero, Janssen had large ears, a receding hairline and his own quirky charm. He easily projected an

---

364. *It was surpassed 11 years later in 1978 by the "Who Shot J.R.?" episode of primetime* soap Dallas

intelligent, bemused and rather Humphrey Bogart-ish sex appeal. Since Harry Orwell was sort of a 1930's *noir* gumshoe in a 1970s bell bottoms and miniskirts world, Janssen was perfect for the role, but it took two pilots to sell the show.

The first pilot, "Such Dust as Dreams Are Made On," didn't sell.[365] In March 1973 like many unsold pilots, it aired as a TV movie. Audiences didn't like the episode but responded well to Janssen as Orwell, so another pilot was commissioned. Almost a year later, ABC aired the second pilot, "Smile Jenny, You're Dead." Ratings were good (so was young guest star Jodie Foster) and *Harry O* got the green light.

In "Smile Jenny," Clu Gulager portrayed Harry's straight-laced former lieutenant, Milt Bosworth. However, it's often the situation that the actors in a pilot aren't in the series. Creator Howard Rodman and executive producer/director Jerry Thorpe wanted Henry Darrow for the lieutenant and when the show went into production in San Diego on July 23, 1974, Darrow had the part. There was only one problem.

"I told the people on *Harry O*, 'I am many things, but I am not a Milt Bosworth,'" says Darrow. "We decided to make my character Mexican-Irish as a tribute to Tony Quinn, so I had the last name of 'Quinlan'— Manuel 'Manny' Quinlan."

Quinlan wasn't laid-back, but filming the first episode, Darrow felt relaxed. "And near the end, Harry comes up and says something and his tie is loose. Then I walk into the frame and loosen my tie. Jerry Thorpe, the producer, came up to me right after and said, 'Henry, David does that. You're the lieutenant. You're the straight guy.' And that was it. I'm there to be different. I'm the sidekick. There aren't two heroes. There's Zorro…and there's Zorro." He laughs. "He doesn't need competition from his costar. If I try to upstage the star I'm cutting my own throat, so I'm not going to do anything extraordinary unless the star gives me some leverage. Then it'll be in my close-up. In the two shot, I play it straight. You learn the rules and you don't cause problems on the set because if you do, you're costing the company money."

Pranks were another matter. Early on, there was an interview in Balboa Park with Don Freeman, the TV/Radio Editor of *The San Diego Union*. David Janssen had gotten *Harry O* t-shirts for everyone, which he and a number of the crew proudly sported for the interview. Henry Darrow decided to arrive in style. "I got a police escort, with siren blaring and

---

365. *Paraphrase of lines in* The Tempest *by William Shakespeare: "We are such stuff as dreams are made on and our little life/Is rounded with a sleep."*

a limo. Then there was a red carpet rolled out for me to walk on to the table. I arranged for a fishing boat to come by and unfurl a big banner that said, 'Where's Manny Q?' When they let the banner out, several of the crew and I took off our *Harry O* shirts and we had 'Manny Q' t-shirts underneath. David looked at us and said, 'You're all fired!'"

Harry O, said Freeman's article, was "a corking good show," Janssen was "just about perfect in the role" and Henry Darrow was an "asset."[366] Freeman was talking about Darrow's performance, but he also brought Janssen's up. When Janssen was tired, his performance could be too understated and the director told Darrow, "Make him work." "Not necessarily go after him, but just keep my energy level up. The tendency is to lower it, but if I took his tone, the scene was down the toilet and David's stuff wasn't effective," he recalls. "But you pick up the rhythms naturally most of the time."

Most people enjoyed working with Janssen and Darrow ranks *Harry O* as one of the best experiences of his career. "I would sometimes bring my son, Tom, to the set with me. David was always kind to him and Tom became good friends with the kids of one of David's girlfriends," he recalls. "On the set, things were super relaxed. There was a lot of give and take with the crew and practical jokes. But it was professional: David and Jerry Thorpe really cared about quality."

The first day of filming, there was a scene in Manny Quinlan's office. "David said, 'I don't think Henry should be standing over me. He should be seated and I should be standing over him with my hand on his desk.' So it's like, okay, that's begun," Darrow says. He sat at the desk and Janssen listened as he said his lines. Then Janssen made a paper airplane and sailed it at Darrow. Nobody yelled 'Cut!' The cameras kept rolling.

"A few days later, it was *my* turn." Darrow laughs. "When we did a scene at my desk, David would fiddle with my stuff and he'd rip off my paperclips." He chuckles delightedly. "So when he wasn't around, I connected all the paperclips and we started doing the scene. David was fiddling with the paper clips and he said, 'You know, Manny...' then he started picking them up...'Manny...I...uh...'" Darrow's devilish chuckle turns into a belly laugh. "He picked them all up and gave me a look, but he smiled. Nobody yelled 'Cut!' and we just went on."

Variety said *Harry O* had a "screwy style that could be a winner." David Janssen was a "strong lead" and "Henry Darrow as the straight arrow cop should be a valuable regular". As an added bonus, there were no deaths or even gunplay, but "violence wasn't needed to hold interest." All in all, the reviewer applauded *Harry O* as "distinctive property" with a 1930s feel "reminiscent of Raymond Chandler."[367] A large part of 1930s feel and the show's uniqueness came from Janssen's narrative voice-over.

"He was the best voice-over guy in the business," says Darrow. "As Harry O, he'd talk about the case. Tom Selleck did that up in *Magnum, P.I.* and he was very good, but Janssen was more precise."

In a review of the episode "Gertrude," *Variety* noted "Henry Darrow particularly stands out as the police detective" but the show "keeps Janssen, an authoritative actor who knows what he's doing, at stage center." Calling it "Janssen's show," the reviewer stated "he carries the major weight without any sign of strain."[368]

The strain of carrying the show and of Janssen's lifestyle were nevertheless present. He compared starring in a television series to making love to a gorilla, "You don't stop when you're tired. You stop when the gorilla's tired." Only two years Henry Darrow's senior, Janssen's lined face and weary eyes made him look more like a man in his sixties than his forties. Overwork and alcoholism weren't his friends, but they were his constant companions. For years he had employed a driver to take him to and from sets because he was often too drunk, too tired or both to safely drive himself. On *Harry O*, he tried to control his drinking at first and wouldn't break out a bottle until 5:30 in the afternoon.

"That all fell apart within a month or so," says Darrow. "Episode after episode, he was in almost every shot. So, he got tired and stressed and started drinking at 4, then 3:30 and pretty soon he was having cocktails with lunch. Then it was 8:30 in the morning and he was having his Dewar's White Label while I was drinking Coors." When booze and fatigue caused Janssen to slur his speech or otherwise mess up dialogue, he'd hunch and put his head down so his moving mouth was hidden. "That way, when he dubbed his speech or looped it later, it would match. Sometimes if he was just really tired, he'd tell the sound guys, 'Let's get this right, because I'm going to come back to loop it.' They'd pay much closer attention because they'd been warned."

Logistics and expense again ended Darrow's run, although the series survived another year. Filming in San Diego was expensive — guest stars, extras and others had to be flown in and housed. The company constantly encountered problems with the mayor's office and city council over

367. *"Television Reviews" by* Mick. *9/18/74*

368. Daily Variety, *"Telefilm Reviews," by* Tone. *9/12/74*

permits to work a location. If the permit was granted from the council, it was a sure bet someone from the mayor's office would show up and tell them the permit had to come from the mayor — or vice versa. The decision was made to move the show to Malibu. Nobody told Darrow, but he figured it out.

"Wardrobe always knows when you're gone," he says. "The word goes to them, don't do Henry's wardrobe, he's not coming back. It goes around after that. You can tell there's something different. The last few days of this particular week, the way the director treated me was just a little off. People were nice, but they were sort of avoiding me. Everyone knew they were dealing with 'dead man walking.' Then I got a call from my agent and he said the show was moving."

"David waited for me," says Darrow. "We went to a bar and had a drink and he told me what was going on." Manny Quinlan, the San Diego cop, couldn't relocate to Malibu with his freelance gumshoe buddy.

Although he was paid for the whole season, Henry Darrow only did fourteen episodes of *Harry O*. Manny Quinlan was killed off in a dramatic *tour de force* for Darrow called "Elegy for a Cop."

Anthony Zerbe became Harry's Malibu cop friend in the second half of the season and won a Supporting Actor Emmy. Meanwhile, Henry Darrow was again without a steady gig. "David Janssen told me I'd been up for the support role in *Police Woman* with Angie Dickinson," he recalls. "I never read for them, but David told me it was between me and Earl Holliman. Angie wasn't sure who to choose and David told her to go with Holliman. He told her I was too strong, that I would overshadow her."

Very few people knew where Manny was going.
Only people who had to know.

HARRY ORWELL

Always the Heart

You can't stop. My friend Brenda Vaccaro says,
"Oh, doll! You gotta keep moving. It creates a
breeze."

ACTRESS SALLY STRUTHERS

Earl Holliman became Angie Dickinson's macho costar on *Police Woman*. Henry Darrow got some solid guest-star parts, then flew to Oshkosh, Wisconsin where he was the only professional actor in a student movie. Straight-arrow cop Manny Quinlan had a following of fans and one was Robert Jacobs, a first year instructor at the University of Wisconsin-Oshkosh.

Jacobs was teaching a class on cinema techniques when his class decided to make "a movie good enough to compete with the crap we're getting on TV." Yeah! Right on! The young professor wrote a script (*Exit Dying*) and decided to find a Hollywood star for the lead. This wasn't as far-fetched as it seems. Bob Jacobs had an undergraduate degree in cinema from the University of Southern California, a Ph.D. in dramatic art from the University of California-Santa Barbara and contacts in the entertainment biz. He picked up the phone and called an old pal who managed publicity at NBC in Burbank.

"He said he had had just the man for me," Jacobs recalls. "A good friend of his had recently lost a continuing role on a series called *Harry O* and happened to be between jobs. I said, 'You mean the guy who played Manny, the cop?' He said, 'Yeah, man, my buddy Henry Darrow. He just might be interested in doing something for college kids right now.'" Jacobs was thrilled. "I'd been so pissed when they killed Manny that I never watched again."

Soon he was at the airport in Oshkosh to greet Henry Darrow. Darrow stepped from the Air Wisconsin prop plane and fixed Jacobs with "his million dollar smile." A crowd of hundreds had been waiting, too. Seeing Darrow, they cheered. The college band played "Hooray for Hollywood."

The budget for *Exit Dying* was $12,000. People told long-haired, bearded Professor Jacobs it wasn't enough money to make a movie. "They didn't know me, Henry Darrow or this remarkable little town in Wisconsin," says Jacobs, who was determined to prove naysayers wrong. Besides writing the screenplay, he was the producer, director and entire accounting department for the film.

Exit Dying was Darrow's first student project. He gave Jacobs' undergraduates advice on making it in Hollywood and had a blast. Jacobs, who later became head of the film department, became a life-long friend. Although you can't have too many friends, it would be easy to discount Darrow's time in Oshkosh. But that would be underestimating Darrow's influence and the gratitude of talented students.

"Many years passed," says the actor. "I was called in to meet with a vice-president at Paramount. He introduced himself and said, 'Listen, I have a big project in Mexico. Are you interested?' I said yeah and he asked if I remembered him. I said, 'I'll be honest, no.' It turned out he was one of the kids from Oshkosh. He remembered all this stuff I told them and it had helped him career wise. He said, 'Now I'm in a position to pay it back.' Then more decades pass and all of a sudden, I'm doing this program *Pioneers of Television* for PBS and two other kids from Oshkosh, who are no longer kids, are working on that."

Henry Darrow's ability to inspire others punctuates his life and career, but 1977 was marked by the death of a man who inspired and supported him — his father. Enrique Delgado was only sixty-eight when a fatal heart attack finished the job his lifestyle had been doing for decades.

"With the men in my family, it's always the heart," says Darrow. "And the alcoholism stayed in the family. Pop passed it to me and I passed it along to my son."

Henry took his son Tom to Puerto Rico for the funeral. "You hear family lore. 'All the Delgado men are quiet.' Pop didn't talk very much. I'm outgoing in public, but at home, I'm quiet. I talked to my son about that and it led us into good conversations we didn't have before." He wanted badly to be a positive part of Tom's and Deedee's lives. Sometimes, they connected. Tom attended Highland Hall, a private school where classmates were the children of celebrities or celebrities themselves, like the singing Jacksons. Since fame was no big deal at Highland Hall, when Tom played basketball Darrow could watch his son play without causing an uproar. But Tom's nonchalance about basketball and everything else perplexed and worried Darrow. "He never took anything seriously," he says. "A girlfriend of mine had connections at UCLA and could have gotten him into a program there, but he refused to go. Then he decided he wanted to be an actor and asked me to help him. So I said, 'Well, you've got to study and you've got take classes' and he said, 'Nah, I can just go in and play stuff.' He could have had a career as a studio musician and made good money, but he walked away from it. He was very likeable and people gave him opportunities but he just didn't care."

Actor/stuntman Denis Lehane met Tom in 1977 when Lehane and Henry Darrow were shooting the movie *Where's Willie* (1978). "You could tell he was taught some serious manners along the way. He wasn't your typical kid. He acted more mature than he was and I guess that was because of Hank, number one, and his mother, number two." To Lehane, Tom had everything going for him. He was a good looking, personable kid with a boatload of musical talent. "I thought he would have a long, full, happy life."

Neither Darrow nor his friend Lehane knew Tom was already drinking and doing drugs.

"It started through friends of Tom's," Darrow says. Their father was a musician and he did drugs. The kids got into his stash and that opened the door to a lot of bad stuff. He never had the impetus to succeed at anything. He and Deedee had been given a lot by Lucy's parents. Trust funds, things like that. It was going to be that way and that was it. And Deedee is so talented and good at pursuing things, but then she turns against them or loses the desire."

From childhood, Deedee was especially close to her grandmother Delgado. "She wrote a poem about Mom, '*Abuelita*'. That is an endearment, "little grandmother," in Spanish," says Darrow. "Deedee wrote some very nice poetry and she danced very well and had wonderful musical abilities. I thought she would stay with her writing, but she lost the desire." College didn't work out, jobs didn't last very long. Deedee's plans and passions were at the mercy of a restless soul. "It's such a hard life. You try to help but you don't know how. I tried to protect her, but every time Lucy talked or I talked with her, it ended up being a critique or a lesson and that only made her angry." He could help aspiring young actors and actresses, hard luck teens in the East L.A. *barrio* and kids in the neighborhood, but his own children had increasingly complex lives and troubles he couldn't fix.

His liaisons were increasingly complicated as well. He hooked up with women in their thirties with kids, ex-husbands or husbands, stressful jobs and economic pressures. His current mistress was pressuring him to leave Lucy. "I was always clear with my girlfriends that I wouldn't divorce my wife, but she started making demands," he says. "She also had kids with problems and I already had kids with problems."

More and more, affairs introduced new troubles instead of respite from a sour marriage. Meanwhile, in his career he was earning well but frustrated. He wasn't advancing and Les Miller, his agent, wasn't helping him advance. The flamboyant ex-fire eater once had "a good little office" and quality clients besides Darrow like singer Natalie Cole, actor Tom Nardini and an actor son of legendary director Preston Sturges. Then something happened and Miller started losing clients. For years, friends told Henry Darrow to get another agent, but Miller had repackaged outdated 1950s Henry Delgado into groovy 1960s Henry Darrow, hustled good gigs for him, guided him into stardom with *Chaparral*, hooked him up with the fantastic Sweden tour and other lucrative ventures. He stuck with Les. He was the only client left.

> *Well, somebody's gotta save him from hisself.*
>
> BUCK CANNON[369]

---

369. The High Chaparral *episode "The Glory Soldiers"*

Million-Dollar Babe

I have something wrong with my hearing. Never in
my whole life have I heard a woman say 'no' to me.
MANOLITO MONTOYA[370]

Tall Texan Morgan Woodward acted in myriad westerns and didn't look much like the cherub on Valentine's cards. But Woodward made a pretty good Cupid and he didn't use an arrow. He had something better—he had a play.

Part owner of a dinner theater in Midland-Odessa, Texas, he was responsible for casting a production of *The Rainmaker*, a romantic comedy set in a drought-stricken, western town. The plot follows twenty-seven-year-old Lizzie Curry, who keeps house for her rancher father and brothers and considers herself too "plain" to attract a husband. Then charismatic flimflam man Bill Starbuck strides into the Curry's house promising rain for $100. To Starbuck, all women are pretty and through his eyes, Lizzie finally sees her own beauty. A review of the Broadway production describes Starbuck as "a man in whom charm is all, who captivates neither to connive nor corrupt but because he must live in the glow of esteem, and what to do in that case but radiate it oneself?"[371]

When Woodward guest-starred in *The High Chaparral*, he and Henry Darrow became friends. They kept in touch and Woodward had followed Darrow's career with interest. "Hank is a marvelous actor," says Woodward. "And so I called him and asked him to play Starbuck. He said, 'What? You want a Puerto Rican to play Starbuck?' And I said, 'You bet! You're going to be great!'"

Darrow had final approval on the actress chosen to play opposite him. Auditions were in a small theater in Hollywood and he says, "I dressed in my 'Zorro outfit', black pants and shirt, and I did the charming bit. But we auditioned people all day and I wasn't feeling especially suave at the

---

370. The High Chaparral *episode, "Once on a Day in Spring"*

371. *http://www.darrenmcgavin.net/darren%27s_theatre_page.htm , retrieved 5/4/11*

end. Finally we were down to the last three actresses. The first one was quite good and the second was better." The final actress was thirty-two-year-old Lauren Levian, winner of the L.A. Drama Critics Award for her portrayal of Zelda Fitzgerald in the play *Scott and Zelda*.

Petite and pretty with a spirited wit and luminous smile, Levian was described by a theatrical reviewer as having "one of the strongest and most remarkably interesting faces of any young actress I've seen." But the day of her audition, the Long Island native wasn't at her best. Marriage to her long-time sweetheart had breathed a last ragged gasp. Division of community property was the last unfinished business. Meanwhile, Levian and her five cats stayed in the home she had lovingly restored and decorated, knowing it would go to her attorney ex-husband since she couldn't afford property taxes and upkeep on an actor's wages. Performing in one play after another, she recalls, "I was your basic basket case."

The night before her audition, she and a pal from New York partied late. In the morning, she gulped a cup of coffee, read the play, threw on clothes and staggered out the door. "Lizzie is always complaining about being 'plain' and I looked right for the part because I looked awful!"

She knew the man playing Starbuck was a "name" actor, but his name didn't mean anything to her. She never saw *The High Chaparral*; it aired when she was busy working on her Master's in Dramatic Arts. After graduation, she never had time to watch television or go to many movies, so she never saw *Harry O*, Darrow's feature films, TV movies or guest-star parts. But when he walked toward her beaming his dimpled grin, Levian says, "I didn't know who he was, but I knew he was *really* something!"

"I remember she was sort of sweaty," Darrow says. Then she auditioned. The scene was the famous tack room scene:

> Starbuck: *There's no such thing as a plain woman! Every real woman is pretty! They're all pretty in a different way — but they're all pretty!*
>
> Lizzie: *Not me! When I look in the looking glass —*
>
> Starbuck: *Don't let Noah be your lookin' glass! It's gotta be inside you! And then one day the lookin' glass will be the man who loves you! It'll be in his eyes maybe! And you'll look in that mirror and you'll be more than pretty! — you'll be beautiful!* [372]

372. The Rainmaker, *p. 78*

When Starbuck kisses Lizzie, "the bonds of her spinsterhood" break away and Lizzie is at first so shaken that she "collapses on the sacks, sobbing" but soon "goes to him with all her giving." [373] But when Darrow kissed Levian, his lip got caught between her teeth.

"Her eyeteeth had a little gap," he says. "They crossed over a bit, like Gene Tierney's." When she pulled away, she took a piece of his skin along. "The blood was certainly a surprise."

Levian laughs. "How could he resist me after that?" She still thought it was an excellent audition and Darrow agrees.

"She was the best. No doubt about it. She finished her audition and everybody said, 'She's Lizzie.'"

"I thought, 'Ooooh! I'm going to be with this hottie and I'm the only woman in the play!'" she says.

Darrow was scheduled to fly to Hawaii to guest-star in *Hawaii Five-O* and when he returned, would barely touch down before heading to Texas for *The Rainmaker*. With time short, he asked Levian if they could run a few scenes at her house. She said yes and couldn't wait to rehearse with the drop-dead sexy man in black.

She drove a decrepit Toyota, but lived in the West Hollywood Hills, an area with some pricey real-estate. Secluded canyons, lakes, creeks, wild spaces and knockout views of Los Angeles below made the Hills attractive to film and television industry glitterati, artists, nudists, nature-lovers, musicians, struggling actors, drug kingpins and hippies. Roads wound past glamorous estates, communes, derelict mansions, artists' colonies and cozy bungalows.

Henry Darrow wasn't sure what kind of place he expected Lauren Levian's home to be, but he didn't expect a Spanish castle. He double-checked the address. Levian's place had three stories and a turret. He collected himself before striding to the massive door.

When Levian answered his knock, she wondered what happened to the hottie in black. Darrow was there to rehearse and came as himself. "Henry thinks he's adorable no matter what, so he was in a crummy Ban-Lon shirt and these stretchy brown pants that were so old they were shiny. They were kind of stained, with separations and pulls in the fabric. And he had these glasses with big, black frames and a Band-Aid around the nosepiece because they broke. Dorky! He could've been Gomer Pyle. I thought okay, so much for the fantasies, let's just work."

They set up scenes without a script and improvised. "It's not like he had his stuff planned and that was that," says Levian. "He wanted to work well

373. Ibid, *p. 79*

with me and he would evaluate and adjust. That's a sign of a really good actor and he is a truly fine actor." One scene was an argument. Making up dialogue, they charged around the living room into the dining room, around the table and halfway up the stairs. Despite Gomer Pyle duds and geeky glasses, Darrow exploded into fiery, charismatic Bill Starbuck. Levian was dazzled.

Rehearsals finished, Darrow got a tour of the 16-room castle. Built in the 1920s by a famous movie set designer, it was so authentic that a theater group held auditions for *Macbeth* there. To Levian, the very best feature was the view from the high turret balcony. On a clear day, you could see across the valley far below all the way to Santa Monica. She led him up the winding staircase to the turret. "I didn't know he had a problem with heights, so I went out on the balcony. I was describing how amazing it was, thinking he was right behind me. But I turned around and he was plastered against the back wall. I said, 'Come take a look, it's really amazing' and he said, 'Nono. This is fine. I can see it from here.' So he went from hero to nerd. He would've said no to begin with, except he didn't want me to think he was a wimp." Figuring she'd have lots of time on her hands, Levian packed plenty of books for the trip to Texas.

The Rainmaker earned high marks for "thorough professionalism in a comedy as engaging and heart-warming as it is entertaining." Henry Darrow was "flamboyant and articulate…poetic, expansive…" and Lauren Levian gave "a fine portrayal."[374]

"I hadn't considered getting anything going with Lauren," says Darrow, who had taken his mistress to Hawaii with him. "But then we went to Texas. I was sort of separated from my wife and when rehearsals began, oh, my goodness!"

Levian captured his attention onstage and off. After they kissed during a rehearsal, he whispered, "You'd better watch out, because you're going to fall in love with me." She remembers thinking he was going to fall in love with her, too.

"I just felt like he was my person," she says, but wasn't sure exactly how that would work out, since he was "dating heavily." His mistress stayed with him for a long weekend. At a memorable dinner-party, Levian sat on Darrow's right. His hand rested on her thigh. His mistress was across the table from them and he was flirting with the girl on his left. "Then Lucy walked in. He had roses for her. It was just too much," says Levian.

374. The Midland *(TX)* Reporter-Telegram, *"'Rainmaker' at Mansion engaging" by Roger Southall, 6/30/77*

"*He* was too much. I got to know Lucy and really liked her. She confided in me about her problems and I was determined not to be one of them." But when the play ended and they returned to Los Angeles, they kept in contact.

Still, Lauren wasn't comfortable with Henry's crowded love life. First there was Lucy. Then there was his mistress. And finally, after years had passed with no word from stalker turned-mistress Eve Black, he got a letter from her. With the letter were a picture of a little girl and a lock of hair. Eve claimed she had given birth to Henry's daughter and said when the child was six, her husband accidentally ran her over with his car and killed her. It was the first Darrow knew anything about a baby and who knew if the story was true or not, but Eve desperately wanted "Manolito" to make her pregnant again. He hopped a plane for a rendezvous near her home. "When she showed up, she was a mess," he says. "She looked haggard and drugged-out and she turned very hostile. It was an ugly little scene. She was cursing me and yelling at me, 'Just get it done!' I, as usual, was drunk. I tried but nothing happened." Back in L.A., Lucy made it clear to Henry that he wasn't very welcome at home and trouble was brewing with Lauren.

Lauren had moved with her cats and sparse belongings from the castle to a one-bedroom apartment. When she wasn't auditioning or acting, she focused on organizing her life. She decided her relationship with Henry Darrow wasn't working out. A few days after his forty-fourth birthday, she sat him down and told him, "I just can't be with a married man."

He nodded, got up and left without saying a word. Levian was stunned. So was he. "Wow, I couldn't believe she wouldn't be there for me anymore," he says. "I profoundly missed her when we weren't together, so it really upset me. I thought, 'I've got the best game in town and it's goodbye, Charlie? What's up with that?'" Then he took a hard look at his life. "It was awful. I couldn't keep living like that and Lauren was the best thing I'd ever had. I didn't want to lose her."

The next day, Levian answered a knock at her door. Henry Darrow was standing there with a suitcase. She shrugs. "What else could I do? I let him in."

He had quietly gathered his things, slipped away from the house in Sun Valley and filed for divorce. "I didn't play it straight. I didn't have the courage to tell Lucy I was leaving. I just disappeared and that's not good, but Lucy was capable of incredible anger and hostility."

Lucy had about twenty years of rage stored up. She burned or threw out everything he left behind. The divorce and aftermath were acrimonious.

"Her anger was very understandable," says Levian. "I was fortunate Deedee and Tom were okay with me. It was at one of those times when Deedee was mad at her mother, so she adored me. Tom was Tom–'Okay, cool, whatever.'"

Henry was delighted when Deedee and Tom attended the Hollywood screening of G-rated film *Where's Willie*. He starred as the worried father of boy-genius Willie and was especially pleased when his kids gave the movie thumbs-up. "In the movie, the father is proud of his son even though he discourages him from being different than the other kids. That has an element of truth," he says. "The father holds back from praising his son or saying 'I love you.' Too often, parents in real life hold back and miss the chance to praise our kids or tell them we love them."

His focus on family improved relations with Deedee and Tom and he was proud when *Where's Willie* won the Award of Excellence from the Film Advisory Board. G-rated movies were a hard sell, but there was talk of a sequel or a TV series. Darrow says, "*Where's Willie* wasn't a great film. They shot out of sequence. The dog in it would be small in one scene, big in the next, then small again. The director was a TV director and he shot *Willie* like TV show. But the movie gave you a good feeling and it was entertaining. I would've been happy making a career out of G-rated movies. You can do a lot with them."

Shot in Kerrville, Texas, *Where's Willie* premiered in nearby San Antonio. When Henry and Lauren came to Texas for the premier, Henry's not so G-rated life was there to meet him. His most recent ex-mistress was around and suddenly, Eve Black appeared. Their last disastrous tryst hadn't dimmed her obsession with "Manolito" and she couldn't stand seeing him with Lauren. Eve offered him a bribe. If he ditched Lauren, she would put a million dollars into a movie just for him.

He told her no.

With Lauren, I sort of straightened my act out.

HENRY DARROW

What A Performer!

Henry Darrow...is a casting agent's dream, handsome enough and macho enough to be a love interest, a villain or an executive. He has the chameleon ability to blend into any role he is given.

RANA GOODMAN[375]

"I was the last client Les had," Darrow says. "It got to the point where we just yelled at each other. I finally said, 'No more. This is it.'" Lester Miller became the only gourmet chef, oenophile, ex-fire eater, ex-hypnotist, ex-talent agent, Chinese opera buff driving a taxi in Los Angeles.

Henry Darrow's new agent had clawed his way up from New York City's Lower East Side to Hollywood's bright lights where he became one of the biggest big time agents. In earlier decades, tireless Mr. Bigtime was perpetually on the phone and on the move promoting the people he represented. The rapid fire wheeler dealer built a client list that read like *Who's Who in Show Business*. He seemed like just the ticket to ramp up Henry Darrow's career.

There was just one problem. Mr. Bigtime and his other clients were so well known, he didn't need to hustle anymore. People called *him*. "He didn't need to sell his stars, he just waited for the phone to ring," says Lauren Levian. "That's what he did with Henry. He waited for the phone to ring. He did nothing to promote him."

Darrow had a part in the blockbuster miniseries *Centennial* (1978), but when he got to the hotel his hotel room wasn't ready. "It was still dirty and the manager told me I'd have to wait. I told them, okay, I'm going home." They cleaned and he stayed. He had one line.

He had a much more prominent role in the Puerto Rico-made film *Isabel La Negra* (1979), released in the States as *A Life of Sin*. Based on

375. The San Fernando Valley *(CA)* Herald, *"Say: Aren't You?"* 9/2/81

legendary madam Isabel Luberza Oppenheimer, a woman of color born into dire poverty who amassed great wealth and power, *Isabel* showcased Puerto Rico and Puerto Rican talent. The stars were striking veteran performer Miriam Colón as Isabel, gifted up and comer Raul Julia as her protégé and Henry Darrow as a reporter. Support players included José Ferrer and Miguel Ángel Suárez. Besides the powerhouse cast *Isabel* had impressive talent behind the cameras and featured beautiful cinematography, but hardly anyone saw it. After a gala premier in Guaynabo, it played a few film festivals and limited run engagements in Puerto Rico and the States, then disappeared from theaters. Although the film was a commercial failure, Clara E. Rodríguez later noted it was interesting as "one of the first films to address issues of race" among Latinos.[376]

Darrow next starred as a youth counselor in a feature film from Universal Studios, *Walk Proud* (1979). Leads in the star-crossed love melodrama were teen heartthrob Robby Benson as a reluctant Chicano gang member and Sarah Holcomb (*Animal House*, 1978) as his rich Anglo girlfriend. Twenty-three-year-old Benson, already a seasoned pro, turned in a good performance and there were a number of outstanding young Latino actors in support roles, including Pepe Serna (*Scarface*, 1983) and Trinidad Silva, Jr. (TV's *Hill Street Blues*).[377] However, the movie sparked outrage in the Hispanic community for having blue-eyed (he wore brown contact lenses), Jewish Robby Benson in the lead and for being yet another "gang picture".

Casting a known "name" won't ensure film success any more than casting a "nobody" dooms a movie to Floptown (1976's blockbuster *Rocky* starring previously unknown Sylvester Stallone is but one example), but Universal wanted an established box office winner in the lead. When the Mexican-American community learned Universal chose Benson, protests began. Other actors were suggested, like soulfully handsome A Martinez, but the studio claimed there were no young, Hispanic hotties with enough horsepower to carry the film.

Besides displeasing Mexican-Americans with a non-Hispanic lead, *Walk Proud* was one of four movies about youth gangs released in 1979. *The Wanderers*, set in 1963 and centered on an Italian gang, won accolades for its insightful coming-of-age storyline. Cinematographically impressive, *The Warriors* was an urban desolation fantasy which had mixed reviews, spawned violence at cinemas and generated a cult following. Innovative *Boulevard Nights*, set in contemporary East Los Angeles, had

---

376. Heroes, Lovers and Others, *p. 182*

377. Variety, *"Film Reviews," by* Har. *5/16/79*

a groundbreaking mostly Latino cast and set a standard for later films dealing sensitively with *barrio* life. On the other hand, *Walk Proud*, a throwback to gang movies of the1950s, had no cutting-edge elements to spark interest. This did not make good box office, especially since *Walk Proud* was already in Dutch for casting choices. Between peaceful protests and riots at theaters, film distributors walked away from *Walk Proud*, but being in the film was wonderful for the young Latino support players.

"The industry was in flux at that time," says Luis Reyes. "There just weren't many well-known Latino actors in their teens and twenties. *Walk Proud* and the other gang movies were major studio releases and they gave us a way to break into films and *become* known. We joined SAG. One guy put himself through college working as an extra, others who started out in those films went far as actors." Reyes, a New York City native with a B.A. in drama,had a small part as a gang member and remembers, "When filming started, we all wondered who had been cast as the youth counselor, Mike Serrano. We found out it was Henry Darrow and it was like, 'Oh, wow! Manolito from *High Chaparral!* He'll be great!' We all admired him and when we met him, he was everything we'd hoped he'd be–very generous, very kind, very supportive of young talent. He'd say hello to everyone and shake hands. He's a very serious actor, he knew what to do and how to do it and he was very, very good. They'd call action and he was *there*. When he found out I was Puerto Rican from New York, we talked and became friends. It was amazing."

Darrow was happy to nurture new talent, but needed more work and his agent Mr. Bigtime wasn't bringing it. His new agent, Alan Goldstein, was Mr. Bigtime's polar opposite. "He was a hustling agent," says the actor with a laugh. "He set me up for stuff I was right for, stuff I was wrong for. It didn't matter. He'd send me out." An agent after Darrow's own heart, Goldstein told him to do anything and everything. "And I did."

He hit gold with memorable TV and theater roles while working in a dizzying number of commercials, feature films, documentaries, indie films, straight to video movies, pilots, theater, public appearances, game shows, soaps, series and miniseries. As star, guest-star, costar, narrator, host and "voice of," he played uptight bureaucrats, lawyers, doctors, gangsters, cops, a Spanish *conquistador*, priests and ministers, judges, a Vulcan, revolutionaries, Zorro, a Native American, the owner of a whorehouse, a politician, a farm worker, a hero's father, an alcoholic archeologist, Don Juan, a Hawaiian cowboy, an incestuous father and a magician. He sang, he danced, he cracked jokes, he jerked tears, he brandished swords, monologues, guns and gavels and he acted, acted, acted. Nosotros took note and in 1983, Darrow won a Golden Eagle Award for consistent outstanding performances by an actor.

As always, his consistently outstanding performances ran the gamut. He guest-starred on hit TV series, moderately successful TV series and flops: *Secrets of Midland Heights* (CBS), *B.J. and the Bear* (NBC), *The Incredible Hulk* (CBS), *Simon & Simon* (twice, CBS), *Quincy, M.E.* (three times, NBC), *Dynasty* (ABC), *Hart to Hart* (ABC), *Trauma Center* (ABC), *Tales of the Gold Monkey* (ABC), *Dallas* (twice, CBS), *Jennifer Slept Here* (NBC), *Scarecrow and Mrs. King* (twice, CBS), *The Fall Guy* (ABC), *Airwolf* (CBS), *Cover Up* (CBS), *This Is the Life* (twice, syndicated religious drama), *Knight Rider* (NBC), *T.J. Hooker* (three times, ABC), *Easy Street* (NBC), *Ohara* (ABC), *Star Trek: The Next Generation* (CBS) and *The Golden Girls* (NBC). Roles were created especially for him in at least two series, *Magnum, P.I.* (CBS) and *True Confessions* (syndicated anthology series).

He co-hosted *Jackpot Bingo* (1985), the first bilingual game show in the U.S. and had continuing roles in three major daytime dramas. One was long-running top tenner *General Hospital*, which cast Darrow as a revolutionary leader in a summer storyline. *GH* hired many young Latinos for that storyline, including Rick Najera. Najera was from San Diego, California and grew up in a solid, working class family where watching *The High Chaparral* was a weekly event. To the young actor and aspiring writer, Henry Darrow was the hero he never imagined he'd ever meet, much less work with. "I remember driving up and wow! There was Henry holding court with all these Latino extras. He must have had every extra on the lot around him," Najera says. "It's like I became a kid again when I saw him! I was just flabbergasted and honored to work with him. We were in a scene together and he didn't break a moment. I was impressed. Then I got to meet him and talk to him and I was impressed with him as a person. He was a gracious gentleman, just pure class."

Darrow became a mentor and father figure to Najera, who was stunned by the older actor's skill. "Henry even brings a soap opera to a higher level. I couldn't believe it. What a performer!" Najera quickly realized he had to tighten up to keep up. "I used a teleprompter. Henry didn't use a teleprompter. *He was live!* He'd force me to be on my best game. If I wasn't, I could feel it coming, a lecture and a lesson. I loved working with him. If you're an okay actor, he's going to make you good. If you're good and you're acting with Henry Darrow, he'll make you a great actor." Najera became so fascinated watching Darrow, he says, "I became the audience when I was onstage with him. It's odd, but he's got this very hypnotic way of performing and he takes you into his world. He will force you to join his reality."

Darrow captured the attention of viewers in made for TV movies like hard hitting, fact based *Attica* (1980). In *Attica*, he co-starred as New York politician Herman Badillo. The first Representative of Puerto Rican descent in Congress, Badillo was on the team of outside observers tasked with resolving the bloody prisoner riots at Attica State Correctional Facility. Shot at Lima State Hospital for the Criminally Insane, *Variety* said *Attica* was "compelling," "a brilliant study in manipulation," "startling drama" with fine acting throughout.[378] The gritty film was nominated for several awards and won an Emmy.

While not award winning, *St. Helens* (1981) was an "interesting… entertaining"[379] fictionalized version of events surrounding the 1980 eruption of Mount St. Helens in Washington state. It starred Art Carney in his last screen role as Harry Truman, the grumpy eccentric who refuses to leave the mountain. Henry Darrow costarred as rule-bound, rather slimy head geologist Lloyd Wagner.

Darrow played a considerably more admirable character in the fact-based PBS *American Playhouse* production *Seguin* (1982). As Don Erasmo Seguin, mayor and quartermaster of Bexar, Texas, Darrow was again the father of A Martinez, in the lead as patriot Juan Seguin. Directed and written by executive producer Jesús Treviño, *Seguin* was a "skilled production"[380] about the San Antonio born *Tejano* hero who helped Texas establish independence from Mexico, became a senator in the Texas Republic and two term mayor of San Antonio, was forced into exile in Mexico by hostile Anglo settlers, fought for Mexico in the Mexican-American War and later pardoned by Gov. Sam Houston, finally returned home to San Antonio. *Seguin* won excellent reviews. *The Sacramento Union* called it "a knockout" with a "remarkably talented cast" including Martinez, Darrow and Rose Portillo, who played the wife of Juan Seguin.[381] *The Sacramento Bee* described the "stirring" performances in an outstanding drama.[382] *The San Jose Mercury* noted the "searing drama," was "superbly made," "powerful," "thought provoking" and crucial for understanding contemporary

378. Daily Variety, *"Telefilm Reviews" by Tone.*, 3/4/80

379. Daily Variety, *"Telefilm Reviews" by Reed*, 9/24/81

380. The Sacramento Bee, *"Drama May Be Latino 'Roots' by Dean Huber*, 1/26/82

381. The Sacramento Union, *"Today's TV" by Jim Carnes*, 1/26/82

382. The Sacramento Bee, *"In Focus: Drama May Be Latino Roots" by Dean Huber*, 1/26/82

cultural conflicts.[383] Following its debut on PBS, *Seguin* has been shown in classrooms as a part of American History curriculum.

"*Seguin* had legs," A Martinez says. "People came up to me years later and they saw it through some non-traditional means and it's very important to people in the Hispanic community." Making *Seguin* was a career highlight and he treasured the special jacket Henry Darrow loaned him. "It was this amazing waist-length leather coat with beautiful inlay on the lapels. He just showed up with it and volunteered it to me. I had my picture taken in it and it was a big part of the image promoted all over the country."[384]

While *Seguin* was filming, plenty of people in the area recognized Henry as Manolito Montoya. Actor/stuntman Denis Lehane, who grew up in Kerrville, Texas, first met Darrow when they worked on *Where's Willie*. Friends since then, they both worked on *Seguin* and Lehane says, "I rented a Lincoln sedan to drive to the location at Ft. Clark Springs and I'd pick Hank up. All the other actors and stuntmen were riding shuttle busses from the San Antonio airport. But we showed up in the Lincoln and when he got out, about fifty Mexicans in the swimming pool started with "Manolito! Manolito!" And I got out of the car and they started yelling, 'Blue Boy!'" Other than his eye and hair color, 6'3" Lehane doesn't look at all like Mark Slade. "So, they're calling me 'Blue Boy' and I'm saying, 'No, no, no.' And Hank said, 'Just shut up and wave at them. Let's *go*.'"

Lehane started out in Hollywood as a wrangler and spent a lot of time around horses. Watching Darrow mount up during *Seguin*, he said, "Hank, I can't believe you still can't ride worth a crap. You were a lead on *High Chaparral* and you say you didn't have stunt guys doing your riding, but you really can't ride very well, can you?"

Darrow said, "You're right. Let's go for a ride to the other side of that hill and you can refresh my memory."

"The next thing I knew, he looked like he'd been riding all his life," Lehane says, then adds, "But I had to keep telling him to put his weight in his stirrups."

Although the setting was rural there were no horses in the modern day saga *Los Alvarez* (1983), a TV pilot made with more hope than money. Luis Reyes wrote the screenplay about a Chicano farming family in the

383. The San Jose Mercury, *"Television: Searing drama probes the life of Juan Seguin"* by Ron Miller, 1/26/82

384. Fans of The High Chaparral *might have recognized it as Manolito Montoya's jacket.*

Salinas Valley and Henry Darrow played the father in the multigenerational *Waltons*-ish Alvarez household. "I wanted to show Hispanic talent in a true manner and try to give meaningful insight into Mexican-American culture, but I didn't have the credentials," Reyes says. "Without Hank, we couldn't have done it. He was supportive all the way through. He was wonderful as Juan Alvarez and his name helped us get the investors." The budget for *Los Alvarez* was still only a miniscule $30,000; Reyes was producer and director. Filming wrapped in four days, but it took almost three years before *Los Alvarez* finally aired. When Reyes tried to sell it, agents and syndicators said the show was "too ethnic."[385] KHJ-TV in Los Angeles eventually ran it in prime time as part of their *Cinco de Mayo* programming after Reyes trimmed it from fifty-five minutes to thirty. In spite of first effort production weaknesses, *The Los Angeles Times* praised *Los Alvarez* for "emotional impact" and *Variety* stated it "scored some worthwhile points, especially through the solid performances of Henry Darrow (as the strict but loving father) and Tony Acierto (as the undisciplined devoted son)."[386] For presenting *Los Alvarez*, KHJ-TV won an Outstanding Community Service Award from Nosotros.

One of Darrow's movies, the independently produced sci-fi flick *Beyond the Universe* (1981) probably had an even smaller budget than *Los Alvarez*. Others were better funded, both direct to video releases (*In Dangerous Company*, 1988 and *L.A. Bounty*, 1989) and feature films. Movie roles took Darrow to South Africa (*Birds of Paradise*, 1981) and Mexico (*The Mission — Kill*, 1987) and he got good reviews ("...solid credit...," "Especially good..."[387]) for playing a Tijuana lawman in *Losin' It* (1983), a teen sex comedy starring Tom Cruise, Jackie Earle Haley and Shelley Long. *Losin' It* was released just after *The Outsiders* and before *Risky Business* (both 1983) and Cruise was a pleasant looking young guy rather than the matinee idol he was in *Top Gun* just two years later or the mega moviestar he became. Another perpetual New Kid whose family moved constantly, Cruise recalled never having the right shoes, clothes and accent for whatever town or school he was in. *Losin' It* was his first starring role.

"He was a nice, kind of bland kid, but a very hard worker," Darrow recalls. "He got to the set on time, did his job well and left." He could

385. The Los Angeles Times, *"The odyssey of 'Los Alvarez'"* by Rick Du Brow, week of 5/1-5/7, 1983

386. Daily Variety, *"Telefilm Review"* by Bier., 5/9/83

387. Variety, *"Film Reviews,"* by Har., 4/13/83

relate to Cruise's diligence. A master of persistent staying power, the Tijuana policemen in *Losin' It* was one of a long string of lawman roles for Darrow, who later played his 100th law enforcement officer in the psychological horror flick *The Hitcher* (1986) starring Rutger Hauer.

Henry and Lauren were seldom together in movies or television shows, but they often acted together on stage. In 1981's *The Queen and the Rebels* (directed by former *High Chaparral* producer James Schmerer), Darrow played the deceitful interpreter and Levian was the prostitute who dies helping the queen. In the metaphorical musical *The Fantasticks* (1982), he portrayed the show stopping mystical Trickster/narrator El Gallo; Lauren, in white face, mimed The Wall.

Los Angeles had nothing like "off-Broadway," but equity waiver theater (ninety-nine seats or less) had "become a respectable outlet and it's not uncommon to see Henry Darrow doing the preem of a new show in a theater that holds only about 60 in the audience."[388]

"I love theater audiences. They charge me up," says Darrow, who certainly never does plays for the money. "With equity waiver, nobody was paid at first. Later, they'd give you enough to buy gas. But major directors and producers went to see equity waver plays and that was an avenue to paying jobs." Equity waiver and other small theater venues also gave a versatile actor like Darrow a showcase for his talent. This was never truer than in productions like 1984's *Corridos*.

Corridos was crafted by Luis Valdez, the son of migrant farm workers who formed *El Teatro Campesino*, a theatrical troupe of and for migrant workers. His first major work was the play *Zoot Suit*, about the infamous Sleepy Lagoon murder and the young Chicanos who were wrongfully convicted of the crime. *Zoot Suit* debuted onstage in Los Angeles in 1978, was later the first play by a Chicano director to hit Broadway and in 1981 became a well-received feature film. Brilliance and early successes like the smash film *La Bamba* (1987) earned Valdez favorable comparison with Orson Wells. Later in life, he became widely respected as the father of Chicano theater.

Like Luis Valdez' other works, *Corridos* drew from the rich heritage of Mexican-Americans. Arising from the folk song tradition of Mexico, the ten ballad anthology expressed the tragedy, comedy and violence of human existence through tales of love, hate, envy, death, sensuality and sex. Henry Darrow, as the folksy Maestro of the Ballad, led the audience from one segment to another, introducing each in time, place and

388. Daily Variety, *"Spotlight on Legit,"* 1/7/77

mood. A "marvelously unifying force," he provided clever insights and "sly commentary" on selections.[389] In "Delgadina," the most dramatic and "especially touching selection," he stepped out of his affable Master of Ceremonies role and was "chillingly effective" as a tortured father whose incestuous desires cause his daughter's death.[390]

"Then Luis Valdez decided he wanted to get up and be on stage," says Darrow. "They let me go immediately instead of giving me two weeks' notice, but they still had to pay me for two more weeks. One of the reviewers wrote, 'as far as Mr. Valdez' acting, he should stay behind the lights.' I was so *glad*." Smug, he chuckles and adds in a poofy, effete tone, "You know, *theatre* is supposed to be honest and direct and that's baloney. It's as cutthroat as anything. Even harder to take, because there's four weeks of rehearsal, all the performances, so much work!" But Darrow's profound theater jones had him starring onstage soon as time allowed and a good project presented.

The Young Lady from Tacna (1985), a tale about the capriciousness of memory and how stories evolve, was written by Peruvian Nobel Laureate Mario Vargas Llosa and produced by the Bilingual Foundation for the Arts, founded by respected actress/activist Carmen Zapata. The play was performed at the BFA's Theatre/Teatro, a building Zapata had transformed from its previous incarnation, the Lincoln Heights jail. Darrow co-starred as Belisario, a writer who delves into the history of his family and discovers the fluidity of time and recollection. "I have a gesture I use a couple of times as Belisario that I got from Paul Muni. Anyone who remembers him will notice the times I gesture to my head as I talk about memories. Muni used it when he played Louis Pasteur and also when he did Juarez," Darrow told *The Hollywood Reporter*, clearly pleased with the play. "There is one scene with kissing in it. You can hear the young members of the audience giggling. That's the feedback an actor loves.[391]

Much as he liked hearing giggles from kids in the audience, in those days Darrow's favorite roles were *uber* heavies: Iago in *Othello* and Judas Iscariot in *Family Portrait* (also one of Gregory Peck's best roles). Yet, he was happily at home in the plays of George Bernard Shaw. *Don Juan in Hell* was his 1987 Shaw; he starred as Don Juan.

389. The Hollywood Reporter, *"Drama-Logue: Theatre Reviews,"* by D. Larry Steckling, 10/18/-10/24, 1984

390. Ibid

391. *"Drama-Logue: Henry Darrow: Under Influence of 'Young Lady From Tacna',"* by Joan Crosby, 6/6 -6/12, 1985

After Hell came *Godman*, Rick Najera's first play. "It was a role I saw for him," Najera says. "I approached him about doing it, because he was a mentor, but to tell you the truth, I never thought I would get him for one of my plays. I thought he would be hard to get in every way, not available for the time or for the money. But Henry honestly liked my plays."

In *Godman*, Darrow starred as a widowed, alcoholic archeology professor who travels to the Chiapas region of Mexico to steal artifacts. Because there is a revolution going on, no outsiders are allowed except priests and medical workers, so the dissolute professor pretends to be a priest. The villagers accept his ruse and treat him as if he was a priest. "He goes from charlatan to truly a priest, a miracle man," Najera says. "So it had religious overtones. The reviewers loved Henry, but they didn't like the Christian meaning in it."

But audiences responded and *Variety's* Frank Nanoia called Darrow "one of our most prestigious performers" and said his performance was explosive. "He's such a fine screen and TV actor…Sure wish he was in another series so we could watch him every week!"[392]

It wasn't for lack of trying. A couple of pilots died on the vine (*Rooster*, 1982; *100 Centre Street*, 1984) and aired as TV movies. He costarred in two short-run series, playing a police lieutenant in *Me and Mom* (ABC, 1985) with Lisa Eilbacher and James Earl Jones and cowardly con artist Indian "Lost Robe" in *Born to the Wind* (ABC, 1982). *Born to the Wind* may have been the most unusual western ever aired. Storylines focused on a band of Plains Indians in the days before the massive westward migration of whites and it featured Native American actors. The lead, Will Sampson, was of the Creek Nation and co-star A Martinez has a mixed heritage of Mexican, Apache, Piegan Blackfoot and European. Native Americans in prominent support roles included Dehl Berti, Linda Redfearn, Geraldine Keams and Nick Ramus. Those who watched *Born to the Wind* remember it as good, culturally sensitive adventure a cut above most programming. As Lost Robe, Darrow played the father of A Martinez for the third time.

More significant, Darrow starred in two Zorro projects, a cartoon for CBS in 1980 and in 1983, the series *Zorro and Son* (CBS). He made television history both times.

392. Daily Variety, *"Under Arturo's Mustache"*, *4/15/88*

A frequent question that I've heard is, "Why haven't you made it bigger?" My answer is that I've worked every month since April of 1981 and in the acting game if you get to work every month without being in a series as a regular you're doing quite well.

HENRY DARROW[393]

393. *Undated press release, files of Henry Darrow*

There's Zorro...
and There's Zorro

As Diego, I pretend to be afraid, but with a mask
as my disguise, I ride into the night and raise my
sword in the name of justice, for I am Zorro.
OPENING VOICE-OVER BY HENRY DARROW
(*THE NEW ADVENTURES OF ZORRO*)[394]

Variety once called Zorro the "do-gooder of all time."[395] The enduring superhero has been fighting injustice in Spanish Colonial California ever since 1919, when he appeared in the pulp magazine serial "The Curse of Capistrano" by Johnston McCulley. Zorro, the original Caped Crusader, was the inspiration for modern superhero Batman and influenced other dual identity superheroes, for El Zorro ("the fox" in Spanish) is wealthy Don Diego de la Vega's secret identity. Through decades of movie, radio, television, *telenovela* and literary incarnations, Diego has played the fop, inept swordsman and effete intellectual to hide the truth–he is also Zorro, mysterious masked defender of the helpless and downtrodden against the vicious and venal.

If you happen to be helpless or downtrodden, handsome Zorro is definitely the guy to have on your side — expert horseman, swordsman, marksman, hand to hand fighter, nimble with a whip, amazingly cunning, stealthy, intelligent and scientifically astute. Of course, Zorro makes the ladies swoon while Don Diego leaves them unimpressed.

Generations of little boys wished they could be Zorro. Unlike most of them, Henry Darrow was working his way up to that. Tati Delgado playing "Zorro" in the streets of New York became the kid transfixed by Tyrone Power's silver screen swashbuckling. By the late 1950s, he had grown into young Hank Delgado, the over actor who lost a reoccurring

---

394. *Quoted in* Zorro Unmasked *by Sandra Curtis, p. 159*

395. Daily Variety *3/31/83*

villain role in Walt Disney's *Zorro* starring Guy Williams. In 1974, he was the mature actor who auditioned for Zorro in the TV movie *The Mark of Zorro* and lost out to Frank Langella. However, it's hard to keep a good swashbuckler down and in 1981, he buckled his swash and auditioned to do the voice of Zorro in *The New Adventures of Zorro*, a new cartoon from animation giant Filmation Studios.

The animated half-hour series would run on CBS-TV's Saturday morning line-up as part of *The Tarzan/Lone Ranger/Zorro Adventure Hour*. Dapper Fernando Lamas was supposed to voice Zorro, but bowed out due to scheduling conflicts. [396]

"I still almost didn't get to do it," Darrow says. He auditioned for producers Lou Scheimer and Norm Prescott, animation industry pioneers and co-founders of Filmation. "When they took my tape to the network, CBS said, 'No, no, no! The way you say '*Buenos noches, señorita*' is much too suggestive for a kids' cartoon.'" Back in the studio, Scheimer told him to read as before without as much expression. "I prepared for the role by watching Saturday morning cartoons. There's a particular sound to all voices on cartoons, a sort of brightness. That's because you rarely tape with another actor there. You sound like you're talking to yourself because you *are* talking to yourself. You just come in, do your stuff and leave. If you have much inflection in your voice, other actors won't know it when they read and they won't match it. When your lines and theirs are put together, it won't sound like you're talking to each other unless you dial it down."

The New Adventures of Zorro ran thirteen episodes as part of *The Tarzan/Lone Ranger/Zorro Adventure Hour*. When bored *hidalgo* Don Diego becomes Zorro to battle tyranny in and around Pueblo de Los Angeles, he's assisted by his faithful horse Tempest and young sidekick Miguel (Julio Medina). Villainous Capitán Ramón (Eric Mason) and dumb bunny sergeant González (Don Diamond) pursue him to no avail. At the end of each episode, Zorro craftily teaches viewers about Californio history and culture.

The series made TV history. It was the first cartoon with a predominantly Latino cast — Darrow, Medina, Christine Avila (Maria), Socorro Valdez (Gov. Gen. Garcia), Carlos Rivas (Don Alejandro de la Vega) and Ismael 'East' Carlo (Gaspar) and the first time Zorro was played — or in the case, voiced — by a person of Hispanic descent. Two years later, Darrow was not just the voice of Zorro, he *was* Zorro. In fact, he was the first *and* the second Hispanic Zorro. It only took him a little over four decades to get there.

396. Daily Variety, 7/6/81

Western spoofs on the silver screen could be big box office. Oscar nominated *Cat Ballou* (1965) won 10 other major awards and was nominated for twelve more. Mel Brooks' satirical western send up *Blazing Saddles* (1974) was nominated for three Oscars, won two other major awards and ranks sixth in the American Film Institute's list of top 100 funniest films of all time. But television audiences weren't historically receptive to western themed comedies; ABC's *F-Troop* (1965), a sitcom set at an Old West fort, was a hit with critics but a loser with viewers and lasted only two seasons. Besides being unreceptive to Old West TV sitcoms, the public usually doesn't lampoon superheroes. An exception was Twentieth Century-Fox's film *Zorro, the Gay Blade* (1981) starring George Hamilton both as Zorro and Zorro's flamboyant gay twin. It earned Hamilton a Golden Globe nomination, but reviews were mixed and the film was only moderately successful. However, TV sitcoms and light adventure shows packed the Nielsen Top Thirty and when CBS-TV got together with Walt Disney Productions to make a new Zorro series, the network wanted it done as a sitcom.[397] The result was 1983's *Zorro and Son*, a limited run, midseason replacement.

Zorro and Son revolved around middle aged Don Diego/Zorro and Don Carlos, his swinging, college aged son. Diego/Zorro has lost some of his zip, so he convinces Carlos to help with the Zorro-ing business. Incredulous then awed to find his old *papacito* is dashing El Zorro, Don Carlos reluctantly dons the mask and joins the action, but he's a modern *caballero* determined to cut Zs his own way. Disney thought they had a sure winner.

The studio tried coaxing Guy Williams out of retirement, but he was serious about Zorro and didn't want to do a sitcom. However, top Latino actors of a certain age (except for Ricardo Montalbán who was starring on ABC's *Fantasy Island*) were falling all over themselves for the part. "It was the best shot at a series I'd had in a long time," Darrow says. "I told Lauren, 'If I can't do this, there isn't anything in this town I can do.'"

Darrow interviewed at Disney for the casting director and the producer, Eric Cohen. They liked him and asked him back to audition at CBS with one of the actors vying for the part of Don Carlos, Paul Regina. A handsome man of Italian, Puerto Rican and Mexican heritage, Regina was in his early twenties and had Eric Cohen's backing. Cohen, who was responsible for casting John Travolta in TV's *Welcome Back, Kotter*, felt Regina had attitude and star quality similar to Travolta. "At CBS, we auditioned for Peter Baldwin, the director and Kevin Corcoran, the

397. The Legend of Zorro, p. 74

producer," Darrow recalls. "Paul knew his dialogue by heart and I had most of mine down and we just hit it off. They liked my style and they liked his. I had bursitis and bad feet and they said, 'That's great. You're perfect for Zorro.'" Cast as over-the-hill Zorro, Henry Darrow was the first Hispanic of nineteen actors to portray the character in live action. The cast also featured veteran Latino character actors as the heavies — Gregory Sierra as villainous Capt. Paco Pico and Richard Beauchamp as Pico's lamebrained *segundo*, Sgt. Sepulveda. Zorro was assisted by his faithful sidekick Bernardo, played by Hungarian-American comedian Bill Dana (best known for his "José Jiménez" character) and magnificent black horse, Toronado.

"Greg Sierra is among the finest actors I've ever worked with," Darrow says. "He's one of the few men who ever upstaged Peter Sellers, during a scene they had in *The Prisoner of Zenda*. And Bill Dana, most people know him as a great comedian but he's also an excellent writer of comedy. On *Zorro and Son*, he wrote very funny stuff for me and then he'd play my straight man."

Darrow's stunt doubles were also tops. For tricky horsemanship, his double was second generation stuntman Jerry Wills, who worked on *The High Chaparral* and *Zorro, the Gay Blade*.[398] For especially athletic fencing scenes, George Marshall Ruge doubled Darrow; Ruge was previously George Hamilton's double in *Gay Blade*.[399] Darrow said it wasn't hard to tell when it was Ruge in the scene and not him: "In those scenes I look much slimmer and move much faster."[400]

Since *Zorro and Son* was produced by Disney, they used some of the sets and costumes from the old series. "I never realized how tall Guy Williams was until they brought me his costume to wear. They had to take it up because he was three inches taller than I am," says Darrow. "I thought it was great. I had Guy Williams' outfit and I told Peter Baldwin I was stealing Douglas Fairbanks' entrance. I wanted to be cocked and seated on the banister, back against a wall or beam like Fairbanks. Then a guy looks up and says 'Who's that?' and all the peasants shout, 'It's Zorro!'"

398. *He was the son of Henry Wills, a stunt coordinator, stuntman, actor, writer and second unit director on* The High Chaparral

399. *Ruge was later Duncan Regehr's fencing opponent when Regehr starred in the Errol Flynn TV biopic* My Wicked, Wicked Ways *(1985), and stunt coordinator for feature film series* Pirates of the Caribbean *(2003, 2006, 2007, 2011) and* Lord of the Rings *(2001, 2002, 2003).*

400. The Honolulu Star-Bulletin, *"The Return of Zorro (and His Son, Too!)," AP Los Angeles, 3/30/83*

"There were legit fencing scenes, a nice father son relationship, great one-liners, pranks and slapstick," he says. He would turn fifty that year and could relate to Zorro's resistance to jumping off balconies ("If God wished us always to jump, why would he have given us stairs?") and swinging from chandeliers (In one scene, his foe Capt. Pico snarls, "I could not help but notice when we dueled that the Spirit of Freedom has bursitis."). "There was even some adult humor. In one episode, I tell my son how Zorro suppresses lustful thoughts: 'Son, I keep thinking about freedom and justice. But if that doesn't work, I just put on the outfit, hit the bars and score like a bandit!'"

"Henry is like a boy set loose in Toyland," Paul Regina told one reporter. "He's playing Zorro for all it's worth."[401]

"I thought it had everything. It was corny, but it was fun corn," Darrow says. He also felt dignity was a given because of Zorro's intrinsic nobility and emphasized this aspect when he talked to *The Los Angeles Herald*. "I very much wanted the series to have dignity even during the slapstick comedy scenes — dignity was the bottom line…Everyone is in agreement and I couldn't be more pleased with that or with the fine ensemble cast and production people Disney selected for the project." As for material possibly demeaning for Latinos, he said, "My background gives me some latitude in dealing with scripts. I can point out what might be offensive and, more today than in the past, people in the industry are willing to listen."[402]

Darrow conferred with Emmy winning comedy writer/producer Garry Marshall. Marshall said the show could work if generational conflicts between Zorro Sr. and Zorro Jr. were played for laughs, but warned, "It's mush if they make fun of Zorro."

The writers, director and producer should have talked with Garry Marshall. They made fun of Zorro. When *Zorro and Son* premiered April 6, 1983, *Variety* first called it a "[d]isturbingly banal extension of the Zorro legend" with "thin material that cries out for Mel Brooks' fine tuning', but noted "…Darrow, Regina and Dana are superior…"[403] A later review commended Darrow as "properly dashing and aching for the senior Zorro" and gave high marks to Regina and Sierra but dunned the series for lack of a "stronger satirical cutting edge."[404]

401. Gannett Westchester Newspapers, "Radio & Cable Week," 4/17/83

402. "TV People" by Frank Torrez, "TV's newest Zorro brings 'dignity' to a slapstick comedy," undated, from private papers of Henry Darrow

403. Daily Variety, "Telefilm Reviews" by Tone., 4/6/83

404. Variety, "Television Reviews" by Bok., 4/13/83

The Hollywood Reporter was kinder to show, but not to TV audiences which were deemed too dim to get the "quick one liners…" since those "take some concentration to catch — a trait not shared by many home viewers."[405] Michael Druxman, Darrow's publicist at the time, has probably never been called dull-witted and says, "Hank would tell me about the scripts. He's a marvelous storyteller and he had me on the floor laughing. Then I saw the show. It was terrible!"

"Paul Regina didn't want to be typecast. That's something you see in young actors," Darrow recalls. "He was worried that *Zorro and Son* would cause him to be typecast, so he didn't want the show to be a big deal. And I thought to myself, 'Oh, God, Paul! What you want to do is work! You *want* to establish yourself! Typecasting is when you have succeeded in embedding your character into the heart of your audience."

Regina needn't have been concerned about being typecast as Zorro Junior. There weren't enough viewers for that. When the Nielsen ratings came out, *Zorro and Son* was second to last. It vanished after five episodes, but you can't keep a good superhero down. Five years later, another Zorro project was in the works.

Gary M. Goodman and Barry Rosen, producers with New World Television, struck a deal with Zorro Productions, Inc. to do a new Zorro series. With John Gertz of Zorro Productions as creative consultant, the group began casting the pilot for *Zorro: The Legend Continues*.[406] Goodman and Rosen approached Henry Darrow about playing the bad guy, the *alcalde* (mayor) of Pueblo de Los Angeles. At the time, Darrow was playing a continuing character on daytime's *One Life to Live* and had other projects in the works. "The alcalde would have been interesting, but the money wasn't quite there so I turned it down," he recalls. "My friend Val de Vargas ended up with it. He had the right look."

De Vargas, a screen veteran with intimidating black eyebrows and menacing scowl, faced off against a young Zorro played by Patrick James. James was dark and athletic looking, but lacked experience and wasn't first choice. Among others, a dashing Canadian actor named Duncan Regehr had been seriously considered for Zorro, but Regehr wasn't available because he was starring in the miniseries *Earth Star Voyager*.[407]

405. *"Televisions" by Richard Hack, undated, from files of Henry Darrow*

406. *From* Zorro Unmasked, *quoted on http://zorrolegend.blogspot.com/2010/07/new-world-zorro-dvd-set-bonus-feature.html retrieved 5/19/11*

407. Zorro Unmasked, *p. 169-70*

In the pilot, Zorro's real-life persona was still an aristocratic dandy, but this time he's Antonio de la Cruz, who dons the mask after Diego de la Vega is killed. In the dual role, Patrick James lacked European refinement as de la Cruz and didn't have sufficient flamboyance as Zorro. The pilot was mostly drab-o except for a sparkling performance by Patrice Martinez (then billed under her married name, Patrice Camhi) as Antonio's feisty fiancée.

John Gertz thought the pilot was humorless, miscast and excessively violent. Would-be financial backers agreed. Funding for a series came up short and *Zorro: The Legend Continues* was shelved. Goodman-Rosen Productions reconnoitered for another crack, this time addressing Gertz's concerns.[408]

Meanwhile, Henry Darrow was deeply concerned with balancing his life. "My involvement in my career was so encompassing in the past that my personal life was adversely affected," he said. "I'm trying to gain a closer relationship to the people that I care for."[409]

They are wonderfully compatible, but Lauren is the glue in that relationship.

DIRECTOR DOROTHY RANKIN

408. Zorro Unmasked, *quoted on http://zorrolegend.blogspot.com/2010/07/new-world-zorro-dvd-set-bonus-feature.html retrieved 5/19/11*

409. *Undated press release, files of Henry Darrow*

A Room Full of Roses

Padre, where are my pants?

MANOLITO MONTOYA[410]

Henry lavished attention on Lauren in his own way. His own way didn't include kitty litter boxes. As a sideline, she had opened a ritzy pet shop called Fabulous Felines which specialized in purebred cats and he says, "I thought I would come in and hang out and drink champagne with my fancy Hollywood friends, but then she handed me a pooper scooper. There went my fantasy!"

"I guarantee, he never scooped even one litter box," she says. "Henry is *not* a worker bee." Fortunately, he has other ways of making her feel loved. "He's a real gentleman: the kind of guy who opens the door for you, the kind of guy who stands until you sit down. And he's very romantic!" Lauren smiles broadly. "He brings me flowers for absolutely nothing. It's Tuesday, here's a bouquet. He tells me he loves me all the time and he's very affectionate and expressive. He holds my hand in public, which seems like nothing, except I wasn't used to that." People in her family were not physical and as for speaking their feelings, they didn't. "It's not that people didn't have feelings," she says with a laugh. "But it was like, 'Okay, I love you. I've said it. Memorize it.'" Getting accustomed to warmth and romance was easier than making peace with Henry's wardrobe.

Not long after he moved in, items he brought with him started vanishing. "I had clothes that I used to wear at the Pasadena Playhouse, stuff like old sweaters with holes in them, bell bottom pants, some kind of silky shirts and stretch pants. I had some work out pants Lauren called 'the goldos', because they were originally yellow. I wore them for everything until she told me I couldn't wear them anywhere. It was like 'Oh, my goodness — you're right.' Then I was unable to find things. I'd say, 'Hey, L? Remember my blue sweater, the one with a couple of holes that I sewed up?' She'd say, 'I think it's gone. I think you got rid of it.'" He wasn't buying that. She

---

410. The High Chaparral, *"A Joyful Noise"*

didn't know then, but he never got rid of anything even if it was old enough to vote and held together with nothing but optimism. Sure enough, she'd applied a little cunning to the problem of Henry's sartorial non-elegance. "She had quietly and without my knowledge, gathered up my clothes and put them in the trunk of her old Toyota and then she sold the car. After the guy took it home, he called her and said, 'Hey, you got some old clothes in the back. Do you want to get them?' Lauren told him, 'Look you got a great deal on the car — keep the clothes or the deal is off.'" Henry laughs.

"It wasn't just the age and disrepair of the clothes. They were completely inappropriate for where he wore them," she notes. "Most of his clothes came from the wardrobe department of shows he'd done. He'd wear see through shirts that he got when he played bad guys, total Vegas sleaze, just no taste. Purple pants just weren't a problem to him. He'd wear stuff like that when we went out to dinner. Around the house he'd wear his swimsuit and then guess what he didn't have when we went to the beach?" Before long, she was head of the household wardrobe department. "That was fine with Henry, because he didn't have to do anything. He's like 'oh, you're going to handle that? Great!'"

Although Lauren quickly realized her man wasn't a fashion plate, she had no real grasp of his celebrity status until the first time they traveled to South Africa. Television had only made its debut in that country in 1975, but by 1980 syndicated American shows had viewers glued to broadcasts from the South African Broadcast Company (SABC), the only TV station. The nighttime soap *Dallas* was the most popular show in the country, but *The High Chaparral* was strong in second and Henry Darrow was one of the presenters for the SABC's annual Artes Awards. Thousands of fans waited for his plane to land at Jan Smuts Airport in Johannesburg and when Lauren saw the crowd, she was stunned. "I felt like I was with one of the Beatles! I couldn't believe it. There were people holding signs, throwing things, trying to cross the barricades, screaming 'Henry! Henry! Manolito! Manolito!'" People wanted his autograph or to touch him or just get a glimpse. He was mobbed by little girls who liked his smile, boys who thought he was terrific and women who liked the way Manolito made love. A local reporter interviewed a young mother trying to cross police barricades who said, "He's brutal, kind, sensuous. He's got everything. He's just my kind of man."[411]

Lauren says with admiration, "When there's a crush of fans, Henry is always pleasant. I wouldn't be anywhere near as gracious as he is."

411. *Undated news clipping, files of Henry Darrow*

"Yeah, and he's quite a character," says Denis Lehane. "When we were doing *Where's Willie*, we were at this place on the Riverwalk in San Antonio — Hank, me and Hank's son Tom. The waiter comes up to us and he's shaking like a leaf. He looks at Hank and he's in awe. He's stuttering, 'A-a-are you w-w-who…a-a-are you w-w-who I think you are?' And Hank looks at him and says, 'If you think I am, I am!'"

Of course, most of the time, they recognize him as "Manolito! Manolito!" Several years after *Chaparral* ended and several years before he met Levian, Darrow was dining in the same New York City restaurant as actor Michael Douglas. The son of legendary film star Kirk Douglas, Michael Douglas was not yet a major movie star, but he was co-starring with Karl Malden in ABC's police drama *The Streets of San Francisco* and well on his way. He was seated with stage and screen actress BarBara Luna (who had guest starred on *Chaparral*) and group of people from Sweden. Suddenly, the Swedes spotted Henry Darrow. So what if they were at the table with Michael Douglas? They were in the same restaurant as Manolito! The Swedes were beyond excited. This was before Darrow guest starred on *The Streets of San Francisco* and Douglas had no idea who he was. Luna clued him in and Darrow recalls, "He sent her over to my table to tell me that this group from Sweden was thrilled to see me."

Being recognized as Manolito was handy when Darrow was shooting a movie in Mexico and lost his passport: after much fanfare, Mexican officials waved him through to the U.S. "Mr. Manolito has been very, very good to me," he observes. When he and Lauren returned to South Africa to shoot *Birds of Paradise* (1981), a French farce starring Darrow and the late Marti Caine ("Britain's clown queen of comedy"), Mr. Manolito rode along but it was Mr. Darrow who galloped to Lauren's rescue.

Lauren had a support role in the movie and while filming a scene on a day when Henry wasn't working, she plummeted from a twelve-foot high platform on the set. A desk below broke a potentially fatal fall to the concrete floor. "I bounced off the desk and onto the concrete, so I was pretty much a mess," she says. "I was screaming, which made me happy because I knew I was still alive." The movie people notified Henry while an ambulance carrying Lauren streaked to the nearest hospital. It was a crowded, understaffed public facility and she was on a gurney in the chaotic emergency ward when Henry arrived. "I'm in a lot of pain and he comes through the doors and everybody who's taking care of me starts screaming, 'It's HIM! It's HIM! It's MANOLITO!' They all left me and mobbed Henry to get autographs."

After quickly working the crowd, he phoned the movie company and unleashed unshirted fury for inadequate safety on the set. "A guard rail could have prevented the whole thing and a lawsuit was definitely possible, so the movie people were terrified," Lauren says. "They did everything they could to calm him down and take really good care of me." That included a transfer to a swank private hospital where Lauren had a private room overlooking beautiful gardens and wine with her meals.

Darrow is never a half-measures guy, especially where Lauren is concerned. "When my mother died, I went to Hawaii for the funeral and Henry was there. Then right after that, I came home and two days later, I went to St. Louis to do a movie. It was really rough working right after Mom passed away and I was in St. Louis for about a month. When I came home, there were flower petals on the walkway up to the door. I opened the door and Henry had filled the entire living room with roses." She smiles, misty eyed. "Then when we got married, we had our honeymoon in Puerto Vallarta, Mexico and we stayed in a resort that had little cabins on cliffs overlooking the ocean–just beautiful! This one night, he said 'We're going out to dinner. Let's get really dressed up because it's going to be special.' So I put on the dress I'd worn to our engagement party and he put on his white suit and we were about to turn into the lobby when he said, 'Let's just take a walk on the beach.'" On the beach, he had a surprise waiting for her. There was a table for two. Flower petals were strewn on the sand and across the table. The sun was setting and a group of musicians were, playing just for them. "He even had our favorite wine brought down to the shore."

"Yeah! It was German wine called Bernkastle," he recalls. "The tide was coming in and I really surprised her. It was wonderful. I brought an extra bottle and she really didn't expect that, because of the cost. She says if it was up to me, we'd still be living in the apartment on Whitworth to save money."

"The apartment was darling, but Henry was too big for it," Lauren says. "He had to hang his clothes in the hall and the only place he could watch TV was this little alcove breakfast area. He would lie on the floor and any time I went from the kitchen to anywhere else, I had to step over him." Something had to give and with both incomes rising, they rented a larger 1920s Spanish-style duplex, then bought a midcentury rancher in the San Fernando Valley but Lauren wasn't too happy with either the Valley or the house. Altadena suited her better and they bought a pretty Spanish-inspired fixer-upper on an attractive suburban street near Mt. Lowe.

"The backyard was just dirt and a few fruit trees," she says. "I wanted to fix it up and Henry said, 'Why? Nobody ever goes back there.' Well, nobody went back there because it was awful!" Lauren's attempts to renovate Henry were only partially successful, but she fared better with the house. "Of course, after I made the gardens in the back, Henry was out there all the time."

"She's so wonderful at those things and without spending much money at all," he says. The latter part especially pleases him.

"Henry can be a cheapskate about some things, but he'll splurge on fine food and wine and really nice hotels," Lauren says, adding "and he does have that thing about Cadillac limousines." His love of limos and fanfare meant when his brother Dennis and wife Olga visited California, Henry had a luxuriously appointed, chauffeured limousine meet them at the airport.

It took a little getting used to, but Lauren happily discovered that Henry's knack for making life grand and glorious ran in the family. Unlike Darrow who "can barely operate a toaster," his brother Dennis inherited their father's love for tools, equipment and fixing things. "But Henry and Dennis are alike in that they're both very social and warm and a lot of fun. That was how everyone in his entire family was. The first time I met Henry's mom, she hugged me and everyone was hugging and kissing. It was so different from my family, but I loved it! It was so wonderful to be with people who weren't afraid of showing their feelings." Irrepressible Gloria Delgado was nothing if not demonstrative. When Henry told Lauren how quiet his father had been, her first thought was, "That was probably good because he definitely couldn't have kept up with Gloria."

"She was a very flamboyant person," Levian says. "She wrote poetry and she would perform her poems. Everybody had to behave at the poetry readings. If you didn't give enough applause, she'd refuse to continue reading. If you gave a rousing round of applause, she'd go to Henry and whisper, 'Tell them I have more.' Then she'd get right back up." When a little conflict arose, it was always grand opera with Henry's mom. "I can't remember the details, but Gloria criticized me about something and Henry scolded her. She threw herself down on her knees in front of me and started crying and wailing, 'Ohhhhhh! Forgive me! Forgive me!' Henry just said very calmly, 'Okay, Mom. Get up. She forgives you. Come on, get up.' With Gloria, it was always over the top, never just 'Oh, sorry. I didn't mean to offend you.'"

Gloria thought Henry had phenomenal artistic talent and excitedly showed Lauren some of his childhood drawings, exclaiming, "He was only twelve when he did these!"

Lauren recalls, "And Henry said, 'Yeah, Mom, they look exactly like a twelve-year-old did them.' But no, no, no! He was the best!"

When Gloria heard about a new movie about the life of dancer Fred Astaire, she thought her son would be perfect for the starring role. Darrow smiles. "I said, 'Mom, I'm in my fifties. I've put on weight. I've got a little pot belly and it's going to stay there.' She said, 'But you can *play* thin!' Mom always thought I was a great dancer," he says. "I would remind her that I only had lessons for nine months when I was eight, but it did no good. She was convinced."

Since Gloria was convinced that Henry was spectacular in all ways, she readily put him on exhibit any chance she got. "Lauren and I were in a store in Puerto Rico with Mom and over the microphone they used to announce things like 'Clean up on Isle Two,' there was singer who was promoting his records for sale. All of a sudden, Mom disappeared and we heard this *voice* over the mike saying, "Attention everybody! *Manolito* is in the store to help Pepino sell his records!'"

"Henry just groaned and said, 'Oh, no! That's *Mom!*' She'd commandeered the mike from the guy who was trying to sell his records," says Lauren. "Henry just wanted to crawl under a rug, but he was always pretty much of a good sport with his mother. She would really embarrass him, but she'd say, 'I do it with love' and that was true."

"Yeah, that time I ended up signing autographs for a bunch of fans. It was not really what I wanted to do, but people in Puerto Rico have always been wonderful to me and it made Mom happy. She was always my biggest fan."

Darrow's own enthusiasm as a promoter remained more focused on organizations and other people than himself. If *Nosotros* needed him, he was there to MC the banquet for incoming board members. If Holy Family Adoption Services needed celebrity oomph for a fund raiser, he was there. Local bank in New Mexico having a "Save-A-Thon" to encourage frugality? He was there. Operación Hermanos telethon for Guatemalan earthquake relief? The organizers could count on Henry Darrow. Puerto Rico could especially count on him.

"Henry is a loyal *Borinquen* and he has always been there when he's needed," says writer Miluka Rivera. He traveled to New York on behalf of Puerto Rican candidates. Any chance he got, he spotlighted the island, worked to grow its film industry and promoted Puerto Rican talent.

He turned the same energies to supporting Lauren's career. Proud of her considerable acting and writing talent, he boosted her efforts although sometimes with unintended results.

Lauren worked regularly in theater and film, but her dedication to writing and performing for children's theater went back to her teen years when she made extra money doing puppet shows for younger children. Grant money that supported her innovative one woman performances in New York City continued in Los Angeles, but venues could be less than ideal. Henry did six months as her sound effects assistant and says, "We went to schools that were so rough we needed an armed guard to escort us in and out. You needed a guard to walk to the restroom and there was one place where we had to drive the van into the auditorium. It would have been vandalized or stolen if we parked on the street."

Other locations weren't dangerous, just wrong for Levian's quiet one-woman shows. "*Women of the West* was about pioneers. *A New Life in a New Land* was about Jewish immigrants, another focused on the Civil War and one targeted environmental issues. I did *A New Life in a New Land* right next to the landing strip at the airport in Ontario, California while the jets were landing and taking off," she recalls. "Then I did *Women of the West* in a school 'cafetorium'. That's a combination of cafeteria and auditorium and during this very dramatic part where the wagon train is crossing the desert and the young mother's baby dies, the pots and pans started banging in the kitchen. You could hear the kitchen staff laughing and talking. When we had a break, I went back to the kitchen and asked them very nicely to hold it down. The cafeteria manager gave me a cold stare, then said, 'All right, but at ten o'clock I fire up the ovens and you're on your own.' Then there was the Los Angeles zoo. I wasn't going to take the job, but Henry kept saying 'Take it, L. It'll look *great* on your résumé.' I still have no idea why a show at the zoo would look good on my résumé."

"You played the Gene Autry Museum. You played galleries." He's holding firm.

"Yeah, but the zoo?"

"It's one of the bigger zoos in the country," he insists.

"But I was in the burro paddock! They had a new Western Animals section and there was a huge festival for the grand opening, so they hired me to do *Women of the West*. I had told them I needed a controlled environment. They put me in the burro paddock right next to the buffet line and there were wandering musicians and children crawling under the fence. Henry was doing my sound and I was so upset, I was whimpering. He literally had to push me out of the makeshift backstage area. 'L, go! Forty five minutes and you'll be through! Whoosh!'"

"It was going to be great on her résumé," he repeats. "Michael Landon and Danny Devito were there."

"Yeah, they had all these celebrities and I was in the worst possible location. It was just horrible. Michael Landon came over and said something like 'I admire your courage.'" She's laughing, but at the time would have been happy if Manolito Montoya had ridden in to save the day. Manolito was nowhere near the burro barn. However, in the late 1980s, it seemed he might once again ride across TV screens.

Encouraged by the successful syndication of *Bonanza: The Next Generation*, in 1988 David Dortort started talking about a *High Chaparral* reunion special. It had been seventeen years since *Chaparral* went off the air and Leif Erickson had died in 1986, but Dortort dreamed of returning Linda Cristal, Cameron Mitchell, Henry Darrow and Mark Slade to the Cannon ranch. "With the new, important Latino audience, Cristal and Darrow (Delgado) would be an added asset," Dortort told *Variety's* Army Archerd.[412]

"David Dortort had written the script," Darrow recalls. "Mark Slade called me about it and he was in favor of getting the project together." But it stalled at the planning stage and never happened. Figuring he no longer needed all his Manolito costumes, in 1989 Darrow gave some items to the Gene Autry Western Heritage Museum[413] and donated a pair of Manolito's pants to a charity event in Tucson. He was at the charity auction when a lady offered several hundred dollars for the pants. That was great, but then she offered two hundred dollars more if he'd put them on. "I said, 'Why don't you just take the pants, because I've got to tell you, I don't fit into them anymore. I've tried! I can't get them past my knees and I'm not an exhibitionist.'"

True, but Patrice Martinez notes, "He is so genuine an actor that he makes every role his own." He did just that with another dashing, somewhat disreputable, somewhat heroic character — this time on the quirky, often comical soap opera *Santa Barbara* (NBC, 1984-1993). He played the father of A Martinez for the fourth time and it would be one of the most significant roles of his career.

I've always enjoyed playing heroic characters, con-men and magicians.

HENRY DARROW

---

412. Daily Variety, *"Just for Variety,"* 3/14/88

413. *Founded by singing cowboy star and business tycoon Gene Autry (1907-1998), it's now known as the The Autry National Center*

Whatever Happens Don't Break Up

El Día del Padre puede ser difícil para ti con tantos recuerdos y sentimientos diferentes...Tan solo recuerda que pienso en ti y que te deseo mucha paz y felicidad...ahora y siempre.[414]

FROM A FATHER'S DAY CARD FROM DEEDEE DELGADO
TO HER DAD, HENRY DARROW

Produced by New World Television, *Santa Barbara* was the first daytime drama with prominent Mexican-American characters and romantic partners from different ethnic groups. It won numerous Daytime Emmys and other honors while enthralling viewers with the lives of the wealthy Capwells, the working class Mexican-American Andrade family and other dysfunctional fictional residents of coastal California.

A Martinez starred as hunky spy turned detective Cruz Castillo and about a year after the show's debut, chemistry between Cruz and socialite Eden Capwell (Marcy Walker) sparked Martinez and Walker to push a star crossed love angle. Resistant at first, the writers eventually made Eden and Cruz central to storylines. When they did, the two fan favorites became a 1980s soap "super couple," jetting Walker and Martinez to megastardom. Like every super couple, Cruz and Eden had passion and problems enough to keep every psychiatrist at General Hospital busy for all the days of our lives. Along with the kidnapping of their baby by Eden's rapist/obstetrician and other troubles too numerous to list, Cruz had Daddy Issues. His father Rafael Castillo had abandoned the family and relocated to Acapulco where he started a new life as Señor Mago the Magician. After Cruz, his brother Ric and Eden tracked down the elder Castillo (played by Henry Darrow)

---

414. *"Father's Day can be difficult for you with so many memories and different feelings...Just remember I think of you and I wish you much peace and happiness...now and forever."*

in Mexico, he returned to Santa Barbara eager to mend his relationship with his kids.

As Rafael Castillo, Darrow was suave, tough and mesmerizing. "He was still the lady killer and just fearless as an actor," says A Martinez. When *Santa Barbara* did a "What if Cruz had never been born?" retelling of *It's A Wonderful Life*, the scene with Rafael took place in a bar. "He was a ruined man, but he didn't have any self-pity. He played the ruination with a sense of indignity that was so compelling." Martinez credits Darrow's positive impact on his own work. "Henry would show up, totally steel trap knowing his stuff. When you're working with someone day after day, that kind of work ethic makes your job so much easier. You know if things get a little squirrelly, he's got your back. That makes you braver and when you're brave, you do better work."

Darrow, who appreciates Martinez' humor and his vision of acting, says the most pressure he's ever felt was in doing soaps. "Shooting an hour's show every day and being on the money is grueling and I had no time to memorize every single day," he says. "Once I had my character down, it was okay. At first, it's easy to forget your lines and you don't know your character well enough to adlib. A Martinez and Marcy Walker said, 'When you're lost, whatever happens don't break up. Don't say cut. Just keep it going and we'll step in.' That made it possible for me to relax."

"I was going to cover him as best I could," says Martinez. "That's essential in soap, because the actors are utterly dependent upon each other. It's like you cough and everybody catches a cold immediately. There's nothing in acting that takes your measure quite like a challenge of that magnitude." After nearly six hundred episodes of *Santa Barbara*, Martinez recalls an unforgettable scene with Darrow. "We were in the desert and Rafael challenged Cruz to stop whining about his broken heart and come to grips with himself. I think he actually knocked me down in one part of the scene and then he threw a *bota* full of some hallucinogenic concoction at me. The next thing you see, Cruz is in a cave out of his mind." Cruz eventually emerged to face ongoing heartache, drama and his father. While he and Rafael explored their tangled onscreen relationship, Henry Darrow negotiated real world complexities with his real life grown children. Television parenting took less of an emotional toll.

"Tom was on drugs and there's nothing that can stop that. It's ruthless," Darrow says. "His friends from Highland Hall all progressed. Those kids and the kids he was friendly with on Remick all got good jobs. Not Tom. He started detailing cars and then he had a partner and they built decks for a time. People liked Tom and they'd hire them to build decks, then that stopped and he started this business repairing the big blenders they use in bars. He called himself 'The Blender Doctor' and was making a marginal living out of it. But what did he do? He hired kids to do the work for $5.50 an hour and he wouldn't show up to work. They messed up and he messed up."

"Henry passionately loved Tom, but Tom put Henry and Lucy through so much grief. They'd bail him out of all kinds of trouble and he just wore them out. He wore everybody out," Lauren says. During high school, he had been so incorrigible that Henry and Lucy almost made him a ward of the court. Then Tom met Bob, a man who dedicated himself to helping troubled youth. The other kids Bob worked with made something of themselves and it seemed Bob might help turn Tom's life around.

"Bob was like a second father to Tom," Darrow says. "Or a first father, more of a father than I was."

Tom called Henry "Pop," but he called Bob "Dad."

Bob had faith that Tom could get off drugs and alcohol, but by his early thirties, Tom was still drinking and using. Then he was diagnosed with multiple sclerosis (MS), an autoimmune disease affecting brain, spinal cord and nerves. Heat makes MS worse.

"Tom was always making self-destructive decisions," Lauren says. "We were really concerned when he decided to move to Las Vegas." It's hot in Las Vegas, Nevada, a city of sparkling casinos built improbably in the middle of the desert. "And of course, Vegas has all the bad stuff. It's a city that feeds addictions. The only plus was that Bob was living there. Bob got Tom a job in a factory and at first he did well, then he flaked out and got even more heavily into drugs." When he cleaned up again, he went back to fixing bar blenders.

"So he was 'The Blender Doctor' again," Darrow says. "I had friends in the hotel business and at the casinos and they said 'yeah, we'll hand your son twenty or thirty blenders a month to fix.' He did okay, for a while. Then it was the same thing again, the drugs and the booze." Sighing, he pauses. "I didn't like his drug stuff, but at times we had good talks and we had fun. Tom would stay with us in Altadena and I would visit him in Vegas and stay for a few days with him. We'd talk, go out."

When times were good, Tom was as warm and expressive as his Pop. "I love you more than I can say," he wrote Darrow one Father's Day. "I love our conversations. I love you! I hope you live forever. Take Lauren out for a wonderful dinner, set a place for me and talk to it as if I was there (I'm there in spirit, so carry on with your conversation)."

When times were bad, addiction ruled. To pay for drugs, Tom stole from his mother. He could become violent toward her. After three arrests for driving under the influence, he served eighteen months in jail and neither Henry nor Lucy visited him there.

"They were both just fed up," Lauren says. "Then when Tom got out of jail, he turned around for a while. He went to Alcoholics Anonymous and Narcotics Anonymous. He got a job at a warehouse. They liked him and he liked the work, but like everything else it didn't last."

"He showed up at our house with a gun and he was talking suicide," says Henry, voice still raw with pain and fury. "I took the gun away from him and I just went crazy with such anger! Lauren was upstairs with a friend who was visiting, and when they heard me yelling Lauren's friend cried. She was so nervous. She never heard anybody that angry. I just reamed into Tom, 'What the *hell* are you going to do!? Oh, my God! You're bad off already and *now* you're going to make it worse for me, for your mother, for your sister, for your friends!'"

"That was one of maybe three times in almost thirty years that Henry has lost his temper," Lauren says. "We tried to help. Henry really tried, but Tom and Deedee were grown people. They each got $125,000 from Lucy's parents when they turned twenty-one and they both ran through it. Tom's went down his throat and up his nose. Deedee handled things very differently. She was never into drugs or parties, but she'd struggled for years with anorexia and bulimia. She spent part of her money living in a very ritzy hotel and then she took the rest and put herself into rehab for her eating disorders."

"Well, she had fun with her money and then to commit herself for treatment, that took courage," Henry says. "And Deedee is very scrupulous with her money. She can live on a dime. She takes care of herself that way. I admire her ability to survive, but I've caused her angst and she's caused me angst." When she visited the house in Altadena, time spent together could be warm and loving, but sooner or later, conflicts arose. Then at one point she completely vanished. Unable to find out from her friends where she was, not knowing if she was dead or alive, Henry was in a panic. He discovered she had entered an ashram. Afraid a cult was holding her against her will, he was ready to send the police to drag her out before Deedee spoke up. "That's how she found her peace and she was there for several years, living a very ascetic life with a little bed, little bureau. She would get up at four o'clock in the morning to prepare meals. It worked for her, so okay, sure. But she isolated herself from her family and that wasn't good. Then later she developed lupus and there were other health problems and always there was the attitude. It got in the way of her ability to find work and keep jobs. She listed people who had fired her as references in her résumé. She'd say 'They said my work was good, but they didn't like my attitude.' So what did she think that person was going to say when somebody called? Lauren helped her build a good résumé, but Deed is perfectly capable of ignoring attempts to help." Old fatigue deepens the lines of his face. "All you can do is gather yourself and go on." He saved every card and every letter that Deedee and Tom ever sent him.

To mine own self be true...and, of course, it's always one day at a time...I'm having a rough patch — the 'fog' has crept back in...I'm doing the best I can.

DEEDEE DELGADO IN A NOTE TO HER FATHER

Good, Clean Family Fun

Zorro has true transgenerational appeal, with every age group having known and loved its own version of the character as interpreted within the spirit of the times.

ZORRO PRODUCTIONS[415]

"I try not to focus on the difficult aspects of life or I'll talk myself into a depression," Henry says. "What I like is getting into a part that's really cooking, one that starts the juices flowing, something positive that I can sink my teeth into." He had a substantial role as a corrupt vice cop in the feature film *The Last of the Finest* (1990), but *Santa Barbara's* reformed reprobate Rafael Castillo was truly Darrow's kind of role. *SB's* audience loved the character. Darrow got a kick out of playing him. Then at the end of the day, he could turn Rafael off and go home. *SB* was such a good gig that when Gary Goodman offered Darrow the part of Zorro's father in the new *Zorro* project, he turned Goodman down again.

"As with the first pilot they did, when my friend Val ended up with the bad guy role, I asked for a certain amount of money and the *Zorro* people said no," he recalls. "I stayed with *Santa Barbara*. *Santa Barbara* extended my contract for a year and I developed my character more fully. Also, *Santa Barbara* was filmed in Burbank and I could drive to Burbank versus *Zorro* which was filmed overseas." The second Goodman-Rosen *Zorro* pilot rolled without Henry Darrow.

This time Goodman and Rosen utilized John Gertz more as story consultant and placed unprecedented attention on technical details and historical accuracy. Zorro historian Bill Yenne later wrote, "In what was to become another milestone in the history of Zorro's depiction, Gary Goodman and Barry Rosen of New World Television…undertook in 1989 to produce what was to be the most thoroughly planned and

---

415. *Undated release "A Brief History of a Living Legend," files of Henry Darrow*

executed project ever."[416] Financial backers responded well and the new *Zorro* series began filming.

A joint venture of Zorro Productions Incorporated, New World Television, The Family Channel, Radiotelevisione Italiana (Italy) and Ellipse Programme-Canal Plus (France), *New World Zorro* was shot on location in Spain and France. The Spanish National Archives and California Historical Society shared manuscripts, sketches and photos pertaining to customs, clothing and weapons of 1820s California. All costumes, props and décor were period replicas or antiques; museums and historical societies loaned the series valuable one of a kind items. Most interiors were filmed at a huge soundstage in Madrid, but some interiors and all exteriors were shot at an intricately designed copy of early Pueblo de Los Angeles on thirty-four acres north of the city. The Pueblo had a church, military garrison, central plaza, tavern and other typical adobe buildings. Façades of outlying haciendas were constructed nearby. Fifty carpenters, fifteen craftsmen, thirty-six laborers and twenty-five painters built the set in seven weeks.

Composer/songwriter Jay Asher and lyricist Dennis Spiegal contributed the stirring theme, sung with gusto by Cathi Campo. The daughter of Cuban born orchestra leader Pupi Campo and singer Betty Clooney, Campo is a member of the famous Clooney family along with movie star George, singer Rosemary and Rosemary's children by her husband, actor José Ferrer. The cast and crew had impressive pedigrees as well.

Stunt coordinator and second unit director Peter Diamond was "unquestionably the world's greatest film stunt coordinator/fencer."[417] Diamond studied acting at the Royal Academy of Dramatic Arts, but acting took a backseat to stunting and directing. As stunt coordinator, fight arranger and choreographer, he had around a thousand stage, film and TV credits. He staged fight sequences at the Royal Opera House, the London Palladium and for films *Star Wars* (1977, 1980, 1983), *Raiders of the Lost Ark* (1981), *Highlander* (1986) and *The Princess Bride* (1987). On *Zorro*, Diamond trained the actors in fencing for the camera. Unlike match fencing, swords weren't tipped and actors weren't protected. Diamond emphasized, "I always try and make it a point that we don't do any dangerous stuff…We work in the entertainment business and we find another way of doing it… But to give the effect on the screen, it has to *look* dangerous."[418]

416. *Quoted in* Riding the Video Range, *p. 563*

417. *http://www.peterdiamond.co.uk/, retrieved 5/22/11*

418. *The Family Channel, quoted on http://newworldzorro.com/Interviews/diamond.html retrieved 5/22/11*

The man who directed the most episodes and produced forty-one was another former stuntman, Londoner Raymond Austin. When Austin began his US career as a stuntman and bit player in the early 1950s, his friend and fellow stuntman/actor Bobby Hoy (who later played Joe Butler on *The High Chaparral*) introduced him to the industry. Austin doubled Cary Grant in 1959's *North by Northwest* and *Operation Petticoat* and by 1967 he was one of the world's highest paid stuntmen. However, his interests turned more to screenwriting, producing and directing. After decades in film and TV on both sides of the Atlantic, he says, "*Zorro* was one of the best gigs that I ever had. The Family Channel left us alone to do the show. Gary Goodman was one of the best executive producers I ever worked with in my life; he chose the cast and he trusted their abilities. They were all *so* good, from the character actors to the lead."

The producers had offered the lead to award-winning Latin screen heartthrob Fernando Allende, but according to Sandra Curtis he passed because the shooting schedule conflicted with his upcoming wedding.[419] Canadian actor Duncan Regehr, who was unavailable for the first pilot, got the part. Tall (6'5"), dark and handsome, Regehr was everything Gary Goodman wanted and then some. A classically trained Shakespearean actor, former champion figure skater, Olympic boxing contender, swordsman, horseman and internationally acclaimed multimedia artist, he had acted in theater, TV and movies. Before filming started on *Zorro*, he said, "We'll do two segs a week, but they will be done in high style in the tradition of Ty Power and Douglas Fairbanks. It's a wonderful legacy to live up to."[420] His enthusiasm continued when the cameras rolled. "Zorro is an actor's dream to play," he said in an interview for A&E *Biography*. "You get to do all of those things you wanted to do as a kid."[421]

Regehr probably wanted to do different things than Patrice Martinez when she was a child. As a little girl, Martinez dreamed of going to Spain and meeting Henry Darrow. Thanks to *Zorro*, she could check off going to Spain. The only actor retained from the first pilot, she was cast as Victoria Escalante, Zorro's love interest. Martinez is from an Albuquerque, New Mexico family of performers — her father was a musician and her mother, Margarita Cannon, founded *La Compania de Teatro de Albuquerque*, a bilingual repertory company. A graduate of the Royal Academy of

419. Behind the Mask, *p. 169*

420. Daily Variety, *"Just for Variety" by Army Archerd, 8/10/89*

421. Zorro: Mark of the "Z" (1996), *quoted on http://newworldzorro.com/Interviews/ Regehr/aebio.html retrieved 5/19/11*

Dramatic Arts, Patrice Martinez earned five of RADA's most important awards while there. In Hollywood, she worked in TV and films but said, "I never had an interview where somebody with the production, the writer, producer, or in this case, John Gertz, wanted to know my input on a character...I was thrilled. They wanted to know how I saw it and they even let me give her the name."[422] When she was a child watching *The High Chaparral*, she wished she could be Victoria Cannon. What better name for her own fiery, headstrong character in *Zorro* than Victoria? As tavern keeper Victoria Escalante, Martinez sweltered under historically accurate costuming much as Linda Cristal did during her stint as Victoria Cannon. Wearing twenty pounds of corsets, undergarments and dresses while filming *Zorro*, Martinez almost cooked when the temperature spiked to one hundred and fifteen degrees. "I don't know how women in those days could wear all this clothing, especially in the heart of Los Angeles," she said.[423]

Along with a love interest, every superhero needs a sidekick. To attract young viewers, Goodman and Rosen picked teenaged Juan Diego Botto as Zorro's sidekick Felipe. Born in Argentina and raised in Spain, Botto spoke no English, but didn't need it since Felipe was mute and Botto already had the acting chops to mime the role effectively. His parents were a well-known actors in Argentina, but only his mother survived the bloody coup d'état which deposed then-President Isabel Perón and began the *Guerra Sucia* (Dirty War), a regime of torture, kidnapping and murder. During *La Guerra Sucia*, alleged enemies of the government were kidnapped and never seen again, presumed dead. Juan Diego was a toddler when his father, Diego Fernando Botto, became one of the estimated thirteen thousand *desaparecidos* (disappeared). His mother, Cristina Rota, rightly feared for the lives of her children and fled to Spain with Juan Diego and his sister. Because he was so young Juan Diego easily adjusted to the new country, but later said, "When a classmate asked me to lunch at her grandmother's house, I thought, 'To go to the house of my grandmother, I would have to travel fourteen thousand kilometers.' It made me aware of the remoteness of our family ties."[424] Following in his parents' footsteps, Juan Diego Botto made his acting debut when he was seven years old.

422. *http://newworldzorro.com/Interviews/camhi.html retrieved 5/19/11*

423. *http://www.newworldzorro.com/presskitinfo/prodnotes.html retrieved 5/23/11*

424. *http://www.lanacion.com.ar/356609-ernesto-alterio-y-juan-botto-actores-que-son-hijos-del-exilio "Ernesto Alterio y Juan Botto, actores que son hijos del exilio" by Néstor Tirri, retrieved 5/22/11*

Zorro's nemesis, Alcalde Luis Ramón, was played by Michael Tylo. Originally from Detroit, Michigan, he almost followed in his father's footsteps. Tylo's dad, a plumber, told his son that plumbers would always be more necessary than actors because people always needed to go to the bathroom, but they didn't always need to watch TV. Good point, but instead of becoming a plumber Tylo earned a Bachelor of Fine Arts in acting and a Master's degree in directing. He never planned to act and said, "I always wanted to direct, but I had one of those faces that at thirty-five I could still play an eighteen-year-old. Nobody wants to trust their budget to a director who looks like he just walked out of public school."[425] *Zorro* was in pre-production without an alcalde when handsome blond Tylo, a veteran of theater, daytime dramas and the miniseries *Lonesome Dove* (1989) read for the part. Winning the role, he enjoyed making discontented Alcalde Luis Ramón "a little evil."

Villains need sidekicks too and Tylo's was Dominican-born James Victor as Sgt. Jaime Mendoza. Victor, "one of the finest character actors in Hollywood"[426] was raised in New York City where he joined Miriam Colón's bilingual theater company and studied Method acting under cinéma vérité virtuoso and close friend John Cassavetes. It took four auditions before Victor was finally cast as Mendoza and his struggles didn't end there. Henry Calvin, who played the analogous part of Sgt. Garcia in Disney's *Zorro*, set a standard for comic foils. When the producers talked to Victor about his portrayal of Sgt. Mendoza, he felt they wanted another Henry Calvin. "They were trying to have me watch Henry Calvin in the other *Zorro* and I said, 'Look, I'm not going to give you any of that. Henry Calvin was a wonderful actor and he gave it his shot. Now I'm going to give you mine." He won that battle and says, "I loved doing *Zorro*. It was probably the highlight of my whole career as far as making a lot of money and getting worldwide attention."

Worldwide attention was novel for Jimmy Victor, but not for Efrem Zimbalist, Jr., the man playing Don Alejandro de la Vega, the father of Don Diego/Zorro. The son of renowned concert violinist Efrem Zimbalist Sr. and world famous soprano Alma Gluck, he had graduated from the Yale University Drama School and New York's Neighborhood Playhouse. In 1950 he won the New York Drama Critics' Award and the Pulitzer Prize as producer of the dramatic opera *The Consul*. Later winning a Tony and a Golden Globe, Zimbalist was best known to television viewers for starring roles in *77 Sunset Strip* and *The FBI*. His refined good looks and smooth baritone brought easy-going class to his portrayal of Don Alejandro.

425. TV Scene, 6th *Edition*, "*Michael Tylo: The Guy You Love to Hate*," *by Janette Hyem*

426. *http://www.newworldzorro.com/presskitinfo/victor.html retrieved 5/10/11*

"He was the best known because he was a movie and television star, but he was a very unassuming man," James Victor recalls. "We went to the opera and out to dinner. He used to call his *per diem* 'play money.' When we went out, he wouldn't let me pick up the check. He would say, 'No no, it's only play money.'" Zimbalist and the rest of cast became close during the first year, with the exception of Duncan Regehr.

"Duncan is wonderful to work with, but the first year he was a pain in the butt," says James Victor. "I throw that off on nerves and playing the dual role. He isolated himself and we left him alone because he was not a pleasant person to be around. He was off-putting. The workman — the lighting guys, the grips — put some cow manure in his dressing room. They took it out before he came in, but the smell lingered. Regehr came in and just blew his stack!"

Everyone else was great from the start as far as Victor was concerned. Juan Diego Botto was a marvelously expressive young actor who wanted badly to go to Hollywood. "He was always talking about Hollywood, asking questions. He was a wonderful kid," Victor says. "Patrice Camhi Martinez, a gorgeous girl with incredible talent. Then there was Michael Tylo. He and I had a chemistry together that was just electric."

Tylo says, "Jimmy was a good buddy from the first second and I got along well with Duncan; he's a very intelligent actor with good physical presence." Tylo was only supposed to be in half the episodes and ended up in nearly all. That's usually a good thing, but not in his case. "I hated working in Spain. I don't speak Spanish so there was the language barrier. Also, my sons were very young and I didn't like being away from my family."

Efrem Zimbalist, Jr. also found working in Spain difficult. His children were adults, but he disliked being abroad for months at a stretch and he suffered in the intense heat.

For Jimmy Victor, it wasn't the heat but the horses. When Sgt. Mendoza moaned that he hated horses, he mirrored Victor's feelings. He was afraid before one almost trampled him in an early episode. He was also allergic, popping an allergy pill anytime there was a horse nearby.[427] Unfortunately for him, spunky Spanish horses were a big part of *Zorro*.

"They treat horses differently in Spain and they're a lot more spirited," says Ray Austin, who learned stunt riding at Ken Johnson's ranch where Johnson didn't give him a saddle until he mastered riding bareback. Riding became one of his best skills and with horsemen like Austin around, there were very few mishaps involving horses. "A groom might drop the rein when he was about to hand it to Duncan and the damn horse would run

427. Daily Variety, *"Just for Variety" by Army Archerd, 4/30/90*

away free. Of course, it would take time to get the blasted thing back so we could shoot. The usual thing with horses — it might go only twenty yards away and just stand there, but when you went ten yards toward it, it would go another twenty yards further." He'd never convince Jimmy Victor, but Austin always found horses very safe for stunts. "If you let the horse have its way, you're safe. He's not going to step on you unless he stumbles or something." Obviously, the adjunct is if the horse stumbles, you may have a twelve-hundred pound weight on you, so stunts are best left to the stuntmen — but Austin was pleased to work on *Zorro* with actors who knew how to ride. "Regehr was a good rider as well as a talented actor, but you have to double the stars because you can't take the risk that they'll be injured. If the star can't work, we're all out of work. That's often the main reason for using stunt doubles."

Expert horsemanship combined with other elements made *Zorro* what Michael Tylo called "good, clean family fun." When the show premiered on January 5, 1990 reviews were mixed, but most concurred with Tylo. David Bianculli of the *New York Post* called it "an instant hit in my household." *The San Diego Union's* Don Freeman complimented Regehr's looks, skill and derring-do and dubbed Martinez a "knockout." For Tom Walter of the *Memphis Commercial Appeal*, it was rip-roaring "fun stuff."[428] However, *Variety* was considerably cooler, calling the show "bright but slight" 1950s fare lacking "suspense or real amusement."[429]

Also displeased was a coalition of Latino actors, producers, politicians and community organizers called United Hispanics of America. Shortly after *Zorro's* debut, the coalition ran a full page "Open Letter to the Industry Regarding Discrimination" in *Variety*. Charging discrimination, the statement complained that leading roles in *New World Zorro* were not being played by Hispanic actors, but noted "Representatives of New World Television claim that Hispanics were offered some of the leading roles and rejected the offers and that in casting all the roles, at least as many Hispanic performers were considered as were non-Hispanic performers." United Hispanics voiced dismay over the "unwritten rule" that — with few exceptions — Hispanics "cannot compete" for non-Hispanic roles while non-Hispanics got Hispanic parts. Emphasizing that they were not asking for the cancellation of *Zorro*, the group declared its desire was only to call attention to "current injustices in discriminatory hiring practices in the motion picture industry" and to work toward

428. *Quoted in* Zorro Unmasked, *p. 182*

429. Variety, *"Television Reviews" by* Tone., *2/7/90*

providing "visible, positive Hispanic role models for our children and future generations."[430]

"Typecasting has existed since the beginning of the movies," James Victor responded in his column in the magazine *Canales*. "No one ever said that prejudice doesn't exist in our country or in our industry. It is a proven fact that this business does not seek out anyone. So if you get in it, you learn to accept…[or] hone in your craft so when those roles come up you are ready to compete in the market place. To the United Hispanics of America I say: Save your money on *Variety* ads and learn your craft so you too can be ready when the opportunity arises."[431]

The United Hispanics protest fizzled and The Family Channel green-lighted *Zorro* for another season, but Efrem Zimbalist, Jr. opted out and the show needed a new Don Alejandro de la Vega. "So one got ready for a change," Ray Austin says. Gary Goodman suggested Henry Darrow, whom Austin first met when he visited Bobby Hoy on the *Chaparral* set. Years later, directing *The Yeagers*, a TV series starring Andy Griffith, Austin needed a Mexican villain and Hoy suggested Darrow. "So I cast Henry as this shady Mexican bandido. That was the first time we worked together and everybody was good on that show, but Henry is absolutely super. I knew if we hired him on *Zorro*, there would be no problems whatsoever."

Meanwhile, after a very good year on *Santa Barbara*, Henry Darrow's contract was coming up for renewal. *SB*'s producers were noncommittal about about extending his option. "Suddenly, I was approached again by Gary Goodman, the executive producer of *Zorro*. We had lunch at the Polo Lounge and talked about my pay and billing and we were in agreement." Darrow watched several episodes with Efrem Zimbalist Jr. and liked his genteel quality, but felt the father of Zorro should have more vigor and spirit. "I wanted to keep the Spanish gentleman aspect, but to give Don Alejandro my interpretation of a more physical man. They were good with that and I was in." He was the first Latino Zorro and now he would one of only two to play both Zorro and Zorro's father.[432]

> *I hear Zorro has a new daddy — Henry Darrow.*
> *I like him a lot. I've always admired his work. Oh,*
> *and I'm so looking forward to throwing him in jail!"*
> MICHAEL TYLO

430. Daily Variety, *2/2/90*

431. *"Hollywood Hotline," 2/2/90*

432. *Douglas Fairbanks, Sr. was the first*

Like a Volcano!

Actors ought to be larger than life. You come across enough ordinary, nondescript people in daily life and I don't see why you should be subjected to them on the stage, too.

FRENCH COURTESAN NINON DE LENCLOS

"Sometimes when you have somebody like Efrem who leaves — he was a wonderful guy — you miss steps," Michael Tylo notes. "But Henry came and it was like not missing a step. He's immediately into whatever he's doing and he's one *hell* of an actor." Tylo was a fan decades before meeting Darrow. "When I was younger, I watched him as Manolito. I even got my hair cut like his at the time, because I thought he was so cool. And meeting him, he's so friendly you feel comfortable with him."

"When Darrow came in the second season, it was like a volcano! Bla-BOOM!" He made Don Alejandro bombastic and *alive!*" exclaims Jimmy Victor. "He's always on! I don't know what vitamins he takes, but man! He'd walk on the set in the morning and yawn and stretch his arms and say, 'Ah, another day in paradise!' He was *very* uplifting." He was also the soul of diplomacy, which was handy when Victor almost went *mano a mano* with former Olympic Boxing Team contender Regehr. "We were shooting and Duncan started giving me line readings. That's when you have a line like 'I'm going to the supermarket.' It's your line. And I try to tell you how you should say your line, "I am…going…to the supermarket!' You don't do that to another actor. I was so pissed off. We were calling each other names and we almost went to it. Duncan would've killed me! He's about seven feet tall and I'm looking up at him and yelling. Henry broke up the fight. He ran out and said, 'Come on guys, don't be silly' and that was it. Regehr respected him. They got along from the start."

Duncan Regehr more than agrees. "Upon meeting certain actors I have always felt an immediate sense of kinship. Henry is one of those. He became a friend at first handshake, a brother without conditions on and off the set."

"Duncan considered me a sort of elder statesman and he is the most dedicated actor I ever worked with," Darrow says. "He worked *all* the time and he could do almost anything, a true Renaissance man. He was extremely precise in everything and very serious about his physical fitness. He didn't drink, he didn't smoke and he would exercise at 4:30 in the morning to be ready for his scenes. He eventually got smoking banned from the set and then there was no wine with lunch and he also had lunch hours reduced by a half hour. The Spanish didn't like any of that, but it did tighten things up. He was indeed intense and initially very on guard with the other actors. He has something of a dark side, which comes through in his wonderful paintings." In many ways, Regehr was Victor's polar opposite, so it shouldn't have been a big surprise when sparks flew between them. "Then there was Jimmy. He's a very warm, emotional person and one of the finest character actors around, but he came out of the Actor's Studio and so he was from a Method background. He would improvise and change things." Darrow was the bridge between those two and other diverse personalities.

"Everybody brought their squabbles to Henry," says Michael Tylo. "We all had our little peccadillos and because we were stuck there for three months together, everybody had their squabbles. Henry believed if you picked on somebody and caused dissention, the collaborative effort would not be there. He was just full of love and common sense for everybody. He had a wonderful sense of humor about everything and he always stood up for what was right. He was friends with everyone as a result, but he and Jimmy were my best buddies."

"Tylo would've made a good Iago," Darrow says. "He was just evil personified as the alcalde and such a good actor, very detailed and dynamic. As a person, he could be emotional and difficult to talk with, but he's also a thoughtful, very introspective man."

After a day's shoot and before dinner, Tylo, Victor and Darrow unwound at the hotel over good Spanish wine and cheese. They watched old American TV shows like *Richard Diamond* on black and white sets in their suites or discussed baseball.

"Henry and I were both into baseball and we locked onto that," Tylo says. "We argued baseball or talked about ballplayers. We both had books about the Dodgers and the Yankees and we exchanged books. My father gave me his baseball card collection with stars from the 1930s to the 1950s and when I told Henry about that, he was really impressed." Besides enjoying baseball and vintage American television shows, they especially appreciated the great view from Darrow's suite of the topless women at the hotel pool.

"So that's why they didn't answer when I called them for dinner!" exclaims Patrice Martinez with a giggle. "Where we stayed was part hotel and part long term residence, and of course, the European ladies tan and swim topless. To them, it's totally natural, but *I* didn't know that! The first time I went to the pool, I looked up and I was the only one *with my top on!*"

"Oh, Patrice — the most beautiful girl!" says Darrow. "The first time I saw her in the casting office, it was like who is that stunning woman? When she let her hair down, she was a lot of fun, too. And we worked well together."

"Henry is extraordinary," she says. "How shall I say this? I have to take off my hat to him for his subtlety and his professionalism in stealing scenes. He's very clever. If you're too overt, then the director can cut it out. But if you're subtle like Henry..." She's laughing. He could steal scenes with a glance or the smallest gesture. "He does it in such a casual way, like 'Oh, I'm here, hello.' I would study him. I wanted to learn a lot from him and I did!" Because of time constraints in a half-hour show with a teaser, tag and room for commercials, *New World Zorro* restricted actors almost completely to the script. Dialogue might be changed at any time, but there was no room for scene stealing improvisation. That didn't stop an old pro like Darrow. "He would wink and say to me, 'I'll get that last scene.' He would throw in something innocuous and *he would be the last shot!*"

"He'd steal scenes like crazy!" Michael Tylo says. And not just scenes. "I'd do something I planned on using in a scene and the little fart would see it and mutter, 'hmm, I like that. How would I do it? Okay, I got it.' And I'd think 'Oh, shit!' because he'd use it before I had a chance and he's so masterful, he'd make it his own.' You really have to do your homework to keep up with him."

Probably no amount of homework could stop Henry Darrow from stealing, but he taught Patrice Martinez how to avoid being upstaged by the horses. "You don't feed them little treats," he says. "If you do, they'll look for it and start nudging. When you're doing a scene, if you just pet the horse calmly he'll stand quietly." He discovered that during *The High Chaparral*, where he also learned that if he was in the master shot, he'd be on the set all day. That was fine if he had a lot of dialogue because he'd be working.

"If you don't have many lines, you want to get out of the master shot," Martinez says. "Henry showed me how to sneak out of the frame so we didn't have to be there for fourteen hours with nothing to do. I learned that one quick! During the rehearsal, it would be clear how much dialogue we had. So if I only had one line or he only had one line, we'd pair up and slip out very graciously. It was new to me, but it was very helpful! I don't know if Ray Austin noticed."

"I don't either!" Darrow laughs. "Ray is so veddy, veddy British. He has this marvelous accent and brought in these wonderful British guest stars like Daniel Craig and Roger Moore's daughter Deborah Barrymore. And Ray is such a stylish man. On the set he would wear red slippers with these little goodies on them."

When Austin directed interior sequences, he always wore velvet opera slippers. Usually bought by his wife in Paris or London, they were embroidered with gold thread and decorated with coronets or a fox's head.

"I was known for them," he says, sounding much like Cary Grant. He was also known for being a hands-off director and producer. "I let the actors have the floor and if it's good, I say 'thank you.' If I don't think it's right, I then make the adjustments. I never say nono, I'm the director, it *must* be done this way. So many times, I've gone to block a scene and I've said to the Henrys and the Duncans, here's the scene, show me what you can do with it. And they've played a scene in a way I never considered and it was good." He could do that that with the highly skilled actors on *Zorro* and Henry Darrow's years of experience, innate talent and personality made him exceptionally adept. "He's not a pain in the backside like some artists. They study for the role, they walk on the set and try to become that person and they drive you insane all day being that person. Henry can switch it off and switch it on. When I said 'Action!' he was there." Darrow's ability to excel at the physical demands of his role were as significant as his professionalism as an actor. "Don Alejandro had to be very physical as the father of Zorro. When it came to swords or a sword routine, Henry was excellent, but put him on a horse and he became part and parcel with the horse. An absolutely wonderful rider! We cast a lot of English actors and we have some good riders in England. But for a ride out of Los Angeles or into the ranch, our English actors would look around for their stunt doubles. I used a lot of doubles for them; otherwise they would have bounced all over the place. But when Henry swung into the saddle, all the English actors would look at him and say 'Ahhh, Manolito!' He was a natural."

Darrow's skill with horses and rah-rah attitude dovetailed in an incident involving Jimmy Victor. Victor was supposed to ride his horse down the steep side of a deep ravine. He wasn't happy about it.

"It was so huge, it was like the horse was going to fall off," he recalls. "So we're all sitting there and they're setting up the shot and I said, 'I'm not going to do this, Henry. I'm not going down that ravine. They've got to double me.' And he says, 'Oh, Jimmy! Those horses are trained. The horse will do it and you just have to hang on. Don't worry about anything, believe me.' I told him I wasn't too sure about that, because it really looked dangerous. So he said, 'But Jimmy, the coverage will be better! It'll really be *you*! It won't be the back of the stunt guy's head!' Badda-badda-badda-badda, the Puerto Rican talked me into doing it. I shut my eyes and just held on and the horse did his thing. He went right down. It turned out great. I felt much more courageous and much more macho after that."

In spite of occasional personality clashes and homesickness, the *Zorro* family was generally collegial, creating a friendly atmosphere when actual family members visited. Duncan Regehr's wife Catherine came to Spain often. Henry brought his mom over and James Victor says, "We went out to dinner and Henry just ballooned with pride to have his mother with him when he was starring in a show in Madrid. I remember she was a very warm, nice lady." Family members who were actors were especially welcome since Zorro had roles to fill. Jimmy Victor's brother had a part in one episode. Patrice Martinez' brother Benito was in two. When Lauren visited Henry the first year he was there, she got a featured guest-star role in the episode "Sanctuary."

Michael Tylo's wife at the time, daytime drama actress Hunter Tylo, visited during *Zorro's* first year and was cast in the episode "Family Business". But while filming the second season, Michael Tylo's urge to return to the States and tend to his own family business reached critical mass.

"My baby son started to speak when I wasn't there," he recalls. "Then my father-in-law died and they wouldn't let me leave for the week to attend his funeral." The capper came one day when Tylo was in Spain and his older son, who was about eight, called him to say the little one had chickenpox. "I was in a panic and I asked him why his mom didn't call. He said, 'Daddy, she's been asleep on the couch for a whole day.'" Tylo was frantically calling friends and relatives to find somebody to take care of his family when time came to shoot his scenes. "Henry came down and said, 'Don't worry about it. I'll tell them you have an emergency and to leave you alone.'"

Although Tylo finally reached a cousin, working in Spain had become completely untenable. Deciding to leave the show, he went to Henry and said, "This is the deal. I just wanted to let you know that I am putting my family first."

"Well, Michael, you have to do that. Jobs will come and go," Darrow answered. "True love in your life is that which you have to work at. You have to put your family first, because it affects everything else you do."

For Michael Tylo, Darrow's affirmation was crucial. "I probably still would have made that decision, but it was nice to be validated by him. We aren't that far apart in age, but Henry was like a wonderful uncle to me. He was very direct and honest and after speaking with him, I told the producers I wouldn't be back for another season."

Before Tylo left, he and Darrow shared a bottle of wine and Henry gave him a special gift. "He gave me a book on the the film history of Zorro and he signed it 'to a wonderful actor and a good man, a true gentleman.' I cherish it."

Being away from home impacted not only Tylo, but everyone in some way. Henry Darrow didn't know he'd won a greatly deserved honor until after the fact, thanks to a lackadaisical Spanish attitude toward telegrams.

Even crusty television critic Cleveland Amory once wrote that Darrow should have gotten an Emmy for his portrayal of Manolito Montoya. Other roles like *Harry O's* Manny Quinlan garnered applause from reviewers and audiences, but through years of outstanding performances, Henry Darrow was never even nominated for an Emmy. Again and again, he was passed over. Finally in 1990, he received a Daytime Emmy nomination for Outstanding Supporting Actor in a Drama Series for his portrayal of Rafael Castillo on *Santa Barbara*. He was in Spain filming *Zorro*, but following his nomination had a full page ad with photo in *Variety*:

TO THE ACADEMY...

What a delightful surprise...
Thank you, Jill, the Castillos
and the entire cast and crew of "SANTA BARBARA"
It was a wonderful year.

HENRY DARROW [433]

Being nominated was itself a huge honor and *Zorro's* producers were willing to work around Henry so he could fly back to California for the awards ceremony, but he'd have to pay for his flight. It was a lot of money to fly to Los Angeles and fly right back to Madrid, especially since he figured he wouldn't win.

The Daytime Emmys came and went and Darrow had no idea he won Outstanding Supporting Actor in a Drama Series. A Martinez had picked up his award for him. The Academy sent a telegram to him at the

---

433. Daily Variety, *6/5/90; Jill refers to executive producer Jill Farren-Phelps*

hotel in Madrid where it sat…and sat…and sat until finally someone got around to handing it to him.

"Damn if I didn't win!" he says. "And I could've been up there for my fifteen minutes of fame to show everybody I really made it." His mother and Lauren were both visiting, so those two very important women knew almost as soon as he did. The ladies were so thrilled they bounced around until they were breathless.

"Gloria and I just kept hugging Henry and hugging each other and she and I jumped up and down on the beds like children," Levian recalls.

Again, Darrow made television history, this time with A Martinez. Martinez had been nominated several times for Outstanding Lead Actor in a Drama Series for his portrayal of Cruz Castillo and 1990 was no exception. The difference was this time he won. "He submitted film clips of scenes with me," says Darrow. "Always before, he submitted scenes with Marcy Walker. She would win and he wouldn't. I think he realized that she was the favorite and it was better to show off with someone else!" He laughs, then adds proudly, "That was the first and only time that two Hispanic actors had won Emmys for lead and supporting from the same show simultaneously." When *Zorro's* producers discovered he won the Emmy, they sent a limo to take him from the hotel to the set. On the set, they unfurled a red carpet for him to walk on.

After *Zorro's* second season wrapped and everyone said their fond farewells, Darrow returned to *Santa Barbara* for an encore year as Rafael Castillo. He had another ad run in *Variety* thanking everyone for his win.

TO THE ACADEMY…

What an even nicer surprise…
Again…thank you, Jill, the Castillos
And the entire cast and crew of "SANTA BARBARA"
I'M TRULY GRATEFUL.

HENRY DARROW [434]

---

434. Daily Variety, *6/5/90*

No Half-Measures

We really did have too much fun.

ACTOR JOHN HERTZLER

When *Zorro* was renewed for a third season, Henry Darrow returned as Don Diego/Zorro's daddy, but Michael Tylo's departure meant Pueblo de Los Angeles needed a new alcalde to throw him in jail. The part of Alcalde Ignacio De Soto went to Savannah, Georgia born John G. Hertzler. An "Air Force brat" who grew up moving from state to state, brawny 6'2" Hertzler played high school and college football. At college he was an outside line-backer. "Outside linebacker means I had absolutely no athletic talent," he told *The Los Angeles Times*.[435] He tossed football aside for acting after wandering into the college drama department during auditions for *Marat/Sade*. "They looked me over, saw I was a big guy and said, 'Hmmm, we could use you.' That did it."[436] He showed more flair for acting than football and by the time he joined the cast of *Zorro* Hertzler's résumé included several movies, TV movies, television series and myriad Shakespearean productions in venues from Broadway to San Francisco's American Conservatory.

A huge "Welcome New Alcalde" banner hung in Pueblo de Los Angeles heralding De Soto's arrival; Hertzler snatched it from the set and nailed it to his dressing room. Another jokester had arrived. In a sword fighting sequence with Regehr, Hertzler suddenly stepped out of character, threw down his sword, flung his arms out and shouted to the surprised star, "Damn, Duncan! Look at you! You're perfect!"

"Hertzler would be a great Falstaff," says Darrow. "His alcalde was very different from Tylo's — bombastic, bellowing and full of bravado. There was no real threat, but there was all that very expansive bluster and it played well."

---

435. *"Theater/Jan Herman: Actor Plays Heavies, Heroes With Equal Ease" 8/20/93 http://articles.latimes.com/1993-08-20/entertainment/ca-25722_1_julius-caesar retrieved 12/7/10*

436. Ibid

"Henry was the one who made my transition into the company," Hertzler says. "He is a tremendous trickster, but he made it easier for me to come into that little pre-existing family and bless him for that."

It was an entertaining little family. Duncan Regehr rose early for his rigorous workout regime, but most of the actors started the day around 5:00 a.m. when their drivers picked them up to take them to the set. With actors aboard the drivers raced down the road, then screeched into a café for coffee and brandy. After downing drinks, they burned highway rubber to be at the set on time. At about six in the morning, sweatsuit clad actors trundled out of the cars and headed into makeup and wardrobe. Once in costume, they were ready to work.

"That was especially true of Henry," Ray Austin says. "When he put that costume on, he *was* Don Alejandro!" Sometimes Don Alejandro and everyone else spent time standing around. That's when Austin put on *his* show.

"There is a lot of waiting around on a set, like while they were setting up the cameras," says John Hertzler. "Ray would just grab a horse and get on it bareback. He'd ride around town sitting backwards or standing on the horse because he's an ex-stuntman and he's a maniac."

The sometimes maniacal English director Austin was part of a multi-national cast and crew. The sound crew was French and the cameramen were British. There was a Spanish explosives crew, Spanish stunt doubles, British and American guest stars, American regulars, a Canadian lead, Spanish extras and bit players. To round things off religion wise, Hertzler is an Amish name. Although his grandfather broke with the Order, he notes the show had "a Mennonite Zorro and an Amish alcalde," a *Zorro* first. Henry Darrow, a sometimes maniacal and always devoted practical joker, latched on to Hertzler's Amish background and ran with it.

Initially, Hertzler did not speak Spanish. The young woman named Maria Luz who did his makeup spoke no English. They depended on Henry to translate; it was an opportunity he couldn't pass up. He convinced the makeup girls that Hertzler was Amish and likewise convinced them that the Amish were polygamous. He confided to the girls that since John's three current wives were blonde, he was shopping for a dark haired one. Maria Luz was a pretty brunette.

"He totally made her believe that I was scoping her out to be another wife and she was scared to death!" Hertzler says. "It took her forever to get anything done and I'd say, 'I gotta go, I gotta go! Hurry, I'm on, I'm on!' It didn't help me at *all* with the producers." He wasn't safe from Darrow's jokes after work, either. "We were going out to eat and I said,

'Let me get it. You always pay and this one's on me.' He said okay and he picked a Japanese place. He kept ordering and ordering and encouraging me to try another little *hors d'oeuvre* and then another. I must not have been counting all the zeros in the prices, because when the bill came it was about four hundred dollars! I said, 'Henry, I don't have enough money!' So he said he'd get it, but he knew what he was doing all along, just driving the price through the roof! I still don't know if he even likes Japanese food, but I'm not a particular fan.'"

Besides pranking Hertzler, Darrow shared acting tips. "I called him 'Gloves' because he tagged his lines with his gloves," Hertzler says. "He'd smack them on his pants or he'd do his thinking with one glove on and one off or if it was a big scene, he'd take them off and wave them around. He said, 'You should always have some sort of signature prop in your hand, John.' He's a master."

He was a master at working Jimmy Victor into what Hertzler calls "a frothing mania." Victor was a champion for the little guys, the behind the scenes workers. "Henry worked like hell to get him excited about some issue, like the drivers weren't being treated well or something equally untrue and Jimmy would just react and go shouting at the producer about nothing to do with reality. And there would be Henry with a big smile on his face." It might seem everyone would have copped to it, but Hertzler says no. "Henry was *good*. He got away with murder and he'll continue to. His sense of humor is just to get people in trouble and stand back and watch. It's his passion in life and he's so *good* at it."

Henry's hijinks broke up tensions on the set and kept things loose. "That's when I do my best work," he says. "I want it on a professional level, but I want to have a good time and for everybody to do their best. If people are tense, that's not going to happen."

"Henry's humor never failed to provide great relief," Duncan Regehr recalls. "His re-enactment of a funny experience will invariably turn into an improvisational performance, offering several different embellishments at one sitting. I think I actually lost weight, laughing at his impression of my swordsmanship." Between becoming more comfortable as series lead and Darrow's upbeat presence, Regehr started to relax.

"By the end of the second year, Duncan really warmed up," says Jimmy Victor. "By the third year he was fine. Then by the last year, he really opened up. He was giving everybody his address and inviting us to visit. He really saved me in one episode where I got a complete block. I got to a certain line and I couldn't get that line out! The director was being a real ass and Duncan came to the rescue. He told the director, 'Hey, the sergeant wouldn't talk like that.' So the director let me say it another way and I got through the scene. And then Duncan and I became great friends. He was available to everyone. We had a very nice camaraderie and I think that was Henry's influence because he's such a fun man."

Spanish culture and the bustle of post-Franco Spain suited Darrow and his fellow cast members. Schedules accommodated Spanish ways like afternoon siestas and dinner at ten p.m. "Nobody worked from about two to five," says John Hertzler. "They'd go out and eat tapas and drink, then come back for a couple of hours." After the work day ended, throngs of people mingled in vibrant Madrid until past midnight. On Sundays and holidays, locals and tourists packed the cobblestone streets of El Rastro, Madrid's huge open-air market. El Rastro's pickpockets and purse snatchers were legendary as the wares; watching a puppet show with Henry, Duncan and Duncan's wife Catherine, Hertzler reached into his pocket for his wallet and was shocked to find a hand already there. Whether petty criminal or young Capitalist, the Spanish worked and played hard. "They don't do anything half-assed," says Hertzler. "If they smoke cigarettes, they don't smoke two or three, they smoke six packs a day. Their national sport isn't like football where there's a winner and a loser. It's bullfighting where either you kill the bull or the bull kills you. There are no half-measures in Spain."

By the fourth season, filming in Spain was a marvelous combo of the foreign and the familiar for the cast and crew. The art, fine food, shopping and culture of Spain and nearby European countries were invigorating, but Madrid was a home away from home, where favorite restaurants and the familiar hotel eagerly anticipated the return of cast and crew. Just arrived on April 27, 1992 Henry Darrow unpacked, showered and arranged his room. The next day, he jotted down notes about grocery shopping, lunch with costars and doing laundry. Then on April 29, he was struck by how far he was from home and Lauren when Los Angeles burst into flames. The four Los Angeles police officers charged with brutality toward DUI suspect Rodney King, an African-American, had been acquitted by a predominantly white jury.[437] Largely black and Hispanic South Central Los Angeles erupted. The 1992 Los Angeles riots would cause fifty-three deaths and thousands of injuries. Over 7,000 fires burned. Fire and looting damaged more than 3,000 businesses.

---

437. *Two were later convicted on federal charges of violating King's civil rights*

International news coverage exploded with footage of chilling destruction. Duncan Regehr, James Victor, Patrice Martinez and Henry Darrow all had family or friends in Los Angeles. Thousands of miles away in Madrid, the actors could only worry, watch terrifying images on CNN, make calls or wait for the phone to ring.

Lauren was at home in Altadena and had been booked to perform one woman shows at schools in areas ripped by violence. Henry scribbled his thoughts on the back of pages of his scripts. "Concerned for The BABES." He underlined his pet name for her with hard strokes. "No shows — more violence — theater, basketball, public events have been cancelled." The last word is dark and heavy. "Riots, burnings, LOOTINGS again like Watts," he wrote, remembering the Watts riots of summer 1965 when it seemed Los Angeles was burning down. "Why destroy your own area? Where you live? You lose jobs, places to buy food. Fire, all night long — Westwood HIT — Lake Arrowhead — Riverside — San Bernardino!!!! What about The Babes?? Everything cancelled — come to Spain?"

After six days federal troops quashed mob violence and although resentments remained a festering sore in the wounded city, Lauren was safe. Darrow and the others concentrated on work and *Zorro's* fourth season filming continued without a hitch. But when it comes to renewing television shows, there are no half-measures. A series is either renewed or it's not. For *Zorro*, the fourth season was also the last, but like Zorro himself, it left its mark.

A teacher of high-risk youth in Kentucky successfully used *New World Zorro* as a teaching tool, earning her a commendation from First Lady Barbara Bush and launching a comprehensive "Zorro in the Classroom" guide for teachers.

"*Zorro* was endorsed by the National Educational Association for encouraging good moral values and achievement and it was rare for that organization to give their approval," says Darrow.

"We kept our violence to a minimum. Zorro wounded people, he very seldom killed anyone. If they got killed it was their very own fault," Ray Austin notes. "And we had marvelous guest-stars, especially famous wrestlers. The children were big fans of wrestlers and we had no trouble getting them as guest-stars because everyone wanted to come to Spain to play with our toys."

Nobody enjoyed the toys more than Henry Darrow. "I got to use my sabre practice and to actually fence in sequences," he recalls. "I made $12,500 a week, the best income I ever had and in my favorite episode, I got to be Zorro again!"

"Like Father, Like Son" was a fourth season episode which has been dubbed one of the "most interesting and original stories" of the series.[438] While reading *Don Quixote*, Don Alejandro accidentally falls into the Zorro cave and hits his head. Coming to, he sees Zorro's costume and decides he must be Zorro. "When I think of Zorro, I think of dash," Darrow says. "Being dashing and romantic and very Spanish." Which is just how he played it, except during his adventures he becomes a little confused as to whether he's Zorro or Don Quixote. As Zorro, he rides into town and dashingly rescues Victoria Escalante from villains. After subduing the bad guys he's promptly arrested by Alcalde de Soto and sentenced to hang as Zorro. However, while in jail he segues into Quixote. He decides Victoria must be the fair Dulcinea and recognizes Sgt. Mendoza as trusty servant Sancho Panza. The real Zorro rescues Don Alejandro from the gallows in the nick of time and luckily, the elder de Vega hits his head again and wakes up as his old self. In a clever exchange at the end, Don Alejandro recalls wistfully his dream of being Zorro and wonders if there actually is a little bit of Zorro in him. Don Diego answers that there is some of Zorro in everyone and even a bit of Don Alejandro in Zorro.

Two other episodes highlighting Henry Darrow featured friends dating back from *The High Chaparral*. In third season episode "Alejandro Rides Again," Bob Hoy guest-starred as one of Don Alejandro's former army buddies (Hoy was also Second Unit Director on several *Zorro* episodes). "A Love Remembered" guest-starred another familiar face from *The High Chaparral* —Donna Baccala.[439] Baccala had guest-starred on *Chaparral* as Manolito's ill-fated love and this time, she played Don Alejandro's old flame. A flashback scene of the first meeting between Don Alejandro and Mercedes Villero is actually footage of Manolito and Mercedes Vega de Granada meeting for the first time as adults in the *Chaparral* episode "A Time to Laugh, A Time to Cry." Since Baccala was there on the *Zorro* set, she voiced over "Alejandro?" where she originally said "Manolito?"

Darrow laughs. "When we cut in with that footage from *Chaparral*, it was like 'Wow! They went back in time! How did they do that?" But some things never change and for the second time, "Mercedes" died in his arms. "Well as you know, in any series, fall in love with a regular and you're either dead or you enter the convent," he observes.

Of course, the most familiar *High Chaparral* face on *New World Zorro* was Henry Darrow's. Visiting London during a *Zorro* hiatus, he was in

438. Yoggy, p. 566 and 567

439. Billed as Donna Bacalla

a cab and saw the cabbie checking him out in the rear view mirror. The gray-haired actor figured the cabbie probably watched *Zorro* with his kids or grandkids and recognized him as Don Alejandro. Then the cabdriver took a long look and said, "I know you! You're Manolito!"

The most used question in Hollywood is "Whatever happened to...?" People who make a living in this business for ten years are really unusual. People who last fifty years are freaks.

ACTOR DENNY MILLER

One-Man Show

Home is wherever you happen to be.

KOLOPAK (HENRY DARROW) IN *STAR TREK: VOYAGER*

When *New World Zorro* ended, Darrow traveled to Australia for guest appearances in the science fiction series *Time Trax*. Back in the U.S. he guest-starred in the crime-drama series *Silk Stalkings* and had a support role in the TV movie *Percy & Thunder* (1993), but he was a star again onstage. In *B/C Historia*, a powerful production covering thirteen centuries of intertwined Latino and black history, he won rave reviews for versatility in multiple roles. He played a "spirited" Arabian general eager to invade Spain, displayed "comic skills as a lascivious court physician" and was a dignified Mexican-American cantina owner who dies saving migrant workers.[440]

He had a different sort of role as star of the English-language version of a bicultural *telenovela* filmed in Mexico. The conjoint project media-mogul billionaires Rupert Murdock and Televisa CEO Emilio Azcárraga Milmo, it employed two companies — one Mexican and one American — for two versions of the same show. In the morning, a Mexican cast shot the Spanish-language version, *Imperio de Cristal*. In the afternoon, the American company had the same set to shoot *Crystal Empire*, starring Darrow as old fox Marcus Lambert.

"I did *Crystal Empire* because of *High Chaparral*," he says. "The producer had been a fan of the show when he was a kid. He flew up to meet me because he wanted to see how I looked. We met and he said, 'Okay, let's do it' and that was that." When Lauren came for a visit, she ended up staying to play his ex-wife.

After six months in Mexico filming *Crystal Empire*, Henry had a solid supporting role stateside as an avuncular police captain in the straight-to-video thriller *Criminal Passion* (1994), which was either a cheesy *Basic Instinct* (1992) rip-off or "smokily sensual and genuinely erotic" depending

---

440. Daily Variety, *"Legit Reviews," by Julio Martinez, 3/5/93*

upon the reviewer.[441] Reviews were also mixed for 1994's big-budget feature film *Maverick* starring Mel Gibson and Jodie Foster, but most critics were charmed and nearly all agreed that half the fun was "keeping an eye peeled for celebrity cameos."[442] Director Richard Donner (who directed Henry Darrow in *Hernandez, Houston P.D.*) cast numerous actors he'd worked with as credited and uncredited background characters. Henry Darrow was one, along with Danny Glover, Denver Pyle, Margot Kidder, Dub Taylor, Bert Remsen, Clint Black, William Marshall, Doug McClure and Robert Fuller.

"It was a wonderful experience," says Darrow. "Alfred Molina was the lead bad-guy and I was sitting there with Bill Marshall, and I played Iago to his Othello decades before. There were all these marvelous character actors from long-ago westerns and the company was so generous. I was supposed to work for four weeks but I got sick and only worked for two, but Donner paid me for three."

When Alfred Molina, who remembered him from *The High Chaparral*, asked, "Why do you take all these little parts?"

"I don't see them as little parts," Darrow responded. "I see them as work and I want to work."

Hispanic Hollywood noted Darrow's long commitment to excellence in parts large and small. He won the National Hispanic Media Coalition Impact Award (1996) and Nosotros' Golden Eagle Award for Lifetime Achievement (1999), both significant honors. However, acting is too often a young person's business and Lifetime Achievement awards can signal someone who is revered as an icon but can't find a job. Although work was harder to get as years passed, Darrow's strength as an actor, versatility and resilient ego kept him in the game.

He guest-starred once on the Emmy and Golden Globe nominated NBC drama series *Sisters* and twice on UPN's *Star Trek: Voyager* (1995-2001) as the Native American Kolopak, father of USS *Voyager*'s First Officer Chakotay (played by Robert Beltran). He costarred in the BBC documentary *Way Out West* (1996) along with James Drury and Tom Selleck. In 1997 he narrated *The Fight in the Fields*, a PBS documentary about César Chávez and the United Farmworkers Union which was nominated for the Grand Jury Prize at the Sundance Film Festival and won both a Golden Apple from the National Educational Media Network

441. http://movies.tvguide.com/criminal-passion/review/130136

442. http://www.washingtonpost.com/wp-srv/style/longterm/movies/videos/maverickpgbrown_a0ae19.htm

and an ALMA (American Latino Media Arts) award for Outstanding Made-for-Television Documentary. As the new millennium drew closer, he voiced a support role in the popular CD-ROM interactive video game, *Tex Murphy Overseer* ("Great game…wonderful concept," "…downright entertaining," "You can't beat Tex!"[443]). Also in 1998, he had a support role in the straight-to-video kidflick *Mom, Can I Keep Her?* about a boy and a stray gorilla. Featuring frequent film gorilla Don McLeod as the ape, it won audiences with its family-friendly humor and Darrow's antics as an off-kilter war veteran. He also contributed a solid performance in the adventure flick *Enemy Action* (1999) starring C. Thomas Howell, with whom he had worked previously (*The Hitcher*, 1986). That same year he was in the teen horror feature *Tequila Body Shots* starring pop sensation Joey Lawrence. Henry had an appealing support role as "Doc" the medicine man, but *Variety's* Robert Koehler noted that out of the whole limp retelling of the Orpheus myth, "Saddest of all is Darrow, a credible medicine man but an actor much too strong to be reduced to this assignment."[444]

However, the theater embraced Darrow like an eager woman and gave the strong actor suitable star-turns. In 1996, he costarred in the Los Angeles Opera production of *Florencia en el Amazones*, a two-act drama by Daniel Catán inspired by Gabriel García Márquez. Co-commissioned by the Houston, Los Angeles and Seattle operas, it was the first Spanish-language opera commissioned by major American opera-houses. He followed with *Tale and Song: A Tribute to Gabriel García Márquez*, then starred in Rick Najera's autobiographical play *A Quiet Love* in San Diego.

"*A Quiet Love* was really the story of my father," Najera explains. "It was a gift to my family, to my father's generation of men and to my father. He was a man I admired and it was great to have Henry, a man we both admired, play him." He began writing *Quiet Love* while his father, Ed Najera, was dying. "Henry was a brave enough actor that he could play a dying man who was dignified and fun and full of love." Najera by that time had written for HBO, Showtime, Paramount, ABC, FOX and Viacom and had written and performed a successful one-man show, but Darrow's facile acting still awed him as it had when he was just starting in the business. "Henry truly lights up the stage and he's performing *for* you. He always had that little sparkle in his eye and he'd look at me like, 'Watch this. I'm about to amaze you.' When we were rehearsing and he did a particularly great job, he'd look at me like, 'Did you see that? Wow,

443. IMDB.com *user reviews, retrieved 7/27/11*

444. Variety, *"Film Reviews" by Robert Koehler, 5/10-5/16, 1999*

pretty good, wasn't it?' Then he'd slip back into character again and it was like talking to my dad. He had this playfulness even though he was serious about his work and that reminded me very much of my father."

"Rick has a wonderful positive energy," says Darrow. "He gave me the freedom to improvise and it was interesting because I'd adlib and he'd say, 'God! That's just what my father would say!'"

Reviewers responded enthusiastically to Najera's touching combination of comedy and drama and superb performances by the cast, but Darrow blew them away. *The Los Angeles Times* deemed his Ed "larger than life with his warmth, wit, loyalty and love."[445] "First rate" declared the *North County Times*, noting that Darrow played Ed "believably from ailing middle age to youth and back without benefit of makeup or costume changes."[446] The *San Diego Union-Tribune* called him "splendid" and "regal" with an "almost magically relaxed" acting style."[447] Darrow, Najera and the outstanding cast copped the *Drama-Logue* Critics Award for Outstanding Achievement in Theatre for their "magical mirror" on a loving and complex family.[448]

Given the chance, Darrow could have wowed 'em on camera, too. But since he wasn't getting that chance, well…Before *A Quiet Love*, he had started a project involving a 20th Century writer working as a waiter and a Spanish novelist who died in 1616. He dove back into it after *A Quiet Love* wrapped.

The writer was Harry Cason, a Midwesterner who moved to Los Angeles to follow his dreams. When Henry, Lauren and Deedee dined at the Pasadena restaurant where he waited tables, he recognized Darrow and introduced himself. Months later, he took a class for nascent directors. His assignment was to direct a scene from *The Dresser*, a knockout melodrama about a ruined actor in his sixties and his self-sacrificing personal assistant. Albert Finney garnered an Oscar nomination as the aged actor in the 1983 film version and Cason thought Henry Darrow would be perfect in the role. He also thought Darrow wouldn't remember him and probably wouldn't do a freebie for a directing class even if he did. He left a message with Darrow's agent anyway. When Darrow returned the call, his only question was, "When do we start?"

445. The Los Angeles Times, *"Theater Review" by Nancy Churnin, 6/16/97*

446. *"Tender comedy 'Quiet Love' marked by first-rate performances" by Bill Fark, undated from files of Henry Darrow*

447. *"A magical mirror on San Diego Family's life" by Michael Phillips, 5/12/97*

448. Ibid

A friend of Cason's named Evan played the dresser and during rehearsals, Cason says, "Hank was blowing Evan out of the water. He wasn't being piggish, but he had that extraordinary magnetism and concentration. I pulled Evan aside and said, 'You know, this guy is a shark and he's going to eat you alive.' Hank chuckled and said, 'Oh, I'm a very old shark. A very old, tired shark.' He brought Evan's performance up about 50%. It was like playing tennis with John McEnroe." For the class and the teacher, it was like *watching* John McEnroe play tennis. The instructor told Cason, "A director can spend his entire career looking for an actor like this guy. He's the real thing and I want you to recognize that."

Cason did. A few months later Darrow said he wanted to do a one-man show and asked Cason to write it. The stunned younger man said he'd try. Darrow said, "Find me somebody with status, somebody flamboyant." They nixed several Spanish *conquistadores* because their bloody exploits weren't appealing, then Cason casually suggested Cervantes. Darrow crows, "And that was it! He was not particularly flamboyant, but he wrote plays and other stuff that were turkeys and then he wrote *Don Quixote*, something that has withstood the test of centuries, with these two *incredible* characters Don Quixote de la Mancha and Sancho Panza!" His voice sizzles with excitement; so what if Cervantes wasn't actually a flamboyant character? Henry Darrow could make him into one! "He lived right after the Spanish Golden Age of Lope de Vega and Calderón de la Barca and when he did *Don Quixote*, it was the best seller of the day all over the world in so many different languages! He had been in prison. He was wounded in the battle of Lepanto and lost the use of his arm. He had to make his living as a tax collector and he was hated! *Hated!* A brave soldier, but a basically a failure, certainly a failure as a writer. Every time he went to bat, bam! He struck out. But he never gave up and he wrote the world's first great novel!"

Cason immersed himself in the life of Cervantes, Darrow gave the first draft a hearty thumbs-up and they started workshopping it. Henry performed before acting classes and solicited input from the students. At theaters around Los Angeles, he performed sections of the play under various titles — *Don Quixote de la Mancha, Cervantes the Patriot, The Mirror of La Mancha* — and friends in the audience gave feedback. After each performance came revisions.

"It's a very painful process," says Cason. "You put your raw material out there and strangers go, 'Well, this part kind of sucks.' Henry never sulked. He'd just say, 'Oh, that was painful.' Rejection is the actor's world and it's hard not to take it personally, but Henry has stayed alive by recognizing, it's not me, it's the role, it's not me, it's the character, let's just go forward, tomorrow is another day." Revision after revision, performance after performance, tomorrow was another day and then another year.

By 1999, sixty-five-year-old Darrow was constantly on the go between performing pieces of Cervantes and other work. He traveled often to Puerto Rico to help Miluka Rivera's SAG delegation establish a branch of the Screen Actors' Guild there; proud of the island's growing presence in the film industry, he was part of nearly every publicity event during the three-year planning stage. He also taught "Acting for the Camera" at the American Academy of Dramatic Arts. "That was a pleasure and a delight," he says. "Teaching the kids and doing live theater have a similar energy and it's a chance to return what has been given to you."

Lauren was likewise busy, writing for the well-regarded UPN series *Legacy*. The post-Civil War family saga was filmed in Virginia and on January 26, 1999 she was upstairs packing to leave for Richmond when Henry trudged into the room. His face was ashen and contorted.

"He was just paler than pale and he said, 'Take me to the doctor,'" she recalls. "We managed to get him down the stairs and to the doctor's office, but once we were there he had to crawl out of the elevator. They knew he was having a heart attack and they started working on him there, and then they rushed him to the emergency room."

In the E.R., with Lauren by his side, the medical team hooked up monitors and settled him in, then they left to tend to another patient. Suddenly the alarms for his monitors shrieked, buzzers bellowed, lights flashed and his eyes rolled back white. Lauren screamed.

His heart had stopped beating. He wasn't breathing. The intercom announced Code Blue, Code Blue as the ER team burst in with the crash cart and hustled Lauren into the hall. She waited while the room swarmed with frantic activity. When CPR didn't work, the crash team hit Henry with defibrillation paddles. Once they got a heartbeat, it was a race to the operating room.

"I ran down the hall after the gurney when they rushed him into surgery," she says. "The doctor came out and asked if he had any children and I couldn't find Deedee's phone number at first. They put in a stent and moved him to ICU. I stayed with him for two nights in intensive care and then they moved him to the cardiac floor. That's when I knew he was going to be okay. I held it together until then, because I didn't want him to think he was dying. But once he was in a room, I went home and just broke down."

Darrow's odds of surviving a cardiac arrest were only a little better than the odds of making a living as an actor. A full fourth of his heart lost all function. Most of the men on his father's side died of heart failure in their sixties.

"I remember being in the ER and then there was just nothing. Then I heard Lauren scream and that brought me back," he recalls. "I heard her footsteps going away and I knew she was gone, but that was it until I came to later in the ICU and she was there."

"We really tried to make sure nobody in the business found out about it in case he could work again," Lauren says. "If they knew, nobody would have hired him. They would have been too worried that he'd die during filming; finding a replacement, reshooting scenes would cost money and time and nobody wants that."

Recuperating at home, Henry was initially too debilitated to think of work. As he grew stronger, he collaborated on the *Cervantes* scripts with Harry Cason and guest-starred on two award-winning series, *Family Law* (CBS) and AMC's *The Lot*. He also guest-starred in the long-running Dick Van Dyke series *Diagnosis Murder* (CBS) in the episode "You Bet Your Life" as high-stakes poker player Sherman Webster, a has-been movie star. The executive producer, a friend of Darrow's, had the part written especially for him. There was a sly moment when Van Dyke looked at Webster and said, "Didn't you used to be somebody?" Webster struck a pose and it suddenly came to Van Dyke. "You were Miguelito on 'The Green Chaparral'…!"

Darrow wasn't ready to be a has-been in real life and decided to prove he could carry a load. It took him six months to memorize the final script for his eighty-minute one-man show, *That Certain Cervantes*.

Harry Cason recalls, "One day I got a call from this gal, Debra De Liso, who had been one of his students. She was a director and she knew a producer. They'd gotten with Henry and *Cervantes* was going to open in three weeks! The theater was already booked! I said, 'Oh my God! Are you kidding?'"

Days later on September 11, 2001, Deedee called Henry and said, "Pop? Are you watching TV? There's something awful happening in New York!" Nineteen radical *al-Queda* terrorists had hijacked four US passenger jets and Deedee just saw footage of American Airlines Flight 11 crashing into the World Trade Center's North Tower. Henry turned on the news in time to see United Airlines Flight 175 blast into the WTC's South Tower. This was not the New York where he'd played Zorro with the boys in the neighborhoods and gone to movies with his mother. The twin towers, consumed with flame and bellowing smoke, collapsed within two hours. Hijacked American Airlines Flight 77 hit the Pentagon minutes later, followed by United Airlines Flight 93 which went down in a Pennsylvania field following intervention by the passengers. Nobody in the airliners survived. This first-ever assault on US soil by a foreign attacker claimed thousands of lives and exacted an economic toll in the billions. Fear had the nation by the throat. Many people were too terrified to leave their homes, but most stuck to routines and tended to their usual business. "I couldn't do anything about terrorist attacks in New York City, but I had a barn to build," said a small-city construction worker. "I saw it on television at the tire store and it was horrible. Everybody was shaken up, but the tire guys went back to work and so did I."

"People on the television were saying we can't change our lives because of this. We couldn't let fear rule us, but it was awful for the whole country," Henry recalls. "We had rented the theater for *Cervantes* with sponsorships from people like the McCrays, David Dortort and Lauren's dad, so we opened about two weeks after 9/11. Nobody showed up, but at least it was a small theater. A small one seems less empty than an empty big one."

The theater didn't grow, but the audience did. His dazzling performance and enthusiastic accolades from reviewers pulled them in.

"Darrow is an actor who projects warmth with his every aspect; his rich voice, his friendly face, his beguiling sense of humor."[449]

He played a deft mélange of parts with an accent, a well-placed scarf, a particular walk or a change of voice. His artistry made a pantheon of characters spring to life: Don Quixote's decrepit horse Rocinante, loyal servant Sancho Panza, the aged, impoverished Cervantes, the young soldier Cervantes at the bloody Battle of Lepanto, Cervantes' wife Catalina, Quixote's idealized Dulcinea, village women, children, Spanish nobles and hated rival, the poet Lope de Vega.

"Darrow makes up a dream cast all by his lonesome!"[450]

"Darrow also displays a wonderfully facile gift for characterization as he embodies the vocal and physical attributes of the many colorful characters who inhabit Cervantes' world…"[451]

There was pure slapstick and sly irony. There was loss and tragedy. There was adventure. There was hope and despair and fantasy. There was Papa Abuelo's (and Manolito Montoya's) little song about the dying hen

449. Back Stage West, *"That Certain Cervantes" by Wenzel Jones, 10/4/01*

450. The Los Angeles Times, *undated review from files of Henry Darrow*

451. Daily Variety, *"Legit Reviews" by Julio Martinez, 10/8/01*

and crying chicks. Tying it together was the "underlying theme of faith supplying the strength to get a man through prison, war, poverty and a houseful of vexatious women…"[452]

"Darrow is captivating throughout…There appears to be no limit to his emotional range as he segues from the passionate sounds of battle to his recollections of being imprisoned and enslaved by Algerian pirates to his deeply felt sadness at the death of his brother, killed at the Battle of Flanders."[453]

"Darrow, with his gleaming white hair and mustache, makes an elegant and dashing Cervantes…the crowning achievement of his career."[454]

"[Cervantes] could find no greater tribute…Darrow doesn't just perform…[he] burrows into the psyche of this complex historical figure who never found true success in his own time."[455]

"Darrow renders a bravura performance…the very embodiment of the great writer he portrays in *That Certain Cervantes*."[456]

"I've just been enthralled by the character of Cervantes," Darrow says. "Maybe in some way, there's an affinity. Some Latino producers wanted more angst and I said, 'No, I want this to be uplifting!' We ended it with him getting teed off. 'I'll show them!' Sure, that's old theater, but it's *good* old theater and it worked."

Not long after, he guest-starred in an episode of *Resurrection Boulevard* with Rita Moreno and showed her *Variety's* review of *That Certain Cervantes*. "I said, 'This is the best review I've ever gotten for anything.' I thought I could share it with her without sounding too self-important, just to say, 'Hey what do you think? Small ninety-nine seat theater and look at the reviews.' Rita started to read it and she began crying. She said, 'Henry, this is the most magnificent review I've ever read.'"

In Showtime's compelling family drama *Resurrection Blvd.* (2000-2002) Darrow and *La Moreno* played husband and wife. One scene brought a chapter in his career full-circle. In that scene, they danced together. "I said, 'Rita, I just want you to know that it's taken me forty years to dance with you. Forty years ago during *Summer and Smoke*, the

452. Back Stage West, *"That Certain Cervantes" by Wenzel Jones, 10/4/01*

453. Daily Variety, *"Legit Reviews" by Julio Martinez, 10/8/01*

454. Valley Scene, *"That Certain Cervantes" by Don Grigware, undated review files of Henry Darrow*

455. Daily Variety, *"Legit Reviews" by Julio Martinez, 10/8/01*

456. The Orange County Register, *"That Certain Cervantes" by Lucille De View, undated from the files of Henry Darrow*

director called for somebody to dance with Miss Moreno and I hesitated for five seconds and when I got up, someone else beat me to it. And now, I finally get to dance with you.' She was very touched and got all choked up," he recalls softly. "I don't usually speak out of anger because I don't function well that way, but when it's a good feeling from the heart, I like to express it." He pauses, then laughs. "Rita is intense and she's done so much great work and she's fun, but she'll chew your head off! I asked the director to hold her off of me. I just couldn't match her! Every time I adlibbed, she came up with a better one. The director said, 'So don't adlib on her. Just keep your mouth shut and stay with the dialogue or she's gonna top you.' Aw, crap! I couldn't do *anything*!"

For Luis Reyes, who ditched acting and became a successful publicist, handling publicity for *Resurrection Blvd.* was the chance to see two top Puerto Rican performers show everyone how it's done. "Young actors waste time on their cell-phones or they're in their trailers; you have to go get them and bring them back to the set and you lose time. Five minutes here or there doesn't seem like much, but at the end of the day, you can be behind an hour if you have a large cast. Henry and Rita are old school. They always knew their lines and they were *always* on the set, sitting by the director, ready to go on."

Reyes wasn't the only one who appreciated Darrow's old-time professionalism and 2001 was a good year for him. Besides performing *That Certain Cervantes* in California, he took the play to Connecticut where old friend Susan McCray hooked him up with a University gig as Resident Guest Artist and to New Mexico, where Val de Vargas, who pointed him to his first agent, was in the audience.

"He'd retired from acting and he came up and said, 'Jesus, Hank! I can't believe it! After all these years, you've never given up. You were fantastic!" Darrow recalls. "Yeah! I'm not through *yet*."

He certainly wasn't. He starred in twelve episodes of the CBS daytime drama *The Bold and the Beautiful* and guest-starred as a priest in Nickelodeon's award-winning series *The Brothers Garcia* ("zesty comedy for the entire family!"[457]). Onstage back in California, he broke from *Cervantes* to star in *Burning Patience* as Chilean poet Pablo Neruda, a compadre of his uncle Emilio. In a radio drama for the BBC *(The Blood of Strangers)*, he voiced an old cowboy with a bad heart, but he played a more vigorous character in the Emmy-nominated PBS drama series *American Family*.

---

457. http://www.commonsensemedia.org/tv-reviews/Brothers-Garcia.html, retrieved 8/5/2011

Filmed in East Los Angeles and Mexico, *American Family* was the saga of the Mexican-American Gonzalez family. Created and directed by Gregory Nava (*El Norte*, 1983; *Selena*, 1997), the all-star cast included Edward James Olmos, Sonia Braga, Esai Morales, Raquel Welch, Patricia Velasquez, Kurt Caceres, Constance Marie, Rachel Ticotin, Kate del Castillo, Liz Torres and A.J. Lamas. Rounding out the show were outstanding character actors and world-class guest stars like Rita Moreno and Henry Darrow. Darrow guest-starred three times as Uncle Léon, the older brother of Jess Gonzalez' (Olmos) departed wife Berta (Braga). Olmos, a notably accomplished actor, held his own well in sequences with Darrow, but Darrow's scene-stealing acumen wasn't dimmed by working with an old friend. Before he made his last appearance on a two-parter filmed in Chiapas, Mexico, the producer wanted to know, "Can you ride a horse?" Darrow said yes and when Uncle Léon, owner of a vast ranch, swung gracefully into the saddle and rode away, it was impressive enough to make everyone sigh, "Oh, Manolito!"

> *Never meddle with play-actors, for they're a favoured race.*
>
> MIGUEL DE CERVANTES SAAVEDRA

From the Top

I am the Ballad. I sing of happiness, tragedies and sorrows...

MAESTRO OF THE BALLAD[458]

Henry Darrow points to *Resurrection Blvd.* as an example of how things changed since audiences originally said, "Oh, Manolito!" in 1967. "There were probably 125-150 Hispanic actors in *Resurrection Blvd.* in just one year compared to *High Chaparral*, which probably used 120-150 over a four-year period," he says, noting that *Resurrection Blvd.'s* stars and principal supporting actors were all Hispanic, as were most of the others on the series. That would have been unimaginable forty years earlier, but Hispanics had become major players in all facets in of the entertainment industry and American society. "Hispanic newscasters were doing real news stories, not just stories about the Mexican market that opened down the street. Hispanic actors had roles in movies and TV that had nothing do with being Hispanic—they were just good roles with Latino actors in them. That's when you know what you started or tried to start decades earlier was succeeding." As for radical organizations that "use racism as a badge of honor," he notes, "It's like, 'Jeez, you said that forty years ago! How can you have the nerve to say nothing has changed? There's a Mexican-American mayor in Los Angeles, Antonio Villaraigosa. There are other Hispanics in high office and business, including the entertainment business. Look around! You see very positive strides in the Spanish-speaking community.'"

But for Darrow himself, things seemed less positive. "When you know everything, all the ends and outs, you're past your prime. Your mortgage is all gone and nobody wants to hire you," he says. "I would go to auditions and it would be the same twelve old guys. The young casting directors had no idea what I'd done. Some people who knew me were still working and I would do wonderful audition and they would say they didn't want

458. *In* Corridos, *by Luis Valdez*

anybody in the role but me, but then I'd learn they hired somebody else. It knocks you down, like, 'Oh, crap! Don't get so up, don't start thinking you'll get a really good part!' There's the stress and there's the pang in my gut when I'm not cast. When I was young, I just thought, it's their loss and I went on to the next one. But later in life, it takes pieces out of you."

James Victor agrees. "It takes a piece of you every time, but you have to perform because that's what you do. You have to perform to get the job. You have to perform while you're doing the job. Sometimes you don't feel like doing it, but you gotta get up there and get that show going." If you have a show, that is.

Although younger, Lauren had her own career disappointments. When Henry was doing *Zorro*, she performed her shows for children 140 times a year or more. As the years passed, the grants she depended upon for funding dried up. She was down to thirty-seven shows a year.

"She just finally wore out," Darrow says tenderly. "She asked, 'Shall we get out of here?' and I said, 'Yeah!' She was shocked, because I don't even want to walk to the corner and all of a sudden, we were thinking of moving across the country. Our friends couldn't believe it, but it just wasn't worth staying in L.A. anymore with the stress and the traffic and the crime."

Character actor Pat Hingle was living in North Carolina and talked up Wilmington. Home to Screen Gems Studios (the largest film and television studio outside California), a thriving arts community and a branch of the University of North Carolina, Wilmington has long attracted Hollywood refugees trading hustle and smog for a more laid-back lifestyle. After Hingle showed Henry and Lauren around, they sold the house in Altadena and bought a neoclassical revival fixer in a graceful historic neighborhood.

Director Dorothy Rankin and her husband actor/director Lee Lowrimore were initially concerned when they heard a "big star" was moving nearby, but fears about having a disruptive diva in their midst soon vanished. "We all became friends rights away. Henry is so unlike you would imagine a movie star or television actor, so welcoming of the world," says Rankin. "The first time we went out to dinner with Henry and Lauren, everybody in the restaurant knew Henry. He'd just moved in and he'd already met half the town."

"I love Wilmington," Darrow says. "There are actors, writers and directors from all over the country who have come here and they're part of the community fabric. The cultural scene is very low-key and friendly, but there's plenty going on."

Lauren threw herself into renovating their home, exploring the new community and tending to her beloved but difficult father. A once-brilliant Wall Street player, Allan Levian was in his early nineties and stricken with Alzheimer's disease; Lauren, his only child, found a care facility for him in Wilmington so she could be close by.

Not long after the move, another senior citizen demanded their attention in Puerto Rico. Gloria Delgado had orchestrated a 90th birthday bash for herself. Friends and family came from near and far. Dennis and his wife Olga were there and their daughters with their families, Gloria's great-grandchildren. After dinner in the huge banquet hall, Gloria got up and performed. She told jokes in Spanish and English (some of them a little risqué) and recited her poetry from memory. After she finished, the dancing started.

"Mom danced a little flamenco and Dennis and I got up and danced with her," Henry says. "She had her arms in the air and she was clapping and Dennis and I were trying to do the flamenco heel-toe and we were out of breath! And Mom wasn't! She got a standing ovation! I asked her, 'How come you're not breathing hard?' She said, 'Sweetheart, it's all in the hands. Look at my feet.' Sure enough, she started to dance again and she wasn't moving her feet. She was just doing the arms."

Lauren selected the perfect present for Gloria Delgado, who had dreamed of being a "toe-dancer" when she was a young girl. "We gave her a real ballerina's outfit with a pink tutu and a pair of toe shoes," Lauren says. Gloria being Gloria, she couldn't wait to put it on. At her apartment after the party, the trim little lady proudly donned her present and smiled brightly as her family snapped pictures.

Back in Wilmington, Henry performed *That Certain Cervantes* to rave reviews, then he and Lauren collaborated with with Harry Cason to make *Cervantes* into a two-person play. Directed by Cason and performed in Santa Fe, New Mexico and in Wilmington at the historic Thalian Hall Center for the Performing Arts, the two-person version was a winner.

"Lauren played Sancho Panza and several other characters including my wife, Catalina and those scenes took on a different perspective because there was somebody else to play off," Darrow says. "It helped the creative process because I'd get bored and a little lazy. That makes you lose precision, but Lauren kept me in line."

He points out, "Some actors as they get older produce or direct when the acting work dries up. I go back to the theater and teaching." He connected with UNC, where he was a guest instructor and performed in the English farce *See How They Run*. He also remained a hot property at western film festivals and science fiction conventions around the country where he enchanted fans with stories, sold autographed photos, reminisced and caught up with old colleagues. The Internet brought fans together for events and hundreds of people attended to meet the stars they admired. In 2003, with *The High Chaparral* airing in the U.S. on the Hallmark Channel, long-time fans of the show held their first big reunion in Los Angeles. Boxing promoter/announcer Al Bernstein, a fan of westerns in general and *Chaparral* in particular, speaks for others when he says of such events, "It completes a circle. You get to meet someone who helped create a great fantasy for you."

The High Chaparral had aired repeatedly all over the world and fans from Europe, Australia, Central and South America and across the U.S. came to the reunion to meet their heroes. There were middle-aged Baby-Boomers and twenty-somethings; female and male; a doctor, a sportscaster, a mayor, secretaries, nurses, students, executives, writers and housewives. All were thrilled to meet Henry Darrow. As one wrote afterward, "I got to speak with Henry Darrow!!!!! Yee-haw! I was (and still am) so excited! He was very sweet and caught me up on what he's been doing. SIGH…"[459]

Settling into Wilmington, Darrow began picking up supporting parts in film and TV. He guest-starred in *Dawson's Creek*, WB's award-winning coming-of-age drama and was also among the huge cast of the Edgar-nominated courtroom thriller *The Runaway Jury* (2003). But he told the local paper, "When I see seniors, older actors working, I love it. I don't have the fire to go after it like I once did."[460]

Lauren turned her considerable energies toward real estate, writing her novel and crafting radio commentaries. She and Henry immersed themselves in the social scene: dining out, monthly dancing and spending time with family and friends. Meeting new friends like Screen Gems CEO Frank Capra, Jr. and reconnecting with old ones brought work Henry's way. In 2005, he guest-starred in an episode of WB's teen drama series *One Tree Hill*, starred in the well-received short thriller *The Writer's Pub* and earned a good review ("earnest character acting from… Henry Darrow") for a support role in the feature film *Angels with Angles* (2005)."[461] In 2006, he starred in the short thriller *Snapshot* (a film festival entry), then played the grandfather in Lifetime Network's TV movie *A Girl Like Me: The Gwen Araujo Story*, based on the true story of a trans-

459. http://thehighchaparral.com/reunion03.htm retrieved 8/10/11

460. The Wilmington Star-News, "A hero at home" by Allison Ballard, 4/4/04

461. Daily Variety, "Film Reviews" by Robert Koeler, 12/19/2005

gendered teen. Starring Mercedes Ruehl, J.D. Pardo, Lupe Ontiveros and Leela Savasta, it earned high marks for fine acting, was nominated for an Imagen Award and won a Media Award from the Gay & Lesbian Alliance Against Defamation.

"But you start to become second or third level again," Darrow says. "You're way in the background. 'Oh, hi gramps!' And there you are taking out your false teeth. Your roles are inconsequential, except in theater where age isn't held against you or when somebody has known you for decades and they have a TV or movie part for you."

At last, there was a meaty movie part waiting in Nevada. Michael Tylo was teaching in the film department at the University of Nevada — Las Vegas and mentioned to department head Francisco Menendez that he was friends with Henry Darrow.

"I was was eight years old in El Salvador when I saw him as Manolito and that was who I wanted to be when I grew up," Menendez says. "When I did my first short feature I called one of the characters Manolito because of him and when I performed Petruccio in a *Taming of the Shrew* adaptation, I stole Manolito for everything. Then Michael said he knew how to get in touch with him and I thought, oh my God! I was making this movie, *Primo*, which had a good role for an older man, so I sent Henry a love-letter and he signed on."

"I played a mean grandpa who tried to control the lives of his grandsons," says Darrow. *Primo* (cousin), the dramatic saga of three cousins separated during the El Salvadoran civil war who reunite when they travel to Las Vegas to see their dying grandfather, had a young cast and considerable student involvement. "What they lacked in experience, they made up for in energy! The energy of the students rubbed off and sometimes I'd work until two in the morning, but it was the best location for shooting I've ever had. We shot it at somebody's house and when I got tired, I could take a nap. When I woke, the set was right there!"

Even though Darrow had to refresh himself with an occasional nap, Menendez says, "I call him 'lightning in the bottle,' because he would show up ready to go. With the students, I reshot sequences until I got the performance I wanted. Henry? Take one, he's there with guns blazing." The talented young cast benefitted. "He has an amazing understanding of film grammar and he'd make adjustments very diplomatically without making anyone feel bad. He was excellent at contributing to their growth."

For Darrow, trips to Las Vegas were bittersweet. Working on *Primo* with Menendez and his students was uplifting, so was spending time with Michael Tylo. But visits with his son Tom were painful. Relentless drug addiction and multiple sclerosis had attacked Tom with a vengeance. Still living with Bob, his friend of many years, Tom went from walking with a cane to wheelchair confinement. Bob wasn't a young man anymore and caring for Tom taxed his physical capabilities. Meanwhile Henry's daughter Deedee was fifty years old, dealing with lupus and an increasingly hostile relationship between herself and Lucy's second husband; Henry could do nothing except listen and offer fatherly advice guaranteed to irritate Deedee.

Boxing promoter/announcer Al Bernstein describes his friend Henry Darrow as having an "inner peace," but tranquility was about to be blown apart. Darrow was booked to attend the Dean Smith Celebrity Rodeo in Abilene, Texas in October 2006, but cancelled when Alzheimer's disease finally claimed Lauren's father. Although Allan Levian's death was expected, Lauren's grief was profound and Henry's concern for her was great. Personal appearances went on hold while he stayed by his wife's side. Then Tom's friend Bob called and said, "Hank, I can't pick Tom up anymore."

"Bob helped so many kids who were serious drug addicts," Darrow says. "He helped them get on their feet and they made it. He had such faith in Tom, but Tom was one of his biggest disappointments. After he called, I phoned Lucy and said, 'I need your okay to put him into a care facility.'"

With plans underway to find a nursing home for Tom, Deedee stepped in. "She wanted to take him home with her and she meant well, but Bob couldn't lift him and she definitely couldn't. So Lucy and I said no."

Lucy found a facility for Tom, soon completely bedridden. Henry flew out to spend time with him and had just returned in March 2007 when he felt he should return. When he called Lucy on March 10 to say he was coming again she said he'd died that morning. Thomas Delgado was forty-five years old.

Denis Lehane remembers, "Hank called me when he passed away. Normally we'll talk for fifteen or twenty minutes, but we talked for about three hours that night. Hank was heartbroken. I just listened and tried to console him as best I could."

Tom had been dead for little over a month when Henry went to Florida. He was up for a part in a TV series filming near Miami and had also been convinced to appear at a new western film festival near Orlando. Neither worked out very well. He was passed over for the part and unlike established festivals drawing hundreds if not thousands of fans, the festival in Florida was poorly attended. With time on his hands, a memorabilia dealer who knew Henry from other events approached him and asked, "Did that son of yours die yet?" Henry just turned and walked away.

He struggled to be positive. He enjoyed swapping tales with Dennis Cole, his old friend from the series *Bearcats!* and discovered the hotel cleaning staff was full of fans. "The maids were all these young girls in their twenties from Guatemala and Honduras and they had seen *Chaparral* in reruns at home. They recognized me right away as Manolito, so there I was in the middle of the hallway signing autographs. They were all shooting photos with their camera phones while I was kneeling on the ground and posing with them. They were thrilled, but they had to go back to work, so they were saying goodbye, thank you and I was still kneeling. I said, 'Nono, my knees are bad! You have to help me up!' They did of course and it was fantastic to be remembered like that after all the years."

After the festival, he says, "I became partly hermit." Deedee began returning his letters unopened. "She really came to despise me and I don't know why. I always tried to be supportive and to send her money, but she just shut me out. She stayed in contact with my brother, but I never came up in the conversation. Dennis says he doesn't go there. It's between me and her."

Asked to be a guest at the 2007 reunion of *The High Chaparral*, he resisted. "I was just worn out and nobody wants to see you not smiling," he says, but cajoled by fans, he relented and flew to Los Angeles. Saturday of the reunion, the hospitality room was packed. Kent McCray had just finished emphasizing Mark Slade's anticipated fifth-season return to the *Chaparral* when trim, silver-haired Henry strode into the room, flashed a dimpled grin and declared, "When Mark left, that meant more lines for me!" His surprise arrival played to enthusiastic applause and adoring sighs. "BAM! I got such a kick out of it! Everyone was asking questions and stories kept rushing to my head and it was fantastic! The whole thing just sparked me up," he says. "I was thinking my God! This is what it was about years and years ago." Being with old friends like Kent and Susan McCray, Bob Hoy, Don Collier, Marie Gomez and Harry Cason and the adoration of fans was invigorating, but upbeat days and late-night parties left him physically crushed and emotionally drained. "You can't sustain that for too long. It's like a theater performance. It's exhilarating, but then there's the letdown. With fan events it's important to be available so you continue to push. You just push yourself to pose for pictures and tell stories. I'm pretty good at that, but all of a sudden I was performing on empty."

On the flight home, he sat next to National Soccer Hall of Famer Mia Hamm. Earlier that year Hamm and her husband became the parents of twin girls and Hamm had her infant daughters with her on the plane.

"We talked and she let me hold the babies and that was nice. Then she asked me if I had any grandchildren and I just burst into tears."

He used to save his sorrow, anger, remorse and despair for performances. Under the protective glow of the Klieg lights, it gave depth and edge to his acting and brought him approving applause. "Then as I got older, my emotions were on my sleeve. If I waste it like that, it won't be available when I need it," he told a friend. But there weren't many roles to save it for. "I got sort of hot and heavy with two auditions I did and one was for a wonderful part," he says. "I wasn't cast, but there's all the stress and I'm thinking, 'This is why I left Hollywood.' This is what I do not want, getting knocked down like that, so I try to focus on how lucky I am to be with Lauren and with the real estate business."

His mother was his inspiration for being upbeat, but her health was failing and Dennis had moved her to a retirement home. "Her memory was in and out, but she was the star of the home. The doctors and nurses all loved her. They all called her *La Reinita*, the little queen," Darrow recalls. "She would recite her poems and she was really the hit of the place." Then after several falls and two strokes, she became bed-bound and less lucid. Sometimes she forgot Dennis' name. When Henry visited for her birthday in November 2008, she stared at Henry, then said to Dennis, "He looks like my son. Don't you think he looks like my son?"

"It's hard to reach ninety-six with your mind completely intact," Dennis says. "Sometimes she remembered him more as Manolito than as a man in his seventies."

Back home, Darrow re-read old cards and letters from Deedee and Tom and tried to "keep on keeping on" like his mother always advised. He thought of his remarkable career, one which had taken to heights few actors ever go. It warmed him when fans remembered him. In some countries, he had second and third generation fans. People around Wilmington — neighbors, doctors, other show business folks, waiters in restaurants and even the mayor—remembered him as Manolito Montoya. As Patrice Martinez says, Darrow has the range to play almost any part, but that iconic character "makes him an actor of legacy. Years and generations can pass and there is still an audience because that actor has had a legacy."

But for the first time in decades, Manolito wasn't paying off in acting work. Neither was fifty years in the business. Just when Darrow's confidence in himself was at low ebb, a friend of his offered him a role in the classic musical *My Fair Lady*. A singing, dancing adaptation of George Bernard Shaw's *Pygmalion*, *My Fair Lady* had a long Broadway run and in 1964, was an Academy Award-winning film starring Rex Harrison as Professor Henry Higgins, Wilfrid Hyde-White as his friend Col. Pickering, Audrey Hepburn as flower-girl turned lady Eliza Doolittle and Stanley Holloway as Eliza's morally unencumbered Cockney dustman father, Alfred P. Doolittle. As a play, it has been a hit with generations of professional and amateur theater companies and audiences.

The Wilmington production by Lou Criscuolo and the Opera House Theatre Company would be directed by Broadway veteran Ray Kennedy. The cast included professional actors Dan Morris as Higgins and Eric Paisley as Pickering along with amateurs, many of them university drama students. It would play at historic Thalian Hall Theatre for the Performing Arts, a twin of the magnificent Ford's Theatre in Washington, D.C. resplendent with towering columns, grand arches and sweeping staircases. They just needed someone with the chops to play the crucial character role of cheerful reprobate Alfred P. Doolittle, like Criscuolo's friend Henry Darrow.

"I'm running it through my mind," he said, singing a few bars of "Get Me to the Church on Time," one of Doolittle's signature tunes. "I don't know if I have the stamina for it and of course, I'd have to work on my accent. I'd have to study Stanley Holloway in the movie. He was brilliant! I'll steal from him totally, but it will come out different, my body language will be different." Criscuolo told Darrow no audition was needed but Darrow said no. "I'd prepare so I could go in and do a little dance routine. I think my memory would hold out, but I'd be testing it. I just need a kick." When he read the script, he got all the kick he needed from lines like this:

Pickering: *Have you no morals, man?*
Doolittle: *No, no. I can't afford 'em, gov'ner. Neither could you if you was as poor as me.*

He worked on the part for three months, memorizing his lines, watching the movie version and studying Stanley Holloway's Doolittle. He researched the lives and costumes of garbage collectors in early twentieth century London. He worked on dance-steps, but said, "I have put on kneepads to clean out the cat-box because if I do it without some protection, I fall over backward. Lauren was afraid I was really going to hurt myself trying to dance."

But he got the part. There were only four weeks of rehearsal before it opened and he practiced songs so much Lauren worried he'd blow out his voice. "I could hit some notes. That went back to my training with Augusto Rodriguez," he says. "His expression was 'from the top down.'

He meant start on the money, don't wave your way into it like a crooner. I can't sustain it anymore, but I can sort of blast it out. Ray Kennedy, the director said, 'You seem to have a good ear' and I said 'I do?' But that was Augusto, start at the top of your head and just hit it!"

He kept his voice but hurt his back dancing too vigorously. Pretty soon, he had a back-brace to match the braces on his painful knees, but Darrow was on fire. "Yeah! I had a script in my hand! It perked my imagination. I wasn't getting paid anything, but it was a good part."

Then Lauren had a lump in her breast biopsied. It was cancer, but she refused to have surgery until the play was over. She was there to help him rehearse, running lines over and over. He loves to act," she says. "And he is *fantastic*."

"If anything happened to her, I'd be devastated," Henry told friends. He would turn to Lauren with tears in his eyes and say, "Babes, I don't want you to be sick. Please don't be sick." She assured him she would be fine.

He shared a dressing room with Dan Morris and Eric Paisley. "We were closeted in the 'star' dressing room," recalls Paisley. "Higgins, Doolittle and Pickering. I knew Henry from only a brief meeting. I had no preconceptions, but he is probably one of the most inventive actors I've come across. He hits the mark, but he never takes the safe route on the boards."

The performance was sold out and Darrow sat alone backstage in a quiet corner of the theater, going over his lines. He felt every creaking bone in his seventy-five-year-old body. Lauren's cancer terrified him. His mother died while he was in rehearsals. The day before she passed away, Dennis told her, "Henry can't come, Mom. He's in a play." She smiled. Her sons were doing exactly what she wanted them to do. Dennis was there to brush her hair and take care of her; Henry was the actor she'd raised him to be.

When it was time to go onstage, decades fell away. His entrance was electric. He radiated unadulterated joy that transcended mere command of the stage. He could see Lauren in the audience and hear her laugh when he delivered a good line. He danced; his mom always said he could. He belted out "With a Little Bit of Luck" and "Get Me to the Church on Time" in a strong baritone like Broadway's best. He adlibbed Shaw, as he had forty years earlier in *The Devil's Disciple*. "It's hard to improve on Bernard Shaw's dialogue or his humor," Eric Paisley notes. "Unless you're Henry Darrow and *he* gets away with it!"

"He stole every scene he was in," says Dan Morris. "But Eric and I had a ball with him. He brought such energy and he has immediate rapport with an audience."

Screenwriter Rich Leder was in the audience and says, "Henry has this quality where you *must* love him. He walks out, he starts talking and you *fall in love. My Fair Lady* was a terrific show, but when Henry came out, it jumped ten levels. It was truly outstanding from that moment on because of Henry. You can't learn that quality. It can't be taught. It has to be born in you and he has it."

When it was all over and Darrow strode onstage to take his bow, the audience scrambled to their feet. The applause was like thunder.

> *Did David Dortort ever tell you how good you really are?*
>
> PRODUCER SAM STRANGIS TO HENRY DARROW[462]

---

462. *Letter dated June 28, 1974, from personal papers of Henry Darrow*

Selected Bibliography

Ayala, César J. and Rafael Bernabe. *Puerto Rico in the American Century: A History Since 1898*. Chapel Hill, NC: University of North Carolina Press, 2007.

Berg, Charles Ramírez. *Latino Images in Film: Stereotypes, Subversion & Resistance*. Austin, TX: University of Texas Press, 2002.

Bogle, Donald. *Toms, Coons, Mulattoes, Mammies & Bucks: An Interpretive History of Blacks in American Films*. 4th ed. New York, London: Continuum Publishing Group, 2009.

Bradbury, Ray. *The Wonderful Ice Cream Suit and Other Plays for Today, Tomorrow and Beyond Tomorrow*. Toronto, New York, London: Bantam Pathfinder, 1972

Curtis, Sandra. *Zorro Unmasked: The Official History*. New York: Hyperion, 1998.

Eppinga, Jane. *Images of America: Tucson Arizona*. Charleston, SC, Chicago IL, Portsmouth NH, San Francisco CA: Arcadia Publishing, 2000.

Loewen, James W. *Sundown Towns: A Hidden Dimension of American Racism*. New York, Touchstone Books, 2006.

Marx, Arthur. *The Secret Life of Bob Hope: An Unauthorized Biography*. New York, Barricade Books, 1993.

Montalbán, Ricardo, with Bob Thomas. *Reflections: A Life in Two Worlds*. Garden City, NY: Doubleday & Company, 1980.

Nash, N. Richard. *The Rainmaker: A Romantic Comedy in Three Acts*. New York, London, Hollywood, Toronto: Samuel French, 1983.

Reyes, Luis, and Peter Rubie. *Hispanics in Hollywood: A Celebration of 100 Years in Film and Television*. Hollywood, CA: Lone Eagle Publishing, 2000.

Rivera, Miluka. *Legado Puertorriqueño en Hollywood: Famosos y Olvidados*. Burbank, CA: Kumaras Center for the Arts and Etiquette, 2010

Rodríguez, Clara E. *Heroes, Lovers and Others: The Story of Latinos in Hollywood*. Washington: Smithsonian Books, 2004.

Rodríguez, Clara E., et al. *Latin Looks: Images of Latinas and Latinos in the U.S. Media*. Boulder, CO and Oxford: Westview Press, 1997.

Soares, André. *Beyond Paradise: The Life of Ramon Novarro*. New York: St. Martin's Press, 2002.

Witney, William. *In a Door, Into a Fight, Out a Door, Into a Chase: Moviemaking Remembered by the Guy at the Door*. Jefferson, NC and London: McFarland & Company, 1996.

Yenne, Bill. *The Legend of Zorro*. Mallard Press, 1991.

Yoggy, Gary A. *Riding the Video Range: The Rise and Fall of the Western on Television*, Vols. I and II. Jefferson, NC and London: McFarland & Company, 1995.

Appendix I

Henry Darrow in Movies, on Television and on Stage

Tale and Song: A Tribute to Gabriel García Márquez (PLAY).............. 1996
Florencia en el Amazones (PLAY)..................................... 1996
Way Out West (TV DOCUMENTARY) 1996
Star Trek: Voyager (TV SERIES) 1996
Sisters (TV SERIES)... 1995
Star Trek: Voyager (TV SERIES) 1995
Crystal Empire (TV SERIES).. 1995
Exit to Eden (MOVIE).. 1994
Criminal Passion (MOVIE).. 1994
Maverick (MOVIE).. 1994
Nurses (TV SERIES).. 1994
B/C Historia (PLAY)... 1993
Percy & Thunder (TV MOVIE).. 1993
Time Trax (TV SERIES) 1993
Zorro (TV SERIES)..1990-1993
Silk Stalkings (TV SERIES) 1993
The Last of the Finest (MOVIE) 1990
Santa Barbara (TV SERIES) 1989-1992
L.A. Bounty (MOVIE) 1989
Godman (PLAY)... 1988
The Golden Girls (TV SERIES)...................................... 1988
In Dangerous Company (MOVIE) 1988
Star Trek: The Next Generation (TV SERIES)........................ 1988
Simon & Simon (TV SERIES) 1988
Don Juan in Hell (PLAY)... 1987
Ohara (TV SERIES)... 1987
One Life to Live (TV SERIES)...................................... 1987
The Mission…Kill (MOVIE) 1987
Easy Street (TV SERIES)... 1986
Fresno (TV MINI-SERIES) 1986
T.J. Hooker (TV SERIES)... 1986
The Hitcher (TV MOVIE).. 1986
The Young Lady from Tacna (PLAY) 1985
Magnum, P.I. (TV SERIES).. 1985
Me and Mom (TV SERIES) 1985
Jackpot Bingo (TV GAME SHOW SERIES) 1985
This is the Life (TV SERIES)...................................... 1985
100 Centre Street (TV MOVIE) 1984
Corridos (PLAY)... 1984
This is the Life (TV SERIES) 1984

True Confessions (TV SERIES).. 1984
Cover Up (TV SERIES)... 1984
Airwolf (TV SERIES)... 1984
The Fall Guy (TV SERIES) 1984
The Scarecrow and Mrs. King (TV SERIES)........................... 1983, 1984
T.J. Hooker (TV SERIES)... 1983
Jennifer Slept Here (TV SERIES) 1983
Trauma Center (TV SERIES).. 1983
Zorro and Son (TV SERIES).. 1983
Losin' It (MOVIE)... 1983
Dallas (TV SERIES)... 1983
Tales of the Gold Monkey (TV SERIES) 1983
Hart to Hart (TV SERIES)... 1983
Los Alvarez (TV SPECIAL) 1983
The Fantasticks (PLAY)... 1982
T.J. Hooker (TV SERIES)... 1982
General Hospital (TV SERIES) 1982
Dynasty (TV SERIES).. 1982
Born to the Wind (TV SERIES).. 1982
Rooster (TV MOVIE).. 1982
Quincy, M.E. (TV SERIES).. 1982
American Playhouse: Seguin (TV MOVIE) 1982
Birds of Paradise (MOVIE).. 1981
The Incredible Hulk (TV SERIES)... 1981
St. Helens (TV MOVIE).. 1981
B.J. and the Bear (TV SERIES) 1981
Simon & Simon (TV SERIES) 1981
The Queen and the Rebels (PLAY)... 1981
Quincy, M.E. (TV SERIES).. 1981
Secrets of Midland Heights (TV SERIES) 1981
Beyond the Universe (MOVIE) 1981
Attica (TV MOVIE) 1980
The Yeagers (TV SERIES).. 1980
The New Adventures of Zorro (TV SERIES) 1980
The Roar of the Greasepaint, the Smell of the Crowd (PLAY)................ 1979
The Waltons (TV SERIES)... 1979
Sunday (PLAY) 1979
Walk Proud (MOVIE) 1979
Hart to Hart (TV SERIES)... 1979
Vega$ (TV SERIES)... 1979

A Life of Sin/Isabel La Negra (MOVIE) 1979
When the West Was Fun: A Western Reunion (TV SPECIAL) 1979
Centennial (TV MINI-SERIES) 1978
Where's Willie? (MOVIE) 1978
The Bionic Woman (TV SERIES) 1978
Police Woman (TV SERIES) 1977
The New Adventures of Wonder Woman (TV SERIES) 1977
Halloween with the New Addams Family (TV MOVIE) 1977
Hawaii Five-O (TV SERIES) 1977
The Rainmaker (PLAY) 1977
Kingston: Confidential (TV SERIES) 1977
Gemini Man (TV SERIES) 1976
Baretta (TV SERIES) 1976
Jigsaw John (TV SERIES) 1976
Sara (TV SERIES) 1976
Quincy, M.E. (TV SERIES) 1976
Hawaii Five-O (TV SERIES) 1976
The Streets of San Francisco (TV SERIES) 1976
Ping-Pong (PLAY) 1976
McMillan & Wife (TV SERIES) 1975
The Invisible Man (TV SERIES) 1975
Harry O (TV SERIES) 1974-1975
Aloha Means Goodbye (TV MOVIE) 1974
Night Games (TV MOVIE) 1974
Kojak (TV SERIES) 1974
Chase (TV SERIES) 1974
The New Dick Van Dyke Show (TV SERIES) 1973-1974
Badge 373 (MOVIE) 1973
The Paul Dixon Show (TV TALK SHOW) 1973
Hernandez, Houston P.D. (TV MOVIE) 1973
Kung Fu (TV SERIES) 1973
Portrait: A Man Whose Name Was John (TV MOVIE) 1973
Brock's Last Case (TV MOVIE) 1973
Insight (TV SERIES) 1973
The Tavern (PLAY) 1973
The F.B. I. (TV SERIES) 1972
Bravo (TV SERIES) 1972
Cancel My Reservation (MOVIE) 1972
The Mod Squad (TV SERIES) 1972
Bearcats! (TV SERIES) 1971

Rod Serling's Night Gallery (TV SERIES) 1971

The Man and the City (TV SERIES)... 1971

Primus (TV SERIES).. 1971

Mission: Impossible (TV SERIES)... 1971

Hawaii Five-O (TV SERIES) 1971

The Paul Dixon Show (TV TALK SHOW) 1971

The High Chaparral (TV SERIES)..1967-1971

Bonanza (TV SERIES) 1967

Gunsmoke (TV SERIES) 1967

Daniel Boone (TV SERIES) 1967

T.H.E. Cat (TV SERIES) 1967

The Wild, Wild West (TV SERIES) 1967

Gunsmoke (TV SERIES) 1966

T.H.E. Cat (TV SERIES) 1966

Iron Horse (TV SERIES).. 1966

Dark of the Moon (PLAY) 1966

Richard III (PLAY)... 1966

Love for Love (PLAY) 1965

The Devil's Disciple (PLAY) 1965

Peer Gynt (PLAY)... 1965

The Shoemaker's Prodigious Wife (PLAY) 1965

The Firebugs (PLAY).. 1965

The Wonderful Ice Cream Suit (PLAY) 1965

Voyage to the Bottom of the Sea (TV SERIES)..................................... 1964

Othello (PLAY).. 1964

The Emperor (PLAY).. 1964

Family Portrait (PLAY) 1964

Arms and the Man (PLAY).. 1963

The Outer Limits (TV SERIES) 1963

Stoney Burke (TV SERIES) 1963

Day in Court (TV SERIES) 1963

Walk on the Wild Side (MOVIE) 1962

Wagon Train (TV SERIES)... 1962

The Dick Powell Show (TV SERIES) 1962

Stovepipe Hat (PLAY) 1961

Sniper's Ridge (MOVIE).. 1961

Summer and Smoke (MOVIE) 1961

Ring of Fire (MOVIE) 1961

The 3rd Voice (MOVIE)... 1960

Cage of Evil (MOVIE) 1960

Duff & Lupino (TV SERIES) 1960
The Garlund Touch/Mr. Garlund (TV SERIES)..................................... 1960
Manhunt (TV SERIES)... 1960
Cimarron City (TV SERIES) 1959
Revenge of the Virgins (MOVIE) 1959
Holiday for Lovers (MOVIE).. 1959
Curse of the Undead (MOVIE).. 1959
Border Patrol (TV SERIES) 1959
Frontier Judge (TV SERIES)... 1959
The Man and the Challenge (TV SERIES) 1959
Wagon Train (TV SERIES).. 1958
77 Sunset Strip (TV SERIES).. 1958
The Tormented (PLAY).. 1957
Nathan the Wise (PLAY).. 1957

Other Professional Theater (Late 1950s–early 1960s)

Blood Wedding, Yerma, Moon in Capricorn, Puss 'n Boots (CHILDREN'S THEATER), *Alice in Wonderland* (CHILDREN'S THEATER), *The King's Cream Puff* (CHILDREN'S THEATER), *Beauty and the Beast* (CHILDREN'S THEATER) and *The Alchemist.*

Appendix II

Honors

1999   Nosotros Golden Eagle Award for Lifetime Achievement

1997   *Drama-Logue* Critics Award for Outstanding Achievement in Theatre (*A Quiet Love*)

1996   National Hispanic Media Coalition Impact Award

1990   Daytime Emmy, Outstanding Supporting Actor in a Drama Series (*Santa Barbara*)

1989   Champion, World Chess Convention Celebrity Tournament

1983   Nosotros Golden Eagle Award for Consistent Excellence in Performances

1970   Bambi (Germany), international award to performers "who affected and inspired the German public."

1967   Most Promising New Actor (*Photoplay* magazine)

Index

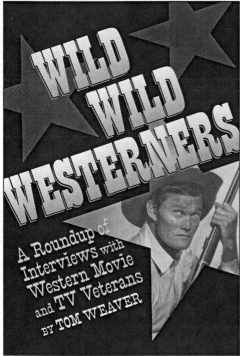

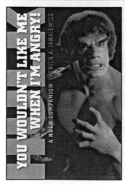